ADAM SMITH

III

Essays on Philosophical Subjects
with
Dugald Stewart's Account of Adam Smith

THE GLASGOW EDITION OF THE WORKS AND CORRESPONDENCE OF ADAM SMITH

Commissioned by the University of Glasgow to celebrate the bicentenary of the Wealth of Nations

I

THE THEORY OF MORAL SENTIMENTS
Edited by A. L. MACFIE *and* D. D. RAPHAEL

II

AN INQUIRY INTO THE NATURE AND CAUSES OF THE WEALTH OF NATIONS
Edited by R. H. CAMPBELL *and* A. S. SKINNER; *textual editor* W. B. TODD

III

ESSAYS ON PHILOSOPHICAL SUBJECTS
(and Miscellaneous Pieces)
Edited by W. P. D. WIGHTMAN

IV

LECTURES ON RHETORIC AND BELLES LETTRES
Edited by J. C. BRYCE
This volume includes the *Considerations concerning the First Formation of Languages*

V

LECTURES ON JURISPRUDENCE
Edited by R. L. MEEK, D. D. RAPHAEL, *and* P. G. STEIN
This volume includes two reports of Smith's course together with the 'Early Draft' of the *Wealth of Nations*

VI

CORRESPONDENCE OF ADAM SMITH
Edited by E. C. MOSSNER *and* I. S. ROSS

Associated volumes:

ESSAYS ON ADAM SMITH
Edited by A. S. SKINNER *and* T. WILSON

LIFE OF ADAM SMITH
By I. S. ROSS

*The Glasgow Edition of the Works and Correspondence of Adam Smith and the associated volumes are published in hardcover by Oxford University Press. The six titles of the Glasgow Edition, but not the associated volumes, are being published in softcover by Liberty*Classics.

ADAM SMITH
Essays on Philosophical Subjects

EDITED BY

W. P. D. WIGHTMAN AND J. C. BRYCE

WITH

Dugald Stewart's
Account of Adam Smith

EDITED BY

I. S. ROSS

GENERAL EDITORS

D. D. RAPHAEL AND A. S. SKINNER

Liberty Classics

INDIANAPOLIS

Liberty*Classics* is a publishing imprint of Liberty Fund, Inc., a foundation established to encourage study of the ideal of a society of free and responsible individuals.

The cuneiform inscription that serves as the design motif for our endpapers is the earliest known written appearance of the word "freedom" (*ama-gi*), or liberty. It is taken from a clay document written about 2300 B.C. in the Sumerian city-state of Lagash.

This Liberty*Classics* edition of 1982 is an exact photographic reproduction of the edition published by Oxford University Press in 1980.

Liberty*Press*/Liberty*Classics*
7440 N. Shadeland
Indianapolis, Indiana 46250

This reprint has been authorized by the Oxford University Press.

Library of Congress Cataloging in Publication Data

Smith, Adam, 1723–1790.
    Essays on philosophical subjects.

    Reprint. Originally published: Oxford [Oxfordshire]: Clarendon Press, 1980. (The Glasgow edition of the works and correspondence of Adam Smith; 3)
    Includes bibliographical references and index.
    I. Stewart, Dugald, 1753–1828. Account of the life and writing of Adam Smith, 1982.   II. Wightman, W. P. D. (William Persehouse Delisle)   III.   Bryce, J. C.
IV. Ross, Ian Simpson.   V. Title.   VI. Series: Glasgow edition of the works and correspondence of Adam Smith; 3.
AC7.S59   1976a, vol. 3   330.15′3s   82–7121
ISBN 0–86597–023–8 (pbk.)   [192]   AACR2

10 9 8 7 6 5 4 3 2 1

Cover design by JMH Corporation, Indianapolis.
Printed & bound by
Rose Printing Company, Inc., Tallahassee, Florida.

Preface

THIS is Volume III of the new edition of the *Works and Correspondence* of Adam Smith undertaken by the University of Glasgow. It contains the *Essays on Philosophical Subjects* and Dugald Stewart's 'Account of the Life and Writings of Adam Smith', together with Smith's contributions to the *Edinburgh Review* and his Preface to William Hamilton's *Poems on Several Occasions*.

The range of subjects covered in this collection is too wide to be edited by any one scholar. The main task of dealing with the essays that are strictly on 'philosophical subjects' was entrusted to W. P. D. Wightman. The editors for the remaining pieces were chosen with an eye to their role in the preparation of other, related, volumes. John Bryce, the editor of the *Lectures on Rhetoric*, has therefore dealt with the essay on 'English and Italian Verses', the articles in the *Edinburgh Review*, and the Preface to Hamilton's *Poems*, while Ian Ross, Smith's biographer and (with E. C. Mossner) editor of the *Correspondence*, has looked after Stewart's 'Account'.

It was also thought desirable to appoint general editors in order to ensure uniformity of practice and to relate the different parts of this volume to each other and to the edition as a whole. We have tried to do so by providing a General Introduction and a number of supplementary notes (enclosed within square brackets). For much of the information in these notes we are indebted to several scholars, including P. Michael Brown, John Bryce, Eric Forbes, A. Rupert Hall, and Donald Malcolm. We owe a special debt to the late Donald Allan, formerly Professor of Greek in the University of Glasgow, for his extensive and invaluable help in dealing with classical sources; many of the supplementary notes concerned with the ancient world have been supplied by him in their entirety.

We should also like to thank Mrs. Therese Campbell, Mrs. Julie Milton, and Miss Eileen O'Donnell for the care with which they have prepared the typescript at different stages.

1978

D. D. R.
A. S. S.

Contents

Key to Abbreviations and References

WORKS OF ADAM SMITH

Corr.	*Correspondence*
EPS	*Essays on Philosophical Subjects*, included among which are:
Ancient Logics	'The History of the Ancient Logics and Metaphysics'
Ancient Physics	'The History of the Ancient Physics'
Astronomy	'The History of Astronomy'
English and Italian Verses	'Of the Affinity between certain English and Italian Verses'
External Senses	'Of the External Senses'
Imitative Arts	'Of the Nature of that Imitation which takes place in what are called the Imitative Arts'
Stewart	Dugald Stewart, 'Account of the Life and Writings of Adam Smith, LL.D.'
Languages	*Considerations Concerning the First Formation of Languages*
TMS	*The Theory of Moral Sentiments*
WN	*The Wealth of Nations*
LJ(A)	*Lectures on Jurisprudence*, Report of 1762–3
LJ(B)	*Lectures on Jurisprudence*, Report dated 1766
LRBL	*Lectures on Rhetoric and Belles Lettres*

References to Corr. give the number of the letter (as listed in the volume of Smith's *Correspondence* in the present edition), the date, and the name of Smith's correspondent.

References to LJ and LRBL give the volume (where applicable) and the page number of the manuscript (shown in the printed texts of the present edition). References to LJ(B) add the page number in Edwin Cannan's edition of the *Lectures on Justice, Police, Revenue and Arms* (1896), and references to LRBL add the page number in John M. Lothian's edition of the *Lectures on Rhetoric and Belles Lettres* (1963).

References to the other works listed above locate the relevant paragraph, not the page, in order that any edition may be consulted (in the present edition, the paragraph numbers are printed in the margin). Thus:

Astronomy, II.4	=	'History of Astronomy', Sect. II, §4
Stewart, I.12	=	Dugald Stewart, 'Account of the Life and Writings of Adam Smith', Sect. I, §12
TMS I.i.5.5	=	*The Theory of Moral Sentiments*, Part I, Sect. I, Chap. 5, §5
WN V.i.f.26	=	*The Wealth of Nations*, Book V, Chap. i, sixth division, §26

OTHER WORKS

Essays on Adam Smith	*Essays on Adam Smith*, edited by Andrew Stewart Skinner and Thomas Wilson (1975)

Rae, *Life*   John Rae, *Life of Adam Smith* (1895)
Scott, *ASSP*   William Robert Scott, *Adam Smith as Student and Professor* (1937)

General Introduction[1]

I

MOST of the essays contained in this book were not prepared for the press by Smith. They are fragments in fact—perhaps, as Black and Hutton suggested in the 'Advertisement' to EPS, parts of 'a plan he had once formed, for giving a connected history of the liberal sciences and elegant arts'. The essays are also diverse both in terms of subject-matter and in the degree of finish they had acquired at the time of Smith's death. Yet, at the same time, there are some common elements.

To begin with, the more important of the essays plainly have a 'philosophical' character, which conforms to Smith's own recommendations regarding the organization of scientific discourse. Smith believed that writers of 'didactical' discourse ought ideally to deliver a system of science by laying down 'certain principles, known or proved, in the beginning, from whence we account for the several phaenomena, connecting all together by the same chain' (LRBL ii.133, ed. Lothian, 140). Smith described this as the 'Newtonian' method, while well aware that it had been used before Newton—most notably by Descartes. This point in itself is an important reminder that Smith drew an implicit distinction between the method used in *expounding* a system of thought and that employed in *establishing* such a system: in the former case, he was able to point out that Descartes and Newton shared a common approach; in the latter, he insisted that the Cartesian sytem was 'fanciful', 'ingenious and elegant, tho' fallacious' (Letter to the Authors of the *Edinburgh Review*, § 5).[2] In short, the task of *establishing* a system of thought must be conducted in terms of the combination of reason *and* experience—although even here he was quick to associate this definition of the term 'method' with Galileo rather than Newton (Astronomy, IV.44).

[1] For a related account of the views expressed in Sections I–IV of this Introduction, see A. S. Skinner, 'Adam Smith: Science and the Role of the Imagination', in W. B. Todd, ed., *Hume and the Enlightenment* (1974). Much of Section V is drawn from part of a paper by D. D. Raphael previously printed (under the title '"The true old Humean philosophy" and its influence on Adam Smith') in G. P. Morice, ed., *David Hume: Bicentenary Papers* (1977) and now reproduced by permission of the Edinburgh University Press.

[2] Smith has been seen by some commentators to have had something of a preoccupation with Descartes. See, for example, S. Moscovici, 'A propos de quelque travaux d'Adam Smith sur l'histoire et la philosophie des sciences' in *Revue d'Histoire des Sciences et de leurs Applications*, ix (1956), section 3.

Secondly, it is at least broadly true that many of the essays provide evidence of Smith's concern with the principles of human nature, again, a wide-ranging interest. For example, Smith himself was to point out that under some conditions the study of grammar could provide the 'best History of the natural progress of the Human mind in forming the most important abstractions upon which all reasoning depends',[3] and John Millar explained his teacher's choice of emphasis in the LRBL by reference to Smith's belief that: 'The best method of explaining and illustrating the various powers of the human mind, the most useful part of metaphysics, arises from an examination of the several ways of communicating our thoughts by speech, and from an attention to the principles of those literary compositions which contribute to persuasion or entertainment.' (Stewart, I.16.) In the same vein, Dugald Stewart suggested that Smith's cultivation of the Fine Arts was developed: 'less, it is probable, with a view to the peculiar enjoyments they convey, (though he was by no means without sensibility to their beauties,) than on account of their connection with the general principles of the human mind; to an examination of which they afford the most pleasing of all avenues' (Stewart, III.13).

Finally, we should recall Smith's overriding interest in historical questions and the fact that he: 'seldom misses an opportunity of indulging his curiosity, in tracing from the principles of human nature, or from the circumstances of society, the origin of the opinions and the institutions which he describes' (Stewart, II.52). Earlier, Stewart had commented on Smith's youthful interest in mathematics[4] and the natural sciences, together with the principles of human nature, both of which: 'enabled him to exemplify some of his favourite theories concerning the natural progress of the mind in the investigation of truth, by the history of those sciences in which the connection and succession of discoveries may be traced with the greatest advantage' (Stewart, I.8).

While the features outlined above are all characteristic of the major essays in this volume, they are combined in one of them to greatest effect—the Astronomy, once described by J. A. Schumpeter as 'the pearl of the collection'.[5] While the essay is one of the best examples of theoretical history, it is perhaps most remarkable as a study of those principles of human nature which 'lead and direct' philosophical inquiry.

[3] Letter 69 addressed to George Baird, dated Glasgow, 7 February 1763.
[4] Interestingly enough, it is remarked in TMS IV.2.7 that: 'It is in the abstruser sciences, particularly in the higher parts of mathematics, that the greatest and most admired exertions of human reason have been displayed.'
[5] *History of Economic Analysis* (1954), 182.

II

One of the characteristics of theoretical history is that it may be applied to situations where direct evidence is lacking. As Stewart put it: 'In this want of direct evidence, we are under a necessity of supplying the place of fact by conjecture; and when we are unable to ascertain how men have actually conducted themselves upon particular occasions, of considering in what manner they are likely to have proceeded, from the principles of their nature, and the circumstances of their external situation.' (II.46.) In the context of the discussion of the *origin* of philosophy, Smith had comparatively little to say about man's external situation, but he did note that philosophical effort could only take place under conditions where subsistence was no longer precarious and where social order and a regular subordination of ranks were established (Astronomy, III.1,5).[6] Elsewhere he also noted the importance of language as a means of expressing ideas while pointing out that language[7] itself developed by virtue of man's intellectual capabilities—for example, his capacity for abstraction and generalization in addition to speech itself.

Given the above conditions, the assumptions employed are fundamentally simple: Smith assumes that *all* men are endowed with certain faculties and propensities such as reason, reflection, and imagination, and that they are motivated by a desire to acquire the sources of pleasure and avoid those of pain. In this context pleasure relates to a state of the imagination: the 'state of . . . tranquillity, and composure' (Imitative Arts, II.20). Such a state, Smith suggested, may be attained even where the objects contemplated are unlike or the processes involved are complex—provided only that the connection is a customary one. He added that the 'indolent' imagination finds satisfaction but no stimulus to thought under such circumstances and duly noted that 'the bulk of mankind' often express no interest in the common-place. For example, the conversion of food into flesh and bone (Astronomy, II.11), even looking-glasses, become 'so familiar' that men typically do not think that 'their effects require any explication' (Imitative Arts, I.17). In the same way, Smith cited the example of the skilled artisan (such as a brewer, dyer, or distiller) who effects the most remarkable transformations in the materials that he uses and yet 'cannot conceive what occasion there is for any connecting events to unite those appearances, which seem to him to succeed each other very naturally. It is their nature, he tells us, to

---

[6] This point is emphasized by Moscovici, op. cit., 5.
[7] See J. F. Becker, 'Adam Smith's Theory of Social Science', *Southern Economic Journal*, xxviii (1961–2).

follow one another in this order, and that accordingly they always do so.' (Astronomy, II.11.)

Three points are worth emphasizing before going further: first, Smith places a good deal of weight on 'conventional' knowledge[8] (i.e. that kind of 'knowledge' which is based on customary connection), and on the fact that the imagination *is* 'indolent'. As Smith put it, men 'have seldom had the curiosity to inquire by what process of intermediate events' a given change is brought about, where 'the passage of the thought from . . . one object to the other is by custom become quite smooth and easy' (Astronomy, II.11). In fact Smith had very little more to say about the origin and nature of 'knowledge' of *this* kind.

Secondly, Smith stressed the difference between the philosopher and the ordinary man, while being careful to add that these differences arise 'not so much from nature, as from habit, custom, and education' (WN I.ii.4). But habit, custom, and education can make the philosopher more perceptive, so that just as the botanist differs from the casual gardener, or the musician from the generality of his auditors, so he 'who has spent his whole life in the study of the connecting principles of nature, will often feel an interval betwixt two objects, which, to more careless observers, seem very strictly conjoined' (Astronomy, II.11).

Finally, it must be emphasized that in the Astronomy Smith was not so much concerned with the state of 'composure' *per se*, as with the sources of its disturbance, and the nature of those processes by virtue of which that state could be re-established. In fact, Smith was largely concerned with a very specific aspect of the problem of 'knowledge', namely, the stimulus given to the undertanding by 'sentiments' such as *surprise, wonder,* or *admiration.* The limited objective of the Astronomy was clearly stated at the outset: 'It is the design of this Essay to consider particularly the nature and causes of each of these sentiments, whose influence is of far wider extent than we should be apt upon a careless view to imagine.' (Introduction, 7.)

Smith's initial argument then is to the effect that when certain objects or events follow in a particular order, 'they come to be so connected together in the fancy, that the idea of the one seems, of its own accord, to call up and introduce that of the other'. But, while the imaginatior finds no stimulus to thought under such conditions, Smith went on to argue that this would not be the case where the 'appearances' studied were in any way *unexpected*: 'We are at first

[8] J. R. Lindgren considers that this point has often been given less than its due weight: *The Social Philosophy of Adam Smith* (1973), 6, and see generally chapter 1 together with the same author's 'Adam Smith's Theory of Inquiry', *Journal of Political Economy,* lxxvii (1969).

surprised by the unexpectedness of the new appearance, and when that momentary emotion is over, we still wonder how it came to occur in that place.' (II.8.) In other words, we feel *surprise* when some object (or number of objects) is drawn to our attention which does not fall into a recognized pattern; a sentiment which is quickly followed by that of *wonder*, where the latter is defined in these terms: 'The stop which is thereby given to the career of the imagination, the difficulty which it finds in passing along such disjointed objects, and the feeling of something like a gap or interval betwixt them, constitute the whole essence of this emotion.' (II.9.) Wonder, in short, involves a source of pain (a disutility); a feeling of discomfort which gives rise to uncertainty and 'anxious curiosity' and even to 'giddiness and confusion'. On the other hand, the *response* to this situation involves the pursuit of some explanation, with a view to relieving the mind from a state of disequilibrium (i.e. lack of 'composure'); a natural reaction, given Smith's assumptions, designed to eliminate the sense of wonder by providing some appropriate ordering of the phenomena in question, or some plausible account of the links between different objects. Finally, Smith suggested that once we have succeeded in providing an acceptable and coherent account of a particular problem, the very existence of that explanation may 'heighten' our appreciation of the 'appearances' in question. In this way, for example, we learn to *admire* a complex social structure once its 'hidden springs' have been exposed, while in the same way a theory of astronomy may help us to admire the heavens through presenting the 'theatre of nature' as a coherent 'and therefore a more magnificent spectacle' (II.12).

Surprise, wonder, and admiration are, therefore, the three *sequential* sentiments on which Smith's account of mental stimulus depends.[9]

Once again, there are a number of points which deserve notice: First, it will be observed, that man is impelled to seek an explanation for observed 'appearances' as a result of a *subjective* feeling of discomfort, and that the resulting explanation or theory is therefore designed to meet some psychological need. Nature as a whole, Smith suggests, 'seems to abound with events which appear solitary and incoherent' and which therefore 'disturb the easy movement of the imagination' (II.12). Under these circumstances, the philosopher feels the disutility involved in the sentiment of wonder; a sentiment which thus emerges as 'the first principle which prompts mankind to the study of Philosophy, of that science which pretends to lay open the concealed connections that unite the various appearances of nature'

---

[9] Vernard Foley has emphasized the importance of classical sources, especially that of Aristotle, in this connection. *The Social Physics of Adam Smith* (1976), chap. 2.

(III.3). It follows from this that the explanation offered can only satisfy the mind if it is coherent, capable of accounting for observed appearances, and stated in terms of principles which are at least plausible.[10]

Secondly, it will be noted that wonder is the *first*, but not the only principle featured and Smith duly went on to emphasize that philosophical effort involved not only an escape from the contemplation of 'jarring and discordant appearances' but also a source of pleasure in its own right; a point made by him in suggesting that men: 'pursue this study for its own sake, as an original pleasure or good in itself, without regarding its tendency to procure them the means of many other pleasures' (III.3). In fact Smith provided many examples of the kinds of pleasure which might be involved in philosophical work. In the LRBL, for example, he noted that 'It gives us a pleasure to see the phaenomena which we reckoned the most unaccountable, all deduced from some principle (commonly a well known one) and all united in one chain' (ii.133–4, ed. Lothian, 140). Likewise, in WN he referred to the beauty of a 'systematical arrangement of different observations connected by a few common principles' (V.i.f.25), and in the Imitative Arts (II.30), likened the pleasure to be derived from the contemplation of a great system of thought to the intellectual and even sensual delights of a 'well composed concerto of instrumental music'.[11]

But, perhaps characteristically, Smith noted that such sources of pleasure were not equally accessible even to those of philosophical pretensions; that scientific thought also involved a *discipline* of which not all were capable and that this discipline could sometimes put too great a strain (i.e. a disutility) on the mind *even where presented with an organized body of thought*. Under some circumstances at least, 'too severe an application to study sometimes brings on lunacy and frenzy, in those especially who are somewhat advanced in life, but whose imaginations, from being too late in applying, have not got those habits which dispose them to follow easily the reasonings in the abstract sciences' (Astronomy, II.10).

III

Most of these points find further illustration in the History of Astronomy itself, where Smith reviewed four main systems of thought, not with a view to judging their 'absurdity or probability,

---

[10] For comment, see T. D. Campbell, *Adam Smith's Science of Morals* (1971), chap. 1.
[11] The importance of aesthetic considerations is particularly noted by H. F. Thomson, 'Adam Smith's Philosophy of Science', *Quarterly Journal of Economics*, lxxix (1965).

their agreement or inconsistency with truth and reality', but rather with a view to considering how far each of them was fitted to 'sooth(e) the imagination'—'that particular point of view which belongs to our subject' (II.12). Looked at in this way, the analysis has a 'static' aspect at least in so far as it is designed to show the extent to which each of the four main astronomical systems reviewed does in fact 'soothe' the imagination, isolating by this means the characteristics which they have in common. But Smith goes further than his stated object in noting that the systems of astronomy reviewed followed each other in a certain historical sequence, and in exposing the causal links which, he felt, might explain that sequence. The essence of Smith's argument would seem to be that each system at the time of its original appearance did satisfy the needs of the imagination, but that each was subject to a process of modification as new problems came to light; a process of modification which resulted in a degree of complexity which ultimately became unacceptable to the imagination. This in turn paves the way for a new kind of response—the production not just of *an* account, but of an *alternative* account (in this case of the heavens); a new thought-system designed to explain the *same* problems as the first, at least in its most complex form.

From one point of view this is the classic pattern of cultural history—human activity released within a given environment ultimately causing a qualitative change in that environment—as illustrated, say, by the development of language or the transition from feudalism to the commercial stage (WN III). But there is a difference, partly because 'environment' here relates to a state of 'knowledge' and partly because the reactions of individuals are now described as *self-conscious*—i.e. designed deliberately to modify an existing thought-system or to replace it with a more acceptable alternative.

As a means of illustrating the burden of the argument, it may be helpful to review the origin, development, and decline of the first astronomical system before going on to say something of those which followed it. Specialist comment on the astronomical *content* (e.g. as to its accuracy) of Smith's treatment is outwith the competence of the general editors, and must be left to the historian of science.

On Smith's argument, the first astronomers were faced with the need to explain the movements of the Stars, Sun, Moon, and five known planets; a task which was fulfilled in terms of a theory of Solid Spheres each of which was thought to have a circular but regular motion.[12] The Stars for example, being fixed in their positions

---

[12] Much later in the argument Smith provided an interesting explanation for such choices.

(*continued*)

relative to one another, while changing with reference to the observer, 'were naturally thought to have all the marks of being fixed, like so many gems, in the concave side of the firmament, and of being carried round by the diurnal revolutions of that solid body' (IV.1). Additional Spheres were used to account for the movements of the Sun and Moon (one inside the other to explain the eclipse) with five more for the planets or 'wandering stars'. The astronomical system which emerged thus represented the Earth as: 'self balanced and suspended in the centre of the universe, surrounded by the elements of Air and Ether, and covered by eight polished and cristalline Spheres, each of which was distinguished by one or more beautiful and luminous bodies, and all of which revolved round their common centre, by varied, but by equable and proportionable motions' (IV.5).

Such a system of thought apparently met the needs of the imagination by providing a coherent and plausible explanation for observed phenomena, and, in connecting by simple and familiar processes the 'grandest and most seemingly disjointed appearances in the heavens', added to man's admiration for them (IV.4).

Indeed, even if some contemporaries recognized that such a system did *not* account for *all* appearances, the degree of completeness was such that the generality of men would be tempted to 'slur over' (IV.6) such problems rather than qualify in any degree the satisfaction derived from the theory itself. In fact, Smith went on to suggest that this beautiful and appealing construction *of the intellect* might 'have stood the examination of all ages, and have gone down triumphant to the remotest posterity' had there been 'no other bodies discoverable in the heavens' (IV.4).

But additional bodies *were* discovered, and this together with the fact that Eudoxus was not one of the 'generality of men' led to the need to modify the existing system and to the addition of more spheres, as a means of accounting for changes in the relative positions of the planets. As a result Eudoxus raised the total number of spheres to 27, Callippus to 34, and Aristotle 'upon a yet more attentive observation' to 56 (until Fracastoro, 'smit with the eloquence of Plato and Aristotle and with the regularity and harmony of their system', felt it necessary to raise the number of spheres to 72, IV.7). In this way the relatively simple system of Eudoxus was gradually modified in order to meet the needs of the imagination when faced with new problems to be explained, until a situation was reached where the

---

The circle was used, he suggests, because it 'is of all curve lines the simplest and the most easily conceived' (IV.51) while 'an equal motion can be more easily attended to, than one that is continually either accelerated or retarded' (IV.52).

explanation offered actually violated the basic prerequisite of simplicity (IV.8).

In consequence, Smith suggests, a second major system was developed—by Apollonius (subsequently refined by Hipparchus and Ptolemy)—that of Eccentric Spheres and Epicycles. Once again, therefore, we are presented with a system which was designed to 'introduce harmony and order into the mind's conception of the movements' of the heavenly bodies and which succeeded in so doing at least at one stage of its development. However, the same argument is advanced by Smith; namely, that a gradual process of modification followed as adherents of the new system came to terms with new observations, or newly perceived problems, until a situation was once more reached where this intellectual system or 'imaginary machine': 'though, perhaps, more simple, and certainly better adapted, to the phaenomena than the Fifty-six Planetary Spheres of Aristotle, was still too intricate and complex for the imagination to rest in it with complete tranquillity and satisfaction' (IV.19). Indeed, Smith considered that the situation became even more complex and thus unsatisfactory as a result of the efforts of the Schoolmen, and especially those of Peurbach, who laboured with perverse ingenuity to reconcile the first astronomical system (of Concentric Spheres) with the second which had been designed to replace it (IV.25).

The response to *this* situation was the system of Copernicus: a system prompted, 'he tells us', by the confusion 'in which the old hypothesis represented the motions of the heavenly bodies' (IV.28).

Like the system which it was to replace, the Copernican managed to account for observed appearances in the manner of a simpler 'machine', requiring 'fewer movements' and by representing: 'the Sun, the great enlightener of the universe, whose body was alone larger than all the Planets taken together, as established immoveable in the center, shedding light and heat on all the worlds that circulated around him in one uniform direction, but in longer or shorter periods, according to their different distances' (IV.32). This was to prove an attractive hypothesis to some, not merely because of the beauty and coherence of the system, but also because of the novelty of the view of nature which it suggested—emphatically the case with an account which 'moved the Earth from its foundations, stopt the revolution of the Firmament, made the Sun stand still' (IV.33).

Yet at the same time, Smith argued that the system was by no means acceptable to all or even to those who confined their attention to astronomical matters, the difficulty being that Copernicus had invested the earth with a velocity which was 'unfamiliar', i.e. which ran counter to normal experience. The imagination tended to think of the earth as ponderous 'and even averse to motion' (IV.38), and it was this difficulty which led to the formulation of the alternative system of Tycho Brahe—a system partly prompted by jealousy of Copernicus, but none the less a system to some extent compounded of those of the latter and of Ptolemy. In this system, 'the Earth continued to be, as in the old account, the immoveable center of the universe' (IV.42). Smith added that Brahe's account was 'more complex and more incoherent than that of Copernicus. Such, however, was the difficulty that mankind felt in conceiving the motion of the Earth, that it long balanced the reputation of that otherwise more beautiful system' (IV.43).

In other words, the coherence and simplicity of the Copernican system was qualified by the unfamiliarity of one of its central principles; a problem which was so important as to render a more complex account more acceptable to some than it could otherwise have been. Interestingly enough, Smith represents subsequent developments as involving an attempt to make the more elegant system (of Copernicus) acceptable to the imagination by removing the basic difficulty—i.e. by providing a plausible explanation for the movement of the Earth. In this connection Smith argued that the astronomical work done by Kepler contributed to the completion of the system, while research on the problem of motion by Galileo helped to remove some of the more telling objections to the idea of a moving Earth. But in terms of the general acceptance of the idea of the Earth spinning at high velocity Smith gave most emphasis to the work of Descartes, who had represented the planets as floating in an immense ocean of ether containing 'at all times, an infinite number of greater and smaller vortices, or circular streams' (IV.62). Once the imagination accepted a hypothesis based on the familiar principle of motion after impulse, it was a short step to the elimination of the central difficulty since 'it was quite agreeable to its usual habits to conceive' that the planets 'should follow the stream of this ocean, how rapid soever' (IV.65). He added, in a significant passage, that under such circumstances: 'the imaginations of mankind could no longer refuse themselves the pleasure of going along with so harmonious an account of things. The system of Tycho Brahe was every day less and less talked of, till at last it was forgotten altogether' (Ibid.).

Yet, as Smith went on to note, the modifications introduced by Descartes were not prompted by *astronomical* knowledge so much as by a desire to produce a plausible explanation for the Copernican thesis. Moreover, he noted that further observations, especially those of Cassini, supported the authority of laws first discovered by Kepler for which the Cartesian 'theory' could provide no explanation. Under such circumstances, the latter system while it 'might continue to amuse the learned in other sciences ... could no longer satisfy those that were skilled in Astronomy' (IV.67).

The Cartesian system was to give way to the Newtonian; a theory which was capable of accounting for observed phenomena in terms of a small number of basic and familiar principles, and of successfully predicting their future movements. Smith wrote of the Newtonian system with real enthusiasm and in his Letter to the *Edinburgh Review* rejoiced as a 'Briton' to find the contributors to the *Encyclopédie* acknowledge its authority as compared to that of Descartes. Characteristically, however, he left readers of the Astronomy with the reminder that 'all philosophical systems' are 'mere inventions of the imagination', even though he had 'insensibly been drawn in' to write as if Newton's system was objectively true (IV.76; cf. Section V below).

IV

While the papers in this volume help to illustrate Smith's wide range of interests, they also confirm that he had an extensive knowledge of literature of a broadly scientific kind. The Astronomy, for example, suggests a very close knowledge of the works of classical authors, together with more modern writers such as Cassini, Kepler, Descartes, Copernicus, and Newton. Other essays extend the list to include Franklin and Linnaeus, while the Letter to the *Edinburgh Review* calls attention to Boyle and Bacon, together with Continental authors such as d'Alembert, Buffon, Daubenton, and Réaumur.[13] It is worth observing in this connection that Dugald Stewart called attention to Smith's unusual knowledge of Continental scientific work (I.25) and considered the 'mathematical sciences' to be 'very favourable subjects for theoretical history'—a fact which may have prompted Smith to undertake 'perfectly analogous' inquiries into the wider fields of language and jurisprudence (II.49,50).[14]

There can be no doubt that Smith regarded such exercises in theoretical history as having a serious scientific purpose or that an essay such as the Astronomy conforms in terms of structure to the general requirements of didactical discourse as set out in LRBL. At the same time, the argument of the Astronomy appears to rely on the use of both reason and experience—partly by virtue of passing in

[13] It is conceivable that Smith's knowledge of contemporary work in biology may have influenced his historical outlook. See Skinner, op. cit., 181–2.

[14] A major direct influence was probably Rousseau, whose work features in the Letter to the *Edinburgh Review*.

review a series of models which had a historical existence, and partly by explaining their appearance, development, and replacement by reference to a number of principles of human nature whose manifestations could be empirically verified. In this sense, Smith's methodology would seem to conform to the requirements of the Newtonian method properly so called in that he used the techniques of analysis and synthesis in the appropriate order. For, as Colin Maclaurin pointed out: 'in any other way, we can never be sure that we assume the principles that really obtain in nature; and that our system, after we have composed it with great labour, is not mere dream and illusion'.[15]

'Dream and illusion' . . . yet it is one thing to suggest that the ('first order') activities of individuals in the field of philosophy or science can be *studied* in a 'scientific way' (the 'second order' enterprise on which Smith was engaged) and another to argue that activity of either kind can always be said to be *scientific* in the sense of conforming to the ideal of objectivity. Moreover, Smith's discussion of the principles which lead and direct philosophical inquiries concentrates, as we have seen, on the needs of the imagination—on broadly psychological needs—so that, as Richard Olson has recently pointed out:

The great significance of Smith's doctrine is that since it measures the value of philosophical systems solely in relation to their satisfaction of the human craving for order, it sets up a human rather than an absolute or natural standard for science, and it leaves all science essentially hypothetical. Furthermore, Smith implied that unceasing change rather than permanence must be the characteristic of philosophy.[16]

While this position does seem accurately to express the burden of Smith's argument as contained in the Astronomy, two points might be suggested by way of qualification. First, it should be noted that Smith did not claim an *exclusive* role for the central principles of surprise, wonder, and admiration, but rather asserted that the part played by these sentiments was 'of far wider extent than we should be apt upon a careless view to imagine'. Secondly, it is worth remarking that while Smith regarded all theoretical constructions as products of the imagination designed to meet its needs, he also indicated that there was a difference between the natural and moral sciences. As he put the point in the TMS (VII.ii.4.14):

A system of natural philosophy may appear very plausible, and be for a long

---

[15] *An Account of Sir Isaac Newton's Philosophical Discoveries* (1748, ed. 3, 1775), 9.
[16] *Scottish Philosophy and British Physics, 1750–1880* (1975), 123. The hypothetical element in Smith's thought is also noted by Moscovici, op. cit.

time very generally received in the world, and yet have no foundation in nature, nor any sort of resemblance to the truth. The vortices of Des Cartes were regarded by a very ingenious nation, for near a century together, as a most satisfactory account of the revolutions of the heavenly bodies. Yet it has been demonstrated, to the conviction of all mankind, that these pretended causes of those wonderful effects, not only do not actually exist, but are utterly impossible, and if they did exist, could produce no such effects as are ascribed to them. But it is otherwise with systems of moral philosophy, and an author who pretends to account for the origin of our moral sentiments, cannot deceive us so grossly, nor depart so very far from all resemblance to the truth.

And yet by way of qualification almost, Smith had earlier remarked that some philosophers, notably mathematicians, 'are frequently very indifferent about the reception which they may meet with from the public', enjoying as they do 'the most perfect assurance, both of the truth and of the importance of their discoveries'. He added: 'Natural philosophers, in their independency upon the public opinion, approach nearly to mathematicians, and, in their judgments concerning the merit of their own discoveries and observations, enjoy some degree of the same security and tranquillity.' (TMS III.2.20.) Passages such as these suggest that 'truth' *is* attainable while at the same time reminding us of the importance of opinion.

But there can be no doubt that Smith did as a matter of fact draw attention to the importance of the subjective side of science both in emphasizing the role of the imagination when reviewing his basic principles, and in illustrating the working of these principles by reference to the history of astronomy. For example, when speaking of the introduction of the ingenious 'equalizing circle' in the system of eccentric spheres, he noted that 'Nothing can more evidently show, how much the repose and tranquillity of the imagination is the ultimate end of philosophy' (Astronomy, IV.13), than this device, and later commented on the ease with which 'the learned give up the evidence of their senses to preserve the coherence of the ideas of their imagination' (IV.35). In the same way, he emphasized the pleasure to be derived from simplicity, order, coherence, and indicated that because men find beauty to be a source of pleasure they may unwittingly give the products of the intellect a form which satisfies purely aesthetic criteria. Hence the Newtonian 'method' as described in LRBL may be used *because* it is 'more ingenious and for that reason more engaging' than any other.

Smith also recognized the importance of *analogy* in suggesting that philosophers, in attempting to explain unusual 'appearances', often did so in terms of knowledge gained in unrelated fields. It was suggested that reasoning by analogy might affect the nature of the work done, in the manner of the Pythagoreans who first studied arithmetic and then explained 'all things by the properties of numbers'—or the modern physician who 'lately gave a system of moral philosophy upon the principles of his own art' (Astronomy, II.12): 'In the same manner also, others have written parallels of painting and poetry, of poetry and music, of music and architecture, of beauty and virtue, of all the fine arts; systems which have universally owed their origin to the lucubrations of those who were acquainted with the one art, but ignorant of the other'. Indeed, Smith went further in noting that in some cases the analogy chosen could become not just a source of 'ingenious similitudes' but even 'the great hinge upon which every thing turned' (ibid.).

This leads on to the discussion of another side of the problem, again illustrated by the Astronomy, namely that different types of philosopher may produce conflicting accounts of the same phenomena. We have already noted that while at a certain stage of development the Cartesian system 'might continue to amuse the learned in other sciences' it could no longer satisfy those who were skilled in Astronomy (IV.67). But Smith also observed that the Copernican system had been adopted by astronomers even though inconsistent with the systems of physics as then known (IV.35), and that the system of eccentric spheres had been accepted by astronomers and mathematicians, but not by philosophers in general: 'Each party of them too, had . . . completed their peculiar system or theory of the universe, and no human consideration could then have induced them to give up any part of it.' (IV.18.) As this implies, there may be a certain unwillingness to accept ideas formulated in a particular way, and even resistance to the reception of new ones as a result of certain 'prejudices'. Some of these are obvious: for example, the 'natural prejudices of the imagination' (IV.52), which partly explained the original resistance to the idea of a moving earth. Others are more complex, especially those which Smith described as prejudices of education.[17] For example, Smith pointed out that resistance to the acceptance of Copernican ideas was partly explained by the 'Peripatetic Philosophy, the only philosophy then known in the world' (IV.38) and added, with reference to the system as a whole that: 'When it appeared in the world, it was almost universally disapproved of, by the learned as well as by the ignorant. The natural

---

[17] Cf. Hume, *A Treatise of Human Nature*, I.iii.x.1: 'But tho' education be disclaim'd by philosophy, as a fallacious ground of assent to any opinion, it prevails nevertheless in the world, and is the cause why all systems are apt to be rejected at first as new and unusual.' Hume's influence on Smith is the subject of the following section.

prejudices of sense, confirmed by education, prevailed too much with both, to allow them to give it a fair examination.' (IV.35.) In the same way, the immediate followers of Copernicus were held to have faced objections which were 'necessarily connected with that way of conceiving things, which then prevailed universally in the learned world' (IV.39).

Smith also noted the constraint on the development of new knowledge represented by reverence for the past (IV.20, 28) and made a good deal of national prejudice in the Letter to the *Edinburgh Review*, observing that the attachment of French philosophers to the system of Descartes had for a time 'retarded and incumbered the real advancement of the science of nature' (§ 5).

Points such as these seem to have been 'confirmed' by those whose business it has been to examine the *behaviour* of philosophers (in Smith's sense of the term). To go no further than the recent past, it is noteworthy that T. S. Kuhn's work on scientific revolutions also emphasized the problems of communication which exist between proponents of different theories (Smith's 'prejudices of education') while explaining the development of ideas in terms of systems (paradigms) each of which was doomed to destruction.[18] Indeed, Kuhn's argument taken as a whole may seem to suggest broad agreement with Smith's assessment of the principles of human nature and to support his belief that these principles were constant through time. It was, of course, this thesis that made it possible for the thinker of Smith's period to conceive of the social sciences as being on a par with the natural, thus matching the achievements of Newton in this field. For Dugald Stewart, the application of this 'fundamental and leading idea' to the various branches of theoretical history was to become 'the peculiar glory of the latter half of the eighteenth century'.[19] What Smith does is to leave the reader of these essays in some doubt as to wherein exactly 'glory' is to be found: in a contribution to knowledge, or to the composure of the imagination, or both.

V

It remains to note the influence of Hume on Adam Smith's philosophy of science. In his youth Smith evidently shared the usual interest of philosophers in the theory of knowledge. His essay on the External Senses is just the kind of thing one would expect from an able young philosopher. Typically, and for this subject very properly,

[18] *The Structure of Scientific Revolutions* (1962).
[19] *Works*, ed. Hamilton (1854), i.70.

Smith brings together evidence from scientists and arguments from philosophers in order to reach his views. A prominent feature of the essay is his acknowledgement of indebtedness to Berkeley's *New Theory of Vision*, from which he is ready to accept much and to criticize a little. There is no reference to the more radical use that Berkeley made of the self-same arguments in the wider theory of his *Principles of Human Knowledge*. Whether or not Smith ever read the latter work, he must surely have learned something of Berkeley's idealist philosophy from Hume's *Treatise of Human Nature*. It therefore seems likely, as Dr. Wightman suggests (133 below), that the essay on the External Senses is a very early piece, written before Smith had read Hume.

If so, the History of Astronomy will have come later. Although it does not mention Hume by name, it shows unmistakable signs of influence from the *Treatise of Human Nature*. Apart from Humean language about the association of ideas and about degrees of vivacity in sensations, Smith's account of the imagination seems to be an adaptation of Hume. He does not simply follow Hume, however, as he largely followed Berkeley when writing of vision in the essay on the External Senses. His view of the imagination in the History of Astronomy adds a significant element of originality by applying to the hypotheses of science a notion which Hume had used to explain the beliefs of common sense. That is one point of historical interest in Smith's account of the imagination here.

Another is that it shows Smith's appreciation of the positive side of Hume's epistemology. Scholars have tended to assume that Hume's contemporaries, like the thinkers of the nineteenth century, saw him as simply a sceptic—in the theory of knowledge at any rate. This was certainly true of his most severe critics, Thomas Reid and James Beattie. Hume's constructive philosophy of human nature, brought out by such twentieth-century scholars as N. Kemp Smith and H. H. Price, was unperceived by Reid and Beattie, and so by the later critics who took their cue from Reid and Beattie.

There is evidence, however, that some of Hume's contemporaries in Scotland, Adam Smith among them, did not share this blind spot. After Smith's death, his heir, David Douglas, evidently wrote to John Millar about the manuscripts which Smith had allowed to remain undestroyed. We know of this letter from the reply which it evoked. After referring to the essay on the Imitative Arts, Millar continues: 'Of all his writings, I have most curiosity about the metaphysical work you mention. I should like to see his powers of illustration employed upon the true old Humean philosophy.' The last words imply that Douglas, in his letter, had seen a connection between a work of Smith and the philosophy of Hume. They do not necessarily imply that Douglas would have agreed with Millar in regarding Hume's philosophy (or the relevant part of Hume's philosophy) as 'true', but they do at least suggest that he would not think the judgement novel or bizarre.

The letter was printed by W. R. Scott in *ASSP*, 311–13. Scott was not sure whether 'the metaphysical work' of Adam Smith that is referred to could be identified. In a note on p. 313 he said there was no trace of the manuscript so described, but in an earlier part of the book (p. 115, note 3) he suggested that it might be either an unknown manuscript or the work entitled 'The Principles which lead and direct Philosophical Enquiries' that was printed in Smith's posthumous *Essays on Philosophical Subjects*. There can be little doubt that this work is what David Douglas was talking about. Each of its three parts carries a title beginning 'The Principles which lead and direct Philosophical Enquiries; illustrated by . . .'. The term 'illustrated by' is picked up in John Millar's phrase, 'I should like to see his powers of illustration employed . . .'. In fact the 'metaphysical' discussion, on Humean lines, occurs only at the beginning of the first and longest essay, the History of Astronomy, but the initial sections of that essay are intended to be a general introduction to the work as a whole. It is these introductory sections that David Douglas must have had in mind when he talked of a 'metaphysical work' in the spirit of Hume.

What, then, is particularly Humean about Adam Smith's view of the history of science and philosophy? Smith follows the dictum of Plato and Aristotle that philosophy begins in wonder, but he gives this a Humean twist. Wonder arises when the smooth course of the imagination is disturbed by an unusual sequence of events. It is assuaged when philosophy (meaning science) shows the unusual event to be part of a system, a customary order, and so enables the imagination to resume an easy passage. Smith describes the work of the imagination in words that recall the doctrine of Hume's *Treatise*:

When two objects, however unlike, have often been observed to follow each other, and have constantly presented themselves to the senses in that order, they come to be so connected together in the fancy, that the idea of the one seems, of its own accord, to call up and introduce that of the other. If the objects are still observed to succeed each other as before, this connection, or, as it has been called, this association of their ideas, becomes stricter and stricter, and the habit of the imagination to pass from the conception of the one to that of the other, grows more and more rivetted and confirmed. . . . When objects succeed each other in the same train in which the ideas of the imagination have thus been accustomed to move, . . . such objects appear all closely connected with one another, and the thought glides easily along them, without effort and without interruption.... There is no break, no stop, no gap, no interval. The ideas excited by so coherent a chain of things seem, as it were, to float through the mind of their own accord, without obliging it to exert itself, or to make any effort in order to pass from one of them to another.

But if this customary connection be interrupted, if one or more objects appear in an order quite different from that to which the imagination has been accustomed, and for which it is prepared, the contrary of all this happens.... The imagination no longer feels the usual facility of passing from the event which goes before to that which comes after.... The fancy is stopped and interrupted in that natural movement or career, according to which it was proceeding. Those two events seem to stand at a distance from each other; it endeavours to bring them together, but they refuse to unite; and it feels, or imagines it feels, something like a gap or interval betwixt them. It ... endeavours to find out something which may fill up the gap, which, like a bridge, may so far at least unite those seemingly distant objects, as to render the passage of the thought betwixt them smooth, and natural, and easy. The supposition of a chain of intermediate, though invisible, events, which succeed each other in a train similar to that in which the imagination has been accustomed to move, and which link together those two disjointed appearances, is the only means by which the imagination can fill up this interval, is the only bridge which, if one may say so, can smooth its passage from the one object to the other.   (Astronomy, II.7–8)

Smith is drawing here on Hume's account both of causation and of our belief in an external world. He writes not only of *constant* conjunction but also of *coherence* in our experience. When he describes the 'interruption' of customary connections and of the 'smooth passage' of the imagination (or 'the fancy' or 'the thought'), and when he proceeds to say that the imagination fills up the gap by supposing a chain of intermediate though invisible events, he is making use of Hume's doctrine in *Treatise*, I.iv.2, the section entitled 'Of scepticism with regard to the senses'. Smith is not simply taking over Hume's theory, for Hume deals with our belief in the continued existence of material things while Smith talks about scientific theory. But Smith is adapting Hume's account of the imagination from the one subject to the other. Smith thinks that philosophy or science is an enlargement of commonsense belief as represented by Hume. Philosophy, 'the science of the connecting principles of nature ... may be regarded as one of those arts which address themselves to the imagination' (§12). Of course Hume himself says that systems of philosophy are also a product of the imagination, but his description of the processes of the imagination in filling up gaps comes into his account of our ordinary belief in an external world, and that is what Adam Smith uses in his account of scientific theory.

The Humean character of this section of Smith's History of Astronomy immediately strikes the modern scholar who is familiar with H. H. Price's book, *Hume's Theory of the External World* (1940). It seems that David Douglas saw it in the same sort of way and that his conception of Hume's philosophy included the role of the imagination in building up our beliefs about the world. There can be little doubt that Adam Smith himself appreciated this side of Hume. Although his debt to Hume is not explicitly acknowledged in the Astronomy, the phrases from the *Treatise* are unmistakable.

Smith takes seriously his conclusion that scientific theory is the work of the imagination. His History of Astronomy leads up to a detailed account of the theory of Newton. While Smith writes in more than one place of the attractions of the Newtonian system to the imagination, his description of it very naturally uses at times the language of objective fact. So he ends by recognizing that a work of imagination can seem to be the discovery of truth.

And even we, while we have been endeavouring to represent all philosophical systems as mere inventions of the imagination, to connect together the otherwise disjointed and discordant phaenomena of nature, have insensibly been drawn in, to make use of language expressing the connecting principles of this one, as if they were the real chains which Nature makes use of to bind together her several operations. Can we wonder then, that it should have gained the general and complete approbation of mankind, and that it should now be considered, not as an attempt to connect in the imagination the phaenomena of the Heavens, but as the greatest discovery that ever was made by man, the discovery of an immense chain of the most important and sublime truths, all closely connected together, by one capital fact, of the reality of which we have daily experience. (IV.76)

Smith seems to be implying here that it is in fact a mistake, though a natural one, to think of Newton's system as the discovery of objective truths and to think of gravity as a 'real chain' that binds operations in nature. This belief is an 'illusion of the imagination', to use a Humean phrase that Smith borrows in *The Theory of Moral Sentiments*,[20] composed a little later than the History of Astronomy. The *Moral Sentiments* is much concerned with the role of the imagination in moral judgement, but there is one place where Smith also relates it to economics. This comes at the beginning of Part IV. Again Smith builds on a doctrine of Hume. Hume, he says, has explained the beauty of utility. The owner of a useful object receives aesthetic pleasure from it by being reminded of its convenience. A spectator receives similar pleasure by sympathy. We find 'the palaces

[20] Hume, *Treatise* (ed. Selby-Bigge), 267; cf. 200, and 'illusion of the fancy', 314, 360: Smith, TMS III.2.4; cf. I.iii.2.2, II.i.5.11, IV.1.9.

of the great' beautiful because we imagine the satisfaction we would get if we owned and used them. Smith then adds his own contribution, that we often come to set a greater value on the convenient means than on the end which they were designed to promote. 'The poor man's son, whom heaven in its anger has visited with ambition,' goes beyond admiration of palaces to envy. He labours all his life to outdo his competitors, only to find in the end that the rich are no happier than the poor in the things that really matter. 'And it is well that nature imposes on us in this manner. It is this deception which rouses and keeps in continual motion the industry of mankind.' The individual does not reap for himself the full benefit of his exertions; there is a benefit to society at large, for the rich 'are led by an invisible hand' to distribute much of their substance among a circle of retainers, and so, 'without intending it, without knowing it, advance the interest of the society, and afford means to the multiplication of the species' (TMS IV.1.8–10).

Smith has an ambivalent attitude to this 'deception' by nature or the imagination. On the one hand, he says it is a deception; the ambition of the poor man's son is unfortunate, a visitation of the anger of heaven, and is succeeded in the end by the discovery that power and riches afford little satisfaction and are dangerous. On the other hand, this realization of the truth is a 'splenetic philosophy' that comes to us only 'in the languour of disease and the weariness of old age'. In a normal healthy state we let our imagination run away with us, and this is just as well because the deception is useful to society and mankind. At any rate Smith is clear that it is a deception and that there is an alternative view which is true, though apparently less preferable.

Would he say quite the same of Newton's scientific theory? He does imply that we are deceived in thinking the theory to be a discovery of truth and not just an 'invention' of the imagination. But would he be ready to add that it is therefore *false* and that there is, or could be, an alternative theory which is true? Apparently not, for he puts all scientific theories in the same boat. Are there then no objective truths of astronomy to be discovered, or is the position rather that there are truths of nature but they cannot be discovered by man because he has to rely on his imagination?

There is one important difference between Hume's view of the external world and Adam Smith's view of Newtonian mechanics. Hume began his discussion by distinguishing two questions. 'We may well ask, *What causes induce us to believe in the existence of body?* but 'tis in vain to ask, *Whether there be body or not?* That is a point, which we must take for granted in all our reasonings.' Smith has endeavoured to answer the Humean question, 'What causes induce us to believe in the existence of gravity?' He would not, however, have added: 'But 'tis in vain to ask, Whether there be gravity or not? That is a point which we must take for granted in all our reasonings.' Earlier theories of astronomy did not include a belief in gravity; and if anyone had suggested to Smith that a later theory might abandon Newton's concept of gravity and explain the observed facts in a different way, Smith would have agreed that this was quite possible. So although he is following Hume in the type of explanation that he gives, there is an important difference in their conclusions. In Smith's time it was a bold thing to say that Newton's mechanics was an 'invention of the imagination' rather than a discovery of truth, but it was far less bold than Hume's theory that belief in a continuing material world is due to 'fiction' by the imagination. Since past systems of astronomy had done without gravity, one could conceive that future systems might dispense with it. There is no analogue in a history of different systems of ordering common experience. The belief in continuing material bodies has not been preceded by one or more different ways of interpreting sense experience, in consequence of which we could conceive of yet another interpretation becoming standard at some future time.

When Smith writes that scientists have imagined inventions he does not say they have invented science fiction—or any other sort of fiction. But he does contrast an invention by the imagination with a discovery of truth, and so he implies that scientific theory cannot be true. The constructions of scientific theory are like the constructions of perceptual belief in Hume's theory of the external world because both are intended to render coherent the data of experience. But they are also unlike in that one scientific theory is succeeded by another; and today we should be more ready than Adam Smith to think that the replacement of the currently favoured theory of physics or astronomy is not just possible but probable. The replacement of one theory by another is not always in order to accommodate new empirical facts. The new facts could often be accommodated within a revised, but more complicated, version of the old theory. The new theory may be preferred because it is simpler or because it can be connected more directly with the theory of a related branch of science. If so, the criteria for preference are quasi-logical and aesthetic, like the criteria that shape the course of the imagination in Hume's theory of the external world. Is it then proper to claim that the preferred theory is more *true* than its rival? In these days of relativity theory, physics itself seems to cast doubt on any idea of strictly objective truths in nature independent of observers at different points of space and time. Adam Smith's view of science appears more perceptive today than it will have done in the eighteenth century.

E S S A Y S

ON

PHILOSOPHICAL SUBJECTS.

BY

The late ADAM SMITH, LL.D.

FELLOW OF THE ROYAL SOCIETIES OF LONDON AND EDINBURGH,
&c. &c.

TO WHICH IS PREFIXED,

An ACCOUNT of the LIFE and WRITINGS of the AUTHOR;

By *DUGALD STEWART*, F.R.S.E.

L O N D O N:

Printed for T. CADELL Jun. and W. DAVIES (Succeffors to Mr. CADELL)
in the Strand; and W. CREECH, Edinburgh.

1795.

The History of Astronomy

The History of the Ancient Physics

The History of the Ancient Logics
and Metaphysics

Introduction

To the inquiring layman, Adam Smith was the author of the *Wealth of Nations*; to the philosopher, of a comparable classic, the *Theory of Moral Sentiments*; these were the only books published in his lifetime. Within five years of his death (1790), however, appeared under the editorship of his two friends, Joseph Black and James Hutton, a substantial volume entitled *Essays on Philosophical Subjects ... to which is prefixed an Account of the Life and Writings of the Author by Dugald Stewart.* Though far less celebrated than the two major works the EPS nevertheless appeared during the next hundred years in at least eight editions, including one from Revolutionary Paris and one from Basel (see Bibliographical Note, Nos. 3, 4). In the present century the book has acquired a renewed interest, attention having been drawn principally to the first three essays, consideration of which has formed the basis of a significant secondary literature. The subject of each of these essays is the history of a branch of science, namely, of Astronomy, of the Ancient Physics, and of the Ancient Logics and Metaphysics. Of these the first alone is of any considerable length; the other two are hardly more than fragments. To none of them would a modern scholar turn for enlightenment on the history of the sciences; at most he could expect to discover what an outstanding mind living in the second half of the eighteenth century *believed* to represent the histories of these subjects. Wherein then lies the attraction to writers during recent decades? It lies in the full titles of the three essays: *The Principles which lead and direct Philosophical Enquiries; illustrated by the History of Astronomy*; the preamble is repeated before each of the other two histories. It might be conjectured from this that the first three essays are to be taken rather as chapters in a book than as separate pieces; that such a conjecture might be correct is supported by the Advertisement of the editors in which they emphasize that though immediately before his death Smith had destroyed many other manuscripts, he had left these 'in the hands of his friends to be disposed of as they thought proper', and that on inspection 'the greater number of them appeared to be parts of a plan he once had formed, for giving a connected history of the liberal sciences and elegant arts' but that he had long since 'found it necessary to abandon that plan as far too extensive'. Though there is now no trace of the manuscripts on which the collection was based, we know from other sources that this is hardly an adequate account.

If the allegedly projected *history* was to embrace the 'elegant arts' why was the telling preamble to the first three essays omitted from the remainder? To the modern reader it seems evident that whereas the former, inadequate though they may now appear, do conform to a unitary and highly significant plan, the remainder, though not without their interesting features, are neither treated historically nor do they illustrate the 'principles which lead and direct philosophical enquiry'. The editors, though in other respects men of high eminence, were not noted for scholarship as such. We must turn to other sources to discover what part the composition of these essays played in the author's intellectual scheme of things.

Fortunately we do not have to look beyond the volume itself: the *Essays* were preceded by a long and detailed 'Account of the Life and Writings of Adam Smith', read to the Royal Society of Edinburgh in 1793 and subsequently published in their *Transactions*. The author was Dugald Stewart, Professor of Moral Philosophy in the University of Edinburgh from 1785 to 1810, and the editor of the first *Collected Works* of Smith published in 1811–12. Towards the end of this 'Account' is cited Smith's earliest reference to the EPS of which we have any knowledge; it was contained in letter (137) to David Hume dated 'Edinburgh, 16th. April 1773' when Smith was preparing to go to London where he expected to remain some time. In the expectation that Hume would in the event of his own earlier death act as his literary executor, Smith insisted that of all the papers he was about to leave behind 'there are none worth the publishing but a fragment of a great work which contains a history of the Astronomical Systems that were successively in fashion down to the time of Des Cartes. Whether that might not be published as a fragment of an intended juvenile work, I leave entirely to your judgment; tho I begin to suspect myself that there is more refinement than solidity in some parts of it.' There is neither here nor anywhere else reference to other 'fragments' such as the Ancient Physics and Ancient Logics that ultimately came to be published in the same volume as the Astronomy; the possible significance of this omission will be discussed later (below, 26–7).

In 1773 Smith was already fifty; it is unlikely, therefore, that he would have referred to any work as 'juvenile' except such as had been written many years earlier. This supposition receives some support from his asking (Astronomy, II.12) 'Why has the chemical philosophy in all ages crept along in obscurity, and been so disregarded by the generality of mankind ... ?' How Smith could have formed such a judgement nearly a century after the prominence of Robert Boyle and Robert Hooke at the Royal Society it is difficult to understand;

but such an opinion would surely have been modified by intercourse with William Cullen with whom Smith is known[1] to have been on intimate terms after he assumed the Glasgow Chair of Logic in 1751. Since by 1748, almost two years after relinquishing the Snell Exhibition at Balliol College, Oxford, he must have been heavily engaged in the preparation and reading of his lectures on belles-lettres at Edinburgh, it has been fairly generally assumed that he at least laid the foundation of the History of Astronomy at Oxford; but from further internal evidence it may be inferred that he did not finish it there. Towards the end of the Astronomy Smith wrote that 'the observations of Astronomers at Lapland and Peru have fully confirmed Sir Isaac's system' (IV.72); Bouguer's account of his observations in Peru confirming Newton's model of the figure of the Earth was published in 1749—three years after Smith left Balliol.

The reader may have noticed a discrepancy between this reference to 'Sir Isaac's [Newton] system' and (in the letter to David Hume) the description of the History as being of the astronomical systems that were successively in fashion down to the time of Descartes: the last ten pages of the original printed text are in fact devoted to establishing 'the superior genius and sagacity of Sir Isaac Newton'. Relevant to this question is the editors' terminal note: 'The Author, at the end of this Essay, left some Notes and Memorandums, from which it appears, that he considered this last part of his History of Astronomy as imperfect, and needing several additions. The Editors, however, chose rather to publish than to suppress it. It must be viewed, not as a History or Account of Sir Isaac Newton's Astronomy, but chiefly as an additional illustration of those Principles in the Human Mind which Mr. Smith has pointed out to be the universal motives of Philosophical Researches.'

This is consistent with the view put forward above that though the Astronomy may well have been largely composed in Oxford the 'last part' of it could have been added after Smith's return to Scotland. That even this 'last part' was written *before* 1758 appears from his statement (Astronomy, IV.74) that Newton's 'followers have, from his principles, ventured even to predict the returns of several of them [sc. comets], particularly of one which is to make its appearance in 1758. We must wait for that time . . .'. Thus the text; a footnote on the same page reads: 'It must be observed, that the whole of this Essay was written previous to the date here mentioned; and that the return of the comet happened agreeably to the prediction.' There is in the

---

[1] Rae, *Life*, 44, states that before the middle of November [1751] he [Smith] and Cullen were 'already deeply immersed in quite a number of little schemes for the equipment of the College' [Glasgow].

original text no indication as to who added this note; but P. Prevost, the translator of the French edition (see Bibliographical Note 3), describes the note as 'de l'editeur anglais'. Since Prevost was a Fellow of the Royal Society of Edinburgh and claimed to be personally acquainted with Dugald Stewart he may have had first-hand information.

The apparent discrepancy in the letter to Hume disappears if it is recalled that Smith was expressing an opinion as to what of his literary remains might be worthy of publication: the 'Notes and Memorandums' referred to in the editors' final note to the Astronomy, suggest that Smith was more than doubtful as to whether the 'last part' should qualify.

The period 1746–8 when Smith was residing at Kirkcaldy with his mother and before he was committed to the reading of lectures on Rhetoric and Belles-Lettres at Edinburgh would seem as likely as any for laying the foundation of a project on the scale that he is known to have envisaged. Whether the other two 'fragments' were composed during that period is a matter of no special consequence; there would, at any rate, be no inconsistency in his having spoken more than once [and presumably much later] to Dugald Stewart of having 'projected, in the earlier part of his life, a history of the other sciences on the same plan' (Stewart, II.52) and of his editors having referred to a 'plan he had once formed, for giving a connected history of the liberal sciences and elegant arts'. There were, of course, neither then nor for a long time afterwards, any Faculties of Science in the Scottish universities and the boundary between 'arts' and 'sciences' was hardly, if at all, clearly drawn. 'Logics and Metaphysics' are still mainly the concern of Faculties of Arts, as would also be the sort of 'ancient physics' that Smith was describing in the essay so entitled.

There is extant one other allusion by Smith which, though somewhat inconsistent with those that have been referred to, cannot be ignored in any attempt to date the composition of the EPS. It occurs in a letter (248) to the Duc de La Rochefoucauld written from Edinburgh in November 1785 but not published until 1895; the relevant section runs as follows:

I have likewise two other great works upon the anvil; the one is a sort of Philosophical History of all the different branches of Literature, of Philosophy, Poetry and Eloquence; the other is a sort of theory and History of Law and Government. The materials of both are in a great measure collected, and some Part of both is put into tollerable good order. But the indolence of old age, tho' I struggle violently against it, I feel coming fast upon me, and whether I shall ever be able to finish either is extremely uncertain.

Now whereas the description of the former of these 'other great works' could well refer to the Histories of Astronomy, Ancient Physics, and Logics and Metaphysics included in the *Essays on Philosophical Subjects*, the remaining essays, though falling under the generous heading of 'Literature, Philosophy, Poetry and Eloquence', are almost wholly devoid of any reference to any historical development. Moreover, the limited range of topics hardly warrants the claim that the 'materials' were 'in a great measure collected'. In the fitful light of such evidence as is now available it seems difficult to avoid the conclusion that after the exacting labour of the *Wealth of Nations* with its successive revisions Smith's 'great work on a sort of philosophical history' existed more in the hope of realizing a youthful ambition than in any adequate progress towards its achievement.[2] Fortunately the impossibility of any precise dating of its components does not preclude further fruitful consideration of the part this ambition continued to play in Smith's intellectual development.

In 1755, four years after Smith had been appointed to the Glasgow Chair, he wrote the two well-known letters to the *Edinburgh Review*. In the second of these letters Smith evidently considered himself so much a master of the state of the sciences in Europe as to include a critical review of 'the new French Encyclopedia' (below, 245–8); and though the modern reader will detect a certain degree of superficiality—not to say even contradiction—in his judgements he had clearly a wide-ranging knowledge relevant to the task. Among the contributors he refers to—'many of them already known to foreign nations by the valuable works which they have published' (Letter, §6)—he singles out 'Mr. Alembert' and 'Mr. Diderot' and refers to the former's famous *Discours préliminaire*.

A perusal of d'Alembert's *Discours* reveals a strong resemblance to Smith's approach to the 'principles which lead and direct philosophical enquiries'. In his stress on what he called Smith's 'Theoretical or Conjectural History' Dugald Stewart (II.49) expressed the view that the 'mathematical sciences, both pure and mixed, afford, in many of their branches, very favourable subjects for theoretical history'; and he went on to note d'Alembert's recommendation of this historical approach for teaching. More striking still, he follows this reference by instancing a passage in Montucla's *Histoire des mathématiques* (Paris, 1758) which included long sections on 'mixed' mathematics (viz. astronomy, mechanics, optics, and their applications) where an attempt is made to 'exhibit the gradual progress of philosophical

---

[2] That Smith himself was far from being consistent in referring to his literary achievements and aims will appear in connection with the dating of the Imitative Arts (172 below).

speculation, from the first conclusions suggested by a general survey
of the heavens, to the doctrines of Copernicus. It is somewhat
remarkable, that a theoretical history of this very science ... was one
of Mr. Smith's earliest compositions'. Since Stewart shared with
Smith the habit of almost total lack of *significant* documentation, we
do not know where he read d'Alembert's reference to Montucla, but
it obviously could not have been in the first (1751) edition of the
Encyclopédie, which we know to have been in Smith's hands before
1755.

Although we can beyond all reasonable doubt reject any charge of
plagiarism, there is nevertheless one feature in Smith's appreciation
of the *Encyclopédie* that must strike us as rather odd: in acclaiming
the outstanding quality of d'Alembert's contributions he makes no
mention of the strong affinity between the latter's views on the nature,
significance, and enlargement of 'philosophy' and those we believe he
had already set forth in the 'historical' essays. Smith's review of the
Encyclopédie was part of the evidence he submitted to the 'Authors'
of the newly founded *Edinburgh Review* in support of the proposal
that they should enlarge the scope of their *Review* to include not only
English but also European letters. Is it not a matter for some surprise
that a young man, little more than thirty, recently established as the
leading philosophical teacher in a small but ancient university,
should not in such circumstances have at least briefly impressed
upon the *Review* the universal significance of the *Discours préliminaire*? D'Alembert, though only six years older than Smith, was
already accepted as one of the most brilliant analytical and
comprehensive of European minds: a mathematician of the first rank,
who appreciated both the power of mathematics and its limitations as
a mode for 'philosophy' in general, and whose concern for this
'philosophy' was primarily in its significance for human welfare. The
broad agreement of the views of such an authority with this 'juvenile'
plan would, one might have supposed, have prompted Smith to a
more enthusiastic welcome to the *Discours* than that 'Mr. Alembert
gives an account of the connection of the different arts and sciences,
their genealogy and filiation, as he calls it; which, a few alterations
and corrections excepted, is nearly the same with that of my Lord
Bacon' (Letter, §6). It is perhaps necessary to emphasize that the
'broad agreement' in the views of Smith and d'Alembert was mainly
(as noted above) in respect of their *approach*. A review of the details
of their argument would here be out of place; but one especially
marked difference in their emphasis may be the clue to the puzzle: it
is that whereas Smith sets so much store on 'wonder' and 'surprise'
(below, 13–14), d'Alembert, following Bacon, stresses the greater

significance of 'need and use' in discovery—a position that the author of the *Wealth of Nations* as dogmatically rejects (Astronomy, III.3). Could it have been that the 'juvenile' author of the *Essays on Philosophical Subjects* held his horses in the hope that an opportunity would later present itself for the systematic refutation of a theory whose wrong-headedness he evidently deplored?

Though this account of the circumstances of time, place, and purpose of the composition of the EPS has been if not wholly negative at least mainly 'conjectural', it may have given some insight into the nature of the undertaking and the reason for its continued interest to scholars. Reference to d'Alembert's *Discours* has shown that Smith's attempt at 'conjectural history' was no isolated phenomenon; Dugald Stewart claims that the 'expression . . . coincides pretty nearly in its meaning with that of *Natural History*, as employed by Mr. Hume [i.e. *The Natural History of Religion*, 1757], and with what some French writers have called *Histoire Raisonnée*' (Stewart, II.48). Among examples of the latter he names Montesquieu's *Esprit des lois* (1748). The title of that great work is itself indicative of what many writers were doing at that time: Paul Hazard reminds us of the numerous attempts to distil the *Esprit* of this, that, and the other; frequently by means of a search for the origin and growth of the 'science' or 'art' concerned. The *Encyclopédie* was not the first to envisage this task: something of the same sort had appeared in Ephraim Chambers's relatively concise *Cyclopaedia; or an Universal Dictionary of Arts and Sciences* (1728), but never before had it been accomplished in such a penetrating manner or on such an immense scale.

The History of Astronomy

The importance of this essay to modern scholars lies mainly in the preamble and the first three sections; these contain a statement and elaboration of the chief 'principles' that Smith believed to 'lead and direct philosophical enquiries'. The History of Astronomy *sensu stricto*, that begins only in Section IV, is of interest partly as an indication of contemporary knowledge of the subject, but mainly for the incidental remarks made by the author in pursuance of his central aim. Though acceptable to a modern historian in its main lines, it contains so many errors of detail and not a few serious omissions as to be no longer more than a museum specimen of its kind. This is not to deny its high merit for an age when systematic study of the history of the sciences was in its infancy. But by 1758 a student would have been better advised to read Jean-Étienne Montucla's *Histoire des mathématiques* (written incidentally in the enlightened spirit characteristic of the young Adam Smith) which by 1802 had been revised

and extended by Jérôme de Lalande. The first history of astronomy
still used as an important work of reference was completed by Jean-
Baptiste-Joseph Delambre in 1827.

In any attempt to assess the success of Smith's enterprise we are
met at the outset by his inconsistent and ill-defined terminology
'philosophy is the science ... Philosophy ... may be regarded as one
of those arts...' (both in Astronomy, II.12). In fact the terms
philosophy, physics, arts, sciences, and natural philosophy are used
almost indiscriminately. In this of course he was not alone: Hume
(*Treatise of Human Nature*, Introduction) speaks of 'philosophy and
the sciences', which seems to promise a distinction more in line with
modern usage; but by including Natural Religion and Criticism
among the 'sciences' he introduced a possible source of confusion.
The actual words 'natural science' in the sense of an 'inquiry by
reason alone into all things in the natural kingdom of God' were first
used by Thomas Hobbes in *Leviathan*; but 'natural philosophy' was
preferred (though not in the restricted sense still current in the
Scottish universities) throughout the seventeenth and eighteenth
centuries. The first demarcation between 'science' and 'art' is
attributed by the *Oxford English Dictionary* to Richard Kirwan:
'Previous to the year 1780 mineralogy tho' tolerably understood as an
art could scarcely be termed a science' (1796). James Hutton about the
same time wrote that 'philosophy must proceed in generalising those
truths which are the objects of particular sciences'. In respect of the
recent blossoming of the so-called 'social sciences' the failure of
English to distinguish the species *Naturwissenschaft* from the genus
Wissenschaft has become even more embarrassing than heretofore.

Had Smith consistently used 'philosophy' to *include* natural
philosophy, leaving it to the context to indicate whether the general
term or the specific application was concerned, there could, in relation
to the period, be no quarrel. When he writes (Astronomy, IV.18)
'Philosophers, long before the days of Hipparchus [*c*. 140 B.C.], seem
to have abandoned the study of nature ...' and to have regarded 'all
mathematicians, among whom they counted astronomers' with
'supercilious and ignorant contempt' his *usage* (whatever we may
think of his judgement) was in general accord with ancient and
medieval practice.

In the Middle Ages the interpretation of 'philosophy' varied from
one university to another. Roughly speaking when the trivium was
enlarged under the term *studia humanitatis* (and in many cases the
quadrivium, as such, disappeared in practice), 'philosophy' meant
moral philosophy. Mathematics and astronomy, together with
'natural philosophy' (more often called 'physics'), became mainly the

concern of the Faculty of Medicine; this was especially the case in the Italian universities. But Smith's judgement cited above follows a brief account of the epicyclic and eccentric systems of planetary motion by which 'those philosophers (IV.9) imagined they could account for the apparently unequal velocities of all those bodies'. Who are 'those philosophers'? It was, we are told, Apollonius (IV.8) who 'invented' the system and Hipparchus who 'afterwards perfected' it. Apollonius was a mathematician of the calibre of Eudoxus and Euclid; Hipparchus pioneered the branch of mathematics that came long afterwards to be known as spherical trigonometry and he was also among the greatest observers of all time. Most of the astronomical works of each were irretrievably lost; but to neither is any interest in 'philosophy' attributed—a fact at which Smith himself hints in another context (Astronomy, IV.25) where he speaks of 'the philosophy of Aristotle, and the astronomy of Hipparchus'. The precise distinction made by the Greeks themselves will be cited in the Introduction to the essay on 'The Ancient Physics'.

It would of course be absurd to demand precisely demarcated categories which would only stifle attempts to reveal latent relationships. But that in relation to the age of Adam Smith there are traps easily fallen into is shown by a recent comment[3] that Smith referred to Isaac Newton 'as a philosopher not scientist'. From Smith's use of the term in this context nothing can be inferred, since the word 'scientist' did not exist before 1839. The use of such expressions as 'Adam Smith's philosophy of science' may similarly be a source of confusion; better to risk a charge of repetitiveness and pedantry than that of circularity; each reference must be explicated on its own merits.

This caveat has an indirect bearing on the introductory sections of the Astronomy. Smith's aim in this and the succeeding essays was to show how these histories illustrate 'the principles which lead and direct philosophical enquiries'. Having in the first three paragraphs given the barest hint of the relevance of 'surprise' and 'wonder' to these 'principles' he reviews at what may seem inordinate length the influence of the sentiments of surprise and wonder on the emotions of joy, grief, panic, frenzy, etc. The modern reader, especially one unfamiliar with the pervasive significance accorded to the 'passions' by Smith and his contemporaries, may feel puzzled to know what all this has to do with the clearly expressed aim of the essays. Smith might have been wise to recall Bacon's words that such observations are 'well inquired and collected in metaphysic, but in physic they are

[3] H. F. Thomson, 'Adam Smith's Philosophy of Science', *Quarterly Journal of Economics*, lxxix (1965), 218.

impertinent' (*Advancement of Learning* II.vii.7). But after a dozen pages the rhetorical fog lifts: the 'surprise' excited in the observer by the motion of a piece of iron 'without any visible impulse, in consequence of the motion of a loadstone at some little distance from it' and the 'wonder' how it came to be 'conjoined to an event with which, according to the ordinary train of things, he could have so little suspected it to have any connection' (II.6) establish the thesis in the clearest possible manner. The further deployment of the thesis, even if unnecessarily prolonged, displays Smith's elegant and imaginative style at its best. Had he but set his own words 'philosophy is the science of the connecting principles of nature' at the beginning instead of near the end, and then avoided the trap in the ill-defined term 'philosophy', this section might well have ranked as the most fundamental in the whole work. Though not free from confusion, the concluding pages of this section reveal in greater emphasis Smith's 'principles of philosophical enquiries'. Central among these is an interpretation of causal investigation as a search for a 'bridge'; the examples here are much more convincing. The special characteristics of this 'bridge' or 'chain' are analogy to more familiar objects, coherence, and—of special significance for the modern scholar— 'without regarding their absurdity or probability, their agreement or inconsistency with truth and reality' (II.12). This remarkable passage is our justification for caution in speaking about what has been called 'Smith's philosophy of science'. For Smith himself who, as we have seen, defines 'philosophy' as 'the science of the connecting principles of nature' the term could have no clear connotation; nor could it for anyone until the term 'science' was restricted to what Smith is here calling 'philosophy'. There is still no general agreement as to the range of the 'philosophy of science'; but that it is essentially *meta*-science, or talk *about* science, would probably not be contested. Of this there could not in Smith's time be any explicit recognition. No doubt the study of his enterprise will shed light on the nature of the problems to be talked about; but in respect of its 'systems' his inquiry was less about their truth than about 'how far each of them was fitted to sooth(e) the imagination, and to render the theatre of nature a more coherent, and therefore a more magnificent spectacle, than otherwise it would have appeared to be' (ibid.). This has certainly a modern ring about it; but a modern 'philosophy of science' that thus ignored the problem of truth would get rather a cold reception. It is thus less the philosophy of science than the history of the *idea* of the 'philosophy of science' that Smith's enterprise is likely to illuminate.[4]

[4] For a further elaboration, see the present writer's 'Adam Smith and the History of Ideas' in *Essays on Adam Smith*. The essay was designed to be read in conjunction with this introduction.

The dubious historiography and scrappy exposition of Section III—'Of the Origin of Philosophy'—are characteristic of the 'Age of Reason': imaginative liveliness creates a colourful stage upon which the drama of Western culture is to take its rise. Regrettably 'imagination'[5] aided and abetted but not controlled by 'reason' takes command; and what was in the circumstances inevitably no more than a 'likely story' is presented with a degree of naïve dogmatism and assurance that would be beguiling if it had not engendered distorted attitudes in the long shadows of which we are still living. The danger of 'conjectural history' is thus made only too plain; justification of this rather critical assessment may most suitably wait on textual commentary.

In Section IV we are plunged rather abruptly into 'The History of Astronomy' proper: abruptly, since Smith has already stated that it is from Plato and Aristotle that he will 'begin to give her history in any detail'. The highly complex and mathematically beautiful system of Eudoxus is thus made to appear fully formed like Pallas from the head of Zeus. For his purpose Smith is perhaps justified in thus proceeding; but not to emphasize the extreme unlikelihood of such a creation without a long preparation of accurate observation and critical correlation is to risk begging the whole question of the genesis of philosophical inquiry. Once launched, however, on the exposition of the 'first regular system of Astronomy' (Astronomy, IV.4) he moves, not indeed with complete mastery, but with a remarkable degree of precision and understanding. Since among the readers of this edition there may be some wholly unfamiliar with the rationale of this system it may be as well to give a necessarily somewhat simplified but also more concise account of it than Smith provides; to facilitate cross-reference this will be set out in a somewhat schematic form.

The celestial phenomena (appearances) were either relatively transitory (e.g. meteors) or eternal; comets, remaining visible for months, were the subjects of some controversy.

The 'eternal' bodies, with seven notable exceptions, were fixed in space relative to each other. The exceptions—Sun, Moon, Mercury, Venus, Mars, Jupiter, and Saturn (to give them their Latinized names)—were all called 'planets' or 'wandering stars', since their positions varied continuously both with respect to each other and to the pattern of the 'fixed' stars.

All the visible objects were seen to move in circles round the Earth in a time constituting a 'day'. The various minor discrepancies among

---

[5] On Smith's attitude to the 'faculty' of imagination see below, 20.

the planets were accounted for by assuming additional circular motions superimposed upon the uniform daily rotation. The 'fixed' stars were thus regarded as being carried round by the rotation of the 'celestial sphere' whose axis, since many of them periodically 'rose' in the east and 'set' in the west, was held to be variously inclined to the surface of the Earth. Contrary to the belief still held in some quarters, the 'flat Earth' had been generally abandoned about a century earlier, and, though reintroduced to conform to biblical cosmology, was probably never again seriously considered among men having any pretension to astronomical knowledge.

Since the Sun and Moon are seen to make a circuit of the stellar sphere once in roughly 365 and 29 days respectively, the motion of each was regarded as being compounded of that of the stellar sphere and that of a second sphere whose axis was inclined to that of the stellar; in the case of the Sun the 'equator' of the second sphere was called the 'ecliptic', and the latter's 'obliquity' represents the observed progressive changes in the Sun's altitude in the course of the year. A third sphere had to be added to account for a further minor irregularity in the observed motion. The Moon's observed motion resisted any adequate representation; it was one of the few problems that gave Newton a headache 2,000 years later.

The motions of the remaining 'planets' were partially accounted for by supposing them to share the daily and (approximate) annual motion of the Sun's two spheres—the third was peculiar to the Sun. But these five bodies—and very obviously those that were believed to be always further from the Earth than is the Sun—possessed a characteristic irregularity of apparently coming to a halt, and then roughly retracing their paths to a second point before once more proceeding in the general direction. These meaningless 'stations' and 'retrogradations' of each of these planets were 'saved' by the ingenious device of 'fixing' each planet on a sphere, the poles of whose axis were also 'fixed' on the surface of the surrounding sphere to whose axis their axes were inclined; and at the same time supposing them to rotate in the opposite sense, each at a characteristic rate different from that of the surrounding sphere. The process could be repeated, and the inclinations and relative rates of rotation varied, to give the closest possible approximation to the 'appearances'.

All this is set out by Smith with only relatively minor historical inaccuracies; but he does not here make clear that the 'constant and equable motions' reported by reliable commentators to have been demanded by Plato were in fact uniform angular motion in perfectly circular paths. Nor, though he has his own view as to the human urge to see coherence and a continuous chain in natural phenomena, does he comment on Plato's postulates in flat opposition to the evidence of the senses, except in respect of the daily revolution. Plato discussed these questions in several dialogues, and his final 'vision' of the cosmos (if he did in fact ever arrive at one) is still a matter of controversy. But his guiding principle, from which he made no fundamental departure, was that the 'visible' heavens have the same relation to 'things divine' as they really exist as do geometrical figures to those 'truths of reason' that they are made to represent.

In proceeding from the concentric systems of Eudoxus to the excentric (and epicyclic) systems that permanently superseded it among the Greeks, Smith missed two points of fundamental importance to his 'principles that lead and direct' philosophical investigation. The first was that Aristotle's addition of twenty-two spheres had nothing to do with the 'insufficiency' of the spheres to represent the motions; the reason was what we should call a philosophical demand for a physical coherence: the additional spheres were so intercalated as to prevent the characteristic motion of each of the planets from being transmitted to the remainder. Another serious physical discrepancy apparently first observed by Autolycus of Pitane but not by Aristotle, was the fact that no system of spheres concentric with the Earth could conceivably account for the marked changes in the apparent size of e.g. Mars and Venus, implying variation in their distances from the Earth. The contrast between 'astronomy' and 'physics' sketched by Aristotle, well known to the Middle Ages and Renaissance through the *Commentaries* of Simplicius, but apparently lost sight of later until stressed by Paul Duhem in his Σώζειν τὰ φαινόμενα, will be discussed more at large in the Introduction to the Ancient Physics.

The first step towards the epicyclic (and incidentally towards the Copernican) theory of planetary motion was taken by Heracleides of Pontus, who, noting the fact that neither Mercury nor Venus is ever seen far from the Sun as the latter makes its annual circuit of the heavens, put forward the hypothesis that the circular paths of the former bodies were centred at the Sun, not the Earth. A century later, when Alexandria had replaced Athens as the centre of 'Greek' culture, this hypothesis was extended by Aristarchus of Samos to include *all* the planets, of which he regarded the Earth instead of the Sun to be one. This revolutionary hypothesis, in which the diurnal rotation of the Earth (already assumed by Heracleides) was also adopted, was summarily rejected by his contemporaries. Nevertheless, since their imaginative leaps achieved the essential basis of that of Copernicus, the omission by Smith of any mention of these two men is quite unaccountable.

Though no motion of the Earth was acceptable to astronomers until the time of Copernicus, and even then but tardily, the concept of epicyclic motion (i.e. the circular motion of a body about another body itself describing a circle about a third) rapidly achieved a dominating influence and received a definitive form in the *Almagest* of Ptolemy (*c.* A.D. 150). Stripped down to the barest essentials this system was based on the following postulates:

(i)   The Earth is the 'centre' of the world.
(ii) The Sun moves at a uniform rate on a circle (the 'eccentric') whose centre is somewhat distant from the Earth.
(iii) The remaining planets (except the Moon) move on circles (epicycles) whose centres move on larger circles ('deferents') centred at the eccentric; but the planets themselves are represented as moving at a uniform rate round a separate point ('equant') on the side of the eccentric remote from the Earth.
(iv) The Moon's motion is especially anomalous.

The eccentric and epicycle had been elaborated by earlier astronomers, notably Hipparchus (*c.* 170 B.C.), but the equant point, concerned not with the shape but with the rate of planetary movement, was the creation of Ptolemy himself. Since their concern was to provide a mathematical model for forecasting celestial events, the Alexandrian (Hellenistic) astronomers took no account of the existence of 'spheres'. The later Islamic astronomers, strongly influenced by Aristotelian and later 'physics', devised means of harmonizing epicyclic and eccentric motion with concentric celestial spheres. This mode of thought achieved its ultimate refinement in the theory of Georg (of) Peurbach. The so-called 'Copernican Revolution' was in fact a retrogression to 'ancient' principles buttressed by superior mathematical technique and the less 'parochial' world-view characteristic of the Renaissance. Far from being technically 'modern', the system of Copernicus was in some respects retrograde in the pejorative sense; this judgement does not detract from the dedication and intellectual courage of the man himself.

By one of those paradoxes that the history of science displays from time to time, Tycho Brahe, 'the great restorer of the science of the heavens' as Smith describes him, spent his life and fortune (aided by royal patronage on a lavish scale) in assembling the data enabling Ioannes Kepler to demolish both his own extension of the system of Heracleides and the details of the Copernican system. Tycho's model, postulating a heliocentric system of all the planets, the Sun and Moon alone describing circles about the Earth, was mathematically equivalent to that of Copernicus, at the same time avoiding any

affront to the physical prejudices of the age, still predominantly
Aristotelian. Endowed with a spirit in which intense religious feeling,
high poetic fancy, and unswerving intellectual integrity were
combined to a degree probably unsurpassed in any man before or
since, Kepler made the first and final break with the Platonic
postulates of 'equable circular motion' for celestial bodies. It is the
Sun, not the Earth, around which the planets describe the only
discoverable simple curve—not a circle, but an ellipse; and it is the
Sun that determines, in a degree corresponding to the harmonics of
the diatonic scale, the speed with which they move in the paths
appointed by God. Stripped of the overtones that Kepler himself
regarded as his supreme act of praise to the living God, his three[6]
'laws' are the basis of the modern astronomy of the solar system.

Within the limits of the available knowledge Smith's account of
the revolution in astronomical thought effected by Copernicus,
Tycho Brahe, and Kepler displays remarkable understanding; there
is however one misleading feature in his exposition—the statements
(Astronomy, IV.29,32) that the Copernican system has no need of
epicycles. It is indeed true that each of these statements is made in the
context of the apparent shape of the planetary motions, but not many
paragraphs later it is made clear that in order to rid his system of the
'incoherence' of the equant point (IV.53) Copernicus had in fact been
compelled to employ a number of epicycles. One of Kepler's earliest
discoveries was that the motion of the Earth demanded just such an
equant point: it is of course a mathematical dodge to represent the
hitherto 'unthinkable' fact that the planets move faster when near the
Sun than when more remote. Smith's account is further notable for
having stressed the possibly decisive nature of Galileo's telescopic
observations—the 'rough' surface of the Moon, the satellites of
Jupiter, sunspots, and the phases of Venus—all phenomena that
could 'appeal to a wide audience', thus enlisting a wider support for
the Copernican hypothesis than Copernicus's own dry mathematical
exposition would have done. Smith's claim that the latter 'was
adopted . . . by astronomers only' (IV.36), though qualified on the
next page, gives a misleading impression of the situation. This and
some relatively minor points are more conveniently dealt with in
footnotes to the text.

The confused state of astronomy during the first half of the
seventeenth century was just such as to give point to Smith's
'principle' that discovery is the fruit of a search for a 'connecting

---

[6] Really four: the first, the demonstration that the planets' orbits, including the Earth's, are
co*planar* with the Sun is unaccountably omitted from the 'text-books'. Kepler himself never set
out the laws in any systematic form.

chain of intermediate objects to link together ... discordant qualities'
(IV.60)—in this case the immensity of the celestial bodies and the
hardly conceivable speeds with which they are hurled round the
Sun. The 'gap' left in the 'imagination' by a purely mathematical
model, however subtle and however accurately representative of the
facts, received expression in the full title of Kepler's *Astronomia Nova*.
The 'physical or if you will metaphysical' element in his system was
supplied by a supposed magnetic 'radiation' emitted by the Sun as it
rotated, thus maintaining the revolutions of the planets at varying
speeds. 'That doctrine,' wrote Smith, 'like almost all those of the
philosophy in fashion during his time, bestowed a name upon this
invisible chain, called it an immaterial virtue, but afforded no
determinate idea of what was its nature.' (Astronomy, IV.60.) In an
age dominated by Newton's proper rejection of 'occult causes' such a
reaction was inevitable. But it is not the whole story. Kepler's
'magnetic virtue' was more than a name; in fact magnetism was not,
in the distinction made by Newton, an 'occult' but a 'manifest' quality.
The fact that it is a different 'manifest' quality—gravitation—that
was later shown to be the controlling factor between Sun and planets
does not detract from Kepler's recognition that a 'chain' must exist.
In his second letter to Richard Bentley, Newton emphasized that 'the
cause of gravity is what I do not pretend to know'. Smith and his
clear-sighted contemporaries failed to realize that the greatest creative
advances in the search for the 'invisible chain' have seldom been free
from the wildest guesses.

The 'first who attempted to ascertain, precisely, wherein this
invisible chain consisted, and to afford the imagination a train of
intermediate events, ...' was, Smith justly states, Descartes (Astronomy, IV.61). The details of the Cartesian system fortunately do not
concern us. But Smith shows remarkable sagacity in emphasizing
that it was he (and not, as is still occasionally stated, Galileo) who
stated three propositions that jointly imply 'Newton's' First Law of
Motion; that his notion of God's conservation of the quantity of
motion in the universe (IV. 61) made a notable advance towards
Newton's Second Law; and that he was 'among the first of the
moderns, who ... took away the boundaries of the Universe'. Not
surprisingly Smith nowhere shows any knowledge of the wide-
ranging mathematical speculation of the fifteenth-century Cardinal
Nicholas of Cues (whom Kepler called 'divine'), nor of the limited
publication of Thomas Digges's theory of stellar distribution in
depth; but his omission of any reference to the ill-supported but
widely publicized 'plurality of worlds' affirmed by Giordano Bruno
is less easy to excuse.

His lengthy treatment of Descartes in a history of astronomy, Smith claims, is justified less by his theory of the heavens that by the time Smith was writing was almost entirely abandoned, than by his demonstration that a coherent 'system of the world' could be based on simple mechanical principles applicable to both celestial and terrestrial bodies. This was a radical departure from the 'natural philosophy' still dominant in the schools: Samuel Pepys was so 'vexed' to discover that his younger brother, John's, knowledge of 'physiques' was based on Descartes instead of Aristotle that he decided to find out 'what it is that he has studied since his going to the University'. So far as 'physiques' were concerned both Samuel and John were wasting their time; for in the same year a young sizar of Trinity College in the same university of Cambridge was also giving less than satisfaction in his undergraduate studies. But within three years he was to think of 'extending gravity to the orbe of the Moon'. Cambridge was slow to appreciate the tremendous revolution that the young Lucasian Professor of Mathematics proceeded to hatch within its walls; but a few years after its publication (1687 —under the imprimatur of Samuel Pepys P.R.S.!) the elements of Newton's *Philosophiae Naturalis Principia Mathematica* were being introduced to the students of the University of Edinburgh by David Gregory.

Despite the lack of any break in the narrative, it seems most probable that it was at this point (Astronomy, IV.67) that Smith's original manuscript ended and the remainder was added at some later date (above, 7–8).

About Smith's account of the Newtonian system, which, despite his doubts, stands least in need of correction at the present day, little need be said. It is clearly written and includes all the 'verifications' available by the middle of the eighteenth century. It is doubtful whether he had ever studied the *Principia* at that time. Voltaire's *Elemens de la philosophie de Neuton* had been published in London by 1737, and, if this section was in fact written some years after the rest of the essay, Colin Maclaurin's *Account of Sir Isaac Newton's Philosophical Discoveries* would have been available to him after 1748; of course he may have been sufficiently well grounded in the qualitative aspects before leaving Glasgow. The only disconcerting feature of his account, taken as a contribution to the 'principles of philosophical investigation', is the facile manner in which he accepts gravitation as an adequate *explanation* of the mutually determined motions of the celestial bodies, simply on the grounds that it has always been 'familiar' to men on the Earth. Taken in conjunction with his remarks (Astronomy, IV.61) in hailing Descartes as having been the first to attempt to 'ascertain, precisely, wherein this invisible chain consisted', this must be regarded as a serious deficiency. It betrays a strange lack of awareness of the fact that what he saw as 'so familiar a principle of connection, which completely removed all the difficulties the imagination had hitherto felt in attending to them [sc. planetary motions]' (IV.67), many continental 'philosophers', notably Leibniz, regarded as either a miracle or a blasphemy. The root of their objections was that celestial gravitation, unlike the 'familiar' form, must be held to act instantaneously across immense distances. Moreover, since the planets showed no sign of slowing down as a result of external resistance, there could be no material medium to transmit the gravitational influence. Such an 'action at a distance' must be regarded as either an inexplicable miracle or an 'occult' property of matter itself. Neither 'solution' was acceptable: not the former, since it removed the question entirely from the realm of natural philosophy; nor the latter, since it reintroduced the 'specific occult qualities' postulated by the Aristotelians, which as Newton himself later remarked 'put a stop to the improvement of natural philosophy' (*Opticks*, Q.30). This fundamental dilemma, and much else of a more technical nature, was ventilated in the famous *Leibniz–Clarke Correspondence* first published in 1707. Newton, on whose behalf (and at the instigation of Princess Caroline) Clarke replied to Leibniz, showed his recognition of the difficulties by adding to the second edition of the *Principia* (1713) the famous General Scholium containing the even more famous (and misunderstood) phrase 'Hypotheses non fingo', and by his letters to the Master of Trinity, Richard Bentley, in one of which he explicitly denied that gravity is 'essential and inherent to matter'. Newton was fully aware of the lack of finality in his 'System of the World' and returned to the question several times; but since Smith was apparently unaware of this, it would be inappropriate to enter into the inevitably long and difficult discussion here.

The History of the Ancient Physics and the History of the Ancient Logics and Metaphysics

The History of Astronomy, though naturally imperfect, was in a sense complete. After the second edition of Newton's *Principia* there was no fundamental change or addition to the 'system of the world', that was Smith's main concern, until long after his death. The mathematical theory was under constant refinement; and Smith shows his continuing interest in the progress of physical astronomy when in the *Edinburgh Review* article he refers to James Bradley's important discovery of the aberration of light. But the titles of the two subsequent essays suggest that the restriction to the 'ancient' period expressed the fact that he had said all that he intended to say.

The two essays now to be considered, though like that on the History of Astronomy both written with an eye to 'philosophical investigation', are in a different class from the first. The title of each reveals a subtle change of aim: the histories of these 'sciences' are to be restricted to their 'ancient' development. For this and other reasons that will appear during the discussion it is convenient to introduce them under a single heading. To a greater extent than in the 'history' of astronomy his account of the 'facts' of pre-Socratic 'physics' is not only without adequate historical foundation but lacks any historical coherence other than that imposed by Smith's own 'likely story', namely that 'from arranging and methodizing the System of the Heavens, Philosophy descended to the consideration of the inferior parts of Nature' (Ancient Physics, 1). There neither is, nor ever was, as far as we know, any evidence for this order of inquiry; on the contrary, Aristotle rightly referred to his predecessors as φυσιολόγοι— those who strove to 'account for nature', which for them was the whole cosmos. Their speculations about the objects above the Earth in fact lacked any 'arrangement or methodizing': they remained crude and ill-supported by reason. The views on the 'elements' (ἀρχαί, Aristotle calls them), on the other hand, put forward separately by the Ionian pioneers embodied a profound insight into the problem of the relation between change and the permanent ground of being. Only later did the Italian, Empedocles, order the elements in such a manner as to make possible the even later 'square of opposite properties' introduced by Aristotle.

As has been hinted already, Smith never made explicit the cardinal distinction between 'physics' and 'astronomy'—a distinction that in fact 'guided and directed philosophical enquiry' from Aristotle onwards, and which, in somewhat altered terms, is still a living issue in the philosophy of science, notably in the interpretation of quantum mechanics. The basic formulation has never been more clearly put than by the sixth-century Neoplatonist, Simplicius, in his commentary on Aristotle's *Physics*, and in which he claims to be quoting the actual words of Geminus summarizing the views of the Stoic Poseidonius, both of them having lived much nearer to the time of Aristotle. After a long and detailed preamble he emphasized that while 'the physicist will in many cases, reach the cause by looking to creative force', 'it is no part of the business of the astronomer to know what is by nature suited to a position of rest and what sort of bodies are apt to move, but he introduces hypotheses under which some bodies remain fixed while others move, and then considers to which hypotheses the phenomena actually observed in the heaven will correspond'.[7] The astronomer, in other words, is satisfied if, given certain physical postulates, such as 'equable motion', he can devise a mathematical scheme from which the motions of the heavenly bodies can be deduced; the question of 'truth' has for him, *qua* astronomer, no relevance. In the History of Astronomy (notably in the introductory Section II) Smith shows his appreciation of this aspect of 'philosophical investigation'. But his failure to explicate the notion of *cause*, latent in the various pre-Socratic speculations and dominating Aristotle's whole philosophy, reduces his Ancient Physics, despite its elegant and persuasive presentation of certain aspects, to a much lower level of cogency. Detailed justification for this judgement would here be out of place; suffice it to say that the reader of the text will find no hint of the pervasive notion of final causation and the grades of 'animation' (the Latin *anima* replaced ψυχή in the transmission of the Aristotelian corpus) in living beings.

Having momentarily forgotten his most promising hypothesis that 'philosophical enquiries' stem from 'surprise and wonder' Smith opens the essay on the 'History of the Ancient Logics and Metaphysics' with a liberal application of the term 'evident' to assumptions that to thinkers in another tradition seem far from evident. This apart, however, he rightly insists that 'philosophy, . . . in considering the general nature of Water, takes no notice of those particularities which are peculiar to this Water, but confines itself to those things which are common to all water'. From which it follows that 'Species, or Universals, and not Individuals, are the objects of Philosophy' (§ 1). In the succeeding passage, amounting to little more than twenty lines, Smith condenses all that he has to say on the relation between the 'ancient' sciences of 'logics' and 'metaphysics'. Restricted to such a compass his account of what came to be regarded as 'logic' and 'metaphysics' might do well enough, though the exclusive emphasis on classification is hardly warranted. But viewed as a stage in the achievement of his historical aim it is quite inadequate. In claiming with some justice that these two sciences 'seem, before the time of Aristotle, to have been regarded as one' and, with less justice, 'to have made up between them that ancient Dialectic of which we hear so much, and of which we understand so little' (Ancient Logics, 1) Smith gives no hint that λογική and its derivatives covered a huge range of meaning as much to do with 'words' as with 'reasoning'; nor that the term 'metaphysics' came only long after Aristotle's death to refer to those of his books which

----

[7] Quoted from T. Heath, *Greek Astronomy* (1932), 124–5.

embodied a consideration of 'those causes and principles the knowledge of which constitutes Wisdom'—'First philosophy' as Aristotle himself described it. The throw-away comment on the 'ancient Dialectic' may have been prompted by Smith's native caution: the subtle and even inconsistent use of the term by Plato and Aristotle is still the subject of scholarly debate. The inappropriateness of the remark becomes even more remarkable in the light of the following *definition* proposed by the Stranger from Elea: 'Dividing according to kinds, not taking the same Form for a difference or a different one for the same—is not that the business of the science of Dialectic?' (Plato, *Sophist*, 253 D.) This 'division by kinds' is precisely the method that Smith himself regarded as being the essence of the 'ancient logics' and one of which he himself makes frequent use. This account of dialectic differs from the more basic requirement stipulated by Socrates (i.e. the effort to attain truth by correction of agreed hypotheses rather than the confutation of an adversary) but is not inconsistent with it. Equally regrettable is Smith's failure to make clear, as Aristotle had, that the pre-Socratic φυσιολόγοι (as Aristotle calls them) were asking 'metaphysical' questions but for the most part (Parmenides being clearly an exception) giving 'physical' answers.

The part of the essay devoted to an exposition of Plato's attitude to Nature and its relation to the general theory of 'Ideas', though disproportionately long, is almost the only part that carries conviction that the author had adequately prepared himself for the ambitious task he had undertaken. But even here he fails to drive home the lesson, so important for his own thesis, that what Plato was for the most part concerned with, even in the dialogue that looks like natural philosophy, the *Timaeus*, is perhaps not even metaphysics, but rather natural theology as it was perhaps understood in the original scheme for the Gifford Lectures. This was far from being without influence on the development of natural philosophy and subsequently of the natural sciences; but by placing 'cause and principle' of nature as it were outwith nature and providing only a 'likely story' of how it (δημιουργός) might have operated, Plato effectively closed the door on further investigation on the lines initiated by the φυσιολόγοι. Or rather he would have closed it, had not his independent-minded pupil, Aristotle, put his foot in the doorway—at least for the sublunary world!

At this stage some readers may reasonably protest that it is an editor's function at most to comment on the text and not to argue with its author. To leave without qualification the rather disparaging remarks which this editor has felt it necessary to make would amount to a failure to view the matter in that historical perspective for the lack of which Smith has been censured. Well versed in the classical tongues as the young Adam Smith undoubtedly was, he cannot be blamed for having failed to transcend the limitations set by the materials available to him. And these were meagre indeed, for though we may think of the eighteenth century as one in which classical scholarship was most highly appreciated and familiarity with the classical authors more widely spread than perhaps at any other time, it is apt to be forgotten that both scholarship and familiarity were almost wholly restricted to grammatical and stylistic aspects; it is probable that Smith's contemporaries were far less conversant with the *matter* of the Greek classics than had been the humanists of three centuries earlier. In his valuable *Greek Studies in England, 1700–1830* (1945) (which in fact includes a knowledgeable chapter on Scotland) M. L. Clarke states that 'the undergraduates at Oxford and Cambridge read only a few isolated dialogues of Plato and learned nothing of his philosophical theories'. Before 1759 there was no English translation, except of the *Phaedo*, to which the Scottish scholar, Spens, added the *Republic* only in 1763. Aristotle was in like case. Smith's dismissal (Astronomy, III.6) of the Ionian φυσιολόγοι on the ground that the extant accounts 'represent the doctrines of those sages as full of the most inextricable confusion' is of a piece with Clarke's judgement that 'of the remarkable speculations of the pre-Socratics there was no appreciation' (op. cit., 114); he would have had to rely upon Aristotle's biased views put forward in the *Metaphysics*. In respect of 'Logics' he was presumably the victim of the 'trivialization' of Aristotle's logic, unavoidable if it was to be taught to the lower end of the teenage stream! His point of view (putting 'objects' into the 'right' classes) seems to be based on the *Topics*, even perhaps mediated through Ramism; but of the structure of inference as expounded by Aristotle himself in the two *Analytics* he gives no hint. If this 'conditioning' was effected at Glasgow it would not have been unique; it is only in our time (by Jan Łukasiewicz and others) that the 'modernity' of Aristotle's canon has been made generally known. Smith was also unlucky in setting forth on this immensely ambitious endeavour at a time when Giambattista Vico's principles of critical historiography based on critical philology (*Scienza Nuova*, 1725-44) were still wholly unappreciated outside Italy. Nevertheless, when all allowance has been made for the handicaps under which Smith must have laboured when composing these 'juvenile' historical pieces, there remains an air of brashness about the two (presumably) later ones that provokes the question whether the author of the *Theory of Moral Sentiments* and the *Wealth of Nations* would have countenanced their publication in the form in which he had left them. It is true that as late as November 1785, in the letter (248) to Rochefoucauld referred to above, the 'sort of Philosophical History' he mentions as still being 'upon the anvil' must have been at least based on the 'great work' mentioned in the letter to Hume twelve years earlier. But in that letter he expressly stated that none of his papers were worth publishing except a fragment—the history of the astronomical systems—and even that one he suspected contained 'more refinement than solidity'. How much more apposite would this judgement be of the two subsequent essays! In view of his repeated request—as he neared his end—for assurance that his papers had been destroyed, it seems more than a little doubtful whether his editors were not doing his memory a disservice in making public these two essays without a more extensive caveat than the rather fulsome and misleading last sentence of their Advertisement.

Bibliographical Note

The survey on which this Note has been based was restricted to the following institutions: British Library (BL), National Library of Scotland (NLS), Bodleian (O), Cambridge University (C), Trinity College, Dublin (D), and the four Scottish universities existing before the recent expansion: St. Andrews (StA), Glasgow (G), Aberdeen (A—see, however, No. 6 below), Edinburgh (E). Eight editions prior to 1900 have been established, at least one copy of each having been examined. Only NLS has a copy of every edition, two of these being accessions from the library of Lauriston Castle near Edinburgh. Thanks are due to members of the library staff at NLS, C, StA, and D for information about their holdings.

The full title-page of the First Edition is provided together with brief descriptions of the remaining editions. Only 'sample' collations have been carried out; no substantial differences in the texts have been discovered.

1. London 1795 4to. First edition. BL, NLS, O, C. StA, G, A, E.
2. Dublin 1795 8vo. Some spelling mistakes have been corrected. BL, NLS, O, C, D. Mr. M. Pollard of Trinity College Library states that the copy of this edition was purchased only in 1962; it contains the bookplate of Eliz. Anne Levinge with the signature 'Elizth. Anne Parkyns 1808' on the title-page. Mr. Pollard emphasizes that reprint by Dublin printers was perfectly legal provided that the books were not offered for sale in England.
3. *Essais philosophiques*; par feu ADAM SMITH, Docteur en droit, de la société royale de Londres, de celle d'Edimbourg, etc. etc. Précédés d'un précis de sa vie et de ses écrits; Par DUGALD STEWART, de la société royale d'Edimbourg. Traduits de l'anglais par P. Prevost, professeur de philosophie à Genève de l'académie de Berlin, de la société des Curieux de la Nature, et de la société royale d'Edimbourg. PREMIERE PARTIE. A Paris, Chez H. AGASSE, imprimeur-librairie, rue des Poitevins, no° 18. An V de la République (1797, vieux style.)
   Fine portrait bust of Adam Smith ('B.L. Prevost *sculp.*') opposite title-page.
   Of this, in some respects the most adequate, edition a rather fuller description seems to be justified. It is unique among editions before 1900 in containing Adam Smith's long letter to the

Edinburgh Review (1756), here in French translation, numerous notes of varying lengths by the translator and mainly relating to the later essays, also a fairly detailed Table of Contents of the whole, the *Seconde Partie* of which is separately signed and paged. The Notes are described (presumably by the publisher) as 'très intéressantes' (ii.316). Of special interest is the translator's statement (i.277) that the note on Halley's comet is de 'l'editeur anglais' (*sic*). BL, NLS.

4. Basel 1799 8vo. *Essays on Philosophical Subjects* by the late ADAM SMITH LL.D.... To which is affixed an account of the Life and Writings of the Author by DUGALD STEWART F.R.S.E.
Basil: printed for the Editor of the Collection of English Classics sold by James Decker, Printer and Bookseller 1799. BL, NLS.
The only point of interest in this edition is the omission of any reference to the original editors, Joseph Black and James Hutton.

5. Volume v of Adam Smith's *Works* edited by Dugald Stewart and dated 1811 (as is vol. iv, vols. i–iii being 1812). Vol. v also contains the essay entitled *Considerations concerning the first Formation of Languages*. BL, NLS, O.

6. *Essays on Philosophical Subjects* by Adam Smith LL.D., F.R.S. etc. London 1822. A new edition.
This apparently very rare edition was printed (title-page verso) by A. Allardice, Leith, for Allardice, Edinburgh; R. Griffin, Glasgow; and several London houses. The copy examined is inscribed 'Biblioth. Classis Physicae in Acad. Mariscallana' and stamped 'Nat. Phil. Clas. Library 1860 University of Aberdeen', i.e. on the union of King's and Marischal Colleges, previously separate universities. NLS. A.

7. London 1869 8vo. *Essays.* The volume is in fact a reprint of both TMS (followed, as usual, by Languages) and EPS. The 'Biographical Notice' is drastically abridged. BL, O, C, StA.

8. London 1880 8vo. *Essays Philosophical and Literary.* Stated in BL catalogue to be a 'duplicate' of No. 7. BL, NLS, O, C, StA.

9. The Essays are included in *The Early Writings of Adam Smith* edited by J. R. Lindgren (Augustus M. Kelley, New York 1967). This edition includes the *Edinburgh Review* articles, the Preface to William Hamilton's *Poems on Several Occasions* (1748), and the Languages. It is not introduced or annotated.

Note on the Text

The present volume follows the text of the first edition (published by Cadell and Davies in 1795, five years after Smith's death), but with printer's errors corrected. Since the essay is designed to illustrate 'the principles which lead and direct philosophical enquiries' rather than to provide a history of astronomy *per se*, no attempt has been made to achieve that completeness of documentation which would be appropriate in a definitive classic.

THE

PRINCIPLES

WHICH LEAD AND DIRECT

PHILOSOPHICAL ENQUIRIES;

ILLUSTRATED BY THE

HISTORY of ASTRONOMY

ADVERTISEMENT

By the EDITORS

The much lamented Author of these Essays left them in the hands of his friends to be disposed of as they thought proper, having immediately before his death destroyed many other manuscripts which he thought unfit for being made public.[1] When these were inspected, the greater number of them appeared to be parts of a plan he once had formed, for giving a connected history of the liberal sciences and elegant arts. It is long since he found it necessary to abandon that plan as far too extensive; and these parts of it lay beside him neglected until his death. His friends are persuaded however, that the reader will find in them that happy connection, that full and accurate expression, and that clear illustration which are conspicuous in the rest of his works; and that though it is difficult to add much to the great fame he so justly acquired by his other writings, these will be read with satisfaction and pleasure.

JOSEPH BLACK
JAMES HUTTON

[1] Details of the executry are given in Stewart, V.8 and note; Rae, *Life*, chap. 32.

THE

HISTORY

OF

ASTRONOMY

1   Wonder, Surprise, and Admiration, are words which, though often confounded, denote, in our language, sentiments that are indeed allied, but that are in some respects different also, and distinct from one another. What is new and singular, excites that sentiment which, in strict propriety, is called Wonder; what is unexpected, Surprise; and what is great or beautiful, Admiration.

2   We wonder at all extraordinary and uncommon objects, at all the rarer phaenomena of nature, at meteors, comets, eclipses, at singular plants and animals, and at every thing, in short, with which we have before been either little or not at all acquainted; and we still wonder, though forewarned of what we are to see.

3   We are surprised at those things which we have seen often, but which we least of all expected to meet with in the place where we find them; we are surprised at the sudden appearance of a friend, whom we have seen a thousand times, but whom we did not imagine we were to see then.

4   We admire the beauty of a plain or the greatness of a mountain, though we have seen both often before, and though nothing appears to us in either, but what we had expected with certainty to see.

5   Whether this criticism upon the precise meaning of these words be just, is of little importance. I imagine it is just, though I acknowledge, that the best writers in our language have not always made use of them according to it. Milton, upon the appearance of Death to Satan, says, that

> The Fiend what this might be admir'd;
> Admir'd, not fear'd.[1]——

But if this criticism be just, the proper expression should have been *wonder'd.*——Dryden, upon the discovery of Iphigenia sleeping, says, that

> The fool of nature stood with stupid eyes
> And gaping mouth, that testified surprise.[2]

---

[1] [*Paradise Lost*, ii.677–8, but Milton wrote 'Th' undaunted Fiend . . .'.]
[2] ['Cymon and Iphigenia', 107–8.]

But what Cimon must have felt upon this occasion could not so much be Surprise, as Wonder and Admiration. All that I contend for is, that the sentiments excited by what is new, by what is unexpected, and by what is great and beautiful, are really different, however the words made use of to express them may sometimes be confounded. Even the admiration which is excited by beauty, is quite different (as will appear more fully hereafter) from that which is inspired by greatness, though we have but one word to denote them.

6　　These sentiments, like all others when inspired by one and the same object, mutually support and enliven one another: an object with which we are quite familiar, and which we see every day, produces, though both great and beautiful, but a small effect upon us; because our admiration is not supported either by Wonder or by Surprise: and if we have heard a very accurate description of a monster, our Wonder will be the less when we see it; because our previous knowledge of it will in a great measure prevent our Surprise.

7　　It is the design of this Essay to consider particularly the nature and causes of each of these sentiments, whose influence is of far wider extent than we should be apt upon a careless view to imagine. I shall begin with Surprise.

SECTION I

Of the Effect of Unexpectedness, or of Surprise

1　When an object of any kind, which has been for some time expected and foreseen, presents itself, whatever be the emotion which it is by nature fitted to excite, the mind must have been prepared for it, and must even in some measure have conceived it before-hand; because the idea of the object having been so long present to it, must have before-hand excited some degree of the same emotion which the object itself would excite: the change, therefore, which its presence produces comes thus to be less considerable, and the emotion or passion which it excites glides gradually and easily into the heart, without violence, pain, or difficulty.[1]

2　　But the contrary of all this happens when the object is unexpected; the passion is then poured in all at once upon the heart, which is thrown, if it is a strong passion, into the most violent and convulsive emotions, such as sometimes cause immediate death; sometimes, by the suddenness of the extacy, so entirely disjoint the whole frame of the imagination, that it never after returns to its former tone and composure, but falls either into a frenzy or habitual lunacy; and such

[1] Cf. Hume, *Treatise of Human Nature*, I.i.4, 'Of the connexion or association of ideas'.

as almost always occasion a momentary loss of reason, or of that attention to other things which our situation or our duty requires.

3   How much we dread the effects of the more violent passions, when they come suddenly upon the mind, appears from those preparations which all men think necessary when going to inform any one of what is capable of exciting them. Who would choose all at once to inform his friend of an extraordinary calamity that had befallen him, without taking care before-hand, by alarming him with an uncertain fear, to announce, if one may say so, his misfortune, and thereby prepare and dispose him for receiving the tidings?

4   Those panic terrors which sometimes seize armies in the field, or great cities, when an enemy is in the neighbourhood, and which deprive for a time the most determined of all deliberate judgments, are never excited but by the sudden apprehension of unexpected danger. Such violent consternations, which at once confound whole multitudes, benumb their understandings, and agitate their hearts, with all the agony of extravagant fear, can never be produced by any foreseen danger, how great soever. Fear, though naturally a very strong passion, never rises to such excesses, unless exasperated both by Wonder, from the uncertain nature of the danger, and by Surprise, from the suddenness of the apprehension.

5   Surprise, therefore, is not to be regarded as an original emotion of a species distinct from all others. The violent and sudden change produced upon the mind, when an emotion of any kind is brought suddenly upon it, constitutes the whole nature of Surprise.

6   But when not only a passion and a great passion comes all at once upon the mind, but when it comes upon it while the mind is in the mood most unfit for conceiving it, the Surprise is then the greatest. Surprises of joy when the mind is sunk into grief, or of grief when it is elated with joy, are therefore the most unsupportable. The change is in this case the greatest possible. Not only a strong passion is conceived all at once, but a strong passion the direct opposite of that which was before in possession of the soul. When a load of sorrow comes down upon the heart that is expanded and elated with gaiety and joy, it seems not only to damp and oppress it, but almost to crush and bruise it, as a real weight would crush and bruise the body. On the contrary, when from an unexpected change of fortune, a tide of gladness seems, if I may say so, to spring up all at once within it, when depressed and contracted with grief and sorrow, it feels as if suddenly extended and heaved up with violent and irresistible force, and is torn with pangs of all others most exquisite, and which almost always occasion faintings, deliriums, and sometimes instant death. For it may be worth while to observe, that though grief be a more violent

passion than joy, as indeed all uneasy sensations seem naturally more pungent than the opposite agreeable ones, yet of the two, Surprises of joy are still more insupportable than Surprises of grief. We are told[2] that after the battle of Thrasimenus, while a Roman lady, who had been informed that her son was slain in the action, was sitting alone bemoaning her misfortunes, the young man who escaped came suddenly into the room to her, and that she cried out and expired instantly in a transport of joy. Let us suppose the contrary of this to have happened, and that in the midst of domestic festivity and mirth, he had suddenly fallen down dead at her feet, is it likely that the effects would have been equally violent? I imagine not. The heart springs to joy with a sort of natural elasticity, it abandons itself to so agreeable an emotion, as soon as the object is presented; it seems to pant and leap forward to meet it, and the passion in its full force takes at once entire and complete possession of the soul. But it is otherways with grief; the heart recoils from, and resists the first approaches of that disagreeable passion, and it requires some time before the melancholy object can produce its full effect. Grief comes on slowly and gradually, nor ever rises at once to that height of agony to which it is increased after a little time. But joy comes rushing upon us all at once like a torrent. The change produced therefore by a Surprise of joy is more sudden, and upon that account more violent and apt to have more fatal effects, than that which is occasioned by a Surprise of grief; there seems too to be something in the nature of Surprise, which makes it unite more easily with the brisk and quick motion of joy, than with the slower and heavier movement of grief. Most men who can take the trouble to recollect, will find that they have heard of more people who died or became distracted with sudden joy, than with sudden grief. Yet from the nature of human affairs, the latter must be much more frequent than the former. A man may break his leg, or lose his son, though he has had no warning of either of these events, but he can hardly meet with an extraordinary piece of good fortune, without having had some foresight of what was to happen.

7   Not only grief and joy but all the other passions, are more violent, when opposite extremes succeed each other. Is any resentment so keen as what follows the quarrels of lovers, or any love so passionate as what attends their reconcilement?

8   Even the objects of the external senses affect us in a more lively manner, when opposite extremes succeed to, or are placed beside each other. Moderate warmth seems intolerable heat if felt after extreme cold. What is bitter will seem more so when tasted after what is very sweet; a dirty white will seem bright and pure when placed by

---

[2] [Livy, XXII.7.13.]

a jet black. The vivacity in short of every sensation, as well as of every sentiment, seems to be greater or less in proportion to the change made by the impression of either upon the situation of the mind or organ; but this change must necessarily be the greatest when opposite sentiments and sensations are contrasted, or succeed immediately to one another. Both sentiments and sensations are then the liveliest; and this superior vivacity proceeds from nothing but their being brought upon the mind or organ when in a state most unfit for conceiving them.

9   As the opposition of contrasted sentiments heightens their vivacity, so the resemblance of those which immediately succeed each other renders them more faint and languid. A parent who has lost several children immediately after one another, will be less affected with the death of the last than with that of the first, though the loss in itself be, in this case, undoubtedly greater; but his mind being already sunk into sorrow, the new misfortune seems to produce no other effect than a continuance of the same melancholy, and is by no means apt to occasion such transports of grief as are ordinarily excited by the first calamity of the kind; he receives it, though with great dejection, yet with some degree of calmness and composure, and without any thing of that anguish and agitation of mind which the novelty of the misfortune is apt to occasion. Those who have been unfortunate through the whole course of their lives are often indeed habitually melancholy, and sometimes peevish and splenetic, yet upon any fresh disappointment, though they are vexed and complain a little, they seldom fly out into any more violent passion, and never fall into those transports of rage or grief which often, upon the like occasions, distract the fortunate and successful.

10   Upon this are founded, in a great measure, some of the effects of habit and custom. It is well known that custom deadens the vivacity of both pain and pleasure, abates the grief we should feel for the one, and weakens the joy we should derive from the other. The pain is supported without agony, and the pleasure enjoyed without rapture: because custom and the frequent repetition of any object comes at last to form and bend the mind or organ to that habitual mood and disposition which fits them to receive its impression, without undergoing any very violent change.

SECTION II

Of Wonder, or of the Effects of Novelty

1 It is evident that the mind takes pleasure in observing the resemblances that are discoverable betwixt different objects. It is by

means of such observations that it endeavours to arrange and methodise all its ideas, and to reduce them into proper classes and assortments. Where it can observe but one single quality, that is common to a great variety of otherwise widely different objects, that single circumstance will be sufficient for it to connect them all together, to reduce them to one common class, and to call them by one general name. It is thus that all things endowed with a power of self-motion, beasts, birds, fishes, insects, are classed under the general name of Animal; and that these again, along with those which want that power, are arranged under the still more general word Substance: and this is the origin of those assortments of objects and ideas which in the schools are called Genera and Species, and of those abstract and general names, which in all languages are made use of to express them.[1]

2   The further we advance in knowledge and experience, the greater number of divisions and subdivisions of those Genera and Species we are both inclined and obliged to make. We observe a greater variety of particularities amongst those things which have a gross resemblance; and having made new divisions of them, according to those newly-observed particularities, we are then no longer to be satisfied with being able to refer an object to a remote genus, or very general class of things, to many of which it has but a loose and imperfect resemblance. A person, indeed, unacquainted with botany may expect to satisfy your curiosity, by telling you, that such a vegetable is a weed, or, perhaps in still more general terms, that it is a plant. But a botanist will neither give nor accept of such an answer. He has broke and divided that great class of objects into a number of inferior assortments, according to those varieties which his experience has discovered among them; and he wants to refer each individual plant to some tribe of vegetables, with all of which it may have a more exact resemblance, than with many things comprehended under the extensive genus of plants. A child imagines that it gives a satisfactory answer when it tells you, that an object whose name it knows not is a thing, and fancies that it informs you of something, when it thus ascertains to which of the two most obvious and comprehensive classes of objects a particular impression ought to be referred; to the class of realities or solid substances which is calls *things*, or to that of appearances which it calls *nothings*.

3   Whatever, in short, occurs to us we are fond of referring to some species or class of things, with all of which it has a nearly exact resemblance; and though we often know no more about them than

[1] [Similar points are made in Languages, 1–2; cf. LRBL i.17–19 (ed. Lothian, 7–8).]

about it, yet we are apt to fancy that by being able to do so, we show ourselves to be better acquainted with it, and to have a more thorough insight into its nature. But when something quite new and singular is presented, we feel ourselves incapable of doing this. The memory cannot, from all its stores, cast up any image that nearly resembles this strange appearance. If by some of its qualities it seems to resemble, and to be connected with a species which we have before been acquainted with, it is by others separated and detached from that, and from all the other assortments of things we have hitherto been able to make. It stands alone and by itself in the imagination, and refuses to be grouped or confounded with any set of objects whatever. The imagination and memory exert themselves to no purpose, and in vain look around all their classes of ideas in order to find one under which it may be arranged. They fluctuate to no purpose from thought to thought, and we remain still uncertain and undetermined where to place it, or what to think of it. It is this fluctuation and vain recollection, together with the emotion or movement of the spirits[2] that they excite, which constitute the sentiment properly called *Wonder*, and which occasion that staring, and sometimes that rolling of the eyes, that suspension of the breath, and that swelling of the heart, which we may all observe, both in ourselves and others, when wondering at some new object, and which are the natural symptoms of uncertain and undetermined thought. What sort of a thing can that be? What is that like? are the questions which, upon such an occasion, we are all naturally disposed to ask. If we can recollect many such objects which exactly resemble this new appearance, and which present themselves to the imagination naturally, and as it were of their own accord, our Wonder is entirely at an end. If we can recollect but a few, and which it requires too some trouble to be able to call up, our Wonder is indeed diminished, but not quite destroyed. If we can recollect none, but are quite at a loss, it is the greatest possible.

4   With what curious attention does a naturalist examine a singular plant, or a singular fossil, that is presented to him? He is at no loss to refer it to the general genus of plants or fossils; but this does not satisfy him, and when he considers all the different tribes or species of either with which he has hitherto been acquainted, they all, he thinks, refuse to admit the new object among them. It stands alone in

----

[2] The notion of 'spirits' associated with material bodies has a long and highly complex history (see, e.g., W. Pagel, *Das medizinische Weltbild des Paracelsus* (1962), under 'Geist' and 'Spiritus' in index). Smith seems here to be assuming some kind of para-material stuff such as Descartes had supposed to flow in the 'hollow' nerves and to 'interact with' the 'extensionless soul' in the unpaired pineal gland in the brain. Cf. Hume, *Treatise*, I.ii.5 (ed. L. A. Selby-Bigge, 61): 'these spirits always excite the idea . . .'.

his imagination, and as it were detached from all the other species of that genus to which it belongs. He labours, however, to connect it with some one or other of them. Sometimes he thinks it may be placed in this, and sometimes in that other assortment; nor is he ever satisfied, till he has fallen upon one which, in most of its qualities, it resembles. When he cannot do this, rather than it should stand quite by itself, he will enlarge the precincts, if I may say so, of some species, in order to make room for it; or he will create a new species on purpose to receive it, and call it a Play of Nature, or give it some other appellation, under which he arranges all the oddities that he knows not what else to do with. But to some class or other of known objects he must refer it, and betwixt it and them he must find out some resemblance or other, before he can get rid of that Wonder, that uncertainty and anxious curiosity excited by its singular appearance, and by its dissimilitude with all the objects he had hitherto observed.

5   As single and individual objects thus excite our Wonder when, by their uncommon qualities and singular appearance, they make us uncertain to what species of things we ought to refer them; so a succession of objects which follow one another in an uncommon train or order, will produce the same effect, though there be nothing particular in any one of them taken by itself.

6   When one accustomed object appears after another, which it does not usually follow, it first excites, by its unexpectedness, the sentiment properly called Surprise, and afterwards, by the singularity of the succession, or order of its appearance, the sentiment properly called Wonder. We start and are surprised at feeling it there, and then wonder how it came there. The motion of a small piece of iron along a plain table is in itself no extraordinary object, yet the person who first saw it begin, without any visible impulse, in consequence of the motion of a loadstone at some little distance from it, could not behold it without the most extreme Surprise; and when that momentary emotion was over, he would still wonder how it came to be conjoined to an event with which, according to the ordinary train of things, he could have so little suspected it to have any connection.

7   [3]When two objects, however unlike, have often been observed to follow each other, and have constantly presented themselves to the senses in that order, they come to be so connected together in the fancy, that the idea of the one seems, of its own accord, to call up and introduce that of the other. If the objects are still observed to succeed each other as before, this connection, or, as it has been called, this

---

[3] The phraseology of this paragraph follows more closely that of Hume; see note 1 to Section I above.

association of their ideas, becomes stricter and stricter, and the habit
of the imagination to pass from the conception of the one to that of
the other, grows more and more rivetted and confirmed. As its ideas
move more rapidly than external objects, it is continually running
before them, and therefore anticipates, before it happens, every event
which falls out according to this ordinary course of things. When
objects succeed each other in the same train in which the ideas of the
imagination have thus been accustomed to move, and in which,
though not conducted by that chain of events presented to the senses,
they have acquired a tendency to go on of their own accord, such
objects appear all closely connected with one another, and the
thought glides easily along them,[4] without effort and without
interruption. They fall in with the natural career of the imagination;
and as the ideas which represented such a train of things would seem
all mutually to introduce each other, every last thought to be called
up by the foregoing, and to call up the succeeding; so when the
objects themselves occur, every last event seems, in the same manner,
to be introduced by the foregoing, and to introduce the succeeding.
There is no break, no stop, no gap, no interval. The ideas excited by
so coherent a chain of things seem, as it were, to float through the
mind of their own accord, without obliging it to exert itself, or to
make any effort in order to pass from one of them to another.

8   But if this customary connection be interrupted, if one or more
objects appear in an order quite different from that to which the
imagination has been accustomed, and for which it is prepared, the
contrary of all this happens. We are at first surprised by the
unexpectedness[5] of the new appearance, and when that momentary
emotion is over, we still wonder how it came to occur in that place.
The imagination no longer feels the usual facility of passing from the
event which goes before to that which comes after. It is an order or
law of succession to which it has not been accustomed, and which it
therefore finds some difficulty in following, or in attending to. The
fancy is stopped and interrupted in that natural movement or career,
according to which it was proceeding. Those two events seem to
stand at a distance from each other; it endeavours to bring them
together, but they refuse to unite; and it feels, or imagines it feels,
something like a gap or interval betwixt them. It naturally hesitates,
and, as it were, pauses upon the brink of this interval; it endeavours

---

[4] [A similar expression is used in Ancient Physics, 2. The idea is derived from Hume; see
especially *Treatise*, I.iv.2.]

[5] Smith's approach to the problem of scientific knowledge has an interesting—perhaps
vital—bearing on 'inductivism' and its denial by Sir Karl Popper and his disciples; cf. A. N.
Whitehead, 'Sometimes we see an elephant and sometimes we do not', *Process and Reality*
(1929), 5.

to find out something which may fill up the gap,[6] which, like a bridge, may so far at least unite those seemingly distant objects, as to render the passage of the thought betwixt them smooth, and natural, and easy. The supposition of a chain of intermediate, though invisible, events, which succeed each other in a train similar to that in which the imagination has been accustomed to move, and which link together those two disjointed appearances, is the only means by which the imagination can fill up this interval, is the only bridge which, if one may say so, can smooth its passage from the one object to the other. Thus, when we observe the motion of the iron, in consequence of that of the loadstone, we gaze and hesitate, and feel a want of connection betwixt two events which follow one another in so unusual a train. But when, with Des Cartes, we imagine certain invisible effluvia[7] to circulate round one of them, and by their repeated impulses to impel the other, both to move towards it, and to follow its motion, we fill up the interval betwixt them, we join them together by a sort of bridge, and thus take off that hesitation and difficulty which the imagination felt in passing from the one to the other. That the iron should move after the loadstone seems, upon this hypothesis, in some measure according to the ordinary course of things. Motion after impulse is an order of succession with which of all things we are the most familiar. Two objects which are so connected seem no longer to be disjoined,[8] and the imagination flows smoothly and easily along them.

9   Such is the nature of this second species of Wonder, which arises from an unusual succession of things. The stop which is thereby given to the career of the imagination, the difficulty which it finds in passing along such disjointed objects, and the feeling of something like a gap or interval betwixt them, constitute the whole essence of this emotion. Upon the clear discovery of a connecting chain of intermediate events, it vanishes altogether. What obstructed the movement of the imagination is then removed. Who wonders at the machinery of the opera-house who has once been admitted behind the scenes? In the Wonders of nature, however, it rarely happens that we can discover so clearly this connecting chain. With regard to a few

     [6] [Smith is again adapting the thought of Hume in *Treatise*, I.iv.2 (ed. Selby-Bigge, 198). A similar idea that a 'gap' in a narration can be a source of discomfort is mentioned in LRBL ii.36 (ed. Lothian, 95–6).]
     [7] Descartes's natural philosophy was based on the denial of empty space in the cosmos. Action at a distance was similarly ruled out, hence the necessity for postulating a 'medium'. The term 'effluvium' had already been used by W. Gilbert for the supposed 'exhalation' uniting 'electrics' (such as amber) to other bodies: he did not apply this concept to magnetic attraction. *De Magnete* (1600), Book II.
     [8] To 'explain' a 'change' is to discover a means of showing that no *real* change has taken place—what E. Meyerson called 'l'identification de l'antécédent et du conséquent' (*Identité et réalité*, ed.3 (1926), xviii).

even of them, indeed, we seem to have been really admitted behind the scenes, and our Wonder accordingly is entirely at an end. Thus the eclipses of the sun and moon, which once, more than all the other appearances in the heavens, excited the terror and amazement of mankind, seem now no longer to be wonderful, since the connecting chain has been found out which joins them to the ordinary course of things. Nay, in those cases in which we have been less successful, even the vague hypotheses of Des Cartes, and the yet more indetermined notions of Aristotle, have, with their followers, contributed to give some coherence to the appearances of nature, and might diminish, though they could not destroy, their Wonder. If they did not completely fill up the interval betwixt the two disjointed objects, they bestowed upon them, however, some sort of loose connection which they wanted before.

10   That the imagination feels a real difficulty in passing along two events which follow one another in an uncommon order, may be confirmed by many obvious observations. If it attempts to attend beyond a certain time to a long series of this kind, the continual efforts it is obliged to make, in order to pass from one object to another, and thus follow the progress of the succession, soon fatigue it, and if repeated too often, disorder and disjoint its whole frame. It is thus that too severe an application to study sometimes brings on lunacy and frenzy, in those especially who are somewhat advanced in life, but whose imaginations, from being too late in applying, have not got those habits which dispose them to follow easily the reasonings in the abstract sciences. Every step of a demonstration, which to an old practitioner is quite natural and easy, requires from them the most intense application of thought. Spurred on, however, either by ambition, or by admiration for the subject, they still continue till they become, first confused, then giddy, and at last distracted. Could we conceive a person of the soundest judgment, who had grown up to maturity, and whose imagination had acquired those habits, and that mold, which the constitution of things in this world necessarily impress upon it, to be all at once transported alive to some other planet, where nature was governed by laws quite different from those which take place here; as he would be continually obliged to attend to events, which must to him appear in the highest degree jarring, irregular, and discordant, he would soon feel the same confusion and giddiness begin to come upon him, which would at last end in the same manner, in lunacy and distraction. Neither, to produce this effect, is it necessary that the objects should be either great or interesting, or even uncommon, in themselves. It is sufficient that they follow one another in an uncommon order. Let any one attempt

to look over even a game of cards, and to attend particularly to every single stroke, and if he is unacquainted with the nature and rules of the game; that is, with the laws which regulate the succession of the cards; he will soon feel the same confusion and giddiness begin to come upon him, which, were it to be continued for days and months, would end in the same manner, in lunacy and distraction. But if the mind be thus thrown into the most violent disorder, when it attends to a long series of events which follow one another in an uncommon train, it must feel some degree of the same disorder, when it observes even a single event fall out in this unusual manner: for the violent disorder can arise from nothing but the too frequent repetition of this smaller uneasiness.

11   That it is the unusualness alone of the succession which occasions this stop and interruption in the progress of the imagination, as well as the notion of an interval betwixt the two immediately succeeding objects, to be filled up by some chain of intermediate events, is not less evident. The same orders of succession, which to one set of men seem quite according to the natural course of things, and such as require no intermediate events to join them, shall to another appear altogether incoherent and disjointed, unless some such events be supposed: and this for no other reason, but because such orders of succession are familiar to the one, and strange to the other. When we enter the work-houses of the most common artizans; such as dyers, brewers, distillers; we observe a number of appearances, which present themselves in an order that seems to us very strange and wonderful. Our thought cannot easily follow it, we feel an interval betwixt every two of them, and require some chain of intermediate events, to fill it up, and link them together. But the artizan himself, who has been for many years familiar with the consequences of all the operations of his art, feels no such interval. They fall in with what custom has made the natural movement of his imagination: they no longer excite his Wonder, and if he is not a genius superior to his profession, so as to be capable of making the very easy reflection, that those things, though familiar to him, may be strange to us, he will be disposed rather to laugh at, than sympathize with our Wonder. He cannot conceive what occasion there is for any connecting events to unite those appearances, which seem to him to succeed each other very naturally. It is their nature, he tells us, to follow one another in this order, and that accordingly they always do so.[9] In the same manner bread has, since the world began, been the common

---

[9] [Cf. Imitative Arts, I.17: 'After a little use and experience, all looking-glasses cease to be wonders altogether; and even the ignorant become so familiar with them, as not to think that their effects require any explication.']

nourishment of the human body, and men have so long seen it, every day, converted into flesh and bones, substances in all respects so unlike it, that they have seldom had the curiosity to inquire by what process of intermediate events this change is brought about. Because the passage of the thought from the one object to the other is by custom become quite smooth and easy, almost without the supposition of any such process. Philosophers, indeed, who often look for a chain of invisible objects to join together two events that occur in an order familiar to all the world, have endeavoured to find out a chain of this kind betwixt the two events I have just now mentioned; in the same manner as they have endeavoured, by a like intermediate chain, to connect the gravity, the elasticity, and even the cohesion of natural bodies, with some of their other qualities. These, however, are all of them such combinations of events as give no stop to the imaginations of the bulk of mankind, as excite no Wonder, nor any apprehension that there is wanting the strictest connection between them. But as in those sounds, which to the greater part of men seem perfectly agreeable to measure and harmony, the nicer ear of a musician will discover a want, both of the most exact time, and of the most perfect coincidence: so the more practised thought of a philosopher, who has spent his whole life in the study of the connecting principles of nature, will often feel an interval betwixt two objects, which, to more careless observers, seem very strictly conjoined. By long attention to all the connections which have ever been presented to his observation, by having often compared them with one another, he has, like the musician, acquired, if one may say so, a nicer ear, and a more delicate feeling with regard to things of this nature. And as to the one, that music seems dissonance which falls short of the most perfect harmony; so to the other, those events seem altogether separated and disjoined, which fall short of the strictest and most perfect connection.

12   Philosophy is the science of the connecting principles of nature.[10] Nature, after the largest experience that common observation can acquire, seems to abound with events which appear solitary and incoherent with all that go before them, which therefore disturb the easy movement of the imagination; which make its ideas succeed each other, if one may say so, by irregular starts and sallies; and which thus tend, in some measure, to introduce those confusions and distractions we formerly mentioned. Philosophy, by representing the invisible chains which bind together all these disjointed objects, endeavours to introduce order into this chaos of jarring and

[10] [Cf. Ancient Logics, 1. A similar definition of moral philosophy in particular is given in WN V.i.f.25.] For a discussion of Smith's indiscriminate use of 'philosophy', etc., see the editor's Introduction, 12–14. [Also T. D. Campbell, *Adam Smith's Science of Morals* (1971), chap. 1.]

discordant appearances, to allay this tumult of the imagination, and to restore it, when it surveys the great revolutions of the universe, to that tone of tranquillity and composure, which is both most agreeable in itself, and most suitable to its nature. Philosophy, therefore, may be regarded as one of those arts which address themselves to the imagination; and whose theory and history, upon that account, fall properly within the circumference of our subject. Let us endeavour to trace it, from its first origin, up to that summit of perfection to which it is at present supposed to have arrived, and to which, indeed, it has equally been supposed to have arrived in almost all former times. It is the most sublime of all the agreeable arts, and its revolutions have been the greatest, the most frequent, and the most distinguished of all those that have happened in the literary world. Its history, therefore, must, upon all accounts, be the most entertaining and the most instructive. Let us examine, therefore, all the different systems of nature, which, in these western parts of the world, the only parts of whose history we know any thing,[11] have successively been adopted by the learned and ingenious; and, without regarding their absurdity or probability, their agreement or inconsistency with truth and reality, let us consider them only in that particular point of view which belongs to our subject; and content ourselves with inquiring how far each of them was fitted to sooth the imagination, and to render the theatre of nature a more coherent, and therefore a more magnificent spectacle, than otherwise it would have appeared to be. According as they have failed or succeeded in this, they have constantly failed or succeeded in gaining reputation and renown to their authors; and this will be found to be the clew that is most capable of conducting us through all the labyrinths of philosophical history: for, in the mean time, it will serve to confirm what has gone before, and to throw light upon what is to come after, that we observe, in general, that no system, how well soever in other respects supported, has ever been able to gain any general credit on the world, whose connecting principles were not such as were familiar to all mankind. Why has the chemical philosophy in all ages crept along in obscurity,[12] and been so disregarded by the generality of mankind, while other systems, less useful, and not more agreeable to experience, have possessed universal admiration for whole centuries together? The connecting principles of the chemical philosophy are such as the generality of mankind know nothing about, have rarely seen, and

---

[11] An exaggeration. Western natural philosophy owed a great deal to Eastern thinkers who wrote in Arabic—a fact well known at that time. Cf. IV.21–3 below.

[12] Smith could hardly have written this in Glasgow, where William Cullen in 1748 began his epoch-making 'popularization' of chemistry in relation to industry and agriculture as well as medicine. It appears to be further evidence for the relatively early composition of this essay.

have never been acquainted with; and which to them, therefore, are incapable of smoothing the passage of the imagination betwixt any two seemingly disjointed objects. Salts, sulphurs, and mercuries, acids, and alkalis, are principles[13] which can smooth things to those only who live about the furnace; but whose most common operations seem, to the bulk of mankind, as disjointed as any two events which the chemists would connect together by them. Those artists, however, naturally explained things to themselves by principles that were familiar to themselves. As Aristotle observes,[14] that the early Pythagoreans, who first studied arithmetic, explained all things by the properties of numbers; and Cicero tells us,[15] that Aristoxenus, the musician, found the nature of the soul to consist in harmony. In the same manner, a learned physician lately gave a system of moral philosophy upon the the principles of his own art,[16] in which wisdom and virtue were the healthful state of the soul; the different vices and follies, the different diseases to which it was subject; in which the causes and symptoms of those diseases were ascertained; and, in the same medical strain, a proper method of cure prescribed. In the same manner also, others have written parallels of painting and poetry, of poetry and music, of music and architecture, of beauty and virtue, of all the fine arts; systems which have universally owed their origin to the lucubrations of those who were acquainted with the one art, but ignorant of the other; who therefore explained to themselves the phaenomena, in that which was strange to them, by those in that which was familiar; and with whom, upon that account, the analogy, which in other writers gives occasion to a few ingenious similitudes, became the great hinge upon which every thing turned.[17]

[13] Modern chemical nomenclature became possible only after Lavoisier's *Traité élémentaire de chimie* (1789; translated into English by Robert Kerr in 1790). The plural 'sulphurs' and 'mercuries' reveal the persistence of alchemical and Paracelsian modes of thought, the former being the 'principle of combustibility', the latter that of 'metallicity'. Smith should have been aware that 'acids and alkalis' had never been regarded as 'principles'; at that time they were regarded as varieties of 'salts'. Nevertheless, his exemplification of Francis Bacon's 'Idols' (*Novum Organum*, aphorism xxxviii ff.) shows an important general insight.

[14] [*Metaphysics*, A, 985^{b}32–986^{a}6.]

[15] [*Tusculan Disputations*, I.10.19, I.18.41.]

[16] [Probably J. O. de La Mettrie, *Discours sur le bonheur* (1748, 1750, 1751, with different titles for substantially the same work). This comes closer to Smith's description than does *Observations on Man* (1749) by David Hartley, likewise a physician turned philosopher. La Mettrie's book, which arose from his translation of Seneca, *De Beata Vita*, is both critical and appreciative of Stoic ethics, and may well have attracted Smith's attention for that reason.]

[17] [In IV.50 below Smith writes of Kepler's 'excessive' tendency to explain by analogy.]

SECTION III

Of the Origin of Philosophy

1 Mankind, in the first ages of society, before the establishment of law, order, and security, have little curiosity to find out those hidden chains of events which bind together the seemingly disjointed appearances of nature.[1] A savage, whose subsistence is precarious, whose life is every day exposed to the rudest dangers, has no inclination to amuse himself with searching out what, when discovered, seems to serve no other purpose than to render the theatre of nature a more connected spectacle to his imagination. Many of these smaller incoherences, which in the course of things perplex philosophers, entirely escape his attention. Those more magnificent irregularities, whose grandeur he cannot overlook, call forth his amazement. Comets, eclipses, thunder, lightning, and other meteors, by their greatness, naturally overawe him, and he views them with a reverence that approaches to fear. His inexperience and uncertainty with regard to every thing about them, how they came, how they are to go, what went before, what is to come after them, exasperate his sentiment into terror and consternation. But our passions, as Father Malbranche observes, all justify themselves;[2] that is, suggest to us opinions which justify them. As those appearances terrify him, therefore, he is disposed to believe every thing about them which can render them still more the objects of his terror. That they proceed from some intelligent, though invisible causes, of whose vengeance and displeasure they are either the signs or the effects, is the notion of all others most capable of enhancing this passion, and is that, therefore, which he is most apt to entertain. To this too, that cowardice and pusillanimity, so natural to man in his uncivilized state, still more disposes him; unprotected by the laws of society, exposed, defenceless, he feels his weakness upon all occasions; his strength and security upon none.

2 But all the irregularities of nature are not of this awful or terrible kind. Some of them are perfectly beautiful and agreeable. These, therefore, from the same impotence of mind, would be beheld with love and complacency, and even with transports of gratitude; for whatever is the cause of pleasure naturally excites our gratitude. A

---

[1] [Cf. IV.21 below, where Smith connects a breakdown of law, order, and security with the neglect of natural science.]

[2] *Recherche de la vérité*, V.11. [TMS III.4.3 cites the same phrase from Malebranche, as did Smith's teacher, Francis Hutcheson, in *Inquiry concerning Moral Good and Evil*, II.4.]

child caresses the fruit that is agreeable to it, as it beats the stone that hurts it.[3] The notions of a savage are not very different. The ancient Athenians, who solemnly punished the axe which had accidentally been the cause of the death of a man,[4] erected altars, and offered sacrifices to the rainbow. Sentiments not unlike these, may sometimes, upon such occasions, begin to be felt even in the breasts of the most civilized, but are presently checked by the reflection, that the things are not their proper objects. But a savage, whose notions are guided altogether by wild nature and passion, waits for no other proof that a thing is the proper object of any sentiment, than that it excites it. The reverence and gratitude, with which some of the appearances of nature inspire him, convince him that they are the proper objects of reverence and gratitude, and therefore proceed from some intelligent beings, who take pleasure in the expressions of those sentiments. With him, therefore, every object of nature, which by its beauty or greatness, its utility or hurtfulness, is considerable enough to attract his attention, and whose operations are not perfectly regular, is supposed to act by the direction of some invisible and designing power. The sea is spread out into a calm, or heaved into a storm, according to the good pleasure of Neptune. Does the earth pour forth an exuberant harvest? It is owing to the indulgence of Ceres. Does the vine yield a plentiful vintage? It flows from the bounty of Bacchus. Do either refuse their presents? It is ascribed to the displeasure of those offended deities. The tree, which now flourishes, and now decays, is inhabited by a Dryad, upon whose health or sickness its various appearances depend. The fountain, which sometimes flows in a copious, and sometimes in a scanty stream, which appears sometimes clear and limpid, and at other times muddy and disturbed, is affected in all its changes by the Naiad who dwells within it. Hence the origin of Polytheism, and of that vulgar superstition which ascribes all the irregular events of nature to the favour or displeasure of intelligent, though invisible beings, to gods, daemons, witches, genii, fairies. For it may be observed, that in all Polytheistic religions, among savages, as well as in the early ages of Heathen antiquity, it is the irregular events of nature only that are ascribed to the agency and power of their gods. Fire burns, and water refreshes; heavy bodies descend, and lighter substances fly upwards, by the necessity of their own nature; nor was the invisible hand of Jupiter[5] ever apprehended to be employed in those matters. But

---

[3] [Cf. TMS II.iii.1.1: 'We are angry, for a moment, even at the stone that hurts us. A child beats it ...']

[4] [Cf. LJ(A) ii.119, LJ(B) 188 (ed. Cannan, 141).]

[5] [For comment on this phrase and its connection with Smith's later use of 'invisible hand',
(*continued*)]

thunder and lightning, storms and sunshine, those more irregular events, were ascribed to his favour, or his anger. Man, the only designing power with which they were acquainted, never acts but either to stop, or to alter the course, which natural events would take, if left to themselves. Those other intelligent beings, whom they imagined, but knew not, were naturally supposed to act in the same manner; not to employ themselves in supporting the ordinary course of things, which went on of its own accord, but to stop, to thwart, and to disturb it. And thus, in the first ages of the world, the lowest and most pusillanimous superstition supplied the place of philosophy.

3   But when law has established order and security, and subsistence ceases to be precarious, the curiosity of mankind is increased, and their fears are diminished. The leisure which they then enjoy renders them more attentive to the appearances of nature, more observant of her smallest irregularities, and more desirous to know what is the chain which links them all together.[6] That some such chain subsists betwixt all her seemingly disjointed phaenomena, they are necessarily led to conceive; and that magnanimity, and cheerfulness, which all generous natures acquire who are bred in civilized societies, where they have so few occasions to feel their weakness, and so many to be conscious of their strength and security, renders them less disposed to employ, for this connecting chain, those invisible beings whom the fear and ignorance of their rude forefathers had engendered.[7] Those of liberal fortunes, whose attention is not much occupied either with business or with pleasure, can fill up the void of their imagination, which is thus disengaged from the ordinary affairs of life, no other way than by attending to that train of events which passes around them. While the great objects of nature thus pass in review before them, many things occur in an order to which they have not been accustomed. Their imagination, which accompanies with ease and delight the regular progress of nature, is stopped and embarrassed by those seeming incoherences; they excite their wonder, and seem to require some chain of intermediate events, which, by connecting them with something that has gone before, may thus render the

---

see A. L. Macfie, 'The Invisible Hand of Jupiter', *Journal of the History of Ideas*, xxxii (1971), 595–9.]

   [6] [Cf. Hume, who says of a republic: 'From law arises security: from security curiosity: and from curiosity knowledge.' 'Of the Rise and Progress of the Arts and Sciences', in *Essays Moral, Political and Literary*, ed. Green and Grose, i.180.]

   [7] [For Smith's views on the relation between scientific and religious explanation, cf. WN V.i.f.24: 'Superstition first attempted to satisfy this curiosity by referring all those wonderful appearances to the immediate agency of the gods. Philosophy afterwards endeavoured to account for them, from more familiar causes ...' But also Ancient Physics, 9, below: 'as ignorance begot superstition, science gave birth to the first theism that arose among those nations, who were not enlightened by divine Revelation.']

whole course of the universe consistent and of a piece. Wonder, therefore, and not any expectation of advantage from its discoveries, is the first principle which prompts mankind to the study of Philosophy, of that science which pretends to lay open the concealed connections that unite the various appearances of nature; and they pursue this study for its own sake, as an original pleasure or good in itself, without regarding its tendency to procure them the means of many other pleasures.[8]

4   Greece, and the Greek colonies in Sicily, Italy, and the Lesser Asia, were the first countries which, in these western parts of the world, arrived at a state of civilized society. It was in them, therefore, that the first philosophers, of whose doctrine we have any distinct account, appeared. Law and order seem indeed to have been established in the great monarchies of Asia and Egypt, long before they had any footing in Greece: yet, after all that has been said concerning the learning of the Chaldeans and Egyptians, whether there ever was in those nations any thing which deserved the name of science, or whether that despotism which is more destructive of security and leisure than anarchy itself, and which prevailed over all the East, prevented the growth of Philosophy, is a question which, for want of monuments, cannot be determined with any degree of precision.[9]

5   The Greek colonies having been settled amid nations either altogether barbarous, or altogether unwarlike, over whom, therefore, they soon acquired a very great authority, seem, upon that account, to have arrived at a considerable degree of empire and opulence before any state in the parent country had surmounted that extreme poverty, which, by leaving no room for any evident distinction of ranks, is necessarily attended with the confusion and misrule which flows from a want of all regular subordination.[10] The Greek islands being secure from the invasion of land armies, or from naval forces, which were in those days but little known, seem, upon that account too, to have got before the continent in all sorts of civility and improvement. The first philosophers, therefore, as well as the first poets, seem all to have been natives, either of their colonies, or of their

[8] This explanation of the origin of philosophy is commonly attributed to Plato. The *locus classicus* is 'The sense of wonder is the mark of the philosopher' (*Theaetetus*, 155 D), but the context suggests 'puzzlement' rather than the conventional sense. [For the complete thought of Smith's sentence cf. Aristotle, *Metaphysics*, A, 982^{b}11–24.]

[9] With the knowledge then available Smith's cautious statement could hardly have been improved upon. Modern research, based on authentic documents (papyrus, steles, etc.), reveals the high sophistication of Egyptian and especially 'Babylonian' mathematics, astronomy, and medicine *sensu lato*. The debt of Greece to these forerunners becomes progressively apparent; nevertheless, the Greek innovation of rigour and abstraction introduced a new dimension.

[10] [Smith comments extensively on the proposition that 'Civil government supposes a certain subordination' in WN V.i.b.3 ff. ('Part II, Of the Expence of Justice'). On the social utility of the 'distinction of ranks' cf. TMS I.iii.2.3, VI.ii.1.20, VI.iii.30.]

islands. It was from thence that Homer, Archilochus, Stesichorus, Simonides, Sappho, Anacreon, derived their birth. The Thales and Pythagoras, the founders of the two earliest sects of philosophy, arose, the one in an Asiatic colony, the other in an island; and neither of them established his school in the mother country.[11]

6   What was the particular system of either of those two philosophers, or whether their doctrine was so methodized as to deserve the name of a system, the imperfection, as well as the uncertainty of all the traditions that have come down to us concerning them, makes it impossible to determine. The school of Pythagoras, however, seems to have advanced further in the study of the connecting principles of nature, than that of the Ionian philosopher. The accounts which are given of Anaximander, Anaximenes, Anaxagoras, Archelaus, the successors of Thales, represent the doctrines of those sages as full of the most inextricable confusion. Something, however, that approaches to a composed and orderly system, may be traced in what is delivered down to us concerning the doctrine of Empedocles, of Archytas, of Timaeus, and of Ocellus the Lucanian, the most renowned philosophers of the Italian school.[12] The opinions of the two last coincide pretty much; the one, with those of Plato; the other, with those of Aristotle; nor do those of the two first seem to have been very different, of whom the one was the author of the doctrine of the Four Elements, the other the inventor of the Categories;[13] who, therefore, may be regarded as the founders, the one, of the ancient Physics; the other, of the ancient Dialectic; and, how closely these were connected,

---

[11] [Cf. WN IV.vii.b.4 ('Causes of the Prosperity of new Colonies'): 'The schools of the two oldest Greek philosophers, those of Thales and Pythagoras, were established, it is remarkable, not in antient Greece, but the one in an Asiatick, the other in an Italian colony.' Smith elaborates the point in LRBL ii.117–19 (ed. Lothian, 132–3), stating that Thales taught in Miletus, Pythagoras in Italy, and Empedocles in Sicily, before 'the Persian expedition' brought commerce and the arts to the mainland of Greece.]

[12] The work on natural philosophy by 'Ocellus the Lucanian' is now (*Oxford Classical Dictionary*, 1970) regarded as supposititious and as dating from *c.*150 B.C., i.e. post-Aristotelian. [See R. Mondolfo's note in his Italian translation of E. Zeller, *History of Greek Philosophy*, ii.384–5.

As regards Timaeus, Smith is making two assumptions usual at that time. (1) He takes Plato's dialogue figure Timaeus to be a historical person. On this, see F. M. Cornford, *Plato's Cosmology* (1937), 2–3. (2) He does not doubt the genuineness of the surviving treatise, ascribed to Timaeus, 'On the World-Soul'. But see A. E. Taylor, *Commentary on Plato's Timaeus* (1928), Appendix II, 655–64, and other literature there cited.

The 'Italian School' refers to the Pythagoreans at Croton in Southern Italy. It is mentioned again in Ancient Physics, 3 ff.]

[13] [Here again Smith's judgement is based on a too ready acceptance of pseudonymous writings. Some genuine fragments of works by Archytas of Tarentum have been preserved; but the logical works acribed to him, with such titles as *On general propositions, On opposites*, are now commonly regarded as productions of much later neo-Pythagoreans. Admittedly, Simplicius and other ancient commentators on Aristotle's *Categories* accepted them as genuine. E. Zeller, *Philosophie der Griechen*, ed. 4, vol. iii b, 114–26; Diels-Kranz, *Fragmente der Vorsokratiker*, ed. 6, i.439.]

will appear hereafter.[14] It was in the school of Socrates, however, from Plato and Aristotle, that Philosophy first received that form, which introduced her, if one may say so, to the general acquaintance of the world. It is from them, therefore, that we shall begin to give her history in any detail. Whatever was valuable in the former systems, which was at all consistent with their general principles, they seem to have consolidated into their own. From the Ionian Philosophy, I have not been able to discover that they derived any thing. From the Pythagorean school, both Plato and Aristotle seem to have derived the fundamental principles of almost all their doctrines. Plato, too, appears to have borrowed something from two other sects of philosophers, whose extreme obscurity seems to have prevented them from acquiring themselves any extensive reputation: the one was that of Cratylus and Heraclitus; the other was that of Xenophanes, Parmenides, Melissus, and Zeno.[15] To pretend to rescue the system of any of those antesocratic sages, from that oblivion which at present covers them all, would be a vain and useless attempt. What seems, however, to have been borrowed from them, shall sometimes be marked as we go along.

7   There was still another school of philosophy, earlier than Plato, from which, however, he was so far from borrowing any thing, that he seems to have bent the whole force of his reason to discredit and expose its principles.[16] This was the Philosophy of Leucippus, Democritus, and Protagoras,[17] which accordingly seems to have submitted to his eloquence, to have lain dormant, and to have been almost forgotten for some generations, till it was afterwards more successfully revived by Epicurus.

SECTION IV

The History of Astronomy

1 Of all the phaenomena of nature, the celestial appearances are, by their greatness and beauty, the most universal objects of the curiosity

---

[14] [Ancient Logics, 1.]

[15] [Cratylus was a pupil of Heracleitus. For his influence on Plato, see Aristotle, *Metaphysics*, A, 987ª32 ff., and Sir David Ross, *Aristotle's Metaphysics*, vol. i, xlvii. In these remarks, Smith greatly underrates the influence of Parmenides upon his immediate successors and upon Plato.]

[16] [This statement is too sweeping. It is likely that Plato knew *something* of the system of Leucippus (see F. M. Cornford, *Plato's Theory of Knowledge* (1935), 231); but when he attacks materialism, as at *Sophist*, 246 A–D, and *Laws*, X, 889 B ff., it is in quite general terms. Protagoras is criticized specifically by Plato, but see next note.]

[17] The inclusion of Protagoras, the Sophist, in the 'school' of the atomists is unwarranted.

of mankind.[1] Those who surveyed the heavens with the most careless attention, necessarily distinguished in them three different sorts of objects; the Sun, the Moon, and the Stars. These last, appearing always in the same situation, and at the same distance with regard to one another, and seeming to revolve every day round the earth in parallel circles,[2] which widened gradually from the poles to the equator,[3] were naturally thought to have all the marks of being fixed, like so many gems, in the concave side of the firmament, and of being carried round by the diurnal revolutions of that solid body: for the azure sky, in which the stars seem to float, was readily apprehended, upon account of the uniformity of their apparent motions, to be a solid body, the roof or outer wall of the universe, to whose inside all those little sparkling objects were attached.

2   The Sun and Moon, often changing their distance and situation, in regard to the other heavenly bodies, could not be apprehended to be attached to the same sphere with them. They assigned, therefore, to each of them, a sphere of its own; that is, supposed each of them to be attached to the concave side of a solid and transparent body, by whose revolutions they were carried round the earth. There was not indeed, in this case, the same ground for the supposition of such a sphere as in that of the Fixed Stars; for neither the Sun nor the Moon appear to keep always at the same distance with regard to any one of the other heavenly bodies. But as the motion of the Stars had been accounted for by an hypothesis of this kind, it rendered the theory of the heavens more uniform, to account for that of the Sun and Moon in the same manner. The sphere of the Sun they placed above that of the Moon; as the Moon was evidently seen in eclipses to pass betwixt the Sun and the Earth. Each of them was supposed to revolve by a motion of its own, and at the same time to be affected by the motion of the Fixed Stars. Thus, the Sun was carried round from east to west by the communicated movement of this outer sphere, which produced his diurnal revolutions, and the vicissitudes of day and night; but at the same time he had a motion of his own, contrary to this, from west

---

[1] [Cf. Ancient Physics, 1. Also WN V.i.f.24 ('Of the Expence of the Institutions for the Education of Youth'): 'The great phenomena of nature, the revolutions of the heavenly bodies, eclipses, comets, thunder, lightning, and other extraordinary meteors; the generation, the life, growth, and dissolution of plants and animals; are objects which, as they necessarily excite the wonder, so they naturally call forth the curiosity of mankind to enquire into their causes.'

In LRBL ii.18–19v (ed. Lothian, 87), Smith says: 'The more lively and striking the impression is which any phaenomenon makes on the mind, the greater curiosity does it excite to know its causes, tho perhaps the phaenomenon may not be intrinsically half so grand or important as another less striking. Thus it is we have a greater curiosity to pry into the cause of thunder and lightning and of the celestial motions, than of gravity, because these naturally make a greater impression on us.']

[2] [See § 51 below on the use of the circle in early astronomical theories.]

[3] For technical terms employed in the 'Ancient Astronomy' see the editor's Introduction, 15–16.

to east, which occasioned his annual revolution, and the continual shifting of his place with regard to the Fixed Stars. This motion was more easy, they thought, when carried on edgeways, and not in direct opposition to the motion of the outer sphere, which occasioned the inclination of the axis of the sphere of the Sun, to that of the sphere of the Fixed Stars; this again produced the obliquity of the ecliptic, and the consequent changes of the seasons. The moon, being placed below the sphere of the Sun, had both a shorter course to finish, and was less obstructed by the contrary movement of the sphere of the Fixed Stars, from which she was farther removed. She finished her period, therefore, in a shorter time, and required but a month, instead of a year, to complete it.

3   The Stars, when more attentively surveyed, were some of them observed to be less constant and uniform in their motions than the rest, and to change their situations with regard to the other heavenly bodies; moving generally eastwards, yet appearing sometimes to stand still, and sometimes even to move westwards. These, to the number of five, were distinguished by the name of Planets, or wandering Stars, and marked with the particular appellations of Saturn, Jupiter, Mars, Venus, and Mercury. As, like the Sun and Moon, they seem to accompany the motion of the Fixed Stars from east to west, but at the same time to have a motion of their own, which is generally from west to east; they were each of them, as well as those two great lamps of heaven, apprehended to be attached to the inside of a solid concave and transparent sphere, which had a revolution of its own, that was almost directly contrary to the revolution of the outer heaven, but which, at the same time, was hurried along by the superior violence and rapidity of this last.

4   This is the system of concentric Spheres, the first regular system of Astronomy, which the world beheld, as it was taught in the Italian school[4] before Aristotle and his two contemporary philosophers, Eudoxus and Callippus,[5] had given it all the perfection which it is capable of receiving. Though rude and inartificial,[6] it is capable of

---

[4] [No objection can be raised to this account of the science of the 'Italian school', since it is not unlike what classical scholars would have said until quite recent times. Today, however, it seems by no means certain that the Pythagoreans deserve the place in the early history of mathematics and astronomy which tradition has given them. It is safer to regard Eudoxus as the originator of the system of concentric spheres.]

[5] [On Eudoxus and Callippus, see Sir T. L. Heath, *Aristarchus of Samos* (1913), chap. 16, 190–224, and G. L. Huxley in *Dictionary of Scientific Biography*, vol. iv (1971); also D. J. Allan, article 'Plato', ibid., vol. xi (1975), 22–31. As Smith says in §7 below, Eudoxus was the friend and auditor of Plato. We learn on good authority that he propounded his system in answer to a problem posed by Plato. Our knowledge of the system comes from Aristotle, *Metaphysics*, Λ, 8, 1073ᵇ1 ff., and the Commentary of Simplicius (5th–6th century A.D.) on Aristotle, *De Caelo*, II.12, 293ᵃ4. Smith was obviously acquainted with the former, probably with the latter also.]

[6] Far from being 'rude and inartificial', the system of Eudoxus is a remarkable piece of
                                                                        (*continued*)

connecting together, in the imagination, the grandest and the most seemingly disjointed appearances in the heavens. The motions of the most remarkable objects in the celestial regions, the Sun, the Moon, and the Fixed Stars, are sufficiently connected with one another by this hypothesis. The eclipses of these two great luminaries are, though not so easily calculated, as easily explained, upon this ancient, as upon the modern system. When these early philosophers explained to their disciples the very simple causes of those dreadful phaenomena, it was under the seal of the most sacred secrecy, that they might avoid the fury of the people, and not incur the imputation of impiety, when they thus took from the gods the direction of those events, which were apprehended to be the most terrible tokens of their impending vengeance. The obliquity of the ecliptic, the consequent changes of the seasons, the vicissitudes of day and night, and the different lengths of both days and nights, in the different seasons, correspond too, pretty exactly, with this ancient doctrine. And if there had been no other bodies discoverable in the heavens besides the Sun, the Moon, and the Fixed Stars, this old hypothesis might have stood the examination of all ages, and have gone down triumphant to the remotest posterity.

5   If it gained the belief of mankind by its plausibility, it attracted their wonder and admiration; sentiments that still more confirmed their belief, by the novelty and beauty of that view of nature which it presented to the imagination. Before this system was taught in the world, the earth was regarded as, what it appears to the eye, a vast, rough, and irregular plain, the basis and foundation of the universe, surrounded on all sides by the ocean, and whose roots extended themselves through the whole of that infinite depth which is below it. The sky was considered as a solid hemisphere, which covered the earth, and united with the ocean at the extremity of the horizon. The Sun, the Moon, and all the heavenly bodies rose out of the eastern, climbed up the convex side of the heavens, and descended again into the western ocean, and from thence, by some subterraneous passages, returned to their first chambers in the east. Nor was this notion confined to the people, or to the poets who painted the opinions of the people: it was held by Xenophanes, the founder of the Eleatic philosophy, after that of the Ionian and Italian schools, the earliest that appeared in Greece. Thales of Miletus too, who, according to Aristotle,[7] represented the Earth as floating upon an immense ocean of water, may have been nearly of the same opinion; notwithstanding

mathematical analysis, virtually a geometrical equivalent of Joseph Fourier's algebraic resolution of a complex curvilinear motion into simpler components.

[7] [*De Caelo*, II.13, 294ᵃ28.]

what we are told by Plutarch[8] and Apuleius[9] concerning his astronomical discoveries, all of which must plainly have been of a much later date. To those who had no other idea of nature, besides what they derived from so confused an account of things, how agreeable must that system have appeared, which represented the Earth as distinguished into land and water, self-balanced and suspended in the centre of the universe, surrounded by the elements of Air and Ether, and covered by eight polished and cristalline Spheres, each of which was distinguished by one or more beautiful and luminous bodies, and all of which revolved round their common centre, by varied, but by equable and proportionable motions. It seems to have been the beauty of this system that gave Plato[10] the notion of something like an harmonic proportion, to be discovered in the motions and distances of the heavenly bodies; and which suggested to the earlier Pythagoreans, the celebrated fancy of the Musick of the Spheres:[11] a wild and romantic idea, yet such as does not ill correspond with that admiration, which so beautiful a system, recommended too by the graces of novelty, is apt to inspire.

6   Whatever are the defects which this account of things labours under, they are such, as to the first observers of the heavens could not readily occur. If all the motions of the Five Planets cannot, the greater part of them may, be easily connected by it; they and all their motions are the least remarkable objects in the heavens; the greater part of mankind take no notice of them at all; and a system, whose only defect lies in the account which it gives of them, cannot thereby be much disgraced in their opinion. If some of the appearances too of the Sun and Moon, the sometimes accelerated and again retarded motions of those luminaries but ill correspond with it; these too, are such as cannot be discovered but by the most attentive observation, and such therefore as we cannot wonder that the imaginations of the first enquirers should slur over, if one may say so, and take little notice of.

7   It was, however, to remedy those defects, that Eudoxus, the friend and auditor of Plato, found it necessary to increase the number of the Celestial Spheres.[12] Each Planet is sometimes observed to advance forward in that eastward course which is peculiar to itself, sometimes to retire backwards, and sometimes again to stand still. To suppose

---

[8] [*De Pythicae Oraculis*, 18, 402 E–F.]

[9] [*Florilegium*, 18; English translation in Heath, *Aristarchus of Samos*. 22.]

[10] [*Republic*, X.616–17; Heath, op. cit., 148–58.]

[11] [Aristotle, *De Caelo*, II.9, 290^{b}12–29; Cicero, *Somnium Scipionis*, 5. See W. K. C. Guthrie, *History of Greek Philosophy* (1962), i.295–301; W. Bürkert, *Weisheit und Wissenschaft* (1962), 328–35.]

[12] [See notes 4–5 above. The phrase is incorrect if Eudoxus was the originator of the spheres.]

that the Sphere of the Planet should by its own motion, if one may
say so, sometimes roll forwards, sometimes roll backwards, and
sometimes do neither the one nor the other, is contrary to all the
natural propensities of the imagination, which accompanies with
ease and delight any regular and orderly motion, but feels itself
perpetually stopped and interrupted, when it endeavours to attend to
one so desultory and uncertain. It would pursue, naturally and of its
own accord, the direct or progressive movement of the Sphere, but is
every now and then shocked, if one may say so, and turned violently
out of its natural career by the retrograde and stationary appearances
of the Planet, betwixt which and its more usual motion, the fancy
feels a want of connection, a gap or interval, which it cannot fill up,
but by supposing some chain of intermediate events to join them.[13]
The hypothesis of a number of other spheres revolving in the
heavens, besides those in which the luminous bodies themselves were
infixed, was the chain with which Eudoxus endeavoured to supply it.
He bestowed four of these Spheres upon each of the Five Planets; one
in which the luminous body itself revolved, and three others above it.
Each of these had a regular and constant, but a peculiar movement of
its own, which it communicated to what was properly the Sphere of
the Planet, and thus occasioned that diversity of motions observable
in those bodies. One of these Spheres, for example, had an oscillatory
motion,[14] like the circular pendulum of a watch. As when you turn
round a watch, like a Sphere upon its axis, the pendulum will, while
turned round along with it, still continue to oscillate, and communicate to whatever body is comprehended within it, both its own
oscillations and the circular motion of the watch; so this oscillating
Sphere, being itself turned round by the motion of the Sphere above
it, communicated to the Sphere below it, that circular, as well as its
own oscillatory motion; produced by the one, the daily revolutions;
by the other, the direct, stationary, and retrograde appearances of the
Planet, which derived from a third Sphere that revolution by which
it performed its annual period. The motions of all these Spheres were
in themselves constant and equable, such as the imagination could
easily attend to and pursue, and which connected together that
otherwise incoherent diversity of movements observable in the
Sphere of the Planet. The motions of the Sun and Moon being more
regular than those of the Five Planets, by assigning three Spheres to

[13] [The account that follows is based on Aristotle, *Metaphysics*, Λ, 8 (see note 5 above):
spheres of the planets, 1073^{b}22; of Sun and Moon, 1073^{b}17; system of Callippus, 1073^{b}32 ff.]
[14] Smith seems to have misunderstood the nature of the 'oscillation', since the currently
accepted characteristics—'constant' and 'equable'—contradict it. He may have failed to
recognize that the 'oscillation' is only relative to the observer.

each of them, Eudoxus imagined he could connect together all the diversity of movements discoverable in either. The motion of the Fixed Stars being perfectly regular, one Sphere he judged sufficient for them all. So that, according to this account, the whole number of Celestial Spheres amounted to twenty-seven. Callippus, though somewhat younger, the cotemporary of Eudoxus, found that even this number was not enough to connect together the vast variety of movements which he discovered in those bodies, and therefore increased it to thirty-four.[15] Aristotle, upon a yet more attentive observation, found that even all these Spheres would not be sufficient, and therefore added twenty-two more, which increased their number to fifty-six.[16] Later observers discovered still new motions, and new inequalities, in the heavens. New Spheres were therefore still to be added to the system, and some of them to be placed even above that of the Fixed Stars. So that in the sixteenth century, when Fracostorio,[17] smit with the eloquence of Plato and Aristotle, and with the regularity and harmony of their system, in itself perfectly beautiful, though it corresponds but inaccurately with the phaenomena, endeavoured to revive this ancient Astronomy, which had long given place to that of Ptolemy and Hipparchus,[18] he found it necessary to multiply the number of Celestial Spheres to seventy-two; neither were all these enough.

8   This system had now become as intricate and complex as those appearances themselves, which it had been invented to render uniform and coherent. The imagination, therefore, found itself but little relieved from that embarrassment, into which those appearances had thrown it, by so perplexed an account of things. Another system, for this reason, not long after the days of Aristotle, was invented by Apollonius,[19] which was afterwards perfected by Hipparchus, and has since been delivered down to us by Ptolemy, the more artificial system of Eccentric Spheres and Epicycles.[20]

9   In this system, they first distinguished betwixt the real and

[15] [Aristotle says that Callippus found it necessary, in order to explain the phenomena, to assign two additional spheres each to the Sun and Moon, and one each to Mars, Venus, and Mercury. Thus his total was 27 + 4 + 3.]

[16] This elaboration of the system is described in Aristotle's *De Caelo*. See the editor's Introduction, 17.

[17] i.e. Girolamo Fracastoro (1483–1553), an outstanding figure linking the humanistic (literary) Renaissance with the so-called 'Scientific Revolution'. The theory referred to by Smith was set out in Fracastoro's *Homocentrica* (1583). [See *Dictionary of Scientific Biography*, vol. v (1972), 104–7.]

[18] [Hipparchus (*fl*. 146–127 B.C.) of course preceded Ptolemy, who is one of the prime sources of our information about him.]

[19] [Apollonius of Perga (3rd century B.C.), 'the Great Geometer'. His theory of planetary motion is known from Ptolemy's *Almagest*.]

[20] [See T. L. Heath, *Manual of Greek Mathematics* (1931), 376, 396–7; W. W. Tarn and G. T. Griffith, *Hellenistic Civilization*, ed. 3 (1952), 296–9, and literature there quoted.]

apparent motion of the heavenly bodies. These, they observed, upon account of their immense distance, must necessarily appear to revolve in circles concentric with the globe of the Earth, and with one another: but that we cannot, therefore, be certain that they really revolve in such circles, since, though they did not, they would still have the same appearance. By supposing, therefore, that the Sun and the other Planets revolved in circles, whose centres were very distant from the centre of the Earth; that consequently, in the progress of their revolution, they must sometimes approach nearer, and sometimes recede further from it, and must, therefore, to its inhabitants appear to move faster in the one case, and slower in the other, those philosophers imagined they could account for the apparently unequal velocities of all those bodies.

10   By supposing, that in the solidity of the Sphere of each of the Five Planets there was formed another little Sphere, called an Epicycle, which revolved round its own centre, at the same time that it was carried round the centre of the Earth by the revolution of the great Sphere, betwixt whose concave and convex sides it was inclosed; in the same manner as we might suppose a little wheel inclosed within the outer circle of a great wheel, and which whirled about several times upon its own axis, while its centre was carried round the axis of the great wheel, they imagined they could account for the retrograde and stationary appearances of those most irregular objects in the heavens. The Planet, they supposed, was attached to the circumference, and whirled round the centre of this little Sphere,[21] at the same time that it was carried round the Earth by the movement of the great Sphere. The revolution of this little Sphere, or Epicycle, was such, that the Planet, when in the upper part of it; that is, when furthest off and least sensible to the eye; was carried round in the same direction with the centre of the Epicycle, or with the Sphere in which the Epicycle was inclosed: but when in the lower part, that is, when nearest and most sensible to the eye; it was carried round in a direction contrary to that of the centre of the Epicycle: in the same manner as every point in the upper part of the outer circle of a coach-wheel revolves forward in the same direction with the axis, while every point, in the lower part, revolves backwards in a contrary direction to the axis. The motions of the Planet, therefore, surveyed from the Earth appeared direct, when in the upper part of the Epicycle, and retrograde, when in the lower. When again it either descended from the upper part to the lower, or ascended from the lower to the upper, it necessarily appeared stationary.

<hr>

[21] The system of Ptolemy took no account of 'spheres'; these were later introduced into it by the Muslim astronomers under the influence of Aristotelian 'physics'.

11   But, though, by the eccentricity of the great Sphere, they were thus
able, in some measure, to connect together the unequal velocities of
the heavenly bodies, and by the revolutions of the little Sphere, the
direct, stationary, and retrograde appearances of the Planets, there
was another difficulty that still remained. Neither the Moon, nor the
three superior Planets, appear always in the same part of the heavens,
when at their periods of most retarded motion, or when they are
supposed to be at the greatest distance from the Earth. The apogeum
therefore, or the point of greatest distance from the Earth, in the
Spheres of each of those bodies, must have a movement of its own,
which may carry it successively through all the different points of the
Ecliptic. They supposed, therefore, that while the great eccentric
Sphere revolved eastwards round its centre, that its centre too
revolved westwards in a circle of its own, round the centre of the
Earth, and thus carried its apogeum through all the different points
of the Ecliptic.

12   But with all those combined and perplexed circles; though the
patrons of this system were able to give some degree of uniformity to
the real directions of the Planets, they found it impossible so to adjust
the velocities of those supposed Spheres to the phaenomena, as that
the revolution of any one of them, when surveyed from its own
centre, should appear perfectly equable and uniform. From that
point, the only point in which the velocity of what moves in a circle
can be truly judged of, they would still appear irregular and
inconstant, and such as tended to embarrass and confound the
imagination. They invented, therefore, for each of them, a new Circle,
called the Equalizing Circle, from whose centre they should all
appear perfectly equable: that is, they so adjusted the velocities of
these Spheres, as that, though the revolution of each of them would
appear irregular when surveyed from its own centre, there should,
however, be a point comprehended within its circumference, from
whence its motions should appear to cut off, in equal times, equal
portions of the Circle, of which that point was the centre.

13   Nothing can more evidently show, how much the repose and
tranquillity of the imagination is the ultimate end of philosophy, than
the invention of this Equalizing Circle. The motions of the heavenly
bodies had appeared inconstant and irregular, both in their velocities
and in their directions. They were such, therefore, as tended to
embarrass and confound the imagination, whenever it attempted to
trace them. The invention of Eccentric Spheres, of Epicycles, and of
the revolution of the centres of the Eccentric Spheres, tended to allay
this confusion, to connect together those disjointed appearances, and
to introduce harmony and order into the mind's conception of the

movements of those bodies. It did this, however, but imperfectly; it
introduced uniformity and coherence into their real directions. But
their velocities, when surveyed from the only point in which the
velocity of what moves in a Circle can be truly judged of, the centre
of that Circle, still remained, in some measure, inconstant as before;
and still, therefore, embarrassed the imagination. The mind found
itself somewhat relieved from this embarrassment, when it conceived,
that how irregular soever the motions of each of those Circles might
appear, when surveyed from its own centre, there was, however, in
each of them, a point, from whence its revolution would appear
perfectly equable and uniform, and such as the imagination could
easily follow. Those philosophers transported themselves, in fancy, to
the centres of these imaginary Circles, and took pleasure in surveying
from thence, all those fantastical motions, arranged, according to that
harmony and order, which it had been the end of all their researches
to bestow upon them. Here, at last, they enjoyed that tranquillity and
repose which they had pursued through all the mazes of this intricate
hypothesis; and here they beheld this, the most beautiful and
magnificent part of the great theatre of nature, so disposed and
constructed, that they could attend, with ease and delight, to all the
revolutions and changes that occurred in it.

14　　These, the System of Concentric, and that of Eccentric Spheres,
seem to have been the two Systems of Astronomy, that had most
credit and reputation with that part of the ancient world, who applied
themselves particularly to the study of the heavens. Cleanthes,[22]
however, and the other philosophers of the Stoical sect who came
after him, appear to have had a system of their own, quite different
from either. But, though justly renowned for their skill in dialectic,
and for the security and sublimity of their moral doctrines, those
sages seem never to have had any high reputation for their knowledge
of the heavens; neither is the name of any one of them[23] ever counted
in the catalogue of the great astronomers, and studious observers of
the Stars, among the ancients. They rejected the doctrine of the Solid
Spheres; and maintained, that the celestial regions were filled with a
fluid ether, of too yielding a nature to carry along with it, by any
motion of its own, bodies so immensely great as the Sun, Moon, and
Five Planets. These, therefore, as well as the Fixed Stars, did not
derive their motion from the circumambient body, but had each of
them, in itself, and peculiar to itself, a vital principle of motion, which
directed it to move with its own peculiar velocity, and its own peculiar
direction. It was by this internal principle, that the Fixed Stars

[22] [Second head of the Stoic school, succeeding its founder, Zeno of Citium, in 263 B.C.]
[23] Poseidonius (c.135–51 B.C.) was a notable exception.

revolved directly from east to west in circles parallel to the Equator, greater or less, according to their distance or nearness to the Poles, and with velocities so proportioned, that each of them finished its diurnal period in the same time, in something less than twenty-three hours and fifty-six minutes. It was, by a principle of the same kind, that the Sun moved westwards, for they allowed of no eastward motion in the heavens, but with less velocity than the Fixed Stars, so as to finish his diurnal period in twenty-four hours, and, consequently, to fall every day behind them, by a space of the heavens nearly equal to that which he passes over in four minutes; that is, nearly equal to a degree. This revolution of the Sun, too, was neither directly westwards, nor exactly circular; but after the Summer Solstice, his motion began gradually to incline a little southwards, appearing in his meridian to-day, further south than yesterday; and to-morrow still further south than to-day; and thus continuing every day to describe a spiral line round the Earth, which carried him gradually further and further southwards, till he arrived at the Winter Solstice. Here, this spiral line began to change its direction, and to bring him gradually, every day, further and further northwards, till it again restored him to the Summer Solstice. In the same manner they accounted for the motion of the Moon, and that of the Five Planets, by supposing that each of them revolved westwards, but with directions, and velocities, that were both different from one another, and continually varying; generally, however, in spherical lines, somewhat inclined to the Equator.

15   This system seems never to have had the vogue. The system of Concentric as well as that of Eccentric Spheres gives some sort of reason, both for the constancy and equability of the motion of the Fixed Stars, and for the variety and uncertainty of that of the Planets. Each of them bestow some sort of coherence upon those apparently disjointed phaenomena. But this other system seems to leave them pretty much as it found them. Ask a Stoic, why all the Fixed Stars perform their daily revolutions in circles parallel to each other, though of very different diameters, and with velocities so proportioned, that they all finish their period at the same time, and through the whole course of it preserve the same distance and situation with regard to one another? He can give no other answer, but that the peculiar nature, or if one may say so, the caprice of each Star[24] directs it to move in that peculiar manner. His system affords him no principle of connection, by which he can join together, in his

---

[24] The notion of the 'caprice of each star' was to play an important part in later natural philosophy and especially medicine.

imagination, so great a number of harmonious revolutions. But either of the other two systems, by the supposition of the solid firmament, affords this easily. He is equally at a loss to connect together the peculiarities that are observed in the motions of the other heavenly bodies; the spiral motion of them all; their alternate progression from north to south, and from south to north; the sometimes accelerated, and again retarded motions of the Sun and Moon; the direct retrograde and stationary appearances of the Planets. All these have, in his system, no bond of union, but remain as loose and incoherent in the fancy, as they at first appeared to the senses, before philosophy had attempted, by giving them a new arrangement, by placing them at different distances, by assigning to each some peculiar but regular principle of motion, to methodize and dispose them into an order that should enable the imagination to pass as smoothly, and with as little embarrassment, along them, as along the most regular, familiar, and coherent appearances of nature.

16   Such were the systems of Astronomy that, in the ancient world, appear to have been adopted by any considerable party. Of all of them, the system of Eccentric Spheres was that which corresponded most exactly with the appearances of the heavens. It was not invented till after those appearances had been observed, with some accuracy, for more than a century together; and it was not completely digested by Ptolemy till the reign of Antoninus,[25] after a much longer course of observations. We cannot wonder, therefore, that it was adapted to a much greater number of the phaenomena, than either of the other two systems, which had been formed before those phaenomena were observed with any degree of attention, which, therefore, could connect them together only while they were thus regarded in the gross, but which, it could not be expected, should apply to them when they came to be considered in the detail. From the time of Hipparchus, therefore, this system seems to have been pretty generally received by all those who attended particularly to the study of the heavens. That astronomer first made a catalogue of the Fixed Stars;[26] calculated, for six hundred years, the revolutions of the Sun, Moon, and Five Planets; marked the places in the heavens, in which, during all that period, each of those bodies should appear; ascertained the times of the eclipses of the Sun and Moon, and the particular places of the Earth in which they should be visible. His calculations were founded

---

[25] ['Claudius Ptolemy ... presumably wrote his great work about the middle of the reign of Antoninus Pius (A.D. 138–61)': Heath, *Manual of Greek Mathematics*, 402.]

[26] The catalogue attributed to Hipparchus was based by him on the earlier one of Aristillus and Timocharis, thus making possible his discovery of the precession of the equinoxes. [For Hipparchus' achievements see Heath, *Manual*, 395–9.]

upon this system, and as the events corresponded to his predictions, with a degree of accuracy which, though inferior to what Astronomy has since arrived at, was greatly superior to any thing which the world had then known, they ascertained, to all astronomers and mathematicians, the preference of his system, above all those which had been current before it.

17   It was, however, to astronomers and mathematicians only, that they ascertained this; for, notwithstanding the evident superiority of this system, to all those with which the world was then acquainted, it was never adopted by any one sect of philosophers.

18   Philosophers, long before the days of Hipparchus, seem to have abandoned the study of nature,[27] to employ themselves chiefly in ethical, rhetorical, and dialectical questions.[28] Each party of them too, had by this time completed their peculiar system or theory of the universe, and no human consideration could then have induced them to give up any part of it. That supercilious and ignorant contempt too, with which at this time they regarded all mathematicians, among whom they counted astronomers, seems even to have hindered them from enquiring so far into their doctrines, as to know what opinions they held. Neither Cicero nor Seneca, who have so often occasion to mention the ancient systems of Astronomy, take any notice of that of Hipparchus. His name is not to be found in the writings of Seneca. It is mentioned but once in those of Cicero, in a letter to Atticus,[29] but without any note of approbation, as a geographer, and not as an astronomer. Plutarch, when he counts up, in his second book, concerning the opinions of philosophers, all the ancient systems of Astronomy,[30] never mentions this, the only tolerable one which was known in his time. Those three authors, it seems, conversed only with the writings of philosophers. The elder Pliny[31] indeed, a man whose curiosity extended itself equally to every part of learning, describes the system of Hipparchus, and never mentions its author, which he has occasion to do often, without some note of that high admiration which he had so justly conceived for his merit. Such profound ignorance[32] in those professed instructors of mankind, with

---

[27] Too sweeping a condemnation; the attitudes of Stoics and Epicureans towards 'Nature' differed from that of the 'astronomers' but were far from negligible.

[28] [Cf. LRBL ii.213–14 (ed. Lothian, 175–6), referring to the time of Cicero: 'Rhetoric and Logic or Dialectic were these undoubtedly which had made the greatest progress amongst the ancients, and indeed, if we except a little of Morals, were the only ones which had been tolerably cultivated. These, therefore, were the fashionable sciences ...']

[29] [*Letters to Atticus*, II.6.1.]

[30] [Like Copernicus (see §28 and note 51 below), Smith assumes the genuineness of the *Placita Philosophorum* preserved among the writings of Plutarch. On its real origin, see J. Burnet, *Early Greek Philosophy*, ed. 3 (1920), 34.]

[31] [*Natural History*, II, especially 54, 95.]

[32] While Cicero would probably have been incapable of following the mathematical

(*continued*)

regard to so important a part of the learning of their own times, is so
very remarkable, that I thought it deserved to be taken notice of, even
in this short account of the revolutions of philosophy.

19   Systems in many respects resemble machines.[33] A machine is a
little system, created to perform, as well as to connect together, in
reality, those different movements and effects which the artist has
occasion for. A system is an imaginary machine invented to connect
together in the fancy those different movements and effects which
are already in reality performed. The machines that are first invented
to perform any particular movement are always the most complex,
and succeeding artists generally discover that, with fewer wheels,
with fewer principles of motion, than had originally been employed,
the same effects may be more easily produced.[34] The first systems, in
the same manner, are always the most complex, and a particular
connecting chain, or principle, is generally thought necessary to unite
every two seemingly disjointed appearances: but it often happens,
that one great connecting principle is afterwards found to be sufficient
to bind together all the discordant phaenomena that occur in a whole
species of things. How many wheels are necessary to carry on the
movements of this imaginary machine, the system of Eccentric
Spheres! The westward diurnal revolution of the Firmament, whose
rapidity carries all the other heavenly bodies along with it, requires
one. The periodical eastward revolutions of the Sun, Moon, and Five
Planets, require, for each of those bodies, another. Their differently
accelerated and retarded motions require, that those wheels, or
circles, should neither be concentric with the Firmament, nor with
one another; which, more than any thing, seems to disturb the
harmony of the universe. The retrograde and stationary appearance
of the Five Planets, as well as the extreme inconstancy of the Moon's
motion, require, for each of them, an Epicycle, another little wheel
attached to the circumference of the great wheel, which still more
interrupts the uniformity of the system. The motion of the apogeum

arguments, his remarks relating to what we might call 'philosophy of science' (e.g. in *De Natura
Deorum, De Divinatione*) have a distinctively modern ring.
[33] [Mechanistic analogies were common in the eighteenth century and Smith used them
widely. He writes of the universe as like a machine in Ancient Physics, 9, and in TMS I.i.4.2,
VII.ii.1.37; and of society similarly in TMS VII.iii.1.2, VII.iii.3.16.]
[34] [Cf. Languages, 41: 'All machines are generally, when first invented, extremely complex
in their principles, and there is often a particular principle of motion for every particular
movement which it is intended they should perform. Succeeding improvers observe, that one
principle may be so applied as to produce several of those movements; and thus the machine
becomes gradually more and more simple, and produces its effects with fewer wheels and fewer
principles of motion.' Smith compares with this the development of languages from original
complexity to later simplicity but considers that, while the process of simplification makes
machines 'more and more perfect', it makes languages 'more and more imperfect'. The whole
passage recurs in summary form in LRBL i.34*v*. (ed. Lothian, 11).]

of each of those bodies requires, in each of them, still another wheel, to carry the centres of their Eccentric Spheres round the centre of the Earth. And thus, this imaginary machine, though, perhaps, more simple, and certainly better adapted to the phaenomena than the Fifty-six Planetary Spheres of Aristotle, was still too intricate and complex for the imagination to rest in it with complete tranquillity and satisfaction.

20   It maintained its authority, however, without any diminution of reputation, as long as science was at all regarded in the ancient world. After the reign of Antoninus, and, indeed, after the age of Hipparchus, who lived almost three hundred years before Antoninus, the great reputation which the earlier philosophers had acquired, so imposed upon the imaginations of mankind, that they seem to have despaired of ever equalling their renown. All human wisdom, they supposed, was comprehended in the writings of those elder sages. To abridge, to explain, and to comment upon them, and thus show themselves, at least, capable of understanding some of their sublime mysteries, became now the only probable road to reputation. Proclus and Theon wrote commentaries upon the System of Ptolemy;[35] but, to have attempted to invent a new one, would then have been regarded, not only as presumption, but as impiety to the memory of their so much revered predecessors.

21   The ruin of the empire of the Romans, and, along with it, the subversion of all law and order, which happened a few centuries afterwards, produced the entire neglect of that study of the connecting principles of nature, to which leisure and security can alone give occasion.[36] After the fall of those great conquerors and civilizers of mankind, the empire of the Califfs seems to have been the first state under which the world enjoyed that degree of tranquillity which the cultivation of the sciences requires. It was under the protection of those generous and magnificent princes, that the ancient philosophy and astronomy of the Greeks were restored and established in the East; that tranquillity, which their mild,[37] just, and religious government diffused over their vast empire, revived the curiosity of mankind, to inquire into the connecting principles of nature. The fame of the Greek and Roman learning, which was then recent in the memories of men, made them desire to know, concerning these

---

[35] [Proclus (A.D. 410–85), the Neoplatonist philosopher. His extant works include 'the *Hypotyposis of Astronomical Hypotheses*, a sort of easy and readable introduction to the astronomical system of Hipparchus and Ptolemy' (Heath, *Manual*, 517).
    Theon of Alexandria (4th century A.D.) wrote a commentary on Ptolemy's *Syntaxis*. Heath, ibid., 516, explains its value.]
[36] [Cf. III.1 above.]
[37] Smith gives a somewhat optimistic view of Muslim 'toleration'.

abstruse subjects, what were the doctrines of the so much renowned
sages of those two nations.

22   They translated, therefore, into the Arabian language, and studied,
with great eagerness, the works of many Greek philosophers,
particularly of Aristotle, Ptolemy, Hippocrates, and Galen.[38] The
superiority which they easily discovered in them, above the rude
essays which their own nation[39] had yet had time to produce, and
which were such, we may suppose, as arise every where in the first
infancy of science, necessarily determined them to embrace their
systems, particularly that of Astronomy: neither were they ever
afterwards able to throw off their authority. For, though the
munificence of the Abassides, the second race of the Califfs, is said to
have supplied the Arabian astronomers with larger and better
instruments, than any that were known to Ptolemy and Hipparchus,
the study of the sciences seems, in that mighty empire, to have been
either of too short, or too interrupted a continuance, to allow them to
make any considerable correction in the doctrines of those old
mathematicians. The imaginations of mankind had not yet got time
to grow so familiar with the ancient systems, as to regard them
without some degree of that astonishment which their grandeur and
novelty excited; a novelty of a peculiar kind, which had at once the
grace of what was new, and the authority of what was ancient. They
were still, therefore, too much enslaved to those systems, to dare to
depart from them, when those confusions which shook, and at last
overturned the peaceful throne of the Califfs, banished the study of
the sciences from that empire. They had, however, before this, made
some considerable improvements: they had measured the obliquity
of the Ecliptic, with more accuracy than had been done before. The
tables of Ptolemy had, by the length of time, and by the inaccuracy of
the observations upon which they were founded, become altogether
wide of what was the real situation of the heavenly bodies, as he
himself indeed had foretold they would do. It became necessary,
therefore, to form new ones, which was accordingly executed by the
orders of the Califf Almamon,[40] under whom, too, was made the first
mensuration of the Earth that we know of, after the commencement

---

[38] [At the period in question, many Greek scientific works, especially those of Galen and
Hippocrates, were translated into Syriac as well as into Arabic: see M. Meyerhof, in Sir T.
Arnold and A. Guillaume (eds.), *The Legacy of Islam* (1931), 316 ff.; E. Gilson, *La Philosophie
au moyen âge* (1944), and R. Walzer, 'On the Arabic versions ... of Aristotle's *Metaphysics*',
Harvard Studies in Classical Philology, lxiii (1958), 218–21.]

[39] The term 'nation' is inappropriate: many of the greatest were Persians.

[40] i.e. al-Ma'mūn (786–833), 7th Abbasid Caliph from 813 until his death. [On the Tables of
al-Ma'mūn, see Baron Carra de Vaux in *The Legacy of Islam*, 380–1, chapter on 'Astronomy and
Mathematics'.]

of the Christian Aera, by two Arabian astronomers, who, in the plain of Sennaar,[41] measured two degrees of its circumference.

23   The victorious arms of the Saracens carried into Spain the learning, as well as the gallantry, of the East; and along with it, the tables of Almamon, and the Arabian translations of Ptolemy and Aristotle; and thus Europe received a second time, from Babylon, the rudiments of the science of the heavens. The writings of Ptolemy were translated from Arabic into Latin;[42] and the Peripatetic philosophy was studied in Averroes and Avicenna with as much eagerness, and with as much submission to its doctrines in the West, as it had been in the East.[43]

24   The doctrine of the Solid Spheres had, originally, been invented, in order to give a physical account of the revolutions of the heavenly bodies, according to the system of Concentric Circles, to which that doctrine was very easily accommodated. Those mathematicians who invented the doctrine of Eccentric Circles and Epicycles, contented themselves with showing, how, by supposing the heavenly bodies to revolve in such orbits, the phaenomena might be connected together, and some sort of uniformity and coherence be bestowed upon their real motions. The physical causes of those motions they left to the consideration of the philosophers; though, as appears from some passages of Ptolemy, they had some general apprehension, that they were to be explained by a like hypothesis. But, though the system of Hipparchus[44] was adopted by all astronomers and mathematicians, it never was received, as we have already observed, by any one sect of philosophers among the ancients. No attempt, therefore, seems to have been made amongst them, to accommodate to it any such hypothesis.

25   The schoolmen, who received, at once, from the Arabians, the philosophy of Aristotle, and the astronomy of Hipparchus, were necessarily obliged to reconcile them to one another, and to connect together the revolutions of the Eccentric Circles and Epicycles of the one, by the solid Spheres of the other. Many different attempts of this kind were made by many different philosophers: but, of them all, that of Purbach,[45] in the fifteenth century, was the happiest and the most esteemed. Though his hypothesis is the simplest of any of them, it

[41] [The Biblical Shinar. Other accounts say that the measurements were made by two companies of astronomers.]

[42] [On these developments see C. H. Haskins, *Studies in the History of Medieval Science* (1927), especially chap. 1 on translators from the Arabic in Spain, and chap. 5 on twelfth-century writers on astronomy. For the versions of Ptolemy see 103 ff.]

[43] [See Gilson, op. cit., 344–67, 377–90.]

[44] Here and elsewhere Smith fails to stress that it was *Ptolemy's* system (embodying the equant and based on the unsurpassed observations of Hipparchus) that was adopted in 'learned' circles. But see §26 below.

[45] Georg von Peuerbach or Peurbach (1423–61) was of course a humanist, not a 'schoolman'.

would be in vain to describe it without a scheme; neither is it easily
intelligible with one: for, if the system of Eccentric Circles and
Epicycles was before too perplexed and intricate for the imagination
to rest in it, with complete tranquillity and satisfaction, it became
much more so, when this addition had been made to it. The world,
justly indeed, applauded the ingenuity of that philosopher, who could
unite, so happily, two such seemingly inconsistent systems. His
labours, however, seem rather to have increased than to have
diminished the causes of that dissatisfaction, which the learned soon
began to feel with the system of Ptolemy. He, as well as all those who
had worked upon the same plan before him, by rendering this
account of things more complex, rendered it still more embarrassing
than it had been before.

26   Neither was the complexness of this system the sole cause of the
dissatisfaction, which the world in general began, soon after the days
of Purbach, to express for it. The tables of Ptolemy having, upon
account of the inaccuracy of the observations on which they were
founded, become altogether wide of the real situation of the heavenly
bodies, those of Almamon,[46] in the ninth century, were, upon the
same hypothesis, composed to correct their deviations. These again,
a few ages afterwards, became, for the same reason, equally useless. In
the thirteenth century, Alphonsus, the philosophical king of Castile,[47]
found it necessary to give orders for the composition of those tables,
which bear his name. It is he, who is so well known for the whimsical
impiety of using to say, that, had he been consulted at the creation of
the universe, he could have given good advice; an apophthegm which
is supposed to have proceeded from his dislike to the intricate system
of Ptolemy. In the fifteenth century, the deviation of the Alphonsine
tables began to be as sensible, as those of Ptolemy and Almamon had
been before. It appeared evident, therefore, that, though the system of
Ptolemy might, in the main, be true, certain corrections were
necessary to be made in it before it could be brought to correspond
with exact precision to the phaenomena.[48] For the revolution of his
Eccentric Circles and Epicycles, supposing them to exist, could not,
it was evident, be precisely such as he represented them; since the
revolutions of the heavenly bodies deviated, in a short time, so widely
from what the most exact calculations, that were founded upon his
hypothesis, represented them. It had plainly, therefore, become

---

[46] [See §22 and note 40 above.]

[47] [Alfonso X (b. 1221), 'the Wise', King of Castile and León, 1252–84. See Haskins, op. cit.,
16–17, and literature there cited. The legend of his 'whimsical impiety' is of late authority.]

[48] Additional spheres (ninth and tenth) were introduced to account for two (actually
imaginary) anomalies in the rotation of the 'eighth sphere' (of the fixed stars). One of these
anomalies was 'trepidation', mentioned by Milton, *Paradise Lost*, iii.483.

necessary to correct, by more accurate observations, both the velocities and directions of all the wheels and circles of which his hypothesis is composed. This, accordingly, was begun by Purbach, and carried on by Regiomontanus,[49] the disciple, the continuator, and the perfecter of the system of Purbach; and one, whose untimely death, amidst innumerable projects for the recovery of old, and the invention and advancement of new sciences, is, even at this day, to be regretted.

27   When you have convinced the world, that an established system ought to be corrected, it is not very difficult to persuade them that it should be destroyed. Not long, therefore, after the death of Regiomontanus, Copernicus began to meditate a new system, which should connect together the celestial appearances, in a more simple as well as a more accurate manner, than that of Ptolemy.

28   The confusion, in which the old hypothesis represented the motions of the heavenly bodies, was, he tells us,[50] what first suggested to him the design of forming a new system, that these, the noblest works of nature, might no longer appear devoid of that harmony and proportion which discover themselves in her meanest productions. What most of all dissatisfied him, was, the motion of the Equalizing Circle, which, by representing the revolutions of the Celestial Spheres, as equable only, when surveyed from a point that was different from their centers, introduced a real inequality into their motions; contrary to that most natural, and indeed fundamental idea, with which all the authors of astronomical systems, Plato, Eudoxus, Aristotle, even Hipparchus and Ptolemy themselves, had hitherto set out, that the real motions of such beautiful and divine objects must necessarily be perfectly regular, and go on, in a manner, as agreeable to the imagination, as the objects themselves are to the senses. He began to consider, therefore, whether, by supposing the heavenly bodies to be arranged in a different order from that in which Aristotle and Hipparchus had placed them, this so much sought for uniformity might not be bestowed upon their motions. To discover this arrangement, he examined all the obscure traditions delivered down to us, concerning every other hypothesis which the ancients had invented, for the same purpose. He found, in Plutarch,[51] that some

---

[49] [Johannes Müller (1436–76) assumed the name of Regiomontanus as the Latinized form of his birthplace, Königsberg (bei Hassfurt, W.Germany). For his life and achievements, see the article in the *Dictionary of Scientific Biography*, vol. xi (1975), 348–52.]

[50] [Preface to *De Revolutionibus Orbium Coelestium.*]

[51] [See Heath, *Aristarchus of Samos*, 301. The relevant passages are in Copernicus' *De Revolutionibus*, I.5, and in the Preface. Copernicus assumed that in the *Placita Philosophorum* he had before him a genuine work of Plutarch (see note 30 above).

He was apparently well aware that in the third century B.C. Aristarchus of Samos had suggested the heliocentric hypothesis, a fact which is unambiguously stated by Archimedes in *The Sand-Reckoner*; but he suppressed a note in which he made reference to this. Thus, in his

(*continued*)

old Pythagoreans had represented the Earth as revolving in the centre of the universe, like a wheel round its own axis; and that others, of the same sect, had removed it from the centre, and represented it as revolving in the Ecliptic like a star round the central fire. By this central fire, he supposed they meant the Sun; and though in this he was very widely mistaken,[52] it was, it seems, upon this interpretation, that he began to consider how such an hypothesis might be made to correspond to the appearances. The supposed authority of those old philosophers, if it did not originally suggest to him his system, seems, at least, to have confirmed him in an opinion, which, it is not improbable, that he had before-hand other reasons for embracing, notwithstanding what he himself would affirm to the contrary.

29   It then occurred to him, that, if the Earth was supposed to revolve every day round its axis, from west to east, all the heavenly bodies would appear to revolve, in a contrary direction, from east to west. The diurnal revolution of the heavens, upon this hypothesis, might be only apparent; the firmament, which has no other sensible motion, might be perfectly at rest; while the Sun, the Moon, and the Five Planets, might have no other movement beside that eastward revolution, which is peculiar to themselves. That, by supposing the Earth to revolve with the Planets, round the Sun, in an orbit, which comprehended within it the orbits of Venus and Mercury, but was comprehended within those of Mars, Jupiter, and Saturn, he could, without the embarrassment of Epicycles,[53] connect together the apparent annual revolutions of the Sun, and the direct, retrograde, and stationary appearances of the Planets: that while the Earth really revolved round the Sun on one side of the heavens, the Sun would appear to revolve round the Earth on the other; that while she really advanced in her annual course, he would appear to advance eastward in that movement which is peculiar to himself. That, by supposing the axis of the Earth to be always parallel to itself, not to be quite perpendicular, but somewhat inclined to the plane of her orbit, and consequently to present to the Sun, the one pole when on the one side

published work, there remains only the mention of *Pythagoreans* who had anticipated him—to the extent that they assigned a planetary movement, as well as axial rotation, to the earth.

Smith has nowhere mentioned the remarkable achievement of Aristarchus. Either it escaped him, or he has deliberately confined himself in this essay to those ancient systems which enjoyed wide influence.]

[52] A perceptive comment in respect of the Sun and 'central fire'—a distinction not always recognized by later historians. But the term 'ecliptic' is here misleading (see the editor's Introduction, 16).

[53] Smith's expression 'without the embarrassment of epicycles', repeated more than once, must be taken to refer only to the shapes and directions of the apparent motions. In order to avoid the use of Ptolemy's equant, Copernicus in fact employed more epicycles than Ptolemy had done. Smith partially corrects this in § 53 below.

of him, and the other when on the other, he would account for the obliquity of the Ecliptic; the Sun's seemingly alternate progression from north to south, and from south to north, the consequent change of the seasons, and different lengths of days and nights in the different seasons.

30   If this new hypothesis thus connected together all these appearances as happily as that of Ptolemy, there were others which it connected together much better. The three superior Planets, when nearly in conjunction with the Sun, appear always at the greatest distance from the Earth, are smallest, and least sensible to the eye, and seem to revolve forward in their direct motion with the greatest rapidity. On the contrary, when in opposition to the Sun, that is, when in their meridian about midnight, they appear nearest the Earth, are largest, and most sensible to the eye, and seem to revolve backwards in their retrograde motion. To explain these appearances, the system of Ptolemy supposed each of the these Planets to be at the upper part of their several Epicycles, in the one case; and at the lower, in the other. But it afforded no satisfactory principle of connection, which could lead the mind easily to conceive how the Epicycles of those Planets, whose spheres were so distant from the sphere of the Sun, should thus, if one may say so, keep time to his motion. The system of Copernicus afforded this easily, and like a more simple machine, without the assistance of Epicycles, connected together, by fewer movements, the complex appearances of the heavens. When the superior Planets appear nearly in conjunction with the Sun, they are then in the side of their orbits, which is almost opposite to, and most distant from the Earth, and therefore appear smallest, and least sensible to the eye. But, as they then revolve in a direction which is almost contrary to that of the Earth, they appear to advance forward with double velocity; as a ship, that sails in a contrary direction to another, appears from that other, to sail both with its own velocity, and the velocity of that from which it is seen. On the contrary, when those Planets are in opposition to the Sun, they are on the same side of the Sun with the Earth, are nearest it, most sensible to the eye, and revolve in the same direction with it; but, as their revolutions round the Sun are slower than that of the Earth, they are necessarily left behind by it, and therefore seem to revolve backwards; as a ship which sails slower than another, though it sails in the same direction, appears from that other to sail backwards. After the same manner, by the same annual revolution of the Earth, he connected together the direct and retrograde motions of the two inferior Planets, as well as the stationary appearances of all the Five.

31   There are some other particular phaenomena of the two inferior

Planets, which correspond still better to this system, and still worse to that of Ptolemy. Venus and Mercury seem to attend constantly upon the motion of the Sun, appearing, sometimes on the one side, and sometimes on the other, of that great luminary; Mercury being almost always buried in his rays, and Venus never receding above forty-eight degrees from him, contrary to what is observed in the other three Planets, which are often seen in the opposite side of the heavens, at the greatest possible distance from the Sun. The system of Ptolemy accounted for this, by supposing that the centers of the Epicycles of these two Planets were always in the same line with those of the Sun and the Earth; that they appeared therefore in conjunction with the Sun, when either in the upper or lower part of their Epicycles, and at the greatest distance from him, when in the sides of them. It assigned, however, no reason why the Epicycles of these two Planets should observe so different a rule from that which takes place in those of the other three, nor for the enormous Epicycle of Venus, whose sides must have been forty-eight degrees distant from the Sun, while its center was in conjunction with him, and whose diameter must have covered more than a quadrant of the Great Circle. But how easily all these appearances coincide with the hypothesis, which represents those two inferior Planets revolving round the Sun in orbits comprehended within the orbit of the Earth, is too obvious to require an explanation.

32   Thus far did this new account of things render the appearances of the heavens more completely coherent than had been done by any of the former systems. It did this, too, by a more simple and intelligible, as well as more beautiful machinery. It represented the Sun, the great enlightener of the universe, whose body was alone larger than all the Planets taken together, as established immoveable in the center, shedding light and heat on all the worlds that circulated around him in one uniform direction, but in longer or shorter periods, according to their different distances. It took away the diurnal revolution of the firmament, whose rapidity, upon the old hypothesis, was beyond what even thought could conceive. It not only delivered the imagination from the embarrassment of Epicycles, but from the difficulty of conceiving these two opposite motions going on at the same time, which the system of Ptolemy and Aristotle bestowed upon all the Planets; I mean, their diurnal westward, and periodical eastward revolutions. The Earth's revolution round its own axis took away the necessity for supposing the first, and the second was easily conceived when by itself. The Five Planets, which seem, upon all other systems, to be objects of a species by themselves, unlike to every thing to which the imagination has been accustomed, when supposed

to revolve along with the Earth round the Sun, were naturally
apprehended to be objects of the same kind with the Earth, habitable,
opaque, and enlightened only by the rays of the Sun. And thus this
hypothesis, by classing them in the same species of things, with an
object that is of all others the most familiar to us, took off that wonder
and uncertainty which the strangeness and singularity of their
appearance had excited; and thus far, too, better answered the great
end of Philosophy.

33   Neither did the beauty and simplicity[54] of this system alone
recommend it to the imagination; the novelty and unexpectedness of
that view of nature, which it opened to the fancy, excited more
wonder and surprise than the strangest of those appearances, which
it had been invented to render natural and familiar, and these
sentiments still more endeared it. For, though it is the end of
Philosophy, to allay that wonder, which either the unusual or
seemingly disjointed appearances of nature excite, yet she never
triumphs so much, as when, in order to connect together a few, in
themselves, perhaps, inconsiderable objects, she has, if I may say so,
created another constitution of things, more natural indeed, and such
as the imagination can more easily attend to, but more new, more
contrary to common opinion and expectation, than any of those
appearances themselves. As, in the instance before us, in order to
connect together some seeming irregularities in the motions of the
Planets, the most inconsiderable objects in the heavens, and of which
the greater part of mankind have no occasion to take any notice
during the whole course of their lives,[55] she has, to talk in the
hyperbolical language of Tycho-Brache, moved the Earth from its
foundations, stopt the revolution of the Firmament, made the Sun
stand still, and subverted the whole order of the Universe.[56]

34   Such were the advantages of this new hypothesis, as they appeared
to its author, when he first invented it. But, though that love of
paradox, so natural to the learned, and that pleasure, which they are
so apt to take in exciting, by the novelty of their supposed discoveries,
the amazement of mankind, may, notwithstanding what one of his
disciples tells us to the contrary, have had its weight in prompting
Copernicus to adopt this system; yet, when he had completed his

[54] 'Simple' only to a first approximation.
[55] It was of course for the more accurate calculations of the positions of the planets that the
greater part of astronomy up to and including the Renaissance had been undertaken.
[56] [This appears to be a distorted report at second hand or possibly a confusion between
Tycho Brahe and someone else. The supposed quotation is uncharacteristic of Tycho, who is
usually respectful to Copernicus, even though he was ready to describe both the Copernican
and the Ptolemaic systems as 'absurd'.]
    Smith's spelling of the name, here and elsewhere, though representing more nearly the
Danish pronunciation, is corrected in the Dublin edition of the same year.

Treatise of Revolutions,[57] and began coolly to consider what a strange doctrine he was about to offer to the world, he so much dreaded the prejudice of mankind against it, that, by a species of continence, of all others the most difficult to a philosopher, he detained it in his closet for thirty years together.[58] At last, in the extremity of old age, he allowed it to be extorted from him,[59] but died as soon as it was printed,[60] and before it was published.

35   When it appeared in the world, it was almost universally disapproved of, by the learned as well as by the ignorant. The natural prejudices of sense, confirmed by education, prevailed too much with both, to allow them to give it a fair examination. A few disciples only, whom he himself had instructed in his doctrine, received it with esteem and admiration. One of them, Reinholdus,[61] formed, upon this hypothesis, larger and more accurate astronomical tables, than what accompanied the Treatise of Revolutions, in which Copernicus had been guilty of some errors in calculation. It soon appeared, that these Prutenic Tables, as they were called, corresponded more exactly with the heavens, than the Tables of Alphonsus. This ought naturally to have formed a prejudice in favour of the diligence and accuracy of Copernicus in observing the heavens. But it ought to have formed none in favour of his hypothesis; since the same observations, and the result of the same calculations, might have been accommodated to the system of Ptolemy, without making any greater alteration in that system than what Ptolemy had foreseen, and had even foretold should be made. It formed, however, a prejudice in favour of both, and the learned begin to examine, with some attention, an hypothesis which afforded the easiest methods of calculation, and upon which the most exact predictions had been made. The superior degree of coherence, which it bestowed upon the celestial appearances, the simplicity and uniformity which it introduced into the real directions and velocities of the Planets, soon disposed many astronomers, first

[57] In fact the *Commentariolus* (not the *De Revolutionibus*), privately circulated in 1514. Only three near-contemporary MSS. of the *Commentariolus* are known, one recently discovered in the University of Aberdeen. It is not to be confused with the *Narratio Prima* written by his disciple Rheticus.

[58] [A striking exception to Smith's generalization, in TMS III.2.20, that mathematicians and natural philosophers, 'who may have the most perfect assurance, both of the truth and of the importance of their discoveries, are frequently very indifferent about the reception they may meet with from the public'.]

[59] Rheticus circulated his *Narratio Prima* in 1540 to test the likely reception of a full account that he was trying to persuade Copernicus to publish. The Lutheran pastor, Andreas Osiander, who saw Copernicus' great work through the press, categorically stated (anonymously, as if by Copernicus himself) that the system was not to be taken as 'physically' true. Erasmus Reinhold, as Smith states, used the system as a basis for calculating the Prutenic tables, but it now appears doubtful whether he accepted the system except as a basis for this calculation.

[60] i.e. the *De Revolutionibus Orbium Coelestium* (1543).

[61] [Erasmus Reinhold (1511–53), author of *Prutenicae Tabulae Coelestium Motum* (1551), which were adopted as the basis for the Gregorian reform of the Julian calendar in 1583.]

to favour, and at last to embrace a system, which thus connected together so happily, the most disjointed of those objects that chiefly occupied their thoughts. Nor can any thing more evidently demonstrate, how easily the learned give up the evidence of their senses to preserve the coherence of the ideas of their imagination, than the readiness with which this, the most violent paradox in all philosophy, was adopted by many ingenious astronomers, notwithstanding its inconsistency with every sistem of physics then known in the world, and notwithstanding the great number of other more real objections, to which, as Copernicus left it, this account of things was most justly exposed.

36   It was adopted, however, nor can this be wondered at, by astronomers only.[62] The learned in all other sciences, continued to regard it with the same contempt as the vulgar. Even astronomers were divided about its merit; and many of them rejected a doctrine, which not only contradicted the established system of Natural Philosophy, but which, considered astronomically only, seemed to labour under several difficulties.

37   Some of the objections against the motion of the Earth, that were drawn from the prejudices of sense, the patrons of this system, indeed, easily enough, got over. They represented, that the Earth might really be in motion, though, to its inhabitants, it seemed to be at rest; and that the Sun, and Fixed Stars, might really be at rest, though from the Earth they seemed to be in motion; in the same manner as a ship,[63] which sails through a smooth sea, seems to those who are in it, to be at rest, though really in motion; while the objects which she passes along, seem to be in motion, though really at rest.

38   But there were some other objections, which, though grounded upon the same natural prejudices, they found it more difficult to get over. The Earth had always presented itself to the senses, not only as at rest, but as inert, ponderous, and even averse to motion. The imagination had always been accustomed to conceive it as such, and suffered the greatest violence, when obliged to pursue, and attend it, in that rapid motion which the system of Copernicus bestowed upon it.[64] To enforce their objection, the adversaries of this hypothesis

---

[62] This is a very interesting and perceptive assessment. The alleged acceptance by 'astronomers only' is indeed a serious historical mis-statement: Thomas Digges, Robert Recorde, Reinerus Gemma, and especially Giordano Bruno, were none of them 'astronomers' except in a loose sense; no 'professional' except Rheticus accepted it until the seventeenth century. Nevertheless, this rather gives force to Smith's *philosophical* approach.

[63] As Copernicus, *De Revolutionibus*, I.8 (following Virgil, *Aeneid*, iii.72), had noticed.

[64] [Cf. External Senses, 12: 'Great masses, perhaps, are, according to the ordinary habits of the imagination, supposed to be more fitted for rest than for motion.' Smith then goes on to say that the teaching of modern science makes it 'scarcely possible to refuse our [rational] assent' to the motion of the earth 'with a rapidity that almost passes all human comprehension'.]

were at pains to calculate the extreme rapidity of this motion. They represented, that the circumference of the Earth had been computed to be above twenty-three thousand miles: if the Earth, therefore, was supposed to revolve every day round its axis, every point of it near the equator would pass over above twenty-three thousand miles in a day; and consequently, near a thousand miles in an hour, and about sixteen miles in a minute; a motion more rapid than that of a cannon ball, or even than the swifter progress of sound. The rapidity of its periodical revolution was yet more violent than that of its diurnal rotation. How, therefore, could the imagination ever conceive so ponderous a body to be naturally endowed with so dreadful a movement? The Peripatetic Philosophy, the only philosophy then known in the world,[65] still further confirmed this prejudice. That philosophy, by a very natural, though, perhaps, groundless distinction, divided all motion into Natural and Violent. Natural motion was that which flowed from an innate tendency in the body, as when a stone fell downwards: Violent motion, that which arose from external force, and which was, in some measure, contrary to the natural tendency of the body, as when a stone was thrown upwards, or horizontally. No violent motion could be lasting; for, being constantly weakened by the natural tendency of the body, it would soon be destroyed. The natural motion of the Earth, as was evident in all its parts, was downwards, in a strait line to the center; as that of fire and air was upwards, in a strait line from the center. It was the heavens only that revolved naturally in a circle. Neither, therefore, the supposed revolution of the Earth round its own center, nor that round the Sun, could be natural motions; they must therefore be violent, and consequently could be of no long continuance. It was in vain that Copernicus replied,[66] that gravity was, probably, nothing else besides a tendency in the different parts of the same Planet, to unite themselves to one another; that this tendency took place, probably, in the parts of the other Planets, as well as in those of the Earth; that it could very well be united with a circular motion; that it might be equally natural to the whole body of the Planet, and to every part of it; that his adversaries themselves allowed, that a circular motion was natural to the heavens, whose diurnal revolution was infinitely more rapid than even that motion which he had bestowed upon the Earth; that though a like motion was natural to the Earth,

---

[65] It is largely true that the 'schools' (i.e. the universities) confined themselves to the Peripatetic (i.e. the Aristotelian) philosophy; but the powerful strain of Neoplatonism (largely mediated through the Hermetic philosophy) should not be overlooked. The consequential 'wind' had been considered by Ptolemy; see §40 below.

[66] [*De Revolutionibus*, I.9.]

it would still appear to be at rest to its inhabitants, and all the parts of
it to tend in a strait line to the center, in the same manner as at
present. But this answer, how satisfactory soever it may appear to be
now, neither did nor could appear to be satisfactory then. By
admitting the distinction betwixt natural and violent motions, it was
founded upon the same ignorance of mechanical principles with the
objection. The systems of Aristotle and Hipparchus supposed,
indeed, the diurnal motion of the heavenly bodies to be infinitely
more rapid than even that dreadful movement which Copernicus
bestowed upon the Earth. But they supposed, at the same time, that
those bodies were objects of a quite different species, from any we are
acquainted with, near the surface of the Earth, and to which,
therefore, it was less difficult to conceive that any sort of motion
might be natural. Those objects, besides, had never presented
themselves to the senses, as moving otherwise, or with less rapidity,
than these systems represented them. The imagination, therefore,
could feel no difficulty in following a representation which the senses
had rendered quite familiar to it. But when the Planets came to be
regarded as so many Earths, the case was quite altered. The
imagination had been accustomed to conceive such objects as tending
rather to rest than motion; and this idea of their natural inertness,
encumbered, if one may say so, and clogged its flight, whenever it
endeavoured to pursue them in their periodical courses, and to
conceive them as continually rushing through the celestial spaces,
with such violent and unremitting rapidity.

39   Nor were the first followers of Copernicus more fortunate in their
answers to some other objections, which were founded indeed in the
same ignorance of the laws of motion, but which, at the same time,
were necessarily connected with that way of conceiving things, which
then prevailed universally in the learned world.

40   If the Earth, it was said, revolved so rapidly from west to east, a
perpetual wind would set in from east to west, more violent than
what blows in the greatest hurricanes; a stone, thrown westwards,
would fly to a much greater distance than one thrown with the same
force eastwards; as what moved in a direction, contrary to the motion
of the Earth, would necessarily pass over a greater portion of its
surface, than what, with the same velocity, moved along with it. A
ball, it was said, dropt from the mast of a ship under sail, does not fall
precisely at the foot of the mast, but behind it; and in the same
manner, a stone dropt from a high tower would not, upon the
supposition of the Earth's motion, fall precisely at the bottom of the
tower, but west of it, the Earth being, in the mean time, carried away
eastward from below it. It is amusing to observe, by what subtile and

metaphysical evasions the followers of Copernicus endeavoured to elude this objection, which, before the doctrine of the Composition of Motion had been explained by Galileo,[67] was altogether unanswerable. They allowed, that a ball dropt from the mast of a ship under sail would not fall at the foot of the mast, but behind it; because the ball, they said, was no part of the ship, and because the motion of the ship was natural neither to itself nor to the ball. But the stone was a part of the earth, and the diurnal and annual revolutions of the Earth were natural to the whole, and to every part of it, and therefore to the stone. The stone, therefore, having naturally the same motion with the Earth, fell precisely at the bottom of the tower. But this answer could not satisfy the imagination, which still found it difficult to conceive how these motions could be natural to the Earth; or how a body, which had always presented itself to the senses as inert, ponderous, and averse to motion, should naturally be continually wheeling about both its own axis and the Sun, with such violent rapidity. It was, besides, argued by Tycho Brache, upon the principles of the same philosophy, which had afforded both the objection and the answer, that even upon the supposition, that any such motion was natural to the whole body of the Earth, yet the stone, which was separated from it, could no longer be actuated by that motion. The limb, which is cut off from an animal, loses those animal motions which were natural to the whole. The branch, which is cut off from the trunk, loses that vegetative motion which is natural to the whole tree. Even the metals, minerals, and stones, which are dug out from the bosom of the Earth, lose those motions which occasioned their production and encrease, and which were natural to them in their original state. Though the diurnal and annual motion of the Earth, therefore, had been natural to them while they were contained in its bosom; it could no longer be so when they were separated from it.

41   Tycho Brache, the great restorer of the science of the heavens, who had spent his life, and wasted his fortune upon the advancement of Astronomy,[68] whose observations were both more numerous and more accurate than those of all the astronomers who had gone before him, was himself so much affected by the force of this objection, that, though he never mentioned the system of Copernicus without some note of the high admiration he had conceived for its author, he could never himself be induced to embrace it: yet all his astronomical observations tended to confirm it. They demonstrated, that Venus

---

[67] [*Discourses on Two New Sciences*, IV; in *Opere* (National Edition, Florence, 1890–1910), viii. 268 ff.]

[68] Tycho Brahe is to be regarded less as the 'restorer' of astronomy than, at least as an observer, the first of the 'moderns'. Also, in the pursuit of his passion he 'wasted' not only his own 'fortunes' but those of his defenceless tenants.

and Mercury were sometimes above, and sometimes below the Sun; and that, consequently, the Sun, and not the Earth, was the center of their periodical revolutions. They showed, that Mars, when in his meridian at midnight, was nearer to the Earth than the Earth is to the Sun; though, when in conjunction with the Sun, he was much more remote from the Earth than that luminary; a discovery which was absolutely inconsistent with the system of Ptolemy, which proved, that the Sun, and not the Earth, was the center of the periodical revolutions of Mars, as well as of Venus and Mercury; and which demonstrated, that the Earth was placed betwixt the orbits of Mars and Venus. They made the same thing probable with regard to Jupiter and Saturn; that they, too, revolved round the Sun; and that, therefore, the Sun, if not the center of the universe, was at least, that of the planetary system. They proved, that Comets were superior to the Moon, and moved through the heavens in all possible directions; an observation incompatible with the Solid Spheres of Aristotle and Purbach, and which, therefore, overturned the physical part, at least, of the established Astronomy.

42   All these observations, joined to his aversion to the system, and perhaps, notwithstanding the generosity of his character, some little jealousy of the fame of Copernicus, suggested to Tycho the idea of a new hypothesis,[69] in which the Earth continued to be, as in the old account, the immoveable center of the universe, round which the firmament revolved every day from east to west, and, by some secret virtue, carried the Sun, the Moon, and the Five Planets along with it, notwithstanding their immense distance, and notwithstanding that there was nothing betwixt it and them but the most fluid ether. But, although all these seven bodies thus obeyed the diurnal revolution of the Firmament, they had each of them, as in the old system, too, a contrary periodical eastward revolution of their own, which made them appear to be every day, more or less, left behind by the Firmament. The Sun was the center of the periodical revolutions of the Five Planets; the Earth, that of the Sun and Moon. The Five Planets followed the Sun in his periodical revolution round the Earth, as they did the Firmament in its diurnal rotation. The three superior Planets comprehended the Earth within the orbit in which they revolved round the Sun, and had each of them an Epicycle to connect together, in the same manner as in the system of Ptolemy, their direct, retrograde, and stationary appearances. As, notwithstanding their immense distance, they followed the Sun in his periodical revolution round the Earth, keeping always at an equal distance from

[69] Tycho's hypothesis was not altogether 'new'. See the editor's Introduction, 18–19.

him, they were necessarily brought much nearer to the Earth when
in opposition to the Sun, than when in conjunction with him. Mars,
the nearest of them, when in his meridian at midnight, came within
the orbit which the Sun described round the Earth, and consequently
was then nearer to the Earth than the Earth was to the Sun. The
appearances of the two inferior Planets were explained, in the same
manner, as in the system of Copernicus, and consequently required
no Epicycle to connect them. The circles in which the Five Planets
performed their periodical revolutions round the Sun, as well as
those in which the Sun and Moon performed theirs round the Earth,
were, as both in the old and new hypothesis, Eccentric Circles, to
connect together their differently accelerated and retarded motions.

43   Such was the system of Tycho Brache, compounded, as is evident,
out of these of Ptolemy and Copernicus; happier than that of Ptolemy,
in the account which it gives of the motions of the two inferior
Planets; more complex, by supposing the different revolutions of all
the Five to be performed round two different centers; the diurnal
round the Earth, the periodical round the Sun; but, in every respect,
more complex and more incoherent than that of Copernicus. Such,
however, was the difficulty that mankind felt in conceiving the
motion of the Earth, that it long balanced the reputation of that
otherwise more beautiful system. It may be said, that those who
considered the heavens only, favoured the system of Copernicus,
which connected so happily all the appearances which presented
themselves there. But that those who looked upon the Earth, adopted
the account of Tycho Brache, which, leaving it at rest in the center of
the universe, did less violence to the usual habits of the imagination.
The learned were, indeed, sensible of the intricacy, and of the many
incoherences of that system; that it gave no account why the Sun,
Moon, and Five Planets, should follow the revolution of the
Firmament; or why the Five Planets, notwithstanding the immense
distance of the three superior ones, should obey the periodical motion
of the Sun; or why the earth, though placed between the orbits of
Mars and Venus, should remain immoveable in the center of the
Firmament, and constantly resist the influence of whatever it was,
which carried bodies that were so much larger than itself, and that
were placed on all sides of it, periodically round the Sun. Tycho
Brahe died before he had fully explained his system. His great and
merited renown disposed many of the learned to believe, that, had his
life been longer, he would have connected together many of these
incoherences, and knew methods of adapting his system to some
other appearances, with which none of his followers could connect it.

44   The objection to the system of Copernicus, which was drawn from

the nature of motion, and that was most insisted on by Tycho Brahe, was at last fully answered by Galileo; not, however, till about thirty years after the death of Tycho, and about a hundred after that of Copernicus. It was then that Galileo, by explaining the nature of the composition of motion, by showing, both from reason and experience, that a ball dropt from the mast of a ship under sail would fall precisely at the foot of the mast, and by rendering this doctrine, from a great number of other instances, quite familiar to the imagination, took off, perhaps, the principal objection which had been made to this hypothesis.

45   Several other astronomical difficulties, which encumbered this account of things, were removed by the same philosopher. Copernicus, after altering the center of the world, and making the Earth, and all the Planets revolve round the Sun, was obliged to leave the Moon to revolve round the Earth as before. But no example of any such secondary Planet having then been discovered in the heavens, there seemed still to be this irregularity remaining in the system. Galileo, who first applied telescopes to Astronomy,[70] discovered, by their assistance, the Satellites of Jupiter, which, revolving round that Planet, at the same time that they were carried along with it in its revolution, round either the Earth, or the Sun, made it seem less contrary to the analogy of nature, that the Moon should both revolve round the Earth, and accompany her in her revolution round the Sun.

46   It had been objected to Copernicus, that, if Venus and Mercury revolved round the Sun, in an orbit comprehended within the orbit of the Earth, they would show all the same phases with the Moon, present, sometimes their darkened, and sometimes their enlightened sides to the Earth, and sometimes part of the one, and part of the other. He answered, that they undoubtedly did all this; but that their smallness and distance hindered us from perceiving it. This very bold assertion of Copernicus was confirmed by Galileo.[71] His telescopes rendered the phases of Venus quite sensible, and thus demonstrated, more evidently than had been done, even by the

---

[70] The absolute priority of Galileo in turning the newly invented telescope on the heavens is now questioned. The Englishman, Thomas Harriot (1560–1621), was observing the Moon independently about the same time.

[71] [Galileo's discovery of the phases of Venus was first announced in his letter of 1 January 1610/11 to Giuliano de' Medici, Ambassador of the Duke of Tuscany at the Court of the Emperor Rudolph II in Prague. It is published in Galileo's *Opere* (National Edition), xi.11–12. His description of the mountains and seas on the Moon had, however, already been published in his *Sidereus Nuncius*, 1610 (*Opere*, iii.59 ff.). Smith's reference to these discoveries in non-chronological order might imply that he followed the description in Colin Maclaurin's *Account of Sir Isaac Newton's Discoveries*, 54. See § 58 and note 94 below.]

observations of Tycho Brahe, the revolutions of these two Planets round the Sun, as well as so far destroyed the system of Ptolemy.

47　　The mountains and seas, which, by the help of the same instrument, he discovered, or imagined he had discovered in the Moon, rendering that Planet, in every respect, similar to the Earth, made it seem less contrary to the analogy of nature, that, as the Moon revolved round the Earth, the Earth should revolve round the Sun.

48　　The spots which, in the same manner, he discovered in the Sun, demonstrating, by their motion, the revolution of the Sun round his axis, made it seem less improbable that the Earth, a body so much smaller than the Sun, should revolve round her axis in the same manner.

49　　Succeeding telescopical observations, discovered, in each of the Five Planets, spots not unlike those which Galileo had observed in the Moon, and thereby seemed to demonstrate what Copernicus had only conjectured, that the Planets were naturally opaque, enlightened only by the rays of the Sun, habitable, diversified by seas and mountains, and, in every respect, bodies of the same kind with the Earth; and thus added one other probability to this system. By discovering, too, that each of the Planets revolved round its own axis, at the same time that it was carried round either the Earth or the Sun, they made it seem quite agreeable to the analogy of nature, that the Earth, which, in every other respect, resembled the Planets, should, like them too, revolve round its own axis, and at the same time perform its periodical motion round the Sun.

50　　While, in Italy, the unfortunate Galileo was adding so many probabilities to the system of Copernicus, there was another philosopher employing himself in Germany, to ascertain, correct, and improve it: Kepler, with great genius, but without the taste, or the order and method of Galileo, possessed, like all his other countrymen, the most laborious industry, joined to that passion for discovering proportions and resemblances betwixt the different parts of nature, which, though common to all philosophers, seems, in him, to have been excessive. He had been instructed, by Maestlinus,[72] in the system of Copernicus; and his first curiosity was, as he tells us, to find out, why the Planets, the Earth being counted for one, were Six in number; why they were placed at such irregular distances from the Sun; and whether there was any uniform proportion betwixt their several distances, and the times employed in their periodical revolutions. Till some reason, or proportion of this kind, could be

---

[72] [Michael Maestlin (1550–1631), Professor of Mathematics at Tübingen, where he taught and became friendly with Kepler.]

discovered, the system did not appear to him to be completely coherent.[73] He endeavoured, first, to find it in the proportions of numbers, and plain figures; afterwards, in those of the regular solids; and, last of all, in those of the musical divisions of the Octave. Whatever was the science which Kepler was studying, he seems constantly to have pleased himself with finding some analogy betwixt it and the system of the universe;[74] and thus, arithmetic and music, plain and solid geometry, came all of them by turns to illustrate the doctrine of the Sphere, in the explaining of which he was, by his profession, principally employed. Tycho Brahe, to whom he had presented one of his books, though he could not but disapprove of his system, was pleased, however, with his genius, and with his indefatigable diligence in making the most laborious calculations. That generous and magnificent Dane invited the obscure and indigent Kepler to come and live with him,[75] and communicated to him, as soon as he arrived, his observations upon Mars, in the arranging and methodizing of which his disciples were at that time employed. Kepler, upon comparing them with one another, found, that the orbit of Mars was not a perfect circle; that one of its diameters was somewhat longer than the other; and that it approached to an oval, or an ellipse, which had the Sun placed in one of its foci. He found, too, that the motion of the Planet was not equable; that it was swiftest when nearest the Sun, and slowest when furthest from him; and that its velocity gradually encreased, or diminished, according as it approached or receded from him. The observations of the same astronomer discovered to him, though not so evidently, that the same things were true of all the other Planets; that their orbits were elliptical, and that their motions were swiftest when nearest the Sun, and slowest when furthest from him. They showed the same things, too, of the Sun, if supposed to revolve round the Earth; and consequently of the Earth, if supposed to revolve round the Sun.[76]

51   That the motions of all the heavenly bodies were perfectly circular, had been the fundamental idea, upon which every astronomical hypothesis, except the irregular one of the Stoics, had been built. A

---

[73] Smith omits to mention the most intractable objection to the Copernican system, the absence of any observed stellar parallax, i.e. the inference that if the Earth moves round the Sun, every star should be seen to make a roughly circular revolution once a year in the opposite sense. The absence of any such observed motion implied a then inconceivable distance of the stars from the Earth. Such stellar parallax was not measured until 1838.

[74] [Cf. II.4 above.]

[75] Kepler was indeed usually 'indigent', since his employers were commonly reluctant or unable to pay up; but when invited by Tycho to join him as an assistant, Kepler was already far from 'obscure'.

[76] Smith's account of Kepler's work, though highly condensed and chronologically 're-arranged', is substantially correct.

circle, as the degree of its curvature is every where the same, is of all curve lines the simplest and the most easily conceived.[77] Since it was evident, therefore, that the heavenly bodies did not move in strait lines, the indolent imagination found, that it could most easily attend to their motions if they were supposed to revolve in perfect circles. It had, upon this account, determined that a circular motion was the most perfect of all motions, and that none but the most perfect motion could be worthy of such beautiful and divine objects; and it had upon this account, so often, in vain, endeavoured to adjust to the appearances, so many different systems, which all supposed them to revolve in this manner.[78]

52   The equality of their motions was another fundamental idea, which, in the same manner, and for the same reason, was supposed by all the founders of astronomical systems. For an equal motion can be more easily attended to, than one that is continually either accelerated or retarded. All inconstancy, therefore, was declared to be unworthy those bodies which revolved in the celestial regions, and to be fit only for inferior and sublunary things. The calculations of Kepler overturned, with regard to the Planets, both these natural prejudices of the imagination; destroyed their circular orbits; and introduced into their real motions, such an inequality as no equalizing circle would remedy. It was, however, to render their motions perfectly equable, without even the assistance of an equalizing circle, that Copernicus, as he himself assures us, had originally invented his system. Since the calculations of Kepler, therefore, overturned what Copernicus had principally in view in establishing his system, we cannot wonder that they should at first seem rather to embarrass than improve it.

53   It is true, by these elliptical orbits and unequal motions, Kepler disengaged the system from the embarrassment of those small Epicycles, which Copernicus, in order to connect the seemingly accelerated and retarded movements of the Planets with their supposed real equality,[79] had been obliged to leave in it. For it is remarkable, that though Copernicus had delivered the orbits of the Planets from the enormous Epicycles of Hipparchus, that though in this consisted the great superiority of his system above that of the ancient astronomers, he was yet obliged, himself, to abandon, in some

---

[77] [Cf. LJ(A) vi.14: 'the constantly varying direction of the circle, which at the same time is allways similar and easily conceived, is preferred to the more varied figures of the elipse, parabola, and hyperbola, and the Archimedean spirrall, ... as it is more easily conceved than these, whose nature can not at first sight be understood.']

[78] There is a good deal of special pleading, if not of actual inconsistency, in the argument as set out here.

[79] For 'equality' read 'uniformity'.

measure, this advantage, and to make use of some small Epicycles, to join together those seeming irregularities. His Epicycles indeed, like the irregularities for whose sake they were introduced, were but small ones, and the imaginations of his first followers seem, accordingly, either to have slurred them over altogether, or scarcely to have observed them. Neither Galileo, nor Gassendi, the two most eloquent of his defenders, take any notice of them. Nor does it seem to have been generally attended to, that there was any such thing as Epicycles in the system of Copernicus, till Kepler, in order to vindicate his own elliptical orbits, insisted, that even, according to Copernicus, the body of the Planet was to be found but at two different places in the circumference of that circle which the center of its Epicycle described.

54   It is true, too, that an ellipse is, of all curves lines after a circle, the simplest and most easily conceived; and it is true, besides all this, that, while Kepler took from the motion of the Planets the easiest of all proportions, that of equality, he did not leave them absolutely without one, but ascertained the rule by which their velocities continually varied; for a genius so fond of analogies, when he had taken away one, would be sure to substitute another in its room. Notwithstanding all this, notwithstanding that his system was better supported by observations than any system had ever been before, yet, such was the attachment to the equal motions and circular orbits of the Planets, that it seems, for some time, to have been in general but little attended to by the learned, to have been altogether neglected by philosophers, and not much regarded even by astronomers.[80]

55   Gassendi,[81] who began to figure in the world about the latter days of Kepler, and who was himself no mean astronomer, seems indeed to have conceived a good deal of esteem for his diligence and accuracy in accommodating the observations of Tycho Brahe to the system of Copernicus. But Gassendi appears to have had no comprehension of the importance of those alterations which Kepler had made in that system, as is evident from his scarcely ever mentioning them in the whole course of his voluminous writings upon Astronomy. Des Cartes, the cotemporary and rival of Gassendi, seems to have paid no attention to them at all, but to have built his Theory of the Heavens,[82] without any regard to them. Even those astronomers, whom a serious

[80] For a recent reassessment of the response to Kepler's 'new astronomy' see J. Russell, S. J., 'Kepler's Laws of Planetary Motion, 1609–1666', *British Journal of the History of Science*, ii (1964), 1–24.

[81] [Pierre Gassendi (1592–1655), best known as a philosopher, but also, as Smith implies, a scientist of some repute.]

[82] [In *Le Monde*, completed in 1633 but not published (presumably because of its acceptance of the Copernican system of astronomy which Galileo had just been forced to recant) until 1664,
(*continued*)

attention had convinced of the justness of his corrections, were still so
enamoured with the circular orbits and equal motions, that they
endeavoured to compound his system with those ancient, but natural
prejudices. Thus, Ward[83] endeavoured to show that, though the
Planets moved in elliptical orbits, which had the Sun in one of their
foci, and though their velocities in the elliptical line were continually
varying, yet, if a ray was supposed to be extended from the center of
any one of them to the other focus, and to be carried along by the
periodical motion of the Planet, it would make equal angles in equal
times, and consequently cut off equal portions of the circle of which
that other focus was the center. To one, therefore, placed in that
focus, the motion of the Planet would appear to be perfectly circular
and perfectly equable, in the same manner as in the Equalizing
Circles of Ptolemy and Hipparchus. Thus Bouillaud,[84] who censured
this hypothesis of Ward, invented another of the same kind, infinitely
more whimsical and capricious. The Planets, according to that
astronomer, always revolve in circles; for that being the most perfect
figure, it is impossible they should revolve in any other. No one of
them, however, continues to move in any one circle, but is perpetually
passing from one to another, through an infinite number of circles, in
the course of each revolution; for an ellipse, said he, is an oblique
section of a cone, and in a cone, betwixt the two vertices[85] of the
ellipse there is an infinite number of circles, out of the infinitely small
portions of which the elliptical line is compounded. The Planet,
therefore, which moves in this line, is, in every point of it, moving in
an infinitely small portion of a certain circle. The motion of each
Planet, too, according to him, was necessarily, for the same reason,
perfectly equable. An equable motion being the most perfect of all
motions. It was not, however, in the elliptical line, that it was equable,
but in any one of the circles that were parallel to the base of that cone,
by whose section this elliptical line had been formed: for, if a ray was
extended from the Planet to any one of those circles, and carried
along by its periodical motion, it would cut off equal portions of that
circle in equal times; another most fantastical equalizing circle,
supported by no other foundation besides the frivolous connection

long after the death of its author. The basic doctrines of the work were nevertheless embodied
in *Principia Philosophiae* (1664).]

[83] Seth Ward (1617–89) Savilian Professor of Astronomy at Oxford, Founder Fellow of the
Royal Society, and Bishop of Exeter.

[84] Ismael Boulliau (various spellings, also known as Bullialdus—1605–94), author of
Astronomia Philolaica (1645), was the first to apply the inverse square to planetary motion.
[Ward criticized it in a work entitled *In Ismaelis Bullialdi Astronomiae Philolaicae Fundamenta
Inquisitio Brevis* (1653) and Boulliau replied in *Astronomiae Philolaicae Fundamenta clarius
explicata ... Adversa ... Sethi Wardi impugnationem* (1657).]

[85] [The text of the original edition has 'vortices', presumably a printer's error.]

betwixt a cone and an ellipse, and recommended by nothing but the natural passion for circular orbits and equable motions. It may be regarded as the last effort of this passion, and may[86] serve to show the force of that principle which could thus oblige this accurate observer, and great improver of the Theory of the Heavens, to adopt so strange an hypothesis. Such was the difficulty and hesitation with which the followers of Copernicus adopted the corrections of Kepler.

56   The rule, indeed, which Kepler ascertained[87] for determining the gradual acceleration or retardation in the movement of the Planets, was intricate, and difficult to be comprehended; it could therefore but little facilitate the progress of the imagination in tracing those revolutions which were supposed to be conducted by it. According to that astronomer, if a strait line was drawn from the center of each Planet to the Sun, and carried along by the periodical motion of the Planet, it would describe equal areas in equal times, though the Planet did not pass over equal spaces; and the same rule, he found, took place nearly with regard to the Moon. The imagination, when acquainted with the law by which any motion is accelerated or retarded, can follow and attend to it more easily, than when at a loss, and, as it were, wandering in uncertainty with regard to the proportion which regulates its varieties; the discovery of this analogy[88] therefore, no doubt, rendered the system of Kepler more agreeable to the natural taste of mankind: it was, however, an analogy too difficult to be followed, or comprehended, to render it completely so.

57   Kepler, besides this, introduced another new analogy into the system,[89] and first discovered, that there was one uniform relation observed betwixt the distances of the Planets from the Sun, and the times employed in their periodical motions. He found, that their periodical times were greater than in proportion to their distances, and less than in proportion to the squares of those distances; but, that they were nearly as the mean proportionals betwixt their distances and the squares of their distances; or, in other words, that the squares of their periodical times were nearly as the cubes of their distances;[90] an analogy, which, though, like all others, it no doubt rendered the system somewhat more distinct and comprehensible, was, however, as well as the former, of too intricate a nature to facilitate very much the effort of the imagination in conceiving it.

---

[86] [The text of the original edition has 'many', again simply a printer's error.]
[87] [*Astronomia Nova* (1609).]
[88] i.e. proportion.
[89] [*De Harmonice Mundi* (1619).]
[90] 'Cubes of their distances' should be 'cubes of their mean distances'.

58   The truth of both these analogies, intricate as they were, was at last
fully established by the observations of Cassini.[91] That astronomer
first discovered, that the secondary Planets of Jupiter and Saturn
revolved round their primary ones, according to the same laws which
Kepler had observed in the revolutions of the primary ones round
the Sun, and that of the Moon round the earth; that each of them
described equal areas in equal times, and that the squares of their
periodic times were as the cubes of their distances. When these two
last abstruse analogies, which, when Kepler at first observed them,
were but little regarded, had been thus found to take place in the
revolutions of the Four Satellites of Jupiter, and in those of the Five
of Saturn, they were now thought not only to confirm the doctrine of
Kepler, but to add a new probability to the Copernican hypothesis.
The observations of Cassini seem to establish it as a law of the system,
that, when one body revolved round another, it described equal areas
in equal times; and that, when several revolved round the same body,
the squares of their periodic times were as the cubes of their distances.
If the Earth and the Five Planets were supposed to revolve round the
Sun, these laws, it was said, would take place universally. But if,
according to the system of Ptolemy, the Sun, Moon, and Five Planets
were supposed to revolve round the Earth, the periodical motions of
the Sun and Moon would, indeed, observe the first of these laws,
would each of them describe equal areas in equal times; but they
would not observe the second, the squares of their periodic times
would not be as the cubes of their distances: and the revolutions of
the Five Planets would observe neither the one law nor the other. Or
if, according to the system of Tycho Brahe, the Five Planets were
supposed to revolve round the Sun, while the Sun and Moon
revolved round the Earth, the revolutions of the Five Planets round
the Sun, would, indeed, observe both these laws; but those of the Sun
and Moon round the Earth would observe only the first of them. The
analogy of nature, therefore, could be preserved completely, according
to no other system but that of Copernicus, which, upon that account,
must be the true one. This argument is regarded by Voltaire,[92] and
the Cardinal of Polignac,[93] as an irrefragable demonstration; even
McLaurin,[94] who was more capable of judging; nay, Newton himself,

[91] Giovanni Domenico Cassini (1625–1712), the first of a family of distinguished astronomers
and virtual Director of the Observatory set up by the Académie Royale des Sciences, of which
he was an early *pensionnaire*.
[92] [*Éléments de la philosophie de Newton* (1738).]
[93] Cardinal Melchior de Polignac (1661–1742).
[94] [Colin Maclaurin (1698–1746), educated at the University of Glasgow, appointed Professor
of Mathematics at Marischal College and the University of Aberdeen in 1717, and then at the
University of Edinburgh in 1725 with the recommendation of Newton. His *Account of Sir
Isaac Newton's Discoveries* was published posthumously in 1748.]

seems to mention it[95] as one of the principal evidences for the truth of that hypothesis. Yet, an analogy of this kind, it would seem, far from a demonstration, could afford, at most, but the shadow of a probability.

59   It is true, that though Cassini supposed the Planets to revolve in an oblong curve, it was in a curve somewhat different from that of Kepler. In the ellipse the sum of the two lines, which are drawn from any one point in the circumference to the two foci, is always equal to that of those which are drawn from any other point in the circumference to the same foci. In the curve of Cassini, it is not the sum of the lines, but the rectangles which are contained under the lines, that are always equal. As this, however, was a proportion more difficult to be comprehended than the other, the curve of Cassini has never had the vogue.

60   Nothing now embarrassed the system of Copernicus, but the difficulty which the imagination felt in conceiving bodies so immensely ponderous as the Earth, and the other Planets, revolving round the Sun with such incredible rapidity. It was in vain that Copernicus pretended, that, notwithstanding the prejudices of sense, this circular motion might be as natural to the Planets, as it is to a stone to fall to the ground. The imagination had been accustomed to conceive such objects as tending rather to rest than motion. This habitual idea of their natural inertness was incompatible with that of their natural motion. It was in vain that Kepler,[96] in order to assist the fancy in connecting together this natural inertness with their astonishing velocities, talked of some vital and immaterial virtue, which was shed by the Sun into the surrounding spaces, which was whirled about with his revolution round his own axis, and which, taking hold of the Planets, forced them, in spite of their ponderousness and strong propensity to rest, thus to whirl about the center of the system. The imagination had no hold of this immaterial virtue, and could form no determinate idea of what it consisted in. The imagination, indeed, felt a gap, or interval, betwixt the constant motion and the supposed inertness of the Planets, and had in this, as in all other cases, some general idea or apprehension that there must be a connecting chain of intermediate objects to link together these discordant qualities. Wherein this connecting chain consisted, it was, indeed, at a loss to conceive; nor did the doctrine of Kepler lend it any assistance in this respect. That doctrine, like almost all those of the philosophy in fashion during his time, bestowed a name upon this

[95] [Newton's discussion, at the beginning of Book III of the *Principia*, contains no definite statement to this effect, but Smith's cautious form of expression does not imply otherwise.]

[96] [*Mysterium Cosmographicum* (1596), chap. 20; *Astronomia Nova* (1609), chaps. 33–4.]

invisible chain, called it an immaterial virtue, but afforded no
determinate idea of what was its nature.

61   Des Cartes[97] was the first who attempted to ascertain, precisely,
wherein this invisible chain consisted, and to afford the imagination
a train of intermediate events, which, succeeding each other in an
order that was of all others the most familiar to it, should unite those
incoherent qualities, the rapid motion, and the natural inertness of
the Planets. Des Cartes was the first who explained wherein consisted
the real inertness of matter; that it was not in an aversion to motion,
or in a propensity to rest, but in a power of continuing indifferently
either at rest or in motion, and of resisting, with a certain force,
whatever endeavoured to change its state from the one to the other.
According to that ingenious and fanciful philosopher, the whole of
infinite space was full of matter, for with him matter and extension
were the same, and consequently there could be no void. This
immensity of matter, he supposed, to be divided into an infinite
number of very small cubes; all of which, being whirled about upon
their own centers, necessarily gave occasion to the production of two
different elements. The first consisted of those angular parts, which,
having been necessarily rubbed off, and grinded yet smaller by their
mutual friction, constituted the most subtile and moveable part of
matter. The second consisted of those little globules that were formed
by the rubbing off of the first. The interstices betwixt these globules
of the second element was filled up by the particles of the first. But in
the infinite collisions, which must occur in an infinite space filled
with matter, and all in motion, it must necessarily happen, that many
of the globules of the second element should be broken and grinded
down into the first. The quantity of the first element having thus
been encreased beyond what was sufficient to fill up the interstices of
the second, it must, in many places, have been heaped up together,
without any mixture of the second along with it. Such, according to
Des Cartes, was the original division of matter. Upon this infinitude
of matter thus divided, a certain quantity of motion was originally
impressed by the Creator of all things, and the laws of motion were
so adjusted as always to preserve the same quantity in it, without
increase, and without diminution.[98] Whatever motion was lost by

[97] [See note 82 above.]
[98] *Principles of Philosophy*, II.36. When combined with Descartes's further statement of the
law of inertia (§63 below—'Newton's' First Law of Motion, only partially envisaged by Galileo),
this corresponds to the principle of the conservation of linear momentum (Newton's Third
Law). Recognizing that this does not apply to certain cases of impact, Leibniz claimed that it
is not momentum (product of mass and velocity) but *vis viva* (product of mass and square of
velocity) that is conserved. This *cause célèbre* among the savants of the eighteenth century was
resolved partly by d'Alembert (see the editor's Introduction, 22) in Smith's lifetime, and finally
by Hermann von Helmholtz in 1847.

one part of matter, was communicated to some other; and whatever was acquired by one part of matter, was derived from some other: and thus, through an eternal revolution, from rest to motion, and from motion to rest, in every part of the universe, the quantity of motion in the whole was always the same.

62   But, as there was no void, no one part of matter could be moved without thrusting some other out of its place, nor that without thrusting some other, and so on. To avoid, therefore, an infinite progress, he supposed, that the matter which any body pushed before it, rolled immediately backwards, to supply the place of that matter which flowed in behind it; as we may observe in the swimming of a fish, that the water, which it pushes before it, immediately rolls backwards, to supply the place of what flows in behind it, and thus forms a small circle or vortex round the body of the fish.[99] It was, in the same manner, that the motion originally impressed by the Creator upon the infinitude of matter, necessarily produced in it an infinity of greater and smaller vortices, or circular streams: and the law of motion being so adjusted as always to preserve the same quantity of motion in the universe, those vortices either continued for ever, or by their dissolution give birth to others of the same kind. There was, thus, at all times, an infinite number of greater and smaller vortices, or circular streams, revolving in the universe.

63   But, whatever moves in a circle, is constantly endeavouring to fly off from the center of its revolution. For the natural motion of all bodies is in a straight line.[1] All the particles of matter, therefore, in each of those greater vortices, were continually pressing from the center to the circumference, with more or less force, according to the different degrees of their bulk and solidity. The larger and more solid globules of the second element forced themselves upwards to the circumference, while the smaller, more yielding, and more active particles of the first, which could flow, even through the interstices of the second, were forced downwards to the center. They were forced downwards to the center, notwithstanding their natural tendency was upwards to the circumference; for the same reason that a piece of wood, when plunged in water, is forced upwards to the surface, notwithstanding its natural tendency is downwards to the bottom;

[99] [Smith has said nothing here about the earlier history of this explanation of motion in a plenum. Descartes took it from ancient Greek philosophers who, having denied the existence of void, had to deal with the same problem. The process described is used in Plato's *Timaeus*, 79 A–E, to explain the mechanism of breathing. It is there termed *periosis*. Lucretius, i.370–83, illustrates it by the swimming of a fish, but only in order to oppose it and to insist upon the necessity for a void. The explanation was maintained by Hobbes in his *De Corpore*, chap. 22.12, chap. 25.3, as well as by Descartes. See A. E. Taylor, *Commentary on Plato's Timaeus* (1928), 558.]

[1] But see the editor's Introduction, 16.

because its tendency downwards is less strong than that of the particles of water, which, therefore, if one may say so, press in before it, and thus force it upwards. But there being a greater quantity of the first element than what was necessary to fill up the interstices of the second, it was necessarily accumulated in the center of each of these great circular streams, and formed there the firey and active substance of the Sun. For, according to that philosopher, the Solar Systems were infinite in number, each Fixed Star being the center of one: and he is among the first of the moderns, who thus took away the boundaries of the Universe; even Copernicus and Kepler, themselves, having confined it within, what they supposed, the vault of the Firmament.

64   The center of each vortex being thus occupied by the most active and moveable parts of matter, there was necessarily among them, a more violent agitation than in any other part of the vortex, and this violent agitation of the center cherished and supported the movement of the whole. But, among the particles of the first element, which fill up the interstices of the second, there are many, which, from the pressure of the globules on all sides of them, necessarily receive an angular form, and thus constitute a third element of particles less fit for motion than those of the other two. As the particles, however, of this third element were formed in the interstices of the second, they are necessarily smaller than those of the second, and are, therefore, along with those of the first, urged down towards the center, where, when a number of them happen to take hold of one another, they form such spots upon the surface of the accumulated particles of the first element, as are often discovered by telescopes upon the face of that Sun, which enlightens and animates our particular system. Those spots are often broken and dispelled, by the violent agitation of the particles of the first element, as has hitherto happily been the case with those which have successively been formed upon the face of our Sun. Sometimes, however, they encrust the whole surface of that fire which is accumulated in the center; and the communication betwixt the most active and the most inert parts of the vortex being thus interrupted, the rapidity of its motion immediately begins to languish, and can no longer defend it from being swallowed up and carried away by the superior violence of some other like circular stream; and in this manner, what was once a Sun, becomes a Planet. Thus, the time was, according to this system, when the Moon was a body of the same kind with the Sun, the firey center of a circular stream of ether, which flowed continually round her; but her face having been crusted over by a congeries of angular particles, the motion of this circular stream began to languish, and could no longer

defend itself from being absorbed by the more violent vortex of the
Earth, which was then, too, a Sun, and which chanced to be placed in
its neighbourhood. The Moon, therefore, became a Planet, and
revolved round the Earth. In process of time, the same fortune, which
had thus befallen the Moon, befell also the Earth; its face was
encrusted by a gross and inactive substance; the motion of its vortex
began to languish, and it was absorbed by the greater vortex of the
Sun: but though the vortex of the Earth had thus become languid, it
still had force enough to occasion both the diurnal revolution of the
Earth, and the monthly motion of the Moon. For a small circular
stream may easily be conceived as flowing round the body of the
Earth, at the same time that it is carried along by that great ocean of
ether which is continually revolving round the Sun; in the same
manner, as in a great whirlpool of water, one may often see several
small whirlpools, which revolve round centers of their own, and at
the same time are carried round the center of the great one. Such was
the cause of the original formation and consequent motions of the
Planetary System. When a solid body is turned round its center,
those parts of it, which are nearest, and those which are remotest
from the center, complete their revolutions in one and the same time.
But it is otherwise with the revolutions of a fluid: the parts of it which
are nearest the center complete their revolutions in a shorter time,
than those which are remoter. The Planets, therefore, all floating in
that immense tide of ether which is continually setting in from west
to east round the body of the Sun, complete their revolutions in a
longer or a shorter time, according to their nearness or distance from
him. There was, however, according to Des Cartes, no very exact
proportion observed betwixt the times of their revolutions and their
distances from the center. For that nice analogy, which Kepler had
discovered betwixt them, having not yet been confirmed by the
observations of Cassini, was, as I before took notice,[2] entirely
disregarded by Des Cartes. According to him, too, their orbits might
not be perfectly circular, but be longer the one way than the other,
and thus approach to an Ellipse. Nor yet was it necessary to suppose,
that they described this figure with geometrical accuracy, or even
that they described always precisely the same figure. It rarely
happens, that nature can be mathematically exact with regard to the
figure of the objects she produces, upon account of the infinite
combinations of impulses, which must conspire to the production of
each of her effects. No two Planets, no two animals of the same kind,
have exactly the same figure, nor is that of any one of them perfectly

[2] [§ 55 above.]

regular. It was in vain, therefore, that astronomers laboured to find that perfect constancy and regularity in the motions of the heavenly bodies, which is to be found in no other parts of nature.[3] These motions, like all others, must either languish or be accelerated, according as the cause which produces them, the revolution of the vortex of the Sun, either languishes, or is accelerated; and there are innumerable events which may occasion either the one or the other of those changes.

65　　It was thus, that Des Cartes endeavoured to render familiar to the imagination, the greatest difficulty in the Copernican system, the rapid motion of the enormous bodies of the Planets. When the fancy had thus been taught to conceive them as floating in an immense ocean of ether, it was quite agreeable to its usual habits to conceive, that they should follow the stream of this ocean, how rapid soever. This was an order of succession to which it had been long accustomed, and with which it was, therefore, quite familiar. This account, too, of the motions of the Heavens, was connected with a vast, an immense system, which joined together a greater number of the most discordant phaenomena of nature, than had been united by any other hypothesis; a system in which the principles of connection, though perhaps equally imaginary, were, however, more distinct and determinate, than any that had been known before; and which attempted to trace to the imagination, not only the order of succession by which the heavenly bodies were moved, but that by which they, and almost all other natural objects, had originally been produced.— The Cartesian philosophy begins now to be almost universally rejected, while the Copernican system continues to be universally received. Yet, it is not easy to imagine, how much probability and coherence this admired system was long supposed to derive from that exploded hypothesis.[4] Till Des Cartes had published his principles, the disjointed and incoherent system of Tycho Brahe, though it was embraced heartily and completely by scarce any body, was yet constantly talked of by all the learned,[5] as, in point of probability,

---

[3] A perceptive recognition of the approximative character of all 'laws' of nature. This implies the removal of the distinction between 'natural' and 'celestial' realms and the necessity for the later theory of perturbations, involving a good deal of heart-searching among theologians regarding the 'perfection' of the Creator.

[4] [Cf. Letter to the Authors of the *Edinburgh Review*, 5, where Smith again writes of Descartes's natural philosophy as 'almost universally exploded' and of the advantages that it initially appeared to have. He also refers in TMS VII.ii.4.14 to the high regard in which Descartes's theory of vortices was long held. In the *Discours préliminaire* to the *Encyclopédie* (1751), d'Alembert writes: 'Si on juge sans partialité ces tourbillons devenus aujourd'hui presque ridicules, on conviendra, j'ose le dire, qu'on ne pouvoit alors imaginer mieux.']

[5] Galileo ignored it in his famous polemical work, *On the Two Chief Systems of the World, Ptolemaic and Copernican*: its consistency with the observed phases of Venus would have weakened his insistence on the movement of the Earth.

upon a level with that of Copernicus. They took notice, indeed, of its inferiority with regard to coherence and connection, expressing hopes, however, that these defects might be remedied by some future improvements. But when the world beheld that complete, and almost perfect coherence, which the philosophy of Des Cartes bestowed upon the syste.n of Copernicus, the imaginations of mankind could no longer refuse themselves the pleasure of going along with so harmonious an account of things. The system of Tycho Brahe was every day less and less talked of, till at last it was forgotten altogether.

66   The system of Des Cartes, however, though it connected together the real motions of the heavenly bodies according to the system of Copernicus, more happily than had been done before, did so only when they were considered in the gross; but did not apply to them, when they were regarded in the detail. Des Cartes, as was said before,[6] had never himself observed the Heavens with any particular application. Though he was not ignorant, therefore, of any of the observations which had been made before his time, he seems to have paid them no great degree of attention; which, probably, proceeded from his own inexperience in the study of Astronomy. So far, therefore, from accommodating his system to all the minute irregularities, which Kepler had ascertained in the movements of the Planets; or from shewing, particularly, how these irregularities, and no other, should arise from it, he contented himself with observing, that perfect uniformity could not be expected in their motions, from the nature of the causes which produced them; that certain irregularities might take place in them, for a great number of successive revolutions, and afterwards give way to others of a different kind: a remark which, happily, relieved him from the necessity of applying his system to the observations of Kepler, and the other Astronomers.

67   [7]But when the observations of Cassini had established the authority of those laws, which Kepler had first discovered in the system, the philosophy of Des Cartes, which could afford no reason, why such particular laws should be observed, might continue to amuse the learned in other sciences, but could no longer satisfy those that were skilled in Astronomy. Sir Isaac Newton first attempted to give a physical account of the motions of the Planets, which should accommodate itself to all the constant irregularities which

---

[6] [Smith did not in fact say this before, but did say, in § 55 (cf. the next sentence here in § 66), that Descartes seems to have paid no attention to Kepler's work on observations made by Tycho Brahe.]

[7] This presumably marks the beginning of the material on Newton mentioned by Smith's editors in the concluding note to this section.

astronomers had ever observed in their motions. The physical connection, by which Des Cartes had endeavoured to bind together the movements of the Planets, was the laws of impulse; of all the orders of succession, those which are most familiar to the imagination; as they all flow from the inertness of matter. After this quality, there is no other, with which we are so well acquainted, as that of gravity. We never act upon matter, but we have occasion to observe it. The superior genius and sagacity of Sir Isaac Newton, therefore, made the most happy, and, we may now say, the greatest and most admirable improvement that was ever made in philosophy, when he discovered, that he could join together the movements of the Planets by so familiar a principle of connection, which completely removed all the difficulties the imagination had hitherto felt in attending to them.[8] He demonstrated, that, if the Planets were supposed to gravitate towards the Sun, and to one another, and at the same time to have had a projecting force originally impressed upon them, the primary ones might all described ellipses in one of the foci of which that great luminary was placed; and the secondary ones might describe figures of the same kind round their respective primaries, without being disturbed by the continual motion of the centers of their revolutions. That if the force, which retained each of them in their orbits, was like that of gravity, and directed towards the Sun, they would, each of them, describe equal areas in equal times. That if this attractive power of the Sun, like all other qualities which are diffused in rays from a center, diminished in the same proportion as the squares of the distances increased, their motions would be swiftest when nearest the Sun, and slowest when farthest off from him, in the same proportion in which, by observation, they are discovered to be; and that, upon the same supposition, of this gradual diminution of their respective gravities, their periodic times would bear the same proportion to their distances, which Kepler and Cassini had established betwixt them. Having thus shown, that gravity might be the connecting principle which joined together the movements of the Planets, he endeavoured next to prove that it really was so. Experience shews us, what is the power of gravity near the surface of the Earth. That it is such as to make a body fall, in the first second of its descent, through about fifteen Parisian feet. The Moon is about sixty semidiameters of the Earth distant from its surface. If gravity, therefore, was supposed to diminish, as the squares of the distance increase, a body, at the Moon, would fall towards the Earth in a minute; that is, in sixty seconds, through the same space, which it

[8] An optimistic assessment. See the editor's Introduction, 21–2.

falls near its surface in one second. But the arch[9] which the Moon describes in a minute, falls, by observation, about fifteen Parisian feet below the tangent drawn at the beginning of it. So far, therefore, the Moon may be conceived as constantly falling towards the Earth.[10]

68   The system of Sir Isaac Newton corresponded to many other irregularities which Astronomers had observed in the Heavens. It assigned a reason, why the centers of the revolutions of the Planets were not precisely in the center of the Sun, but in the common center of gravity of the Sun and the Planets. From the mutual attraction of the Planets, it gave a reason for some other irregularities in their motions; irregularities, which are quite sensible in those of Jupiter and Saturn, when those Planets are nearly in conjunction with one another. But of all the irregularities in the Heavens, those of the Moon had hitherto given the greatest perplexity to Astronomers; and the system of Sir Isaac Newton corresponded, if possible, yet more accurately with them than with any of the other Planets. The Moon, when either in conjunction, or in opposition to the Sun, appears furthest from the Earth, and nearest to it when in her quarters. According to the system of that philosopher, when she is in conjunction with the Sun, she is nearer the Sun than the Earth is; consequently, more attracted to him, and, therefore, more separated from the Earth. On the contrary, when in opposition to the Sun, she is further from the Sun than the Earth. The Earth, therefore, is more attracted to the Sun; and, consequently, in this case, too, further separated from the Moon. But, on the other hand, when the Moon is in her quarters, the Earth and the Moon, being both at equal distance from the Sun, are equally attracted to him. They would not, upon this account alone, therefore, be brought nearer to one another. As it is not in parallel lines, however, that they are attracted towards the Sun, but in lines which meet in his center, they are, thereby, still further approached to one another. Sir Isaac Newton computed the difference of the forces, with which the Moon and the Earth ought, in all those different situations, according to his theory, to be impelled towards one another; and found, that the different degrees of their approaches, as they had been observed by Astronomers, corresponded exactly to his computations. As the attraction of the Sun, in the conjunctions and oppositions, diminishes the gravity of the Moon towards the Earth, and, consequently, makes her necessarily extend her orbit, and, therefore, require a longer periodical time to finish it. But, when the Moon and the Earth are in that part of the orbit which is nearest the Sun, this attraction of the Sun will be the greatest;

---

[9] i.e. arc; a common spelling at that time.
[10] [*Principia*, Book III, prop. 4, theorem 4.]

consequently, the gravity of the Moon towards the Earth, will there be most diminished; her orbit be most extended; and her periodic time be, therefore, the longest. This is, also, agreeable to experience, and in the very same proportion, in which, by computation, from these principles, it might be expected.

69   The orbit of the Moon is not precisely in the same Plane with that of the Earth; but makes a very small angle with it. The points of intersection of those two Planes, are called, the Nodes of the Moon. These Nodes of the Moon are in continual motion, and in eighteen or nineteen years, revolve backwards, from east to west, through all the different points of the Ecliptic. For the Moon, after having finished her periodical revolution, generally intersects the orbit of the Earth somewhat behind the point where she had intersected it before. But, though the motion of the Nodes is thus generally retrograde, it is not always so, but is sometimes direct, and sometimes they appear even stationary; the Moon generally intersects the Plane of the Earth's orbit, behind the point where she had intersected it in her former revolution; but she sometimes intersects it before that point, and sometimes in the very same point. It is the situation of those Nodes which determines the times of Eclipses, and their motions had, upon this account, at all times, been particularly attended to by Astronomers. Nothing, however, had perplexed them more, than to account for these so inconsistent motions, and, at the same time, preserve their so much sought-for regularity in the revolutions of the Moon. For they had no other means of connecting the appearances together, than by supposing the motions which produced them, to be, in reality, perfectly regular and equable. The history of Astronomy, therefore, gives an account of a greater number of theories invented for connecting together the motions of the Moon, than for connecting together those of all the other heavenly bodies taken together. The theory of gravity, connected together, in the most accurate manner, by the different actions of the Sun and the Earth, all those irregular motions; and it appears, by calculation, that the time, the quantity, and the duration of those direct and retrograde motions of the Nodes, as well as of their stationary appearances, might be expected to be exactly such, as the observations of Astronomers have determined them.

70   The same principle, the attraction of the Sun, which thus accounts for the motions of the Nodes, connects, too, another very perplexing irregularity in the appearances of the Moon; the perpetual variation in the inclination of her orbit to that of the Earth.

71   As the Moon revolves in an ellipse, which has the centre of the Earth in one of its foci, the longer axis of its orbit is called the Line of

its Apsides. This line is found, by observation, not to be always directed towards the same points of the Firmament, but to revolve forwards, from west to east, so as to pass through all the points of the Ecliptic, and to complete its period in about nine years; another irregularity, which had very much perplexed Astronomers, but which the theory of gravity sufficiently accounted for.

72   The Earth had hitherto been regarded as perfectly globular, probably for the same reason which had made men imagine, that the orbits of the Planets must necessarily be perfectly circular. But Sir Isaac Newton,[11] from mechanical principles, concluded, that, as the parts of the Earth must be more agitated by her diurnal revolution at the Equator, than at the Poles, they must necessarily be somewhat elevated at the first, and flattened at the second. The observation, that the oscillations of pendulums were slower at the Equator than at the Poles, seeming to demonstrate, that gravity was stronger at the Poles, and weaker at the Equator, proved, he thought, that the Equator was further from the centre than the Poles. All the measures, however, which had hitherto been made of the Earth, seemed to show the contrary, that it was drawn out towards the Poles, and flattened towards the Equator. Newton, however, preferred his mechanical computations to the former measures of Geographers and Astronomers; and in this he was confirmed by the observations of Astronomers on the figure of Jupiter, whose diameter at the Pole seems to be to his diameter at the Equator, as twelve to thirteen; a much greater inequality than could be supposed to take place betwixt the correspondent diameters of the Earth, but which was exactly proportioned to the superior bulk of Jupiter, and the superior rapidity with which he performs his diurnal revolutions. The observations of Astronomers at Lapland and Peru have fully confirmed Sir Isaac's system,[12] and have not only demonstrated, that the figure of the Earth is, in general, such as he supposed it; but that the proportion of its axis to the diameter of its Equator is almost precisely such as he had computed it. And of all the proofs that have ever been adduced of the diurnal revolution of the Earth, this perhaps is the most solid and satisfactory.

73   Hipparchus,[13] by comparing his own observations with those of

---

[11] [Ibid., prop. 19, problem 3.]

[12] See the editor's Introduction, 7. [Smith had in his personal library a copy of the English translation of the book describing the results of the Lapland expedition: P.-L. M. de Maupertuis, *The Figure of the Earth, determined from observations made by order of the French King at the polar circle* (1738). See H. Mizuta, *Adam Smith's Library* (1967), 40. The results of the Peruvian expedition were given in Pierre Bouguer, *La Figure de la terre* (1749).]

[13] [For Hipparchus' discovery of the precession, and his estimate of its period, see Heath, *Aristarchus of Samos*, 172–3.]

some former Astronomers, had found that the equinoxial points were not always opposite to the same part of the Heavens, but that they advanced gradually eastward by so slow a motion, as to be scarce sensible in one hundred years, and which would require thirty-six thousand to make a complete revolution of the Equinoxes, and to carry them successively through all the different points of the Ecliptic. More accurate observations discovered that this precession[14] of the Equinoxes was not so slow as Hipparchus had imagined it, and that it required somewhat less than twenty-six thousand years to give them a complete revolution. While the ancient system of Astronomy, which represented the Earth as the immoveable centre of the universe, took place, this appearance was necessarily accounted for, by supposing that the Firmament, besides its rapid diurnal revolution round the poles of the Equator, had likewise a slow periodical one round those of the Ecliptic. And when the system of Hipparchus was by the schoolmen united with the solid Spheres of Aristotle, they placed a new christaline Sphere above the Firmament, in order to join this motion to the rest. In the Copernican system, this appearance had hitherto been connected with the other parts of that hypothesis, by supposing a small revolution in the Earth's axis from east to west. Sir Isaac Newton connected this motion by the same principle of gravity, by which he had united all the others, and shewed, how the elevation of the parts of the Earth at the Equator must, by the attraction of the Sun, produce the same retrograde motion of the Nodes of the Ecliptic, which it produced of the Nodes of the Moon. He computed the quantity of motion which could arise from this action of the Sun, and his calculations here too entirely corresponded with the observations of Astronomers.

74   Comets had hitherto, of all the appearances in the Heavens, been the least attended to by Astronomers. The rarity and inconstancy of their appearance, seemed to separate them entirely from the constant, regular, and uniform objects in the Heavens, and to make them resemble more the inconstant, transitory, and accidental phaenomena of those regions that are in the neighbourhood of the Earth. Aristotle,[15] Eudoxus, Hipparchus, Ptolemy, and Purbach, therefore, had all degraded them below the Moon, and ranked them among the meteors of the upper regions of the air. The observations of Tycho Brahe demonstrated, that they ascended into the celestial regions, and were often higher than Venus or the Sun. Des Cartes, at random, supposed them to be always higher than even the orbit of Saturn; and seems, by the superior elevation he thus bestowed upon them, to have

---

[14] [The text of the original edition has 'procession', no doubt a printer's error.]
[15] [*Meteorologica*, I.6–7; 342^b–345^a.]

been willing to compensate that unjust degradation which they had suffered for so many ages before. The observations of some later Astronomers[16] demonstrated, that they too revolved about the Sun, and might therefore be parts of the Solar System. Newton accordingly applied his mechanical principle of gravity to explain the motions of these bodies. That they described equal areas in equal times, had been discovered by the observations of some later Astronomers; and Newton endeavoured to show how from this principle, and those observations, the nature and position of their several orbits might be ascertained, and their periodic times determined. His followers have, from his principles, ventured even to predict the returns of several of them, particularly of one which is to make its appearance in 1758*.[17] We must wait for that time before we can determine, whether his philosophy corresponds as happily to this part of the system as to all the others. In the mean time, however, the ductility of this principle, which applied itself so happily to these, the most irregular of all the celestial appearances, and which has introduced such complete coherence into the motions of all the Heavenly Bodies, has served not a little to recommend it to the imaginations of mankind.

75   But of all the attempts of the Newtonian Philosophy, that which would appear to be the most above the reach of human reason and experience, is the attempt to compute the weights and densities of the Sun, and of the Several Planets. An attempt, however, which was indispensibly necessary to complete the coherence of the Newtonian system. The power of attraction which, according to the theory of gravity, each body possesses, is in proportion to the quantity of matter contained in that body. But the periodic time in which one body, at a given distance, revolves round another that attracts it, is shorter in proportion as this power is greater, and consequently as the quantity of matter in the attracting body. If the densities of Jupiter and Saturn were the same with that of the Earth, the periodic times of their several Satellites would be shorter than by observation they are found to be. Because the quantity of matter, and consequently the attracting power of each of them, would be as the cubes of their diameters. By comparing the bulks of those Planets, and the periodic times of their Satellites, it is found that, upon the hypothesis of gravity, the density of Jupiter must be greater than that of Saturn, and the density of the

---

* It must be observed, that the whole of this Essay was written previous to the date here mentioned; and that the return of the comet happened agreeably to the prediction.

---

[16] [Smith may be alluding here to the observations of Johann Hevelius published in *Prodromus Cometicus* (1665), those of John Flamsteed in *Historia Coelestis Britannica* (1725), and those of Edmund Halley in *Astronomiae Cometicae Synopsis* (1705).]

[17] The omission of the name of Edmund Halley (1656–1742) is unaccountable. For a discussion of the original footnote see the editor's Introduction, 7–8.

Earth greater than that of Jupiter. This seems to establish it as a law
in the system, that the nearer the several Planets approach to the Sun,
the density of their matter is the greater: a constitution of things
which would seem to be the most advantageous of any that could
have been established; as water of the same density with that of our
Earth, would freeze under the Equator of Saturn, and boil under that
of Mercury.

76　　Such is the system of Sir Isaac Newton, a system whose parts are
all more strictly connected together, than those of any other
philosophical hypothesis. Allow his principle, the universality of
gravity, and that it decreases as the squares of the distance increase,
and all the appearances, which he joins together by it, necessarily
follow. Neither is their connection merely a general and loose
connection, as that of most other systems, in which either these
appearances, or some such like appearances, might indifferently have
been expected. It is every where the most precise and particular that
can be imagined, and ascertains the time, the place, the quantity, the
duration of each individual phaenomenon, to be exactly such as, by
observation, they have been determined to be. Neither are the
principles of union, which it employs, such as the imagination can
find any difficulty in going along with. The gravity of matter is, of all
its qualities, after its inertness, that which is most familiar to us.[18] We
never act upon it without having occasion to observe this property.
The law too, by which it is supposed to diminish as it recedes from its
centre, is the same which takes place in all other qualities which are
propagated in rays from a centre, in light, and in every thing else of
the same kind. It is such, that we not only find that it does take place
in all such qualities, but we are necessarily determined to conceive
that, from the nature of the thing, it must take place. The opposition
which was made in France, and in some other foreign nations, to the
prevalence of this system, did not arise from any difficulty which
mankind naturally felt in conceiving gravity as an original and
primary mover in the constitution of the universe. The Cartesian
system, which had prevailed so generally before it, had accustomed
mankind to conceive motion as never beginning, but in consequence
of impulse, and had connected the descent of heavy bodies, near the
surface of the Earth, and the other Planets, by this more general bond
of union; and it was the attachment the world had conceived for this
account of things, which indisposed them to that of Sir Isaac Newton.
His system, however, now prevails over all opposition, and has
advanced to the acquisition of the most universal empire that was
ever established in philosophy. His principles, it must be acknow-

[18] But see the editor's Introduction, 21–2.

ledged, have a degree of firmness and solidity that we should in vain look for in any other system. The most sceptical cannot avoid feeling this. They not only connect together most perfectly all the phaenomena of the Heavens, which had been observed before his time, but those also which the persevering industry and more perfect instruments of later Astronomers have made known to us; have been either easily and immediately explained by the application of his principles, or have been explained in consequence of more laborious and accurate calculations from these principles, than had been instituted before. And even we, while we have been endeavouring to represent all philosophical systems as mere inventions of the imagination,[19] to connect together the otherwise disjointed and discordant phaenomena of nature, have insensibly been drawn in, to make use of language expressing the connecting principles of this one, as if they were the real chains which Nature makes use of to bind together her several operations. Can we wonder then, that it should have gained the general and complete approbation of mankind, and that it should now be considered, not as an attempt to connect in the imagination the phaenomena of the Heavens, but as the greatest discovery that ever was made by man, the discovery of an immense chain of the most important and sublime truths, all closely connected together, by one capital fact, of the reality of which we have daily experience.

NOTE by the EDITORS

The Author, at the end of this Essay, left some Notes and Memorandums, from which it appears, that he considered this last part of his History of Astronomy as imperfect, and needing several additions. The Editors, however, chose rather to publish than to suppress it. It must be viewed, not as a History or Account of Sir Isaac Newton's Astronomy, but chiefly as an additional illustration of those Principles in the Human Mind which Mr. Smith has pointed out to be the universal motives of Philosophical Researches.

[19] [Cf. II.12 above.]

THE
PRINCIPLES
WHICH LEAD AND DIRECT
PHILOSOPHICAL ENQUIRIES;
ILLUSTRATED BY THE
HISTORY of the ANCIENT PHYSICS

1 From arranging and methodizing the System of the Heavens, Philosophy descended to the consideration of the inferior parts of Nature, of the Earth, and of the bodies which immediately surround it.[1] If the objects, which were here presented to its view, were inferior in greatness or beauty, and therefore less apt to attract the attention of the mind, they were more apt, when they came to be attended to, to embarrass and perplex it, by the variety of their species, and by the intricacy and seeming irregularity of the laws or orders of their succession. The species of objects in the Heavens are few in number; the Sun, the Moon, the Planets, and the Fixed Stars, are all which those philosophers could distinguish. All the changes too, which are ever observed in these bodies, evidently arise from some difference in the velocity and direction of their several motions; but the variety of meteors in the air, of clouds, rainbows, thunder, lightning, winds, rain, hail, snow, is vastly greater;[2] and the order of their succession seems to be still more irregular and unconstant. The species of fossils, minerals, plants, animals, which are found in the Waters, and near the surface of the Earth, are still more intricately diversified; and if we regard the different manners of their production, their mutual influence in altering, destroying, supporting one another, the orders of their succession seem to admit of an almost infinite variety. If the imagination, therefore, when it considered the appearances in the Heavens, was often perplexed, and driven out of its natural career, it would be much more exposed to the same embarrassment, when it directed its attention to the objects which the Earth presented to it, and when it endeavoured to trace their progress and successive revolutions.

[1] [Cf. WN V.i.f.24.]   [2] [See Astronomy, III.1.]

2   To introduce order and coherence into the mind's conception of this seeming chaos of dissimilar and disjointed appearances, it was necessary to deduce all their qualities, operations, and laws of succession, from those of some particular things, with which it was perfectly acquainted and familiar, and along which its imagination could glide smoothly and easily, and without interruption.[3] But as we would in vain attempt to deduce the heat of a stove from that of an open chimney, unless we could show that the same fire which was exposed in the one, lay concealed in the other; so it was impossible to deduce the qualities and laws of succession, observed in the more uncommon appearances of Nature, from those of such as were more familiar, if those customary objects were not supposed, however disguised in their appearance, to enter into the composition of those rarer and more singular phaenomena. To render, therefore, this lower part of the great theatre of nature a coherent spectacle to the imagination, it became necessary to suppose, first, That all the strange objects of which it consisted were made up out of a few, with which the mind was extremely familiar: and secondly, That all their qualities, operations, and rules of succession, were no more than different diversifications of those to which it had long been accustomed, in these primary and elementary objects.

3   Of all the bodies of which these inferior parts of the universe seem to be composed, those with which we are most familiar, are the Earth, which we tread upon; the Water, which we every day use; the Air, which we constantly breath; and the Fire, whose benign influence is not only required for preparing the common necessaries of life, but for the continual support of that vital principle which actuates both plants and animals. These, therefore, were by Empedocles, and the other philosophers of the Italian school, supposed to be the elements, out of which, at least, all the inferior parts of nature were composed. The familiarity of those bodies to the mind, naturally disposed it to look for some resemblance to them in whatever else was presented to its consideration. The discovery of some such resemblance united the new object to an assortment of things, with which the imagination was perfectly acquainted. And if any analogy could be observed betwixt the operations and laws of succession of the compound, and those of the simple objects, the movement of the fancy, in tracing their progress, became quite smooth, and natural, and easy. This natural anticipation, too, was still more confirmed by such a slight and inaccurate analysis of things, as could be expected in the infancy of science, when the curiosity of mankind, grasping at an account of

[3] [Cf. Astronomy, II.7.]

all things before it had got full satisfaction with regard to any one, hurried on to build, in imagination, the immense fabric of the universe. The heat, observed in both plants and animals, seemed to demonstrate, that Fire made a part of their composition. Air was not less necessary for the subsistance of both, and seemed, too, to enter into the fabric of animals by respiration, and into that of plants by some other means. The juices which circulated through them showed how much of their texture was owing to Water. And their resolution into Earth by putrefaction, discovered that this element had not been left out in their original formation. A similar analysis seemed to shew the same principles in most other compound bodies.

4   The vast extent of those bodies seemed to render them, upon another account, proper to be the great stores out of which nature compounded all the other species of things. Earth and Water divide almost the whole of the terrestrial globe between them. The thin transparent covering of the Air surrounds it to an immense height upon all sides. Fire, with its attendant, light, seems to descend from the celestial regions, and might, therefore, either be supposed to be diffused through the whole of those aetherial spaces, as well as to be condensed and conglobated in those luminous bodies, which sparkle across them, as by the Stoics; or, to be placed immediately under the sphere of the Moon, in the region next below them, as by the Peripatetics, who could not reconcile the devouring nature of Fire with the supposed unchangeable essence of their solid and crystalline spheres.

5   The qualities, too, by which we are chiefly accustomed to characterize and distinguish natural bodies, are all of them found, in the highest degree in those Four Elements. The great divisions of the objects, near the surface of the Earth, are those into hot and cold, moist and dry, light and heavy. These are the most remarkable properties of bodies; and it is upon them that many of their other most sensible qualities and powers seem to depend. Of these, heat and cold were naturally enough regarded by those first enquirers into nature, as the active, moisture and dryness, as the passive qualities of matter. It was the temperature of heat and cold which seemed to occasion the growth and dissolution of plants and animals; as appeared evident from the effects of the change of the seasons upon both. A proper degree of moisture and dryness was not less necessary for these purposes; as was evident from the different effects and productions of wet and dry seasons and soils. It was the heat and cold, however, which actuated and determined those two otherwise inert qualities of things, to a state either of rest or motion. Gravity and levity were regarded as the two principles of motion, which directed

all sublunary things to their proper place: and all those six qualities, taken together, were, upon such an inattentive view of nature, as must be expected in the beginnings of philosophy, readily enough apprehended to be capable of connecting together the most remarkable revolutions, which occur in these inferior parts of the universe. Heat and dryness were the qualities which characterized the element of Fire; heat and moisture that of Air; moisture and cold that of Water; cold and dryness that of Earth. The natural motion of two of these elements, Earth and Water, was downwards, upon account of their gravity. This tendency, however, was stronger in the one than in the other, upon account of the superior gravity of Earth. The natural motion of the two other elements, Fire and Air, was upwards, upon account of their levity; and this tendency, too, was stronger in the one than in the other, upon account of the superior levity of Fire. Let us not despise those ancient philosophers, for thus supposing, that these two elements had a positive levity, or a real tendency upwards. Let us remember, that this notion has an appearance of being confirmed by the most obvious observations; that those facts and experiments, which demonstrate the weight of the Air, and which no superior sagacity, but chance alone,[4] presented to the moderns, were altogether unknown to them;[5] and that, what might, in some measure, have supplied the place of those experiments, the reasonings concerning the causes of the ascent of bodies, in fluids specifically heavier than themselves, seem to have been unknown in the ancient world, till Archimedes discovered them,[6] long after their system of physics was completed, and had acquired an established reputation: that those reasonings are far from being obvious, and that by their inventor, they seem to have been thought applicable only to the ascent of Solids in Water, and not even to that of Solids in air, much less to that of one fluid in another. But it is this last only which could explain the ascent of flame, vapours, and fiery exhalations, without the supposition of a specific levity.

6   Thus, each of those Four Elements had, in the system of the universe, a place which was peculiarly allotted to it, and to which it naturally tended. Earth and Water rolled down to the centre; the Air spread itself above them; while the Fire soared aloft, either to the

---

[4] Smith gives no indication of what he means by 'chance' in this context. The experiments on the weight of the air were amongst the first and best documented of the 'new experimental philosophy'.

[5] [Anaxagoras showed experimentally that air was corporeal (Aristotle, *Physics*, VI.6,213^{a}22, and *De Caelo*, II.13,294^{b}21), but it seems to be true that no ancient thinker proved that it had weight.]

[6] [Archimedes 'discovered them' in his treatise *On Floating Bodies*: T. L. Heath, *Manual of Greek Mathematics*, 332–6.]

celestial region, or to that which was immediately below it. When each of those simple bodies had thus obtained its proper sphere, there was nothing in the nature of any one of them to make it pass into the place of the other, to make the Fire descend into the Air, the Air into the Water, or the Water into the Earth; or, on the contrary, to bring up the Earth into the place of the Water, the Water into that of the Air, or the Air into that of the Fire. All sublunary things, therefore, if left to themselves, would have remained in an eternal repose. The revolution of the heavens, those of the Sun, Moon, and Five Planets, by producing the vicissitudes of Day and Night, and of the Seasons, prevented this torpor and inactivity from reigning through the inferior parts of nature; inflamed by the rapidity of their circumvolutions, the element of Fire, and forced it violently downwards into the Air, into the Water, and into the Earth, and thereby produced those mixtures of the different elements which kept up the motion and circulation of the lower parts of nature; occasioned, sometimes, the entire transmutation of one element into another, and sometimes the production of forms and species different from them all, and in which, though the qualities of them all might be found, they were so altered and attempered by the mixture, as scarce to be distinguishable.

7   Thus, if a small quantity of Fire was mixed with a great quantity of Air, the moisture and moderate warmth of the one entirely surmounted and changed into their own essence the intense heat and dryness of the other; and the whole aggregate became Air. The contrary of which happened, if a small quantity of Air was mixed with a great quantity of Fire: the whole, in this case, became Fire. In the same manner, if a small quantity of Fire was mixed with a great quantity of Water, then, either the moisture and cold of the Water might surmount the heat and dryness of the Fire, so as that the whole should become Water; or, the moisture of the Water might surmount the dryness of the Fire, while in its turn, the heat of the Fire surmounted the coldness of the Water, so as that the whole aggregate, its qualities being heat and moisture, should become Air, which was regarded as the more natural and easy metamorphosis of the two. In the same manner they explained how like changes were produced by the different mixtures of Fire and Earth, Earth and Water, Water and Air, Air and Earth; and thus they connected together the successive transmutations of the elements into one another.

8   Every mixture of the Elements, however, did not produce an entire transmutation. They were sometimes so blended together, that the qualities of the one, not being able to destroy, served only to attemper those of the other. Thus Fire, when mixed with water, produced

sometimes a watery vapour, whose qualities were heat and moisture; which partook at once of the levity of the Fire, and of the gravity of the Water, and which was elevated by the first into the Air, but retained by the last from ascending into the region of Fire. The relative cold, which they supposed prevailed in the middle region of the Air, upon account of its equal distance, both from the region of Fire, and from the rays that are reflected by the surface of the Earth, condensed this vapour into Water; the Fire escaped it, and flew upwards, and the Water fell down in rain, or, according to the different degrees of cold that prevailed in the different seasons, was sometimes congealed into snow, and sometimes into hail. In the same manner, Fire, when mixed with Earth, produced sometimes a fiery exhalation, whose qualities were heat and dryness, which being elevated by the levity of the first into the Air condensed by the cold, so as to take fire, and being at the same time surrounded by watery vapours, burst forth into thunder and lightning, and other fiery meteors. Thus they connected together the different appearances in the Air, by the qualities of their Four Elements; and from them, too, in the same manner, they endeavoured to deduce all the other qualities in the other homogeneous bodies, that are near the surface of the Earth. Thus, to give an example, with regard to the hardness and softness of bodies; heat and moisture, they observed, were the great softners of matter. Whatever was hard, therefore, owed that quality either to the absence of heat, or to the absence of moisture. Ice, crystal, lead, gold, and almost all metals, owed their hardness to the absence of heat, and were, therefore, dissolveable by Fire. Rock-salt, nitre, alum, and hard clay, owed that quality to the absence of moisture, and were, therefore, dissolveable in water. And, in the same manner, they endeavoured to connect together most of the other tangible qualities of matter. Their principles of union, indeed, were often such as had no real existence, and were always vague and undetermined in the highest degree; they were such, however, as might be expected in the beginnings of science, and such as, with all their imperfections, could enable mankind both to think and to talk, with more coherence, concerning those general subjects, than without them they would have been capable of doing. Neither was their system entirely devoid either of beauty or magnificence. Each of the Four Elements having a particular region allotted to it, had a place of rest, to which it naturally tended, by its motion, either up or down, in a straight line, and where, when it had arrived, it naturally ceased to move. Earth descended, till it arrived at the place of Earth; Water, till it arrived at that of Water; and Air, till it arrived at that of Air; and there each of them tended to a state of eternal repose and inaction.

The Spheres consisted of a Fifth Element,[7] which was neither light nor heavy, and whose natural motion made it tend, neither to the center, nor from the center, but revolve round it in a circle. As, by this motion, they could never change their situation with regard to the center, they had no place of repose, no place to which they naturally tended more than to any other, but revolved round and round for ever. This Fifth Element was subject neither to generation nor corruption, nor alteration of any kind; for whatever changes may happen in the Heavens, the senses can scarce perceive them, and their appearance is the same in one age as in another. The beauty, too, of their supposed crystalline spheres seemed still more to entitle them to this distinction of unchangeable immortality. It was the motion of those Spheres, which occasioned the mixtures of the Elements, and from thence, the production of all the forms and species, that diversify the world. It was the approach of the Sun and of the other Planets, to the different parts of the Earth, which, by forcing down the element of Fire, occasioned the generation of those forms.[8] It was the recess of those bodies, which, by allowing each Element to escape to its proper sphere, brought about, in an equal time, their corruption. It was the periods of those great lights of Heaven, which measured out to all sublunary things, the term of their duration, of their growth, and of their decay, either in one, or in a number of seasons, according as the Elements of which they were composed, were either imperfectly or accurately blended and mixed with one another. Immortality, they could bestow upon no individual form, because the principles out of which it was formed, all tending to disengage themselves, and to return to their proper spheres, necessarily, at last, brought about its dissolution. But, though all individuals were thus perishable, and constantly decaying, every species was immortal, because the subject matter out of which they were made, and the revolution of the Heavens, the cause of their successive generations, were always the same.

9   In the first ages of the world, the seeming incoherence of the appearances of nature, so confounded mankind, that they despaired of discovering in her operations any regular system. Their ignorance, and confusion of thought, necessarily gave birth to that pusillanimous superstition, which ascribes almost every unexpected event, to the arbitrary will of some designing, though invisible beings, who

---

[7] [Aristotle's view of the Aether was never as widely accepted as the following account implies, being criticized not only by the Epicureans but by many of his own successors. It should not be assumed that all who accepted the concentric spheres as an astronomical hypothesis subscribed to it. See P. Moraux, article 'Quinta Essentia', in Pauly's *Real-Encyclopädie der classischen Alterthumswissenschaft*, Halbband 47 (1963), col. 1231a ff.]

[8] [Aristotle, *De Generatione et Corruptione*, II.10, 336ᵃ14 ff.; *Metaphysics*, Λ, 1071ᵃ15.]

produced it for some private and particular purpose.[9] The idea of an
universal mind, of a God of all, who originally formed the whole, and
who governs the whole by general laws, directed to the conservation
and prosperity of the whole, without regard to that of any private
individual, was a notion to which they were utterly strangers. Their
gods, though they were apprehended to interpose, upon some
particular occasions, were so far from being regarded, as the creators
of the world, that their origin was apprehended to be posterior to that
of the world. The Earth, according to Hesiod,[10] was the first
production of the chaos. The Heavens arose out of the Earth, and
from both together, all the gods, who afterwards inhabited them. Nor
was this notion confined to the vulgar, and to those poets who seem
to have recorded the vulgar theology. Of all the philosophers of the
Ionian school, Anaxagoras, it is well known, was the first who
supposed, that mind and understanding were requisite to account for
the first origin of the world, and who, therefore, compared with the
other philosophers of his time, talked, as Aristotle observes, like a
sober man among drunkards;[11] but whose opinion was, at that time,
so remarkable, that he seems to have got a sirname from it.[12] The
same notion, of the spontaneous origin of the world, was embraced,
too, as the same author tells us,[13] by the early Pythagoreans, a sect,
which, in the antient world, was never regarded as irreligious. Mind,
and understanding, and consequently Deity, being the most perfect,
were necessarily, according to them, the last productions of Nature.
For in all other things, what was most perfect, they observed, always
came last. As in plants and animals, it is not the seed that is most
perfect, but the complete animal, with all its members, in the one;
and the complete plant, with all its branches, leaves, flowers, and
fruits, in the other. This notion, which could take place only while
Nature was still considered as, in some measure, disorderly and
inconstant in her operations, was necessarily renounced by those
philosophers, when, upon a more attentive survey, they discovered,
or imagined they had discovered, more distinctly, the chain which
bound all her different parts to one another. As soon as the Universe
was regarded as a complete machine, as a coherent system, governed
by general laws, and directed to general ends, viz. its own preservation
and prosperity, and that of all the species that are in it; the
resemblance which it evidently bore to those machines which are

---

[9] [Cf. Astronomy, III.2.]
[10] [*Theogony*, 116 ff., noted by Aristotle in *Metaphysics*, A, 984^{b}27–9 and 989^{a}10–11.]
[11] [*Metaphysics*, A, 984^{b}15–19.]
[12] [Diogenes Laertius, II.6, reports that Anaxagoras was nicknamed *Nous*, and confirms this by some lines from the satirical poet Timon of Phlius.]
[13] [*Metaphysics*, Λ, 1072^{b}30–1073^{a}3.]

produced by human art, necessarily impressed those sages with a belief, that in the original formation of the world there must have been employed an art resembling the human art, but as much superior to it, as the world is superior to the machines which that art produces. The unity of the system, which, according to this ancient philosophy, is most perfect, suggested the idea of the unity of that principle, by whose art it was formed; and thus, as ignorance begot superstition, science gave birth to the first theism that arose among those nations, who were not enlightened by divine Revelation. According to Timaeus, who was followed by Plato,[14] that intelligent Being, who formed the world, endowed it with a principle of life and understanding, which extends from its centre to its remotest circumference, which is conscious of all its changes, and which governs and directs all its motions to the great end of its formation. This Soul of the world was itself a God, the greatest of all the inferior, and created deities; of an essence that was indissoluble, by any power but by that of him who made it, and which was united to the body of the world, so as to be inseparable by every force, but his who joined them, from the exertion of which his goodness secured them. The beauty of the celestial spheres attracting the admiration of mankind, the constancy and regularity of their motions seeming to manifest peculiar wisdom and understanding, they were each of them supposed to be animated by an Intelligence of a nature that was, in the same manner, indissoluble and immortal, and inseparably united to that sphere which it inhabited. All the mortal and changeable beings which people the surface of the earth were formed by those inferior deities; for the revolutions of the heavenly bodies seemed plainly to influence the generation and growth of both plants and animals, whose frail and fading forms bore the too evident marks of the weakness of those inferior causes, which joined their different parts to one another. According to Plato and Timaeus,[15] neither the Universe, nor even those inferior deities, who govern the Universe, were eternal, but were formed in time, by the great Author of all things, out of that matter which had existed from all eternity. This at least their words seem to import, and thus they are understood by Cicero,[16] and by all the other writers of earlier antiquity, though some of the later Platonists have interpreted them differently.[17]

---

[14] [Timaeus Locrus, 94 D, but see note 12 to Astronomy, III, above; Plato, *Timaeus*, 30 B, 34 B.]

[15] [Plato, *Timaeus*, 28 B, 37 D, 41 A; Timaeus Locrus, 93 A–95 A.]

[16] [Perhaps *De Natura Deorum*, I.8.19. But the work is a dialogue, and Cicero himself is not speaking.]

[17] [The Neoplatonists followed the interpretation of Xenocrates—that Plato used temporal language in describing the formation of the world only as a device of exposition. See A. E. Taylor, *Commentary on Plato's Timaeus*, 66, 68.]

10   According to Aristotle, who seems to have followed the doctrine of
Ocellus,[18] the world was eternal; the eternal effect of an eternal cause.
He found it difficult, it would seem, to conceive what could hinder
the First Cause from exerting his divine energy from all eternity. At
whatever time he began to exert it, he must have been at rest during
all the infinite ages of that eternity which had passed before it. To
what obstruction, from within or from without, could this be owing?
or how could this obstruction, if it ever had subsisted, have ever been
removed?[19] His idea of the nature and manner of existence of this
First Cause, as it is expressed in the last book of his Physics, and the
five last chapters of his Metaphysics,[20] is indeed obscure and
unintelligible in the highest degree, and has perplexed his commentators more than any other parts of his writings. Thus far, however,
he seems to express himself plainly enough: that the First Heaven,[21]
that of the Fixed Stars, from which are derived the motions of all the
rest, is revolved by an eternal, immoveable, unchangeable, unextended being, whose essence consists in intelligence, as that of a body
consists in solidity and extension; and which is therefore necessarily
and always intelligent, as a body is necessarily and always extended:
that this Being was the first and supreme mover of the Universe: that
the inferior Planetary Spheres derived each of them its peculiar
revolution from an inferior being of the same kind; eternal,
immoveable, unextended, and necessarily intelligent: that the sole
object of the intelligence of those beings was their own essence, and
the revolution of their own spheres; all other inferior things being
unworthy of their consideration; and that therefore whatever was
below the Moon was abandoned by the gods to the direction of
Nature, and Chance, and Necessity.[22] For though those celestial
beings were, by the revolutions of their several Spheres, the original
causes of the generation and corruption of all sublunary forms, they
were causes who neither knew nor intended the effects which they

[18] See note 12 to Astronomy, III, above.
[19] [This hardly represents Aristotle's reasoning. In the text presumably referred to (*Physics*,
VIII.5), Aristotle does not ask 'what could hinder the First Cause from exerting his divine
energy from all eternity'; his argument is that the eternal motion, which is an evident fact,
positively requires a First Cause, of which activity or actuality is the essence.]
[20] [*Physics*, VIII; *Metaphysics*, Λ, 6–10, 1071^{b}3 ff. Smith seems to forget that this is not the last
book of the *Metaphysics*. Or he may intend to dispute the traditional order of books.]
[21] [The text of the original edition has 'Heavens,' presumably a printer's error since the verb,
'is revolved', is singular.]
[22] [This is verbally correct, but one must consider what Nature means for Aristotle. He holds
that 'all things have by nature some part in the divine' (*Nicomachean Ethics*, VII.13,1153^{b}32),
and develops this thought in *De Partibus Animalium*, I.5,644^{b}22 ff. See translation of the
chapter by D. M. Balme, *Aristotle's De Partibus Animalium I and De Generatione Animalium I*,
Clarendon Aristotle (1972), 17–18. Further, Nature aims without conscious prevision at ends
or purposes, and in this respect the human arts are said to imitate her while falling short of the
accuracy of her operations (*Physics*, Book II).]

produced. This renowned philosopher seems, in his theological
notions, to have been directed by prejudices which, though extremely
natural, are not very philosophical. The revolutions of the Heavens,
by their grandeur and constancy, excited his admiration, and seemed,
upon that account, to be effects not unworthy a Divine Intelligence.
Whereas the meanness of many things, the disorder and confusion of
all things below,[23] exciting no such agreeable emotion, seemed to
have no marks of being directed by that Supreme Understanding.
Yet, though this opinion saps the foundations of human worship, and
must have the same effects upon society as Atheism itself, one may
easily trace, in the Metaphysics upon which it is grounded, the origin
of many of the notions, or rather of many of the expressions, in the
scholastic theology, to which no notions can be annexed.

11   The Stoics, the most religious of all the ancient sects of
philosophers,[24] seem in this, as in most other things, to have altered
and refined upon the doctrine of Plato.[25] The order, harmony, and
coherence which this philosophy bestowed upon the Universal
System, struck them with awe and veneration. As, in the rude ages of
the world, whatever particular part of Nature excited the admiration
of mankind, was apprehended to be animated by some particular
divinity; so the whole of Nature having, by their reasonings, become
equally the object of admiration, was equally apprehended to be
animated by a Universal Deity, to be itself a Divinity, an Animal; a
term which to our ears seems by no means synonimous with the
foregoing; whose body was the solid and sensible parts of Nature,
and whose soul was that aetherial Fire, which penetrated and
actuated the whole. For of all the four elements, out of which all
things were composed, Fire or Aether seemed to be that which bore
the greatest resemblance to the Vital Principle which informs both
plants and animals, and therefore most likely to be the Vital Principle
which animated the Universe. This infinite and unbounded Aether,
which extended itself from the centre beyond the remotest circumference of Nature, and was endowed with the most consummate
reason and intelligence, or rather was itself the very essence of reason

[23] 'Disorder and confusion' is a travesty of Aristotle's views on 'all things below'. See *De
Partibus Animalium*, 645ᵃ, and also the editor's Introduction, 23–4.
    [24] [Smith writes again, in TMS I.ii.3.4, of the religious character of the Stoic doctrine of
cosmic harmony. His long account of Stoic ethics, in TMS VII.ii.1.15–47, also contains frequent
references to religion.]
    [25] [A similar judgment recurs in Ancient Logics, 9, below. It is perhaps derived from Cicero's
statements (*De Finibus*, III.3,10; IV.2,3) that Zeno was not justified in founding a new school
since he had little to contribute but a novel vocabulary. The originality of Stoic formal logic was
not appreciated until the twentieth century. Expositions which emphasize the originality of
many Stoic doctrines have been given by M. Pohlenz, *Die Stoa* (1948), and S. Samburksy, *The
Physics of the Stoics* (1959).]

and intelligence, had originally formed the world, and had communicated a portion, or ray, of its own essence to whatever was endowed with life and sensation, which, upon the dissolution of those forms, either immediately or sometime after, was again absorbed into that ocean of Deity from whence it had originally been detached. In this system, the Sun, the Moon, the Planets, and the Fixed Stars, were each of them also inferior divinities, animated by a detached portion of that aetherial essence which was the soul of the world. In the system of Plato, the Intelligence which animated the world was different from that which originally formed it. Neither were these which animated the celestial spheres, nor those which informed inferior terrestrial animals, regarded as portions of this plastic soul of the world. Upon the dissolution of animals, therefore, their souls were not absorbed in the soul of the world, but had a separate and eternal existence, which gave birth to the notion of the transmigration of souls. Neither did it seem unnatural, that, as the same matter which had composed one animal body might be employed to compose another, that the same intelligence which had animated one such being should again animate another. But in the system of the Stoics, the intelligence which originally formed, and that which animated the world, were one and the same, all inferior intelligences were detached portions of the great one; and therefore, in a longer, or in a shorter time, were all of them, even the gods themselves, who animated the celestial bodies, to be at last resolved into the infinite essence of this almighty Jupiter, who, at a destined period, should, by an universal conflagration, wrap up all things, in that aetherial and fiery nature, out of which they had originally been deduced, again to bring forth a new Heaven and a new Earth, new animals, new men, new deities; all of which would again, at a fated time, be swallowed up in a like conflagration, again to be re-produced, and again to be re-destroyed, and so on without end.

THE
PRINCIPLES
WHICH LEAD AND DIRECT
PHILOSOPHICAL ENQUIRIES;
ILLUSTRATED BY THE HISTORY OF THE
ANCIENT LOGICS and
METAPHYSICS

1 In every transmutation, either of one element into another, or of one compound body, either into the elements out of which it was composed, or into another compound body, it seemed evident, that, both in the old and in the new species, there was something that was the same, and something that was different. When Fire was changed into Air, or Water into Earth, the Stuff, or Subject-matter of this Air and this Earth, was evidently the same with that of the former Fire or Water; but the Nature or Species of those new bodies was entirely different. When, in the same manner, a number of fresh, green, and odoriferous flowers were thrown together in a heap, they, in a short time, entirely changed their nature, became putrid and loathsome, and dissolved into a confused mass of ordure, which bore no resemblance, either in its sensible qualities or in its effects, to their former beautiful appearance. But how different soever the species, the subject-matter of the flowers, and of the ordure, was, in this case too, evidently the same. In every body, therefore, whether simple or mixed, there were evidently two principles, whose combination constituted the whole nature of that particular body. The first was the Stuff, or Subject-matter, out of which it was made; the second was the Species, the Specific Essence, the Essential, or, as the schoolmen have called it, the Substantial Form of the Body. The first seemed to be the same in all bodies, and to have neither qualities nor powers of any kind, but to be altogether inert and imperceptible by any of the senses, till it was qualified and rendered sensible by its union with some species or essential form. All the qualities and powers of bodies seemed to depend upon their species or essential forms. It was not the stuff or matter of Fire, or Air, or Earth, or Water, which enabled

those elements to produce their several effects, but that essential form
which was peculiar to each of them. For it seemed evident, that Fire
must produce the effects of Fire, by that which rendered it Fire; Air,
by that which rendered it Air; and that in the same manner all other
simple and mixed bodies must produce their several effects, by that
which constituted them such or such bodies; that is, by their specific
Essence or essential forms. But it is from the effects of bodies upon
one another, that all the changes and revolutions in the material
world arise. Since these, therefore, depend upon the specific essences
of those bodies, it must be the business of philosophy,[1] that science
which endeavours to connect together all the different changes that
occur in the world, to determine wherein the specific Essence of each
object consists, in order to foresee what changes or revolutions may
be expected from it. But the specific Essence of each individual object
is not that which is peculiar to it as an individual, but that which is
common to it, with all other objects of the same kind. Thus the
specific Essence of the Water, which now stands before me, does not
consist in its being heated by the Fire, or cooled by the Air, in such
a particular degree; in its being contained in a vessel of such a form,
or of such dimensions. These are all accidental circumstances, which
are altogether extraneous to its general nature, and upon which none
of its effects as Water depend. Philosophy, therefore, in considering
the general nature of Water, takes no notice of those particularities
which are peculiar to this Water, but confines itself to those things
which are common to all water. If, in the progress of its enquiries, it
should descend to consider the nature of Water that is modified by
such particular accidents, it still would not confine its consideration
to this water contained in this vessel, and thus heated at this fire, but
would extend its views to Water in general contained in such kind of
vessels, and heated to such a degree at such a fire. In every case,
therefore, Species, or Universals, and not Individuals, are the objects
of Philosophy. Because whatever effects are produced by individuals,
whatever changes can flow from them, must all proceed from some
universal nature that is contained in them. As it was the business of
Physics, or Natural Philosophy, to determine wherein consisted the
Nature and Essence of every particular Species of things, in order to
connect together all the different events that occur in the material
world; so there were two other sciences, which, though they had
originally arisen out of that system of Natural Philosophy I have just
been describing, were, however, apprehended to go before it, in the
order in which the knowledge of Nature ought to be communicated.

---

[1] i.e. natural philosophy. [For the words that follow, cf. Astronomy, II.12, where (natural)
philosophy is described as 'the science of the connecting principles of nature'.]

The first of these, Metaphysics, considered the general nature of Universals, and the different sorts or species into which they might be divided. The second of these, Logics,[2] was built upon this doctrine of Metaphysics; and from the general nature of Universals, and of the sorts into which they were divided, endeavoured to ascertain the general rules by which we might distribute all particular objects into general classes, and determine to what class each individual object belonged; for in this, they justly enough apprehended, consisted the whole art of philosophical reasoning. As the first of these two sciences, Metaphysics, is altogether subordinate to the second, Logic, they seem, before the time of Aristotle, to have been regarded as one, and to have made up between them that ancient Dialectic of which we hear so much, and of which we understand so little: neither does this separation seem to have been much attended to, either by his own followers, the ancient Peripatetics, or by any other of the old sects of philosophers. The later schoolmen, indeed, have distinguished between Ontology and Logic; but their Ontology contains but a small part of what is the subject of the metaphysical books of Aristotle, the greater part of which, the doctrines of Universals, and every thing that is preparatory to the arts of defining and dividing, has, since the days of Porphery,[3] been inserted into their Logic.[4]

2. According to Plato and Timaeus,[5] the principles out of which the Deity formed the World, and which were themselves eternal, were three in number. The Subject-matter of things, the Species or specific Essences of things, and what was made out of these, the sensible objects themselves. These last had no proper or durable existence, but were in perpetual flux and succession. For as Heraclitus had said, that no man ever passed the same river twice,[6] because the water which he had passed over once was gone before he could pass over it a second time; so, in the same manner, no man ever saw, or heard, or touched the same sensible object twice. When I look at the window, for example, the visible species, which strikes my eyes this moment, though resembling, is different from that which struck my eyes the immediately preceding moment. When I ring the bell, the sound, or audible species which I hear this moment, though resembling in the same manner, is different, however, from that which I heard the

---

[2] The use of the word 'logics' is unusual, but consistent with the strictly plural form of 'physics' and 'metaphysics', the Latin form of each of which was originally a neuter plural corresponding to the Greek sense of 'physical things'. See also the editor's Introduction, 24–5.

[3] [i.e. Porphyry.]

[4] [In WN V.i.f.29 Smith describes rather differently the confusing character of Ontology. He says that it was supposed to deal with qualities and attributes common to Metaphysics and Physics but was sometimes itself called Metaphysics.]

[5] [Plato, *Timaeus*, 48 E ff.; Timaeus Locrus, 94 A–B. See note 12 to Astronomy, III.]

[6] [Aristotle, *Metaphysics*, Γ, 1010ª13–14.]

moment before. When I lay my hand on the table, the tangible
species which I feel this moment, though resembling, in the same
manner, is numerically different too from that which I felt the
moment before. Our sensations, therefore, never properly exist or
endure one moment; but, in the very instant of their generation,
perish and are annihilated for ever. Nor are the causes of those
sensations more permanent. No corporeal substance is ever exactly
the same, either in whole or in any assignable part, during two
successive moments, but by the perpetual addition of new parts, as
well as loss of old ones, is in continual flux and succession. Things of
so fleeting a nature can never be the objects of science, or of any
steady or permanent judgment. While we look at them, in order to
consider them, they are changed and gone, and annihilated for ever.
The objects of science, and of all the steady judgments of the
understanding, must be permanent, unchangeable, always existent,
and liable neither to generation nor corruption, nor alteration of any
kind.[7] Such are the species or specific essences of things. Man is
perpetually changing every particle of his body; and every thought
of his mind is in continual flux and succession. But humanity, or
human nature, is always existent, is always the same, is never
generated, and is never corrupted. This, therefore, is the object of
science, reason, and understanding, as man is the object of sense, and
of those inconstant opinions which are founded upon sense. As the
objects of sense were apprehended to have an external existence,
independent of the act of sensation, so these objects of the
understanding were much more supposed to have an external
existence independent of the act of understanding. Those external
essences were, according to Plato,[8] the exemplars, according to which
the Deity formed the world, and all the sensible objects that are in it.
The Deity comprehended within his infinite essence, all these species,
or eternal exemplars, in the same manner as he comprehended all
sensible objects.

3   Plato, however, seems to have regarded the first of those as equally
distinct with the second from what we would now call the Ideas or
Thoughts of the Divine Mind*, and even to have supposed, that they

* He calls them, indeed, Ideas, a word which, in him, in Aristotle, and all the other writers of
earlier antiquity, signifies a Species, and is perfectly synonimous with that other word Εἶδος,
more frequently made use of by Aristotle. As, by some of the later sects of philosophers,
particularly by the Stoics, all species, or specific essences, were regarded as mere creatures of the
mind, formed by abstraction, which had no real existence external to the thoughts that
conceived them, the word Idea came, by degrees, to its present signification, to mean, first, an
abstract thought or conception; and afterwards, a thought or conception of any kind; and thus
became synonymous with that other Greek word Ἔννοια, from which it had originally a very
(continued)

[7] [Plato, *Timaeus*, 52 A–B.]   [8] [*Timaeus*, 29 A.]

had a particular place of existence, beyond the sphere of the visible corporeal world; though this has been much controverted, both by

different meaning. When the later Platonists, who lived at a time when the notion of the separate existence of specific essences were universally exploded, began to comment upon the writings of Plato, and upon that strange fancy that, in his writings, there was a double doctrine; and that they were intended to seem to mean one thing, while at bottom they meant a very different, which the writings of no man in his senses ever were, or ever could be intended to do;[9] they represented his doctrine as meaning no more, than that the Deity formed the world after what we would now call an Idea, or plan conceived in his own mind, in the same manner as any other artist.[10] But, if Plato had meant to express no more than this most natural and simple of all notions, he might surely have expressed it more plainly, and would hardly, one would think, have talked of it with so much emphasis, as of something which it required the utmost reach of thought to comprehend. According to this representation, Plato's notion of Species, or Universals, was the same with that of Aristotle. Aristotle, however, does not seem to understand it as such; he bestows a great part of his Metaphysics upon confuting it, and opposes it in all his other works; nor does he, in any one of them, give the least hint, or insinuation, as if it could be suspected that, by the Ideas of Plato, was meant the thoughts or conceptions of the Divine Mind. Is it possible that he, who was twenty years in his school, should, during all that time, have misunderstood him, especially when his meaning was so very plain and obvious? Neither is this notion of the separate existence of Species, distinct both from the mind which conceives them, and from the sensible objects which are made to resemble them, one of those doctrines which Plato would but seldom have occasion to talk of. However it may be interpreted, it is the very basis of his philosophy; neither is there a single dialogue in all his works which does not refer to it. Shall we suppose, that that great philosopher, who appears to have been so much superior to his master in every thing but eloquence, wilfully, and upon all occasions, misrepresented, not one of the deep and mysterious doctrines of the philosophy of Plato, but the first and most fundamental principle of all his reasonings; when the writings of Plato were in the hands of every body; when his followers and disciples were spread all over Greece; when almost every Athenian of distinction, that was nearly of the same age with Aristotle, must have been bred in his school; when Speusippus, the nephew and successor of Plato, as well as Xenocrates, who continued the school in the Academy, at the same time that Aristotle held his in the Lyceum, must have been ready, at all times, to expose and affront him for such gross disingenuity. Does not Cicero, does not Seneca understand this doctrine in the same manner as Aristotle has represented it? Is there any author in all antiquity who seems to understand it otherwise, earlier than Plutarch, an author, who seems to have been as bad a critic in philosophy as in history, and to have taken every thing at second-hand in both, and who lived after the origin of that eclectic philosophy, from whence the later Platonists[11] arose, and who seems himself to have been one of that sect? Is there any one passage in any Greek author, near the time of Aristotle and Plato, in which the word Idea is used in its present meaning, to signify a thought or conception? Are not the words, which in all languages express reality or existence, directly opposed to those which express thought, or conception only? Or, is there any other difference betwixt a thing that exists, and a thing that does not exist, except this, that the one is a mere conception, and that the other is something more than a conception? With what propriety, therefore, could Plato talk of those eternal species, as of the only things which had any real existence, if they were no more than the conceptions of the Divine Mind? Had not the Deity, according to Plato, as well as according to the Stoics, from all eternity, the idea of every individual, as well as of every species, and of the state in which every individual was to be, in each different instance of its existence? Were not all the divine ideas, therefore, of each individual, or of all the different states, which each individual was to be in during the course of its existence, equally eternal and unalterable with those of the species? With what sense, therefore, could Plato say, that the first were eternal, because the Deity had conceived

---

[9] The coexistence of esoteric and exoteric writings is pretty well attested among men far from being 'out of their senses'. There are plausible grounds for believing that Plato may in his later years have been among them, though probably not in respect of the Ideas, where he was doing no more than change his mind. Cf. *Theaetetus*, 152 C, for a suggestion by 'Socrates'.

[10] [The question 'Are Plato's Ideas thoughts of the Divine Mind?' is answered in the negative by E. Zeller, *Plato and the Older Academy* (English translation, 1888, made from the 3rd edition of Zeller's *Philosophie der Griechen*), 243–8. His general line of argument is in fact very similar to Smith's.]

[11] [In TMS VII.ii.3.1 Smith identifies the 'Eclectics' with the 'later Platonists'.]

the later Platonists, and by some very judicious modern critics,[12] who have followed the interpretation of the later Platonists, as what did most honour to the judgment of that renowned philosopher. All the objects in this world, continued he, are particular and individual. Here, therefore, the human mind has no opportunity of seeing any Species, or Universal Nature. Whatever ideas it has, therefore, of such beings, for it plainly has them, it must derive from the memory of what it has seen, in some former period of its existence, when it had an opportunity of visiting the place or Sphere of Universals.[15] For some time after it is immersed in the body, during its infancy, its childhood, and a great part of its youth, the violence of those passions which it derives from the body, and which are all directed to the particular and individual objects of this world, hinder it from turning its attention to those Universal Natures, with which it had been conversant in the world from whence it came. The Ideas, of these, therefore, seem, in this first period of its existence here, to be overwhelmed in the confusion of those turbulent emotions, and to be almost entirely wiped out of its remembrance. During the continuance of this state, it is incapable of Reasoning, Science and Philosophy, which are conversant about Universals. Its whole attention is turned

them from all eternity, since he had conceived the others from all eternity too, and since his ideas of the Species could, in this respect, have no advantage of those of the individual? Does not Plato, in many different places, talk of the Ideas of Species or Universals as innate, and having been impressed upon the mind in its state of pre-existence, when it had an opportunity of viewing these Species as they are in themselves, and not as they are expressed in their copies, or representative upon earth? But if the only place of the existence of those Species was the Divine Mind, will not this suppose, that Plato either imagined, like Father Malbranche, that in its state of pre-existence, the mind saw all things in God;[13] or that it was itself an emanation of the Divinity? That he maintained the first opinion, will not be pretended by any body who is at all versed in the history of science. That enthusiastic notion, though it may seem to be favoured by some passages in the Fathers, was never, it is well known, coolly and literally maintained by any body before that Cartesian philosopher. That the human mind was itself an emanation of the Divine, though it was the doctrine of the Stoics, was by no means that of Plato; though, upon the notion of a pretended double doctrine, the contrary has lately been asserted. According to Plato, the Deity formed the soul of the world out of that substance which is always the same, that is, out of Species or Universals; out of that which is always different, that is, out of corporeal substances; and out of a substance that was of a middle nature between these, which it is not easy to understand what he meant by. Out of a part of the same composition, he made those inferior intelligences who animated the celestial spheres, to whom he delivered the remaining part of it, to form from thence the souls of men and animals. The souls of those inferior deities, though made out of a similar substance or composition, were not regarded as parts, or emanations of that of the world; nor were those of animals, in the same manner, regarded as parts or emanations of those inferior deities; much less were any of them regarded as parts, or emanations of the great Author of all things.[14]

[12] Presumably the so-called 'Cambridge Platonists', of whom Henry More (1614–87) and Ralph Cudworth (1617–88) were the most significant in this connection. Smith mentions Cudworth in §6 below. [In TMS VII.ii.3.3 Smith names Cudworth, More, and John Smith (1618–52) as leading members of the group.]

[13] [Malebranche, *Recherche de la vérité*, III.ii.6.]

[14] On this long and searching footnote, see the editor's Introduction, 25.

[15] [This view is defended by Plato in the *Meno* and in the *Phaedo*, 73 A–76 E.]

towards particular objects, concerning which, being directed by no general notions, it forms many vain and false opinions, and is filled with error, perplexity, and confusion. But, when age has abated the violence of its passions, and composed the confusion of its thoughts, it then becomes more capable of reflection, and of turning its attention to those almost forgotten ideas of things with which it had been conversant in the former state of its existence. All the particular objects in this sensible world, being formed after the eternal exemplars in that intellectual world, awaken, upon account of their resemblance, insensibly, and by slow degrees, the almost obliterated ideas of these last. The beauty, which is shared in different degrees among terrestrial objects, revives the same idea of that Universal Nature of beauty which exists in the intellectual world: particular acts of justice, of the universal nature of justice; particular reasonings, and particular sciences, of the universal nature of science, and reasoning; particular roundnesses, of the universal nature of roundness; particular squares, of the universal nature of squareness. Thus science, which is conversant about Universals, is derived from memory; and to instruct any person concerning the general nature of any subject, is no more than to awaken in him the remembrance of what he formerly knew about it. This both Plato and Socrates imagined they could still further confirm, by the fallacious experiment, which shewed, that a person might be led to discover himself, without any information, any general truth, of which he was before ignorant, merely by being asked a number of properly arranged and connected questions concerning it.[16]

4　　The more the soul was accustomed to the consideration of those Universal Natures, the less it was attached to any particular and individual objects; it approached the nearer to the original perfection of its nature, from which, according to this philosophy, it had fallen. Philosophy, which accustoms it to consider the general Essence of things only, and to abstract from all their particular and sensible circumstances, was, upon this account, regarded as the great purifier of the soul. As death separated the soul from the body, and from the bodily senses and passions, it restored it to that intellectual world, from whence it had originally descended, where no sensible Species called off its attention from those general Essences of things. Philosophy, in this life, habituating it to the same considerations, brings it, in some degree, to that state of happiness and perfection, to which death restores the souls of just men in a life to come.

5　　Such was the doctrine of Plato concerning the Species or Specific

---

[16] A reference to the well-known elicitation by Socrates of a geometrical proof from a slave (*Meno*, 82 B–85 C).

Essence of things. This, at least, is what his words seem to import, and thus he is understood by Aristotle, the most intelligent and the most renowned of all his disciples. It is a doctrine, which, like many of the other doctrines of abstract Philosophy, is more coherent in the expression than in the idea; and which seems to have arisen, more from the nature of language, than from the nature of things.[17] With all its imperfections it was excusable, in the beginnings of philosophy, and is not a great deal more remote from the truth, than many others which have since been substituted in its room by some of the greatest pretenders to accuracy and precision. Mankind have had, at all times, a strong propensity to realize their own abstractions, of which we shall immediately see an example,[18] in the notions of that very philosopher who first exposed the ill-grounded foundation of those Ideas, or Universals, of Plato and Timaeus. To explain the nature, and to account for the origin of general Ideas, is, even at this day, the greatest difficulty in abstract philosophy. How the human mind, when it reasons concerning the general nature of triangles, should either conceive, as Mr. Locke imagines it does,[19] the idea of a triangle, which is neither obtusangular, nor rectangular, nor acutangular; but which was at once both none and all of those together; or should, as Malbranche thinks necessary for this purpose,[20] comprehend at once, within its finite capacity, all possible triangles of all possible forms and dimensions, which are infinite in number, is a question, to which it is surely not easy to give a satisfactory answer. Malbranche, to solve it, had recourse to the enthusiastic and unintelligible notion of the intimate union of the human mind with the divine, in whose infinite essence the immensity of such species could alone be comprehended; and in which alone, therefore, all finite intelligences could have an opportunity of viewing them. If, after more than two thousand years reasoning about this subject, this ingenious and sublime philosopher was forced to have recourse to so strange a fancy, in order to explain it, can we wonder that Plato, in the very first dawnings of science, should, for the same purpose, adopt an hypothesis, which has been thought, without much reason, indeed, to have some affinity to that of Malbranche, and which is not more out of the way?

6   What seems to have misled those early philosophers, was, the notion, which appears, at first, natural enough, that those things, out of which any object is composed, must exist antecedent to that object. But the things out of which all particular objects seem to be composed, are the stuff or matter of those objects, and the form or specific

[17] Cf. §7 below.
[18] [Presumably the discussion, in §7 below, of Aristotle's doctrine of potential existence.]
[19] [*Essay concerning Human Understanding*, IV.vii.9.]
[20] [*Recherche de la vérité*, III.ii.6.]

Essence, which determines them to be of this or that class of things. These, therefore, it was thought, must have existed antecedent to the object which was made up between them. Plato, who held, that the sensible world, which, according to him, is the world of individuals, was made in time, necessarily conceived, that both the universal matter, the object of a spurious reason,[21] and the specific essence, the object of proper reason and philosophy out of which it was composed, must have had a separate existence from all eternity. This intellectual world, very different from the intellectual world of Cudworth,[22] though much of the language of the one has been borrowed from that of the other, was necessarily, and always existent; whereas the sensible world owed its origin to the free will and bounty of its author.

7   A notion of this kind, as long as it is expressed in very general language; as long as it is not much rested upon; nor attempted to be very particularly and distinctly explained, passes easily enough, through the indolent imagination, accustomed to substitute words in the room of ideas; and if the words seem to hang easily together, requiring no great precision in the ideas. It vanishes, indeed; is discovered to be altogether incomprehensible, and eludes the grasp of the imagination, upon an attentive consideration. It requires, however, an attentive consideration; and if it had been as fortunate as many other opinions of the same kind, and about the same subject, it might, without examination, have continued to be the current philosophy for a century or two. Aristotle, however, seems immediately to have discovered, that it was impossible to conceive, as actually existent, either that general matter, which was not determined by any particular species, or those species which were not embodied, if one may say so, in some particular portion of matter. Aristotle, too, held, as we have already observed,[23] the eternity of the sensible world. Though he held, therefore, that all sensible objects were made up of two principles, both of which, he calls, equally, substances, the matter and the specific essence, he was not obliged to hold, like Plato, that those principles existed prior in the order of time to the objects which they afterwards composed. They were prior, he said, in nature, but not in time, according to a distinction which was of use to him upon some other occasions.[24] He distinguished, too, betwixt actual and

[21] [Plato, *Timaeus*, 51 A, 52 B.]
[22] [A reference to the title, as well as the content, of Cudworth's metaphysical treatise, mainly inspired by his interpretation of Plato: *The True Intellectual System of the Universe* (1678).]
[23] [Ancient Physics, 10.]
[24] [While this remark leaves a correct general impression, Aristotle nowhere seems to say explicitly that his principles (matter and specific essence) are prior in nature but not in time.]

potential existence.[25] By the first, he seems to have understood, what is commonly meant, by existence or reality; by the second, the bare possibility of existence. His meaning, I say, seems to amount to this; though he does not explain it precisely in this manner. Neither the material Essence of body could, according to him, exist actually without being determined by some specific Essence, to some particular class of things, nor any specific Essence without being embodied in some particular portion of matter. Each of these two principles, however, could exist potentially in this separate state. That matter existed potentially, which, being endowed with a particular form, could be brought into actual existence; and that form, which, by being embodied in a particular portion of matter, could, in the same manner, be called forth into the class of complete realities. This potential existence of matter and form, he sometimes talks of, in expressions which very much resemble those of Plato, to whose notion of separate Essence it bears a very great affinity.

8   Aristotle, who seems in many things original, and who endeavoured to seem to be so in all things, added the principle of privation to those of matter and form, which he had derived from the ancient Pythagorean school. When Water is changed into Air, the transmutation is brought about by the material principle of those two elements being deprived of the form of Water, and then assuming the form of Air. Privation, therefore, was a third principle opposite to form, which entered into the generation of every Species, which was always from some other Species. It was a principle of generation, but not of composition, as is obvious.

9   The Stoics, whose opinions were, in all the different parts of philosophy, either the same with, or very nearly allied to those of Aristotle and Plato, though often disguised in very different language, held, that all things, even the elements themselves, were compounded of two principles,[26] upon one of which depended all the active; and upon the other, all the passive powers of these bodies.[27] The last of these, they called the Matter; the first, the Cause, by which they

---

[25] [Matter and specific essence as substances: *Metaphysics*, Z, and H (especially 1042^{a}24–^{b}6), also Λ, 1079^{a}9 ff. Actual and potential existence: *Metaphysics*, Θ. See in general Sir David Ross, *Aristotle's Metaphysics* (1924), vol. i, Introduction, xci–cxxx, and J. Owens, *The Doctrine of Being in Aristotelian Metaphysics*, ed. 2 (1963).]

[26] [Perhaps taken from Diogenes Laertius, VII.134.]

[27] [Perhaps derived from Seneca, *Epistulae Morales*, 65.2: 'Dicunt, ut scis, Stoici nostri duo esse in rerum natura ex quibus omnia fiant, causam et materiam. Materia iacet iners, res ad omnia parata, cessatura si nemo moveat. Causa autem, id est ratio, materiam format et quocumque vult versat, ex illa varia opera producit. Esse ergo debet, unde fiat aliquid, deinde a quo fiat.'

But whereas Smith is maintaining that this amounts to the same as the Platonic-Aristotelian account, the drift of Seneca's Epistle is that the Stoics by no means agreed with Plato and Aristotle, and were able to give a simpler account of the Cause. The essence of things, he says (§§ 11–13), cannot properly be regarded as a cause; it is at best an ingredient in one.]

meant the very same thing which Aristotle and Plato understood, by their specific Essences. Matter, according to the Stoics, could have no existence separate from the cause or efficient principle which determined it to some particular class of things. Neither could the efficient principle exist separately from the material, in which it was always necessarily embodied. Their opinion, therefore, so far coincided with that of the old Peripatetics. The efficient principle, they said, was the Deity. By which they meant, that it was a detached portion of the etherial and divine nature, which penetrated all things, that constituted what Plato would have called the specific Essence of each individual object; and so far their opinion coincides pretty nearly with that of the latter Platonists, who held, that the specific Essences of all things were detached portions of their created deity, the soul of the world; and with that of some of the Arabian and Scholastic Commentators of Aristotle, who held, that the substantial forms of all things descended from those Divine Essences which animated the Celestial Spheres. Such was the doctrine of the four principal Sects of the ancient Philosophers, concerning the specific Essences of things, of the old Pythagoreans, of the Academical, Peripatetic, and Stoical Sects.[28]

10   As this doctrine of specific Essences seems naturally enough to have arisen from that ancient system of Physics, which I have above described, and which is, by no means, devoid of probability, so many of the doctrines of that system, which seem to us, who have been long accustomed to another, the most incomprehensible, necessarily flow from this metaphysical notion. Such are those of generation, corruption, and alteration; of mixture, condensation, and rarefaction. A body was generated or corrupted, when it changed its specific Essence, and passed from one denomination to another. It was altered when it changed only some of its qualities, but still retained the same specific Essence, and the same denomination. Thus, when a flower was withered, it was not corrupted; though some of its qualities were changed, it still retained the specific Essence, and therefore justly passed under the denomination of a flower. But, when, in the further progress of its decay, it crumbled into earth, it was corrupted; it lost the specific Essence, or substantial form of the flower, and assumed that of the earth, and therefore justly changed its denomination.

11   The specific Essence, or universal nature that was lodged in each particular class of bodies, was not itself the object of any of our senses,

---

[28] Since Smith wrote in an age when 'physical' (not yet 'chemical') atomism was a dominant mode of thought, it is surprising that the essay should break off without any reference to the Greek atomists—Leucippus and Democritus, mainly 'physical', and the later Epicurus (also strongly 'moral'), as set forth in the poem *De Rerum Natura* by Lucretius.

but could be perceived only by the understanding. It was by the sensible qualities, however, that we judged of the specific Essence of each object. Some of these sensible qualities, therefore, we regarded as essential, or such as showed, by their presence or absence, the presence or absence of that essential form from which they necessarily flowed: Others were accidental, or such whose presence or absence had no such necessary consequences. The first of these two sorts of qualities was called Properties; the second, Accidents.

12   In the Specific Essence of each object itself, they distinguished two parts; one of which was peculiar and characteristical of the class of things of which that particular object was an individual, the other was common to it with some other higher classes of things. These two parts were, to the Specific Essence, pretty much what the Matter and the Specific Essence were to each individual body. The one, which was called the Genus, was modified and determined by the other, which was called the Specific Difference, pretty much in the same manner as the universal matter contained in each body was modified and determined by the Specific Essence of that particular class of bodies. These four, with the Specific Essence or Species itself, made up the number of the Five Universals, so well known in the schools by the names of Genus, Species, Differentia, Proprium, and Accidens.

Of the External Senses

Introduction

Of all the *Essays on Philosophical Subjects* this alone might pass for philosophical in the more restricted sense now current. At any rate it is written in the style we have come to associate with the great philosophical classics of the period beginning with Descartes: characterized by 'full and accurate expression' and 'clear illustration' and controlled by a more adequate acquaintance with the relevant facts of 'natural philosophy' than is evident in much of the 'philosophical' writing of the recent past. Yet of all the essays it is the most difficult to assess. Neither in its title nor in its text is there any hint of what part, if any, Smith intended it to play in his 'grand design'; it is devoid alike of any reference to historical development or 'principles of philosophical investigation'. In the absence of any certain evidence that it was written at, or even near, the same time as the 'historical' essays it is perhaps best to regard it as literally an *essai* or attempt to set out the author's ideas on a subject that remained of central concern throughout his lifetime. Thus it could not avoid being derived from Locke's *Essay*, which it resembles in being set forth in the same 'historical plain method'. The Cartesian 'machine' theory of sensation (in a corpuscularian variant) is given cautious acceptance. But neither Locke nor anyone else (except a passing reference to Gassendi and Newton) is mentioned until the 'Sense of SEEING' is discussed; here Smith refers at once to Berkeley's 'New Theory of Vision, one of the finest examples of philosophical analysis that is to be found, either in our own, or in any other language' (External Senses, 43). Unfortunately, he does not seem to realize that Berkeley's analysis had vitiated[1] the distinction between primary and secondary qualities which he is at pains to establish in the first sixteen pages of his own essay. It is therefore probable that he wrote the essay before digesting Hume's *Treatise* (1739) or even before becoming closely acquainted with Hume, as there is reason to believe he did before 1752 (Stewart, I.13).

Though not unambiguously related to Smith's 'grand design', this essay is not without significance for the general assessment of his appreciation of the nature of 'philosophical' thinking. With the exception just noted it would pass for a very fair résumé of the contemporary state of knowledge of the 'external senses', such as

[1] Explicitly only in the later *Principles of Human Knowledge* that Smith may not have seen.

might have provided an encyclopedia article, and looked at of course from the point of view of philosophical psychology rather than that of natural philosophy; as such it is no more than competent. There are, however, two sections of considerable significance for any assessment of Smith's own intellectual development as also of his place in the history of ideas.

The first of these sections begins at §60, where Smith seizes on Berkeley's ingenious theory (*New Theory of Vision*, 139–47, and *Principles of Human Knowledge*, 30–1) of regarding the association and sequence of 'external' sensations or ideas as a language employed by 'the Author of our being' to guide our behaviour as may best conduce to the welfare of our bodies and minds. In the course of his exposition Berkeley had considered the analogous relationship between 'signs' (letters and words) and objects in languages of human origin and use. Smith was to consider this correspondence in greater depth in *Considerations concerning the First Formation of Languages*, first published in 1761. Professor Ralph Lindgren has seen in this frequent reference to linguistic origin and structure a major factor in Smith's whole methodology.[2]

The other section of special significance in this essay is comprised in the concluding pages where a side of Smith's genius is revealed for which the other 'philosophical' essays had given no scope: this was his appeal to careful 'field' observations on animals in which he displays an appreciation of the power of the comparative method to correlate data and control theory.

[2] J. R. Lindgren, 'Adam Smith's Theory of Inquiry', *Journal of Political Economy*, lxxvii (1969).

EXTERNAL SENSES

1   The Senses, by which we perceive external objects, are commonly reckoned Five in Number; Seeing, Hearing, Smelling, Tasting, and Touching.

2   Of these, the four first mentioned are each of them confined to particular parts or organs of the body; the Sense of Seeing is confined to the Eyes; that of Hearing to the Ears; that of Smelling to the Nostrils; and that of Tasting to the Palate. The Sense of Touching alone seems not to be confined to any particular organ, but to be diffused through almost every part of the body; if we except the hair and the nails of the fingers and toes, I believe through every part of it. I shall say a few words concerning each of these Senses; beginning with the last, proceeding backwards in the opposite order to that in which they are commonly enumerated.

Of the Sense of TOUCHING

3   THE objects of Touch always present themselves as pressing upon, or as resisting the particular part of the body which perceives them, or by which we perceive them. When I lay my hand upon the table, the table presses upon my hand, or resists the further motion of my hand, in the same manner as my hand presses upon the table. But pressure or resistance necessarily supposes externality in the thing which presses or resists. The table could not press upon, or resist the further motion of my hand, if it was not external to my hand. I feel it accordingly, as something which is not merely an affection of my hand, but altogether external to, and independant of my hand. The agreeable, indifferent, or painful sensation of pressure, according as I happen to press hardly or softly, I feel, no doubt, as affections of my hand; but the thing which presses and resists I feel as something altogether different from those affections, as external to my hand, and as altogether independent of it.

4   In moving my hand along the table it soon comes, in every direction, to a place where this pressure or resistance ceases. This place we call the boundary, or end of the table; of which the extent and figure are determined by the extent and direction of the lines or surfaces which constitute this boundary or end.

5   It is in this manner that a man born blind, or who has lost his sight so early that he has no remembrance of visible objects, may form the

most distinct idea of the extent and figure of all the different parts of his own body, and of every other tangible object which he has an opportunity of handling and examining. When he lays his hand upon his foot, as his hand feels the pressure or resistance of his foot, so his foot feels that of his hand. They are both external to one another, but they are, neither of them, altogether so external to him. He feels in both, and he naturally considers them as parts of himself, or at least as something which belongs to him, and which, for his own happiness and comfort, it is necessary that he should take some care of.

6   When he lays his hand upon the table, though his hand feels the pressure of the table, the table does not feel, at least he does not know that it feels, the pressure of his hand. He feels it therefore as something external, not only to his hand, but to himself, as something which makes no part of himself, and in the state and condition of which he has not necessarily any concern.

7   When he lays his hand upon the body either of another man, or of any other animal, though he knows, or at least may know, that they feel the pressure of his hand as much as he feels that of their body: Yet as this feeling is altogether external to him, he frequently gives no attention to it, and at no time takes any further concern in it than he is obliged to do by that fellow-feeling which Nature has, for the wisest purposes, implanted in man, not only towards all other men, but (though no doubt in a much weaker degree) towards all other animals. Having destined him to be the governing animal in this little world, it seems to have been her benevolent intention to inspire him with some degree of respect, even for the meanest and weakest of his subjects.

8   This power or quality of resistance we call Solidity; and the thing which possesses it, the Solid Body or Thing. As we feel it as something altogether external to us, so we necessarily conceive it as something altogether independent of us. We consider it, therefore, as what we call a Substance, or as a thing that subsists by itself, and independent of any other thing. Solid and substantial, accordingly, are two words which, in common language, are considered either as altogether, or as nearly synonimous.

9   Solidity necessarily supposes some degree of extension, and that in all the three directions of length, breadth, and thickness. All the solid bodies, of which we have any experience, have some degree of such bulk or magnitude. It seems to be essential to their nature, and without it, we cannot even conceive how they should be capable of pressure or resistance;[1] the powers by which they are made known

[1] Cf. Locke, *Essay concerning Human Understanding*, especially II.iv.3.

to us, and by which alone they are capable of acting upon our own, and upon all other bodies.

10   Extension, at least any sensible extension, supposes divisibility. The body may be so hard, that our strength is not sufficient to break it: we still suppose, however, that if a sufficient force were applied, it might be so broken; and, at any rate, we can always, in fancy at least, imagine it to be divided into two or more parts.

11   Every solid and extended body, if it be not infinite, (as the universe may be conceived to be,) must have some shape or figure, or be bounded by certain lines and surfaces.

12   Every such body must likewise be conceived as capable both of motion and of rest; both of altering its situation with regard to other surrounding bodies, and of remaining in the same situation. That bodies of small or moderate bulk, are capable of both motion and rest we have constant experience. Great masses, perhaps, are, according to the ordinary habits of the imagination, supposed to be more fitted for rest than for motion.[2] Provided a sufficient force could be applied, however, we have no difficulty in conceiving that the greatest and most unwieldy masses might be made capable of motion. Philosophy teaches us, (and by reasons too to which it is scarcely possible to refuse our assent,) that the earth itself, and bodies much larger than the earth, are not only moveable, but are at all times actually in motion, and continually altering their situation, in respect to other surrounding bodies, with a rapidity that almost passes all human comprehension. In the system of the universe, at least according to the imperfect notions which we have hitherto been able to attain concerning it, the great difficulty seems to be, not to find the most enormous masses in motion, but to find the smallest particle of matter that is perfectly at rest, with regard to all other surrounding bodies.[3]

13   These four qualities, or attributes of extension, divisibility, figure, and mobility, or the capacity of motion or rest, seem necessarily involved in the idea or conception of a solid substance. They are, in reality, inseparable from that idea or conception, and the solid substance cannot possibly be conceived to exist without them. No other qualities or attributes seem to be involved, in the same manner, in this our idea or conception of solidity. It would, however, be rash from thence to conclude that the solid substance can, as such, possess no other qualities or attributes. This very rash conclusion, notwithstanding, has been not only drawn, but insisted upon, as an axiom of

---

[2] [Cf. Astronomy, IV.38.]
[3] This surmise as to the absence of any 'privileged' body in the universe is of course connected with the question of the relativity of all motion; cf. *Leibniz–Clarke Correspondence* (ed. H. G. Alexander, 1956) and Berkeley, *Principles of Human Knowledge*, § 113.

the most indubitable certainty, by philosophers of very eminent reputation.[4]

14   Of these external and resisting substances, some yield easily, and change their figure, at least in some degree, in consequence of the pressure of our hand: others neither yield nor change their figure, in any respect, in consequence of the utmost pressure which our hand alone is capable of giving them. The former we call soft, the latter hard, bodies. In some bodies the parts are so very easily separable, that they not only yield to a very moderate pressure, but easily receive the pressing body within them, and without much resistance allow it to traverse their extent in every possible direction. These are called Fluid, in contradistinction to those of which the parts not being so easily separable, are upon that account peculiarly called Solid Bodies; as if they possessed, in a more distinct and perceptible manner, the characteristical quality of solidity or the power of resistance. Water, however, (one of the fluids with which we are most familiar,) when confined on all sides, (as in a hollow globe of metal, which is first filled with it, and then sealed hermetically,) has been found to resist pressure as much as the hardest, or what we commonly call the most solid bodies.

15   Some fluids yield so very easily to the slightest pressure, that upon ordinary occasions we are scarcely sensible of their resistance; and are upon that account little disposed to conceive them as bodies, or as things capable of pressure and resistance. There was a time, as we may learn from Aristotle and Lucretius,[5] when it was supposed to require some degree of philosophy to demonstrate that air was a real solid body, or capable of pressure and resistance. What, in ancient times, and in vulgar apprehensions, was supposed to be doubtful with regard to air, still continues to be so with regard to light, of which the rays, however condensed or concentrated, have never appeared capable of making the smallest resistance to the motion of other bodies, the characteristical power or quality of what are called bodies, or solid substances. Some philosophers accordingly doubt, and some even deny, that light is a material or corporeal substance.[6]

---

[4] Presumably Descartes and his followers.

[5] [Aristotle, *Physics*, IV.6, 213ª27; *De Caelo*, II.13, 294ᵇ21–3. Lucretius, *De Rerum Natura*, i.269 ff.]

[6] Smith's cautious comment shows remarkable sagacity. Though probably the majority of the contemporary 'philosophers' adopted what they took to be Newton's 'material corpuscular' hypothesis rather than the somewhat loosely-named 'wave theory' mainly associated with Hooke and Huygens, the choice is now recognized to be far from simple. Newton himself with his customary caution set out his views in the form of Queries appended to the later editions of his *Opticks*. Though he regarded 'all hypotheses as erroneous in which light is supposed to consist in pression or motion propagated through a fluid medium' (Q.28), nevertheless he had to have recourse to a subsidiary hypothesis of waves in an 'etherial' medium acting on the light rays to account for certain anomalous forms of behaviour in the latter. Finally—very relevant

16   Though all bodies or solid substances resist, yet all those with
which we are acquainted appear to be more or less compressible, or
capable of having, without any diminution in the quantity of their
matter, their bulk more or less reduced within a smaller space than
that which they usually occupy. An experiment of the Florentine
academy[7] was supposed to have demonstrated that water was
absolutely incompressible. The same experiment, however, having
been repeated with more care and accuracy, it appears, that water,
though it strongly resists compression, is, however, when a sufficient
force is applied, like all other bodies, in some degree liable to it. Air,
on the contrary, by the application of a very moderate force, is easily
reducible within a much smaller portion of space than that which it
usually occupies. The condensing engine, and what is founded upon
it, the wind-gun, sufficiently demonstrate this: and even without the
help of such ingenious and expensive machines, we may easily satisfy
ourselves of the truth of it, by squeezing a full-blown bladder of
which the neck is well tied.

17   The hardness or softness of bodies, or the greater or smaller force
with which they resist any change of shape, seems to depend
altogether upon the stronger or weaker degree of cohesion with which
their parts are mutually attracted to one another. The greater or
smaller force with which they resist compression may, upon many
occasions, be owing partly to the same cause: but it may likewise be
owing to the greater or smaller proportion of empty space comprehended within their dimensions, or intermixed with the solid parts
which compose them. A body which comprehended no empty space
within its dimensions, which, through all its parts, was completely
filled with the resisting substance, we are naturally disposed to
conceive as something which would be absolutely incompressible,
and which would resist, with unconquerable force, every attempt to
reduce it within narrower dimensions. If the solid and resisting
substance, without moving out of its place, should admit into the
same place another solid and resisting substance, it would from that
moment, in our apprehension, cease to be a solid and resisting
substance, and would no longer appear to possess that quality, by

to Smith's comment—he asked 'Are not gross bodies and light convertible into one another?'
(Q.30). The issue was apparently resolved in favour of transverse vibrations of an 'ether' by
Thomas Young a few years after Smith's death. Once again discrepancies appeared which only
the advent of the Quantum Theory was able to resolve—if that is the word!
    [7] i.e. the Accademia del Cimento in Florence. See *Essayes of Natural Experiments made in the
Academie del Cimento*, the English translation of their *Saggi*, by Richard Waller (1648), 204.
That views opposed to atomism are not in themselves to be so hastily dismissed was proved in
1758, when there appeared Roger Boscovich's *Philosophiae Naturalis Theoria*, a work in which
'atoms' were entirely replaced by 'forces', and which exerted a notable influence on Davy,
Faraday, Lord Kelvin, and Maxwell.

which alone it is made known to us, and which we therefore consider as constituting its nature and essence, and as altogether inseparable from it. Hence our notion of what has been called impenetrability of matter; or of the absolute impossibility that two solid resisting substances should occupy the same place at the same time.

18   This doctrine, which is as old as Leucippus, Democritus, and Epicurus, was in the last century revived by Gassendi,[8] and has since been adopted by Newton and the far greater part of his followers. It may at present be considered as the established system, or as the system that is most in fashion, and most approved of by the greater part of the philosophers of Europe. Though it has been opposed by several puzzling arguments, drawn from that species of metaphysics which confounds every thing and explains nothing, it seems upon the whole to be the most simple, the most distinct, and the most comprehensible account that has yet been given of the phaenomena which are meant to be explained by it. I shall only observe, that whatever system may be adopted concerning the hardness or softness, the fluidity or solidity, the compressibility or incompressibility, of the resisting substance, the certainty of our distinct sense and feeling of its Externality, or of its entire independency upon the organ which perceives it, or by which we perceive it, cannot in the smallest degree be affected by any such system. I shall not therefore attempt to give any further account of such systems.

19   Heat and cold being felt by almost every part of the human body, have commonly been ranked along with solidity and resistance, among the qualities which are the objects of Touch. It is not, however, I think, in our language proper to say that we touch, but that we feel, the qualities of heat and cold. The word *feeling*, though in many cases we use it as synonimous to *touching*, has, however, a much more extensive signification, and is frequently employed to denote our internal, as well as our external, affections. We feel hunger and thirst, we feel joy and sorrow, we feel love and hatred.

20   Heat and cold, in reality, though they may frequently be perceived by the same parts of the human body, constitute an order of sensations altogether different from those which are the proper objects of Touch. They are naturally felt, not as pressing upon the organ, but as in the organ. What we feel while we stand in the sunshine during a hot, or in the shade during a frosty, day, is evidently felt, not as pressing upon the body, but as in the body. It does not necessarily suggest the presence of any external object, nor could we from thence alone infer the existence of any such object. It is a sensation which neither does nor can exist any where but either in the organ which feels it, or in

[8] [Notably in *Syntagma Philosophicum*, Part II.]

the unknown principle of perception, whatever that may be, which feels in that organ, or by means of that organ. When we lay our hand upon a table, which is either heated or cooled a good deal beyond the actual temperature of our hand, we have two distinct perceptions: first, that of the solid or resisting table, which is necessarily felt as something external to, and independent of, the hand which feels it: and secondly, that of the heat or cold, which by the contact of the table is excited in our hand, and which is naturally felt as nowhere but in our hand, or in the principle of perception which feels in our hand.[9]

21   But though the sensations of heat and cold do not necessarily suggest the presence of any external object, we soon learn from experience that they are commonly excited by some such object; sometimes by the temperature of some external body immediately in contact with our own body, and sometimes by some body at either a moderate or a great distance from us; as by the fire in a chamber, or by the sun in a Summer's day. By the frequency and uniformity of this experience, by the custom and habit of thought which that frequency and uniformity necessarily occasion, the Internal Sensation, and the External Cause of that Sensation, come in our conception to be so strictly connected, that in our ordinary and careless way of thinking, we are apt to consider them as almost one and the same thing, and therefore denote them by one and the same word. The confusion, however, is in this case more in the word than in the thought; for in reality we still retain some notion of the distinction, though we do not always evolve it with that accuracy which a very slight degree of attention might enable us to do. When we move our hand, for example, along the surface of a very hot or of a very cold table, though we say that the table is hot or cold in every part of it, we never mean that, in any part of it, it feels the sensations either of heat or of cold, but that in every part of it, it possesses the power of exciting one or other of those sensations in our bodies. The philosophers who have taken so much pains to prove that there is no heat in the fire, meaning that the sensation or feeling of heat is not in the fire, have laboured to refute an opinion which the most ignorant of mankind never entertained. But the same word being, in common language, employed to signify both the sensation and the power of exciting that sensation, they, without knowing it perhaps, or intending it, have taken advantage of this ambiguity, and have triumphed in their own superiority, when by irresistible arguments they establish an opinion which, in words indeed, is diametrically opposite to the most obvious

[9] Smith was of course right to separate sensations of heat, etc., from those of touch: separate nervous receptors were later demonstrated.

judgments of mankind, but which in reality is perfectly agreeable to those judgments.

Of the Sense of TASTING

22   WHEN we taste any solid or liquid substance, we have always two distinct perceptions; first, that of the solid or liquid body, which is naturally felt as pressing upon, and therefore as external to, and independent of, the organ which feels it; and secondly, that of the particular taste, relish, or savour which it excites in the palate or organ of Tasting, and which is naturally felt, not as pressing upon, as external to, or as independent of, that organ; but as altogether in the organ, and nowhere but in the organ, or in the principle of perception which feels in that organ. When we say that the food which we eat has an agreeable or disagreeable taste in every part of it, we do not thereby mean that it has the feeling or sensation of taste in any part of it, but that in every part of it, it has the power of exciting that feeling or sensation in our palates. Though in this case we denote by the same word (in the same manner, and for the same reason, as in the case of heat and cold) both the sensation and the power of exciting that sensation, this ambiguity of language misleads the natural judgments of mankind in the one case as little as in the other. Nobody ever fancies that our food feels its own agreeable or disagreeable taste.

Of the Sense of SMELLING

23   EVERY smell or odour is naturally felt as in the nostrils;[10] not as pressing upon or resisting the organ, not as in any respect external to, or independent of, the organ, but as altogether in the organ, and nowhere else but in the organ, or in the principle of perception which feels in that organ. We soon learn from experience, however, that this sensation is commonly excited by some external body; by a flower, for example, of which the absence removes, and the presence brings back, the sensation. This external body we consider as the cause of this sensation, and we denominate by the same words both the sensation and the power by which the external body produces this sensation. But when we say that the smell is in the flower, we do not thereby mean that the flower itself has any feeling of the sensation which we feel; but that it has the power of exciting this sensation in our nostrils, or in the principle of perception which feels in our nostrils. Though the sensation, and the power by which it is excited, are thus denoted by the same word, this ambiguity of language

[10] This is certainly true only in respect of strong odours.

misleads, in this case, the natural judgments of mankind as little as in the two preceding.

Of the Sense of HEARING

24   EVERY sound is naturally felt as in the Ear, the organ of Hearing.[11] Sound is not naturally felt as resisting or pressing upon the organ, or as in any respect external to, or independent of, the organ. We naturally feel it as an affection of our Ear, as something which is altogether in our Ear, and nowhere but in our Ear, or in the principle of perception which feels in our Ear. We soon learn from experience, indeed, that the sensation is frequently excited by bodies at a considerable distance from us; often at a much greater distance than those ever are which excite the sensation of Smelling. We learn too from experience, that this sound or sensation in our Ears receives different modifications, according to the distance and direction of the body which originally causes it. The sensation is stronger, the sound is louder, when that body is near. The sensation is weaker, the sound is lower, when that body is at a distance. The sound, or sensation, too undergoes some variation according as the body is placed on the right hand or on the left, before or behind us. In common language we frequently say, that the sound seems to come from a great or from a small distance, from the right hand or from the left, from before or from behind us. We frequently say too that we hear a sound at a great or a small distance, on our right hand or on our left. The real sound, however, the sensation in our ear, can never be heard or felt any where but in our ear, it can never change its place, it is incapable of motion, and can come, therefore, neither from the right nor from the left, neither from before nor from behind us. The Ear can feel or hear nowhere but where it is, and cannot stretch out its powers of perception, either to a great or to a small distance, either to the right or to the left. By all such phrases we in reality mean nothing but to express our opinion concerning either the distance, or the direction of the body, which excites the sensation of sound. When we say that the sound is in the bell, we do not mean that the bell hears its own sound, or that any thing like our sensation is in the bell, but that it possesses the power of exciting that sensation in our organ of Hearing. Though in this, as well as in some other cases, we express by the same word, both the Sensation, and the Power of exciting that Sensation; this ambiguity of language occasions scarce any confusion in the thought, and when the different meanings of the word are properly

---

[11] An example of 'psychologism'. As a statement of fact it is just plain false. Sensation and inference are reversed. See also §§65, 77, below.

distinguished, the opinions of the vulgar, and those of the philosopher, though apparently opposite, turn out to be exactly the same.

25   These four classes of secondary qualities, as philosophers have called them, or to speak more properly, these four classes of Sensations; Heat and Cold, Taste, Smell, and Sound; being felt, not as resisting or pressing upon the organ; but as in the organ, are not naturally perceived as external and independant substances; or even as qualities of such substances; but as mere affections of the organ, and what can exist nowhere but in the organ.

26   They do not possess, nor can we even conceive them as capable of possessing, any one of the qualities, which we consider as essential to, and inseparable from, the external solid and independant substances.

27   First, They have no extension. They are neither long nor short; they are neither broad nor narrow; they are neither deep nor shallow. The bodies which excite them, the spaces within which they may be perceived, may possess any of those dimensions; but the Sensations themselves can possess none of them. When we say of a Note in Music, that it is long or short, we mean that it is so in point of duration. In point of extension we cannot even conceive, that it should be either the one or the other.

28   Secondly, Those Sensations have no figure. They are neither round nor square, though the bodies which excite them, though the spaces within which they may be perceived, may be either the one or the other.

29   Thirdly, Those Sensations are incapable of motion. The bodies which excite them may be moved to a greater or to a smaller distance. The Sensations become fainter in the one case, and stronger in the other. Those bodies may change their direction with regard to the organ of Sensation. If the change be considerable, the Sensations undergo some sensible variation in consequence of it. But still we never ascribe motion to the Sensations. Even when the person who feels any of those Sensations, and consequently the organ by which he feels them, changes his situation, we never, even in this case, say, that the Sensation moves, or is moved. It seems to exist always, where alone it is capable of existing, in the organ which feels it. We never even ascribe to those Sensations the attribute of rest; because we never say that any thing is at rest, unless we suppose it capable of motion. We never say that any thing does not change its situation with regard to other things, unless we suppose it capable of changing that situation.

30   Fourthly, Those Sensations, as they have no extension, so they can have no divisibility. We cannot even conceive that a degree of Heat or Cold, that a Smell, a Taste, or a Sound, should be divided (in the

same manner as the solid and extended substance may be divided) into two halves, or into four quarters, or into any other number of parts.

31   But though all these Sensations are equally incapable of division; there are three of them, Taste, Smell, and Sound; which seem capable of a certain composition and decomposition. A skilful cook will, by his taste, perhaps, sometimes distinguish the different ingredients, which enter into the composition of a new sauce, and of which the simple tastes make up the compound one of the sauce. A skilful perfumer may, perhaps, sometimes be able to do the same thing with regard to a new Scent. In a concert of vocal and instrumental music, an acute and experienced Ear readily distinguishes all the different sounds which strike upon it at the same time, and which may, therefore, be considered as making up one compound sound.

32   Is it by nature, or by experience, that we learn to distinguish between simple and compound Sensations of this kind? I am disposed to believe that it is altogether by experience; and that naturally all Tastes, Smells, and Sounds, which affect the organ of Sensation at the same time, are felt as simple and uncompounded Sensations. It is altogether by experience, I think, that we learn to observe the different affinities and resemblances which the compound Sensation bears to the different simple ones, which compose it, and to judge that the different causes, which naturally excite those different simple Sensations, enter into the composition of that cause which excites the compounded one.

33   It is sufficiently evident that this composition and decomposition is altogether different from that union and separation of parts, which constitutes the divisibility of solid extension.

34   The Sensations of Heat and Cold seem incapable even of this species of composition and decomposition. The Sensations of Heat and Cold may be stronger at one time and weaker at another. They may differ in degree, but they cannot differ in kind. The Sensations of Taste, Smell, and Sound, frequently differ, not only in degree, but in kind. They are not only stronger and weaker, but some Tastes are sweet and some bitter; some Smells are agreeable, and some offensive; some Sounds are acute, and some grave; and each of these different kinds or qualities too is capable of an immense variety of different modifications. It is the combination of such simple Sensations, as differ not only in degree but in kind, which constitutes the compounded Sensation.

35   These four classes of Sensations, therefore, having none of the qualities which are essential to, and inseparable from, the solid, external, and independant substances which excite them, cannot be

qualities or modifications of those substances. In reality we do not naturally consider them as such; though in the way in which we express ourselves on the subject, there is frequently a good deal of ambiguity and confusion. When the different meanings of words, however, are fairly distinguished, these Sensations are, even by the most ignorant and illiterate, understood to be, not the qualities, but merely the effects of the solid, external, and independant substances upon the sensible and living organ, or upon the principle of perception which feels in that organ.

36 Philosophers, however, have not in general supposed that those exciting bodies produce those Sensations immediately, but by the intervention of one, two, or more intermediate causes.

37 In the Sensation of Taste, for example, though the exciting body presses upon the organ of Sensation, this pressure is not supposed to be the immediate cause of the Sensation of Taste. Certain juices of the exciting body are supposed to enter the pores of the palate, and to excite, in the irritable and sensible fibres of that organ, certain motions or vibrations, which produce there the Sensation of Taste. But how those juices should excite such motions, or how such motions should produce, either in the organ, or in the principle of perception which feels in the organ, the Sensation of Taste; or a Sensation, which not only does not bear the smallest resemblance to any motion, but which itself seems incapable of all motion, no philosopher has yet attempted, nor probably ever will attempt to explain to us.

38 The Sensations of Heat and Cold, of Smell and Sound, are frequently excited by bodies at a distance, sometimes at a great distance, from the organ which feels them. But it is a very antient and well-established axiom in metaphysics, that nothing can act where it is not;[12] and this axiom, it must, I think, be acknowledged, is at least perfectly agreeable to our natural and usual habits of thinking.

39 The Sun, the great source of both Heat and Light, is at an immense distance from us. His rays, however, (traversing, with inconceivable rapidity, the immensity of the intervening regions,) as they convey the Sensation of Light to our eyes, so they convey that of Heat to all the sensible parts of our body. They even convey the power of exciting that Sensation to all the other bodies that surround us. They warm the earth, and air, we say; that is, they convey to the earth and the air the power of exciting that Sensation in our bodies. A common fire produces, in the same manner, all the same effects; though the sphere of its action is confined within much narrower limits.

40 The odoriferous body, which is generally too at some distance from us, is supposed to act upon our organs by means of certain small

[12] But apparently this does not apply to gravity. See the editor's Introduction, 21-2.

particles of matter, called Effluvia, which being sent forth in all possible directions, and drawn into our nostrils by the inspiration of breathing, produce there the Sensation of Smell. The minuteness of those small particles of matter, however, must surpass all human comprehension. Inclose in a gold box, for a few hours, a small quantity of musk. Take out the musk, and clean the box with soap and water as carefully as it is possible. Nothing can be supposed to remain in the box, but such effluvia as, having penetrated into its interior pores, may have escaped the effects of this cleansing. The box, however, will retain the smell of musk for many, I do not know for how many years; and these effluvia, how minute soever we may suppose them, must have had the powers of subdividing themselves, and of emitting other effluvia of the same kind, continually, and without any interruption, during so long a period. The nicest balance, however, which human art has been able to invent, will not show the smallest increase of weight in the box immediately after it has been thus carefully cleaned.

41   The Sensation of Sound is frequently felt at a much greater distance from the sounding, than that of Smell ever is from the odoriferous body. The vibrations of the sounding body, however, are supposed to produce certain correspondent vibrations and pulses in the surrounding atmosphere, which being propagated in all directions, reach our organ of Hearing, and produce there the Sensation of Sound. There are not many philosophical doctrines, perhaps, established upon a more probable foundation, than that of the propagation of Sound by means of the pulses or vibrations of the air. The experiment of the bell, which, in an exhausted receiver, produces no sensible Sound, would alone render this doctrine somewhat more than probable. But this great probability is still further confirmed by the computations of Sir Isaac Newton,[13] who has shown that, what is called the velocity of Sound, or the time which passes between the commencement of the action of the sounding body, and that of the Sensation in our ear, is perfectly suitable to the velocity with which the pulses and vibrations of an elastic fluid of the same density with the air, are naturally propagated. Dr. Franklin has made objections to this doctrine, but, I think, without success.[14]

42   Such are the intermediate causes by which philosophers have endeavoured to connect the Sensations in our organs, with the distant

[13] *Principia*, Book II, Section 8. Newton's result was of the right *order* only. By assuming volume changes to be at constant temperature (isothermal) instead of at constant heat-content (adiabatic), he failed to apply the appropriate law. This was corrected by Laplace in *Annales de Chimie et de Physique*, iii (1816), 20.

[14] [Benjamin Franklin, *Experiments and Observations on Electricity, made at Philadelphia* (1751).]

bodies which excite them. How those intermediate causes, by the different motions and vibrations which they may be supposed to excite on our organs, produce there those different Sensations, none of which bear the smallest resemblance to vibration or motion of any kind, no philosopher has yet attempted to explain to us.

Of the Sense of SEEING

43   DR. BERKLEY,[15] in his New Theory of Vision, one of the finest examples of philosophical analysis that is to be found, either in our own, or in any other language, has explained, so very distinctly, the nature of the objects of Sight: their dissimilitude to, as well as their correspondence and connection with those of Touch, that I have scarcely any thing to add to what he has already done. It is only in order to render some things, which I shall have occasion to say hereafter, intelligible to such readers as may not have had an opportunity of studying his book, that I have presumed to treat of the same subject, after so great a Master. Whatever I shall say upon it, if not directly borrowed from him, has at least been suggested by what he has already said.

44   That the objects of Sight are not perceived as resisting or pressing upon the organ which perceives them, is sufficiently obvious. They cannot therefore suggest, at least in the same manner, as the objects of Touch, the externality and independency of their existence.

45   We are apt, however, to imagine that we see objects at a distance from us, and that consequently the externality of their existence is immediately perceived by our Sight. But if we consider that the distance of any object from the eye, is a line turned endways to it; and that this line must consequently appear to it, but as one point; we shall be sensible that distance from the eye cannot be the immediate object of Sight, but that all visible objects must naturally be perceived as close upon the organ, or more properly, perhaps, like all other Sensations, as in the organ which perceives them.[16] That the objects of Sight are all painted in the bottom of the eye, upon a membrane called the *retina*, pretty much in the same manner as the like objects are painted in a Camera Obscura, is well known to whoever has the slightest tincture of the science of Optics; and the principle of perception, it is probable, originally perceives them, as existing in

[15] Smith uses this spelling throughout. The *Essay towards a New Theory of Vision* appeared in 1709, the *Principles of Human Knowledge* in 1710. Smith seems to take no account of the radical 'immaterialism' of the latter; there is no evidence that he ever read it. [Smith did, however, own a copy of Berkeley's *Works*.]

[16] Confusion between 'seeing' (which we are said to 'imagine'—an ambiguous word still productive of more fundamental confusions—see the editor's Introduction, 14–15) and the inference from analysis. Cf. § 53 below, 'seem to float'.

that part of the organ, and nowhere but in that part of the organ. No Optician, accordingly, no person who has ever bestowed any moderate degree of attention upon the nature of Vision, has ever pretended that distance from the eye was the immediate object of Sight. How it is that, by means of our Sight, we learn to judge of such distances, Opticians have endeavoured to explain in several different ways. I shall not, however, at present, stop to examine their systems.

46   The objects of Touch are solidity, and those modifications of solidity which we consider as essential to it, and inseparable from it; solid extension, figure, divisibility, and mobility.

47   The objects of Sight are colour, and those modifications of colour which, in the same manner, we consider as essential to it, and inseparable from it; coloured extension, figure, divisibility, and mobility. When we open our eyes, the sensible coloured objects, which present themselves to us, must all have a certain extension, or must occupy a certain portion of the visible surface which appears before us. They must too have all a certain figure, or must be bounded by certain visible lines, which mark upon that surface the extent of their respective dimensions. Every sensible portion of this visible or coloured extension must be conceived as divisible, or as separable into two, three, or more parts. Every portion too of this visible or coloured surface must be conceived as moveable, or as capable of changing its situation, and of assuming a different arrangement with regard to the other portions of the same surface.

48   Colour, the visible, bears no resemblance to solidity, the tangible object. A man born blind, or who has lost his Sight so early as to have no remembrance of visible objects, can form no idea or conception of colour. Touch alone can never help him to it. I have heard, indeed, of some persons who had lost their Sight after the age of manhood, and who had learned to distinguish, by the Touch alone, the different colours of cloths or silks, the goods which it happened to be their business to deal in. The powers by which different bodies excite in the organs of Sight the Sensations of different colours, probably depend upon some difference in the nature, configuration, and arrangement of the parts which compose their respective surfaces. This difference may, to a very nice and delicate touch, make some difference in the feeling, sufficient to enable a person, much interested in the case, to make this distinction in some degree, though probably in a very imperfect and inaccurate one. A man born blind might possibly be taught to make the same distinctions. But though he might thus be able to name the different colours, which those different surfaces reflected, though he might thus have some imperfect notion of the remote causes of these Sensations, he could

have no better idea of the Sensations themselves, than that other blind man, mentioned by Mr. Locke,[17] had, who said that he imagined the Colour of Scarlet resembled the Sound of a Trumpet. A man born deaf may, in the same manner, be taught to speak articulately. He is taught how to shape and dispose of his organs, so as to pronounce each letter, syllable, and word. But still, though he may have some imperfect idea of the remote causes of the Sounds which he himself utters, of the remote causes of the Sensations which he himself excites in other people; he can have none of those Sounds or Sensations themselves.

49   If it were possible, in the same manner, that a man could be born without the Sense of Touching, that of Seeing could never alone suggest to him the idea of Solidity, or enable him to form any notion of the external and resisting substance. It is probable, however, not only that no man, but that no animal was ever born without the Sense of Touching, which seems essential to, and inseparable from, the nature of animal life and existence. It is unnecessary, therefore, to throw away any reasoning, or to hazard any conjectures, about what might be the effects of what I look upon as altogether an impossible supposition. The eye when pressed upon by any external and solid substance, feels, no doubt, that pressure and resistance, and suggests to us (in the same manner as every other feeling part of the body) the external and independent existence of that solid substance. But in this case, the eye acts, not as the organ of Sight, but as an organ of Touch; for the eye possesses the Sense of Touching in common with almost all the other parts of the body.

50   The extension, figure, divisibility, and mobility of Colour, the sole object of Sight, though, on account of their correspondence and connection with the extension, figure, divisibility, and mobility of Solidity, they are called by the same name, yet seem to bear no sort of resemblance to their namesakes. As Colour and Solidity bear no sort of resemblance to one another, so neither can their respective modifications. Dr. Berkley very justly observes,[18] that though we can conceive either a coloured or a solid line to be prolonged indefinitely, yet we cannot conceive the one to be added to the other. We cannot, even in imagination, conceive an object of Touch to be prolonged into an object of Sight, or an object of Sight into an object of Touch. The objects of Sight and those of Touch constitute two worlds, which, though they have a most important correspondence and connection with one another, bear no sort of resemblance to one another. The tangible world, as well as all the different parts which compose it, has three dimensions, Length, Breadth, and Depth. The visible world, as

[17] [*Human Understanding*, III.iv.11.]   [18] [*New Theory of Vision*, § 131.]

well as all the different parts which compose it, has only two, Length and Breadth. It presents to us only a plain or surface, which, by certain shades and combinations of Colour, suggests and represents to us (in the same manner as a picture does) certain tangible objects which have no Colour, and which therefore can bear no resemblance to those shades and combinations of Colour. Those shades and combinations suggest those different tangible objects as at different distances, according to certain rules of Perspective, which it is, perhaps, not very easy to say how it is that we learn, whether by some particular instinct, or by some application of either reason or experience, which has become so perfectly habitual to us, that we are scarcely sensible when we make use of it.

51   The distinctness of this Perspective, the precision and accuracy with which, by means of it, we are capable of judging concerning the distance of different tangible objects, is greater or less, exactly in proportion as this distinctness, as this precision and accuracy are of more or less importance to us. We can judge of the distance of near objects, of the chairs and tables, for example, in the chamber where we are sitting, with the most perfect precision and accuracy; and if in broad day-light we ever stumble over any of them, it must be, not from any error in the Sight, but from some defect in the attention. The precision and accuracy of our judgment concerning such near objects are of the utmost importance to us, and constitute the great advantage which a man who sees has over one who is unfortunately blind. As the distance increases, the distinctness of this Perspective, the precision and accuracy of our judgment gradually diminish. Of the tangible objects which are even at the moderate distance of one, two, or three miles from the eye, we are frequently at a loss to determine which is nearest, and which remotest. It is seldom of much importance to us to judge with precision concerning the situation of the tangible objects which are even at this moderate distance. As the distance increases, our judgments become more and more uncertain; and at a very great distance, such as that of the fixed stars, it becomes altogether uncertain. The most precise knowledge of the relative situation of such objects could be of no other use to us than to satisfy the most unnecessary curiosity.

52   The distances at which different men can by Sight distinguish, with some degree of precision, the situation of the tangible objects which the visible ones represent, is very different; and this difference, though it, no doubt, may sometimes depend upon some difference in the original configuration of their eyes, yet seems frequently to arise altogether from the different customs and habits which their respective occupations have led them to contract. Men of letters, who

live much in their closets, and have seldom occasion to look at very distant objects, are seldom far-sighted. Mariners, on the contrary, almost always are; those especially who have made many distant voyages, in which they have been the greater part of their time out of sight of land, and have in day-light been constantly looking out towards the horizon for the appearance of some ship, or of some distant shore. It often astonishes a land-man to observe with what precision a sailor can distinguish in the Offing, not only the appearance of a ship, which is altogether invisible to the land-man, but the number of her masts, the direction of her course, and the rate of her sailing. If she is a ship of his acquaintance, he frequently can tell her name, before the land-man has been able to discover even the appearance of a ship.

53   Visible objects, Colour, and all its different modifications, are in themselves mere shadows or pictures, which seem to float, as it were, before the organ of Sight. In themselves, and independent of their connection with the tangible objects which they represent, they are of no importance to us, and can essentially neither benefit us nor hurt us. Even while we see them we are seldom thinking of them. Even when we appear to be looking at them with the greatest earnestness, our whole attention is frequently employed, not upon them, but upon the tangible objects represented by them.

54   It is because almost our whole attention is employed, not upon the visible and representing, but upon the tangible and represented objects, that in our imaginations we are apt to ascribe to the former a degree of magnitude which does not belong to them, but which belongs altogether to the latter. If you shut one eye, and hold immediately before the other a small circle of plain glass, of not more than half an inch in diameter, you may see through that circle the most extensive prospects; lawns and woods, and arms of the sea, and distant mountains. You are apt to imagine that the Landscape which is thus presented to you, that the visible Picture which you thus see, is immensely great and extensive. The tangible objects which this visible Picture represents, undoubtedly are so. But the visible Picture which represents them can be no greater than the little visible circle through which you see it. If while you are looking through this circle, you could conceive a fairy hand and a fairy pencil to come between your eye and the glass, that pencil could delineate upon that little glass the outline of all those extensive lawns and woods, and arms of the sea, and distant mountains, in the full and exact dimensions with which they are really seen by the eye.[19]

[19] [Cf. TMS III.3.2, where Smith compares the role of imagination in perception and in moral judgement: 'In my present situation an immense landscape of lawns, and woods, and

55 Every visible object which covers from the eye any other visible object, must appear at least as large as that other visible object. It must occupy at least an equal portion of that visible plain or surface which is at that time presented to the eye. Opticians accordingly tell us, that all the visible objects which are seen under equal angles must to the eye appear equally large. But the visible object, which covers from the eye any other visible object, must necessarily be seen under angles at least equally large as those under which that other object is seen. When I hold up my finger, however, before my eye, it appears to cover the greater part of the visible chamber in which I am sitting. It should therefore appear as large as the greater part of that visible chamber. But because I know that the tangible finger bears but a very small proportion to the greater part of the tangible chamber, I am apt to fancy that the visible finger bears but a like proportion to the greater part of the visible chamber. My judgment corrects my eyesight, and, in my fancy, reduces the visible object, which represents the little tangible one, below its real visible dimensions; and, on the contrary, it augments the visible object which represents the great tangible one a good deal beyond those dimensions. My attention being generally altogether occupied about the tangible and represented, and not at all about the visible and representing objects, my careless fancy bestows upon the latter a proportion which does not in the least belong to them, but which belongs altogether to the former.

56 It is because the visible object which covers any other visible object must always appear at least as large as that other object, that Opticians tell us that the sphere of our vision appears to the eye always equally large; and that when we hold our hand before our eye in such a manner that we see nothing but the inside of the hand, we still see precisely the same number of visible points, the sphere of our vision is still as completely filled, the retina is as entirely covered with the object which is thus presented to it, as when we survey the most extensive horizon.

57 A young gentleman who was born with a cataract upon each of his eyes was, in one thousand seven hundred and twenty-eight, couched by Mr. Cheselden,[20] and by that means for the first time made to see

distant mountains, seems to do no more than cover the little window which I write by'. (In the first printing of the Glasgow edition of TMS, 135, the word 'mountains' is incorrectly given as 'mountain'.) Smith goes on to say that a man must know something of 'the philosophy of vision' to appreciate these matters. It seems probable that the TMS passage recalls the present one rather than vice versa, and this tends to confirm the hypothesis (editor's Introduction, 133) of an early date for the composition of this essay.]

20 William Cheselden (or Chesselden) (1688–1752), the most distinguished British surgeon before John Hunter. This famous case-history effectually answered the question put to Locke by William Molyneux (1656–98) after he had read the first edition of Locke's *Human Understanding*, viz. could a person born blind, whose sight was subsequently restored, be able, by sight alone, to distinguish and identify objects already familiar to him by touch? For a full

(*continued*)

distinctly. 'At first,' says the operator, 'he could bear but very little
Sight, and the things he saw he thought extremely large; but upon
seeing things larger, those first seen he conceived less, never being
able to imagine any lines beyond the bounds he saw; the room he was
in, he said, he knew to be but part of the house, yet he could not
conceive that the whole house would look bigger.'21 It was
unavoidable that he should at first conceive, that no visible object
could be greater, could present to his eye a greater number of visible
points, or could more completely fill the comprehension of that organ,
than the narrowest sphere of his vision. And when that sphere came
to be enlarged, he still could not conceive that the visible objects
which it presented could be larger than those which he had first seen.
He must probably by this time have been in some degree habituated
to the connection between visible and tangible objects, and enabled
to conceive that visible object to be small which represented a small
tangible object; and that to be great, which represented a great one.
The great objects did not appear to his Sight greater than the small
ones had done before; but the small ones, which, having filled the
whole sphere of his vision, had before appeared as large as possible,
being now known to represent much smaller tangible objects, seemed
in his conception to grow smaller. He had begun now to employ his
attention more about the tangible and represented, than about the
visible and representing objects; and he was beginning to ascribe to
the latter, the proportions and dimensions which properly belonged
altogether to the former.

58   As we frequently ascribe to the objects of Sight a magnitude and
proportion which does not really belong to them, but to the objects of
Touch which they represent, so we likewise ascribe to them a
steadiness of appearance, which as little belongs to them, but which
they derive altogether from their connection with the same objects of
Touch. The chair which now stands at the farther end of the room,
I am apt to imagine, appears to my eye as large as it did when it stood
close by me, when it was seen under angles at least four times larger

discussion see A. D. Ritchie, *George Berkeley, a Reappraisal* (ed. G. E. Davie, 1967), 13–18.
[Locke reports Molyneux's query in *Human Understanding*, II.ix.8. See also the note by A. S.
Pringle-Pattison on the passage in his abridged edition of the work (1924), 75.
    Smith's quotations, here and in §§63 ff. below, are from 'An Account of Some Observations
made by a young Gentleman, who was born blind, or lost his Sight so early, that he had no
Remembrance of ever having seen, and who was couch'd between 13 and 14 Years of Age.' By
Mr Will. Chesselden, F.R.S. Surgeon to Her Majesty, and to St. Thomas's Hospital.
Philosophical Transactions, xxxv (1727–8), 447–50, 451–2. H. Mizuta, *Adam Smith's Library*, 45–
6, lists Smith's extensive holdings of this work, including 'The philosophical transactions.
From the year 1720 to the year 1723, abridged, and disposed under general heads, by Reid and
Gray ... London 1733.']
    21 [Op. cit., 449. Here, as in the remainder of the quotations from this source, Smith has
'modernized' the spelling and punctuation.]

than those under which it is seen at present, and when it must have occupied, at least, sixteen times that portion which it occupies at present, of the visible plain or surface which is now before my eyes. But as I know that the magnitude of the tangible and represented chair, the principal object of my attention, is the same in both situations, I ascribe to the visible and representing chair (though now reduced to less than the sixteenth part of its former dimensions) a steadiness of appearance, which certainly belongs not in any respect to it, but altogether to the tangible and represented one. As we approach to, or retire from, the tangible object which any visible one represents, the visible object gradually augments in the one case, and diminishes in the other. To speak accurately, it is not the same visible object which we see at different distances, but a succession of visible objects, which, though they all resemble one another, those especially which follow near after one another; yet are all really different and distinct. But as we know that the tangible object which they represent remains always the same, we ascribe to them too a sameness which belongs altogether to it: and we fancy that we see the same tree at a mile, at half a mile, and at a few yards distance. At those different distances, however, the visible objects are so very widely different, that we are sensible of a change in their appearance. But still, as the tangible object which they represent remains invariably the same, we ascribe a sort of sameness even to them too.

59   It has been said, that no man ever saw the same visible object twice; and this, though, no doubt, an exaggeration, is, in reality, much less so than at first view it appears to be. Though I am apt to fancy that all the chairs and tables, and other little pieces of furniture in the room where I am sitting, appear to my eye always the same, yet their appearance is in reality continually varying, not only according to every variation in their situation and distance with regard to where I am sitting, but according to every, even the most insensible variation in the attitude[22] of my body, in the movement of my head, or even in that of my eyes. The perspective necessarily varies according to all, even the smallest of these variations; and consequently the appearance of the objects which that perspective presents to me. Observe what difficulty a portrait painter finds, in getting the person who sits for his picture to present to him precisely that view of the countenance from which the first outline was drawn. The painter is scarce ever completely satisfied with the situation of the face which is presented to him, and finds that it is scarcely ever precisely the same with that from which he rapidly sketched the first outline. He endeavours, as well as he can, to correct the difference from memory, from fancy,

[22] [The text of the original edition has 'altitude', presumably a printer's error.]

and from a sort of art of approximation, by which he strives to express as nearly as he can, the ordinary effect of the look, air, and character of the person whose picture he is drawing. The person who draws from a statue, which is altogether immoveable, feels a difficulty, though, no doubt, in a less degree, of the same kind. It arises altogether from the difficulty which he finds in placing his own eye precisely in the same situation during the whole time which he employs in completing his drawing. This difficulty is more than doubled upon the painter who draws from a living subject. The statue never is the cause of any variation or unsteadiness in its own appearance. The living subject frequently is.

60   The benevolent purpose of nature in bestowing upon us the sense of seeing, is evidently to inform us concerning the situation and distance of the tangible objects which surround us. Upon the knowledge of this distance and situation depends the whole conduct of human life, in the most trifling as well as in the most important transactions. Even animal motion depends upon it; and without it we could neither move, nor even sit still, with complete security. The objects of sight, as Dr. Berkley finely observes,[23] constitute a sort of language which the Author of Nature addresses to our eyes, and by which he informs us of many things, which it is of the utmost importance to us to know. As, in common language, the words or sounds bear no resemblance to the things which they denote, so, in this other language, the visible objects bear no sort of resemblance to the tangible object which they represent, and of whose relative situation, with regard both to ourselves and to one another, they inform us.

61   He acknowledges,[24] however, that though scarcely any word be by nature better fitted to express one meaning than any other meaning, yet that certain visible objects are better fitted than others to represent certain tangible objects. A visible square, for example, is better fitted than a visible circle to represent a tangible square. There is, perhaps, strictly speaking, no such thing as either a visible cube, or a visible globe, the objects of sight being all naturally presented to the eye as upon one surface. But still there are certain combinations of colours which are fitted to represent to the eye, both the near and the distant, both the advancing and the receding lines, angles, and surfaces of the tangible cube; and there are others fitted to represent, in the same

---

[23] [*New Theory of Vision*, § 147.] The paragraphs that follow in Smith's essay are perhaps the most important for the further consideration of his views on language and his general approach to the nature of 'philosophical investigation'. [Smith's 'Considerations Concerning the First Formation of Languages' was first published in 1761. The subject is also considered in LRBL, lecture 3.]

[24] [§§ 142, 152.]

manner, both the near and the receding surface of the tangible globe. The combination which represents the tangible cube, would not be fit to represent the tangible globe; and that which represents the tangible globe, would not be fit to represent the tangible cube. Though there may, therefore, be no resemblance between visible and tangible objects, there seems to be some affinity or correspondence between them sufficient to make each visible object fitter to represent a certain precise tangible object than any other tangible object. But the greater part of words seem to have no sort of affinity or correspondence with the meanings or ideas which they express; and if custom had so ordered it, they might with equal propriety have been made use of to express any other meanings or ideas.

62   Dr. Berkley, with that happiness of illustration which scarcely ever deserts him, remarks,[25] that this in reality is no more than what happens in common language; and that though letters bear no sort of resemblance to the words which they denote, yet that the same combination of letters which represents one word, would not always be fit to represent another; and that each word is always best represented by its own proper combination of letters. The comparison, however, it must be observed, is here totally changed. The connection between visible and tangible objects was first illustrated by comparing it with that between spoken language and the meanings or ideas which spoken language suggests to us; and it is now illustrated by the connection between written language and spoken language, which is altogether different. Even this second illustration, besides, will not apply perfectly to the case. When custom, indeed, has perfectly ascertained the powers of each letter; when it has ascertained, for example, that the first letter of the alphabet shall always represent such a sound, and the second letter such another sound; each word comes then to be more properly represented by one certain combination of written letters or characters, than it could be by any other combination. But still the characters themselves are altogether arbitrary, and have no sort of affinity or correspondence with the articulate sounds which they denote. The character which marks the first letter of the alphabet, for example, if custom had so ordered it, might, with perfect propriety, have been made use of to express the sound which we now annex to the second, and the character of the second to express that which we now annex to the first. But the

[25] [Smith is referring to *New Theory of Vision*, § 143, but does not bring out Berkeley's point clearly enough. Berkeley's argument is that visible figures represent tangible figures as written words represent sounds: it is arbitrary that written letters should represent sounds, but if letters are used for that purpose, the particular combination of letters in a written word must have a certain correlation with the elements of the sound represented. Smith's criticism is not impaired by his compression of Berkeley's argument.]

visible characters which represent to our eyes the tangible globe, could not so well represent the tangible cube; nor could those which represent the tangible cube, so properly represent the tangible globe. There is evidently, therefore, a certain affinity and correspondence between each visible object and the precise tangible object represented by it, much superior to what takes place either between written and spoken language, or between spoken language and the ideas or meanings which it suggests. The language which nature addresses to our eyes, has evidently a fitness of representation, an aptitude for signifying the precise things which it denotes, much superior to that of any of the artificial languages which human art and ingenuity have ever been able to invent.

63   That this affinity and correspondence, however, between visible and tangible objects could not alone, and without the assistance of observation and experience, teach us, by any effort of reason, to infer what was the precise tangible object which each visible one represented, if it is not sufficiently evident from what has been already said, it must be completely so from the remarks of Mr. Cheselden upon the young gentleman above-mentioned, whom he had couched for a cataract. 'Though we say of this gentleman, that he was blind,' observes Mr. Cheselden, 'as we do of all people who have ripe cataracts; yet they are never so blind from that cause but that they can discern day from night; and for the most part, in a strong light, distinguish black, white, and scarlet; but they cannot perceive the shape of any thing; for the light by which these perceptions are made, being let in obliquely through the aqueous humour, or the anterior surface of the crystalline, (by which the rays cannot be brought into a focus upon the retina,) they can discern in no other manner than a sound eye can through a glass of broken jelly, where a great variety of surfaces so differently refract the light, that the several distinct pencils of rays cannot be collected by the eye into their proper foci; wherefore the shape of an object in such a case cannot be at all discerned, though the colour may: and thus it was with this young gentleman, who, though he knew those colours asunder in a good light, yet when he saw them after he was couched, the faint ideas he had of them before were not sufficient for him to know them by afterwards; and therefore he did not think them the same which he had before known by those names.'[26] This young gentleman, therefore, had some advantage over one who from a state of total blindness had been made for the first time to see. He had some imperfect notion of the distinction of colours; and he must have

[26] ['Account of Observations', 447–8. The original has 'the gentleman', not 'this gentleman', at the beginning of the quotation, and 'these colours', not 'those colours', later.]

known that those colours had some sort of connection with the tangible objects which he had been accustomed to feel. But had he emerged from total blindness, he could have learnt this connection only from a very long course of observation and experience. How little this advantage availed him, however, we may learn partly from the passages of Mr. Cheselden's narrative, already quoted, and still more from the following:

64   'When he first saw,' says that ingenious operator, 'he was so far from making any judgment about distances, that he thought all objects whatever touched his eyes (as he expressed it) as what he felt did his skin; and thought no objects so agreeable as those which were smooth and regular, though he could form no judgment of their shape, or guess what it was in any object that was pleasing to him. He knew not the shape of any thing, nor any one thing from another, however different in shape or magnitude; but upon being told what things were, whose form he before knew from feeling, he would carefully observe, that he might know them again; but having too many objects to learn at once, he forgot many of them; and (as he said) at first learned to know, and again forgot a thousand things in a day. One particular only (though it may appear trifling) I will relate: Having often forgot which was the cat, and which the dog, he was ashamed to ask; but catching the cat (which he knew by feeling) he was observed to look at her stedfastly, and then setting her down, said, So, puss! I shall know you another time.'[27]

65   When the young gentleman said, that the objects which he saw touched his eyes, he certainly could not mean that they pressed upon or resisted his eyes; for the objects of sight never act upon the organ in any way that resembles pressure or resistance. He could mean no more than that they were close upon his eyes, or, to speak more properly, perhaps, that they were in his eyes. A deaf man, who was made all at once to hear, might in the same manner naturally enough say, that the sounds which he heard touched his ears, meaning that he felt them as close upon his ears, or, to speak, perhaps, more properly, as in his ears.

66   Mr. Cheselden adds afterwards: 'We thought he soon knew what pictures represented which were shewed to him, but we found afterwards we were mistaken; for about two months after he was couched, he discovered at once they represented solid bodies, when, to that time, he considered them only as party-coloured planes, or surfaces diversified with variety of paints; but even then he was no less surprised, expecting the pictures would feel like the things they represented, and was amazed when he found those parts, which by

[27] [448.]

their light and shadow appeared now round and uneven, felt only flat like the rest; and asked which was the lying sense, feeling or seeing?'[28]

67   Painting, though, by combinations of light and shade, similar to those which Nature makes use of in the visible objects which she presents to our eyes, it endeavours to imitate those objects; yet it never has been able to equal the perspective of Nature, or to give to its productions that force and distinctness of relief and projection which Nature bestows upon hers. When the young gentleman was just beginning to understand the strong and distinct perspective of Nature, the faint and feeble perspective of Painting made no impression upon him, and the picture appeared to him what it really was, a plain surface bedaubed with different colours. When he became more familiar with the perspective of Nature, the inferiority of that of Painting did not hinder him from discovering its resemblance to that of Nature. In the perspective of Nature, he had always found that the situation and distance of the tangible and represented objects, corresponded exactly to what the visible and representing ones suggested to him. He expected to find the same thing in the similar, though inferior perspective of Painting, and was disappointed when he found that the visible and tangible objects had not, in this case, their usual correspondence.

68   'In a year after seeing,' adds Mr. Cheselden, 'the young gentleman being carried upon Epsom-downs, and observing a large prospect, he was exceedingly delighted with it, and called it a new kind of seeing.'[29] He had now, it is evident, come to understand completely the language of Vision. The visible objects which this noble prospect presented to him did not now appear as touching, or as close upon his eye. They did not now appear of the same magnitude with those small objects to which, for some time after the operation, he had been accustomed, in the little chamber where he was confined. Those new visible objects at once, and as it were of their own accord, assumed both the distance and the magnitude of the great tangible objects which they represented. He had now, therefore, it would seem, become completely master of the language of Vision, and he had become so in the course of a year; a much shorter period than that in which any person, arrived at the age of manhood, could completely acquire any foreign language. It would appear too, that he had made very considerable progress even in the two first months. He began at that early period to understand even the feeble perspective of Painting; and though at first he could not distinguish it from the

---

[28] [449. The original has 'paint', not 'paints'.]

[29] ['Account of Observations', 450. The original reads: 'A year after first seeing, being carried upon Epsom-downs ...']

strong perspective of Nature, yet he could not have been thus imposed upon by so imperfect an imitation, if the great principles of Vision had not beforehand been deeply impressed upon his mind, and if he had not, either by the association of ideas, or by some other unknown principle, been strongly determined to expect certain tangible objects in consequence of the visible ones which had been presented to him. This rapid progress, however, may, perhaps, be accounted for from that fitness of representation, which has already been taken notice of, between visible and tangible objects. In this language of Nature, it may be said, the analogies are more perfect; the etymologies, the declensions, and conjugations, if one may say so, are more regular than those of any human language. The rules are fewer, and those rules admit of no exceptions.

69 But though it may have been altogether by the slow paces of observation and experience that this young gentleman acquired the knowledge of the connection between visible and tangible objects; we cannot from thence with certainty infer, that young children have not some instinctive perception of the same kind. In him this instinctive power, not having been exerted at the proper season, may, from disuse, have gone gradually to decay, and at last have been completely obliterated. Or, perhaps, (what seems likewise very possible,) some feeble and unobserved remains of it may have somewhat facilitated his acquisition of what he might otherwise have found it much more difficult to acquire.

70 That, antecedent to all experience, the young of at least the greater part of animals possess some instinctive perception of this kind, seems abundantly evident. The hen never feeds her young by dropping the food into their bills, as the linnet and the thrush feed theirs. Almost as soon as her chickens are hatched, she does not feed them, but carries them to the field to feed, where they walk about at their ease, it would seem, and appear to have the most distinct perception of all the tangible objects which surround them. We may often see them, accordingly, by the straightest road, run to and pick up any little grains which she shews them, even at the distance of several yards; and they no sooner come into the light than they seem to understand this language of Vision as well as they ever do afterwards. The young of the partridge and of the grouse seem to have, at the same early period, the most distinct perceptions of the same kind. The young partridge, almost as soon it comes from the shell, runs about among long grass and corn; the young grouse among long heath, and would both most essentially hurt themselves if they had not the most acute, as well as distinct perception of the tangible objects which not only surround them but press upon them on all sides. This is the case too

with the young of the goose, of the duck, and, so far as I have been able to observe,[30] with those of at least the greater part of the birds which make their nests upon the ground, with the greater part of those which are ranked by Linnaeus in the orders of the hen and the goose, and of many of those long-shanked and wading birds which he places in the order that he distinguishes by the name of Grallae.[31]

71   The young of those birds that build their nests in bushes, upon trees, in the holes and crevices of high walls, upon high rocks and precipices, and other places of difficult access; of the greater part of those ranked by Linnaeus in the orders of the hawk, the magpie, and the sparrow, seem to come blind from the shell, and to continue so for at least some days thereafter. Till they are able to fly they are fed by the joint labour of both parents. As soon as that period arrives, however, and probably for some time before, they evidently enjoy all the powers of Vision in the most complete perfection, and can distinguish with most exact precision the shape and proportion of the tangible objects which every visible one represents. In so short a period they cannot be supposed to have acquired those powers from experience, and must therefore derive them from some instinctive suggestion. The sight of birds seems to be both more prompt and more acute than that of any other animals. Without hurting themselves they dart into the thickest and most thorny bushes, fly with the utmost rapidity through the most intricate forests, and while they are soaring aloft in the air, discover upon the ground the little insects and grains upon which they feed.

72   The young of several sorts of quadrupeds seem, like those of the greater part of birds which make their nests upon the ground, to enjoy as soon as they come into the world the faculty of seeing as completely as they ever do afterwards. The day, or the day after they are dropt, the calf follows the cow, and the foal the mare, to the field; and though from timidity they seldom remove far from the mother, yet they seem to walk about at their ease; which they could not do unless they could distinguish, with some degree of precision, the shape and proportion of the tangible objects which each visible one represents. The degree of precision, however, with which the horse is capable of making this distinction, seems at no period of his life to be very complete. He is at all times apt to startle at many visible objects, which, if they distinctly suggested to him the real shape and proportion of the tangible objects which they represent, could not be the objects of fear; at the trunk or root of an old tree, for example,

[30] The record of these comparative field studies casts an important light on the nature of Smith's method.

[31] [In his *Systema Naturae*.]

which happens to be laid by the road side, at a great stone, or the fragment of a rock which happens to lie near the way where he is going. To reconcile him, even to a single object of this kind, which has once alarmed him, frequently requires some skill, as well as much patience and good temper, in the rider. Such powers of sight, however, as Nature has thought proper to render him capable of acquiring, he seems to enjoy from the beginning, in as great perfection as he ever does afterwards.

73   The young of other quadrupeds, like those of the birds which make their nests in places of difficult access, come blind into the world. Their sight, however, soon opens, and as soon as it does so,[32] they seem to enjoy it in the most complete perfection, as we may all observe in the puppy and the kitten. The same thing, I believe, may be said of all other beasts of prey, at least of all those concerning which I have been able to collect any distinct information. They come blind into the world; but as soon as their sight opens, they appear to enjoy it in the most complete perfection.

74   It seems difficult to suppose that man is the only animal of which the young are not endowed with some instinctive perception of this kind. The young of the human species, however, continue so long in a state of entire dependency, they must be so long carried about in the arms of their mothers or of their nurses, that such an instinctive perception may seem less necessary to them than to any other race of animals. Before it could be of any use to them, observation and experience may, by the known principle of the association of ideas, have sufficiently connected in their young minds each visible object with the corresponding tangible one which it is fitted to represent. Nature, it may be said, never bestows upon any animal any faculty which is not either necessary or useful, and an instinct of this kind would be altogether useless to an animal which must necessarily acquire the knowledge which the instinct is given to supply, long before that instinct could be of any use to it. Children, however, appear at so very early a period to know the distance, the shape, and magnitude of the different tangible objects which are presented to them, that I am disposed to believe that even they may have some instinctive perception of this kind; though possibly in a much weaker degree than the greater part of other animals. A child that is scarcely a month old, stretches out its hands to feel any little play-thing that is presented to it. It distinguishes its nurse, and the other people who are much about it, from strangers. It clings to the former, and turns away from the latter. Hold a small looking-glass before a child of not more than two or three months old, and it will stretch out its little

[32] This may be questioned; degree of mobility may be relevant.

arms behind the glass, in order to feel the child which it sees, and which it imagines is at the back of the glass. It is deceived, no doubt; but even this sort of deception sufficiently demonstrates that it has a tolerably distinct apprehension of the ordinary perspective of Vision, which it cannot well have learnt from observation and experience.

75   Do any of our other senses, antecedently to such observation and experience, instinctively suggest to us some conception of the solid and resisting substances which excite their respective sensations; though these sensations bear no sort of resemblance to those substances?

76   The sense of Tasting certainly does not. Before we can feel the sensation, the solid and resisting substance which excites it must be pressed against the organs of Taste, and must consequently be perceived by them. Antecedently to observation and experience, therefore, the sense of Tasting can never be said instinctively to suggest some conception of that substance.

77   It may, perhaps, be otherwise with the sense of Smelling. The young of all suckling animals, (of the Mammalia of Linnaeus,) whether they are born with sight or without it, yet as soon as they come into the world apply to the nipple of the mother in order to suck. In doing this they are evidently directed by the Smell. The Smell appears either to excite the appetite for the proper food, or at least to direct the new-born animal to the place where that food is to be found. It may perhaps do both the one and the other.

78   That when the stomach is empty, the Smell of agreeable food excites and irritates the appetite, is what we all must have frequently experienced. But the stomach of every new-born animal is necessarily empty. While in the womb it is nourished, not by the mouth, but by the navel-string. Children have been born apparently in the most perfect health and vigour, and have applied to suck in the usual manner; but immediately, or soon after, have thrown up the milk, and in the course of a few hours have died vomiting and in convulsions. Upon opening their bodies it has been found that the intestinal tube or canal had never been opened or pierced in the whole extent of its length; but, like a sack, admitted of no passage beyond a particular place. It could not have been in any respect by the mouth, therefore, but altogether by the navel-string, that such children had been nourished and fed up to the degree of health and vigour in which they were born. Every animal, while in the womb, seems to draw its nourishment, more like a vegetable, from the root, than like an animal from the mouth; and that nourishment seems to be conveyed to all the different parts of the body by tubes and canals in many respects different from those which afterwards perform the

same function. As soon as it comes into the world, this new set of tubes and canals, which the providential care of Nature had for a long time before been gradually preparing, is all at once and instantaneously opened. They are all empty, and they require to be filled. An uneasy sensation accompanies the one situation, and an agreeable one the other. The smell of the substance which is fitted for filling them, increases and irritates that uneasy sensation, and produces hunger, or the appetite for food.

79   But all the appetites which take their origin from a certain state of the body, seem to suggest the means of their own gratification; and, even long before experience, some anticipation or preconception of the pleasure which attends that gratification. In the appetite for sex, which frequently, I am disposed to believe almost always, comes a long time before the age of puberty,[33] this is perfectly and distinctly evident. The appetite for food suggests to the new-born infant the operation of sucking, the only means by which it can possibly gratify that appetite. It is continually sucking. It sucks whatever is presented to its mouth. It sucks even when there is nothing presented to its mouth, and some anticipation or preconception of the pleasure which it is to enjoy in sucking, seems to make it delight in putting its mouth in the shape and configuration by which it alone can enjoy that pleasure. There are other appetites in which the most unexperienced imagination produces a similar effect upon the organs which Nature has provided for their gratification.

80   The Smell not only excites the appetite, but directs to the object which can alone gratify that appetite. But by suggesting the direction towards that object, the Smell must necessarily suggest some notion of distance and externality, which are necessarily involved in the idea of direction; in the idea of the line of motion by which the distance can best be overcome, and the mouth brought into contact with the unknown substance which is the object of the appetite. That the Smell should alone suggest any preconception of the shape or magnitude of the external body to which it directs, seems not very probable. The sensation of Smell seems to have no sort of affinity or correspondence with shape or magnitude; and whatever preconception the infant may have of these, (and it may very probably have some such preconception,) is likely to be suggested, not so much directly by the Smell, and indirectly by the appetite excited by that Smell; as by the principle which teaches the child to mould its mouth into the conformation and action of sucking, even before it reaches

[33] A remarkable anticipation of Freud's claim, received by his contemporaries with scepticism, if not categorical denial.

the object to which alone that conformation and action can be usefully applied.

81　　The Smell, however, as it suggests the direction by which the external body must be approached, must suggest at least some vague idea or preconception of the existence of that body; of the thing to which it directs, though not perhaps of the precise shape and magnitude of that thing. The infant, too, feeling its mouth attracted and drawn as it were towards that external body, must conceive the Smell which thus draws and attracts it, as something belonging to or proceeding from that body, or what is afterwards denominated and obscurely understood to be as a sort of quality or attribute of that body.

82　　The Smell, too, may very probably suggest some even tolerably distinct perception of the Taste of the food to which it directs. The respective objects of our different external senses seem, indeed, the greater part of them, to bear no sort of resemblance to one another. Colour bears no sort of resemblance to Solidity, nor to Heat, nor to Cold, nor to Sound, nor to Smell, nor to Taste. To this general rule, however, there seems to be one, and perhaps but one exception. The sensations of Smell and Taste seem evidently to bear some sort of resemblance to one another. Smell appears to have been given to us by Nature as the director of Taste. It announces, as it were, before trial, what is likely to be the Taste of the food which is set before us. Though perceived by a different organ, it seems in many cases to be but a weaker sensation nearly of the same kind with that of the Taste which that announces. It is very natural to suppose, therefore, that the Smell may suggest to the infant some tolerably distinct preconception of the Taste of the food which it announces, and may, even before experience, make its mouth, as we say, water for that food.

83　　That numerous division of animals which Linnaeus ranks under the class of *worms*, have, scarcely any of them, any head. They neither see nor hear, have neither eyes nor ears; but many of them have the power of self-motion, and appear to move about in search of their food. They can be directed in this search by no other sense than that of Smelling. The most accurate microscopical observations, however, have never been able to discover in such animals any distinct organ of Smell. They have a mouth and a stomach, but no nostrils. The organ of Taste, it is probable, has in them a sensibility of the same kind with that which the olfactory nerves have in more perfect animals. They may, as it were, taste at a distance, and be attracted to their food by an affection of the same organ by which they afterwards enjoy it; and Smell and Taste may in them be no otherwise distinguished than as weaker or stronger sensations derived from the same organ.

84   The sensations of Heat and Cold, when excited by the pressure of some body either heated or cooled beyond the actual temperature of our own organs, cannot be said, antecedently to observation and experience, instinctively to suggest any conception of the solid and resisting substance which excites them. What was said of the sense of Taste may very properly be said here. Before we can feel those sensations, the pressure of the external body which excites them must necessarily suggest, not only some conception, but the most distinct conviction of its own external and independent existence.

85   It may be otherwise, perhaps, when those sensations are either of them excited by the temperature of the external air. In a calm day when there is no wind, we scarcely perceive the external air as a solid body; and the sensations of Heat and Cold, it may be thought, are then felt merely as affections of our own body, without any reference to any thing external. Several cases, however, may be conceived, in which it must be allowed, I imagine, that those sensations, even when excited in this manner, must suggest some vague notion of some external thing or substance which excites them. A new-born animal, which had the power of self-motion, and which felt its body, either agreeably or disagreeably, more heated or more cooled on the one side than on the other, would, I imagine, instinctively, and antecedently to all observation and experience, endeavour to move towards the side in which it felt the agreeable, and to withdraw from that in which it felt the disagreeable sensation. But the very desire of motion supposes some notion or preconception of externality; and the desire to move towards the side of the agreeable, or from that of the disagreeable sensation, supposes at least some vague notion of some external thing or place which is the cause of those respective sensations.

86   The degrees of Heat and Cold which are agreeable, it has been found from experience, are likewise healthful; and those which are disagreeable, unwholesome. The degree of their unwholesomeness, too, seems to be pretty much in proportion to that of their disagreeableness. If either of them is so disagreeable as to be painful, it is generally destructive; and that, too, in a very short period of time. Those sensations appear to have been given us for the preservation of our own bodies. They necessarily excite the desire of changing our situation when it is unwholesome or destructive; and when it is healthy, they allow us, or rather they entice us, to remain in it. But the desire of changing our situation necessarily supposes some idea of externality; or of motion into a place different from that in which we

actually are; and even the desire of remaining in the same place supposes some idea of at least the possibility of changing. Those sensations could not well have answered the intention of Nature, had they not thus instinctively suggested some vague notion of external existence.

87   That Sound, the object of the sense of Hearing, though perceived itself as in the ear, and nowhere but in the ear, may likewise, instinctively, and antecedently to all observation and experience, obscurely suggest some vague notion of some external substance or thing which excites it, I am much disposed to believe.[34] I acknowledge, however, that I have not been able to recollect any one instance in which this sense seems so distinctly to produce this effect, as that of Seeing, that of Smelling, and even that of Heat and Cold, appear to do in some particular cases. Unusual and unexpected Sound alarms always, and disposes us to look about for some external substance or thing as the cause which excites it, or from which it proceeds. Sound, however, considered merely as a sensation, or as an affection of the organ of Hearing, can in most cases neither benefit nor hurt us. It may be agreeable or disagreeable, but in its own nature it does not seem to announce any thing beyond the immediate feeling. It should not therefore excite any alarm. Alarm is always the fear of some uncertain evil beyond what is immediately felt, and from some unknown and external cause. But all animals, and men among the rest, feel some degree of this alarm, start, are roused and rendered circumspect and attentive by unusual and unexpected Sound. This effect, too, is produced so readily and so instantaneously that it bears every mark of an instinctive suggestion of an impression immediately struck by the hand of Nature, which does not wait for any recollection of past observation and experience. The hare, and all those other timid animals to whom flight is the only defence, are supposed to possess the sense of Hearing in the highest degree of activeness. It seems to be the sense in which cowards are very likely to excel.[35]

88   The three senses of Seeing, Hearing, and Smelling, seem to be given to us by Nature, not so much in order to inform us concerning the actual situation of our bodies, as concerning that of those other external bodies, which, though at some distance from us, may sooner or later affect that actual situation, and eventually either benefit or hurt us.

[34] Though based on a dubious premiss, Smith's point is well taken in regard to the general question of the sensory origin of knowledge.
[35] Smith seems to have had an obsession about 'cowards' (cf. Astronomy, III.1). 'Hunters' might be similarly endowed.

Of the Nature of that Imitation which takes place in what are called The Imitative Arts

Of the Affinity between Music, Dancing, and Poetry

Introduction

That Adam Smith 'had never neglected to cultivate a taste for the fine arts' we are assured by Dugald Stewart (III.13); that he was writing a book on the imitative arts about ten years before his death we know from Smith's own admission; but what was the precise relation of that work to well-attested earlier efforts on the one hand, and to the essay posthumously published on the other, is a question to which we shall probably never know the answer. Since the sources of our information concerning this matter cast some light on the larger question of the 'great work' Smith at one time contemplated it may be worth while to study them in some detail.

Neither in his early letter to Hume (Letter 137 dated 16 April 1773) nor in the later one to La Rochefoucauld (Letter 248 dated 1 November 1785) did Smith refer specifically to any study of the imitative arts. But in October 1780 in a letter (208) to Andreas Holt, Commissioner of the Danish Board of Trade, occurs a passage that casts light on more than one question relating to the *Essays on Philosophical Subjects*, and above all on the one we are at present concerned with. In 1773, Smith recalls, he had had to go to London in connection with an 'office' that on the Duke of Buccleuch's advice he had turned down. 'For four years after this', Smith continued, 'London was my principal residence, where I finished and published my Book [sc. *Wealth of Nations*]. I had returned to my old retirement at Kirkaldy and was employing myself in writing another Work concerning the imitative arts . . .' He concluded this letter with an expression of regret that owing to the duties of his new office (Commissioner of H.M. Customs in Edinburgh) 'Several Works which I had projected are likely to go on much more slowly than they otherwise would have done'.

In the year (1781) following that of the letter just quoted, Henry Mackenzie wrote to a Mr. Carmichael that Smith had 'lying by him, several essays, some finished, but the greater part not quite completed on subjects of criticism and Belles Lettres'. Mackenzie, author of *The Man of Feeling*, was one of the most distinguished of contemporary Scottish men of letters. In commenting on this letter Scott (*ASSP*, 284 and note) says that 'He acted on behalf of Adam Smith's literary executors in preparing his *Essays* for publication'. Unfortunately Mackenzie's reference to the essays is limited to the above quotation.

Apart from Smith's letter to La Rochefoucauld (above, p. 171), no evidence as to the progress of the essays is available before the time of their author's death (1790) when letters of condolence were written to Smith's nephew and principal legatee. In one of these letters, from Lord Loughborough, there occurs the following paragraph:

The disposition of his unprinted Works is exactly what I expected as he told me it was his determination to destroy the greater part of them, and He particularly excepted the History of Astronomy and his Treatise on the imitative Arts. The last I had seen when he was in London, but, I understood it had since received some alterations. The first I had not seen for many years, but understood from conversation that he had been employed in correcting it.   (Scott, *ASSP*, 313.)

Unfortunately there is no indication which year it was during Smith's residence in London that Lord Loughborough had seen the 'Arts' essay, but Smith's proposed preservation of it (in addition to the Astronomy, the only one named in Letter 137 to Hume) implies that it was on a later visit than the one Smith refers to in the letter addressed to Andreas Holt—perhaps during the visit of 1787 referred to by Professor E. C. Mossner in *The Biographical Approach* (1969, 20).

   If this were all the evidence we had on the composition of the essay on the imitative arts the conclusion would be tolerably clear—it was 'written' at Kirkcaldy about 1777, 'seen' in London thereafter, and subsequently 'altered'. Unfortunately an element of doubt—though not a conclusive one—is introduced by John Millar, Professor of Law at Glasgow, who in a letter (Scott, *ASSP*, 312–13) to David Douglas written a few days before that of Lord Loughborough stated that 'Of the discourses which he intended upon the imitative arts, he read two to our Society at Glasgow, but the third was not then finished.' This reference to two parts and an unfinished third is a plausible description of the essay and appendix as posthumously printed. Now Smith left the Glasgow Chair in 1764, about fourteen years before he 'wrote' it. At its face value, then, Millar's evidence implies either that Smith 'composed' it long before he 'wrote' it, or that he communicated to the Glasgow Society during a later visit what he had written in 1777. Since Scott could find no record of these papers in the printed extracts from the minutes of the Glasgow society, it is impossible to decide between these alternatives. Professor D. D. Raphael regards it as most probable that Smith read earlier versions to the society and was subsequently able to amplify and confirm his theories as a result of his visit to France (below, 173). That this was a not uncommon procedure is evidenced by the fact that Joseph Black's only 'publication' of his epoch-making discovery of latent heat was to 'a

Society of professors' at Glasgow in 1762. Millar's description may have been a conflation of two reminiscences separated by a long period of time.[1]

Though Dugald Stewart's 'Life' deals with Smith's work on the imitative arts in terms too general to yield any significant guide to its dating, the continuation of the passage quoted above (171) provides an important insight into the working of Smith's mind: 'he had never neglected to cultivate a taste for the Fine Arts;—less, it is probable, with a view to the peculiar enjoyments they convey ... than on account of their connexion with the general principles of the human mind ... To those who speculate on this very delicate subject, a comparison of the modes of taste that prevail among different nations, affords a valuable collection of facts ... Mr. Smith ... may naturally be supposed to have availed himself of every opportunity which a foreign country afforded him of illustrating his former theories.' (Stewart, III.13.) The 'foreign country' to which Stewart refers was of course France, where Smith travelled as the companion of the Duke of Buccleuch during the greater part of the period 1764-6. Among the 'former theories' Stewart included Smith's 'peculiar notions' 'with respect to the imitative arts', especially his belief that the pleasure provided by these arts was chiefly due to the 'difficulty of the imitation' (III.14). That Stewart must at least have discussed these matters with Smith from time to time we may infer from his reference to the latter's sustained interest in the 'principles of dramatic composition' and 'the history of the theatre' that 'had furnished him with some of the most remarkable facts on which his theory of the imitative arts was founded' (III.15). He had, so Stewart claimed, devoted leisure hours to the study of the drama and 'he intended, if he had lived, to have prepared the result of these labours for the press. Of this work, he has left for publication a short fragment; but he had not proceeded far enough to apply his doctrine to versification and to the theatre' (III.15). What the relation was between this 'short fragment' and the essay on the 'Imitative Arts', to which Stewart makes no specific reference, is not made clear. The appendix on the 'Affinity between Music, Dancing, and Poetry' could have been

---

[1] In the same letter Millar wrote: 'Of all his writing I have most curiosity about the metaphysical work you mention. I should like to see his powers of illustration employed upon the true old Humean philosophy.' On this Scott comments, 'There is no trace of this MS.' (*ASSP*, 313n.). But I agree with Professor Raphael (who kindly drew my attention to this letter) that in view of the word 'illustration' (cf. the titles of the three 'historical' essays) the 'metaphysical' MS. could have been no other than that of these essays. Professor Raphael sees in Millar's comment some confirmation of his own view that Smith was greatly influenced by Hume's new attitude to the 'faculty' of imagination. I have dealt with this more fully in my essay, 'Adam Smith and the History of Ideas'; see also D. D. Raphael's 'Impartial Spectator', both in *Essays on Adam Smith*. See further *16-21*, above.

conceived as a 'bridge-passage' between the main essay and the unachieved work on dramatic composition and the theatre. If this was not the case, then Smith's editors must have decided not to print the 'fragment' to which Stewart refers. In view of such occasional imprecision—and in some cases even inconsistency—Stewart's account should not be relied on exclusively for the detailed facts of Smith's life and works.

The date of the composition of this essay has a special interest in relation to one of those asides that some modern readers may find the most rewarding features of these early works. Towards the end of his discussion of the visual arts Smith draws attention to the significance of rarity and costliness in the appreciation of works of art especially of those 'arts which address themselves, not to the prudent and the wise, but to the rich and the great, to the proud and the vain' (Imitative Arts, I.13; cf. WN I.xi.c.31). Smith illustrates this point by reminding the reader of the esteem in which topiary had 'some years ago' been held. The alleged ground of its contemporary rejection— 'unnaturalness'—was, he maintained, unconvincing; the true reason was that 'the rich and the great ... will not admit into their gardens an ornament which the meanest of the people can have as well as they' (I.14). This judgement, supported by cogent analysis and just analogy, was surely an early appreciation of one aspect of Thorstein Veblen's 'Pecuniary Canons of Taste' (chap. iv of his *Theory of the Leisured Class*, 1899) where he writes, 'the marks of expensiveness come to be accepted as beautiful features of the expensive articles'. Smith's emphasis is on exclusiveness rather than on money-value; but he was writing of England and France in the eighteenth century, Veblen of America more than a century later.

This remarkable insight into the social relativity of aesthetic norms is accompanied in the same context by what may have been an almost second-sight into a changing *Zeitgeist*. In an uncommonly familiar vein Smith begs the reader next time he sees examples of topiary to 'restrain for a few minutes the foolish passion for playing the critic', when he 'will be sensible that they are not without some degree of beauty'. In fact Smith is not asking for a suspension of criticism but for a flexibility in relation to critical standards. In 1797 Wackenroder would in effect censure the age for condemning the Middle Ages 'because they did not build the same kind of temples as Greece'; twelve years later August von Schlegel rejected the 'despotism of good taste'. As the nineteenth century advanced, the form of medieval hierarchialism characteristic of eighteenth-century 'classicism' was giving way to the Romantic adventure of ideas.

In 1776 Adam Smith had reminded the world of the still unrealized possibilities of economic expansion and cultural change consequent on the discovery of America; it would be interesting to know when there came to him the first urge to extend the horizon of taste in the arts. Whenever it may have been it remained an incongruity in an essay that, as some of the subsequent notes will show, remained firmly set in the unimaginative cultural atmosphere of the 'Age of Reason'. There is, however, in the question implied in the title 'what are called the imitative arts' one other aspect of the essay which has a relevance outwith the context in which it is applied: this is Smith's recognition of the possibility of what we might call an innate semantic confusion. For his analysis of the nature of the 'imitation' shows that although (at least for the age in which he was writing) a degree of 'imitation' is an essential aim, yet its complete achievement, as in mechanical duplication, is self-defeating.

Though each reader may have some reservations as to the correctness of Smith's individual judgements, the polished lucidity of their expression and the unified structure in which they are embedded lend support to the belief that this essay is the product of a mature understanding. Its preservation adds an important item to the evidence that the author of the *Wealth of Nations* was not only a genius, but one of unusual complexity and fascination about whom the last word will not be spoken for a long time to come.

OF THE

NATURE OF THAT IMITATION
WHICH TAKES PLACE IN WHAT ARE CALLED
THE IMITATIVE ARTS

Part I

1 The most perfect imitation of an object of any kind must in all cases, it is evident, be another object of the same kind, made as exactly as possible after the same model. What, for example, would be the most perfect imitation of the carpet which now lies before me?—Another carpet, certainly, wrought as exactly as possible after the same pattern. But, whatever might be the merit or beauty of this second carpet, it would not be supposed to derive any from the circumstance of its having been made in imitation of the first. This circumstance of its being not an original, but a copy, would even be considered as some diminution of that merit; a greater or smaller, in proportion as the object was of a nature to lay claim to a greater or smaller degree of admiration. It would not much diminish the merit of a common carpet, because in such trifling objects, which at best can lay claim to so little beauty or merit of any kind, we do not always think it worth while to affect originality: it would diminish a good deal that of a carpet of very exquisite workmanship. In objects of still greater importance, this exact, or, as it would be called, this servile imitation, would be considered as the most unpardonable blemish. To build another St. Peter's, or St. Paul's church, of exactly the same dimensions, proportions, and ornaments with the present buildings at Rome, or London, would be supposed to argue such a miserable barrenness of genius and invention as would disgrace the most expensive magnificence.

2 The exact resemblance of the correspondent parts of the same object is frequently considered as a beauty, and the want of it as a deformity; as in the correspondent members of the human body, in the opposite wings of the same building, in the opposite trees of the same alley, in the correspondent compartments of the same piece of carpet-work, or of the same flower-garden, in the chairs or tables which stand in the correspondent parts of the same room, etc. But in objects of the same kind, which in other respects are regarded as

altogether separate and unconnected, this exact resemblance is seldom considered as a beauty, nor the want of it as a deformity. A man, and in the same manner a horse, is handsome or ugly, each of them, on account of his own intrinsic beauty or deformity, without any regard to their resembling or not resembling, the one, another man, or the other, another horse. A set of coach-horses, indeed, is supposed to be handsomer when they are all exactly matched; but each horse is, in this case, considered not as a separated and unconnected object, or as a whole by himself, but as a part of another whole, to the other parts of which he ought to bear a certain correspondence: Separated from the set, he derives neither beauty from his resemblance, nor deformity from his unlikeness to the other horses which compose it.

3   Even in the correspondent parts of the same object, we frequently require no more than a resemblance in the general outline. If the inferior members of those correspondent parts are too minute to be seen distinctly, without a separate and distinct examination of each part by itself, as a separate and unconnected object, we should sometimes even be displeased if the resemblance was carried beyond this general outline. In the correspondent parts of a room we frequently hang pictures of the same size; those pictures, however, resemble one another in nothing but the frame, or, perhaps, in the general character of the subject: If the one is a landscape, the other is a landscape too; if the one represents a religious or a Bacchanalian subject, its companion represents another of the same kind. Nobody ever thought of repeating the same picture in each correspondent frame. The frame, and the general character of two or three pictures, is as much as the eye can comprehend at one view, or from one station. Each picture, in order to be seen distinctly, and understood thoroughly, must be viewed from a particular station, and examined by itself as a separate and unconnected object. In a hall or portico, adorned with statues, the nitches, or perhaps the pedestals, may exactly resemble one another, but the statues are always different. Even the masks which are sometimes carried upon the different key-stones of the same arcade, or of the correspondent doors and windows of the same front, though they may all resemble one another in the general outline, yet each of them has always its own peculiar features, and a grimace of its own. There are some Gothic buildings in which the correspondent windows resemble one another only in the general outline, and not in the smaller ornaments and subdivisions. These are different in each, and the architect had considered them as too minute to be seen distinctly, without a particular and separate examination of each window by itself, as a separate and unconnected

object. A variety of this sort, however, I think, is not agreeable. In objects which are susceptible only of a certain inferior order of beauty, such as the frames of pictures, the nitches or the pedestals of statues, etc. there seems frequently to be affectation in the study of variety, of which the merit is scarcely ever sufficient to compensate the want of that perspicuity and distinctness, of that easiness to be comprehended and remembered, which is the natural effect of exact uniformity. In a portico of the Corinthian or Ionic order, each column resembles every other, not only in the general outline, but in all the minutest ornaments; though some of them, in order to be seen distinctly, may require a separate and distinct examination in each column, and in the entablature of each intercolumnation. In the inlaid tables, which, according to the present fashion, are sometimes fixed in the correspondent parts of the same room, the pictures only are different in each. All the other more frivolous and fanciful ornaments are commonly, so far at least as I have observed the fashion, the same in them all. Those ornaments, however, in order to be seen distinctly, require a separate and distinct examination of each table.

4   The extraordinary resemblance of two natural objects, of twins, for example, is regarded as a curious circumstance; which, though it does not increase, yet does not diminish the beauty of either, considered as a separate and unconnected object. But the exact resemblance of two productions of art, seems to be always considered as some diminution of the merit of at least one of them; as it seems to prove, that one of them, at least, is a copy either of the other, or of some other original. One may say, even of the copy of a picture, that it derives its merit, not so much from its resemblance to the original, as from its resemblance to the object which the original was meant to resemble. The owner of the copy, so far from setting any high value upon its resemblance to the original, is often anxious to destroy any value or merit which it might derive from this circumstance. He is often anxious to persuade both himself and other people that it is not a copy, but an original, of which what passes for the original is only a copy. But, whatever merit a copy may derive from its resemblance to the original, an original can certainly derive none from the resemblance of its copy.

5   But though a production of art seldom derives any merit from its resemblance to another object of the same kind, it frequently derives a great deal from its resemblance to an object of a different kind, whether that object be a production of art or of nature. A painted cloth, the work of some laborious Dutch artist, so curiously shaded and coloured as to represent the pile and softness of a woollen one, might derive some merit from its resemblance even to the sorry

carpet which now lies before me. The copy might, and probably would, in this case, be of much greater value than the original. But if this carpet was represented as spread, either upon a floor or upon a table, and projecting from the back ground of the picture, with exact observation of perspective, and of light and shade, the merit of the imitation would be still greater.

6   In Painting, a plain surface of one kind is made to resemble, not only a plain surface of another, but all the three dimensions of a solid substance. In Statuary and Sculpture, a solid substance of one kind, is made to resemble a solid substance of another. The disparity between the object imitating, and the object imitated, is much greater in the one art that in the other; and the pleasure arising from the imitation seems to be greater in proportion as this disparity is greater.

7   In Painting, the imitation frequently pleases, though the original object be indifferent, or even offensive. In Statuary and Sculpture it is otherwise. The imitation seldom pleases, unless the original object be in a very high degree either great, or beautiful, or interesting. A butcher's stall, or a kitchen-dresser, with the objects which they commonly present, are not certainly the happiest subjects, even for Painting. They have, however, been represented with so much care and success by some Dutch masters, that it is impossible to view the pictures without some degree of pleasure. They would be most absurd subjects for Statuary or Sculpture, which are, however, capable of representing them. The picture of a very ugly or deformed man, such as Aesop, or Scarron, might not make a disagreeable piece of furniture. The statue certainly would. Even a vulgar ordinary man or woman, engaged in a vulgar ordinary action, like what we see with so much pleasure in the pictures of Rembrant, would be too mean a subject for Statuary. Jupiter, Hercules, and Apollo, Venus and Diana, the Nymphs and the Graces, Bacchus, Mercury, Antinous and Meleager, the miserable death of Laocoon, the melancholy fate of the children of Niobe, the Wrestlers, the fighting, the dying gladiator, the figures of gods and goddesses, of heroes and heroines, the most perfect forms of the human body, placed either in the noblest attitudes, or in the most interesting situations which the human imagination is capable of conceiving, are the proper, and therefore have always been the favourite subjects of Statuary: that art cannot, without degrading itself, stoop to represent any thing that is offensive, or mean, or even indifferent. Painting is not so disdainful; and, though capable of representing the noblest objects, it can, without forfeiting its title to please, submit to imitate those of a much more humble nature. The merit of the imitation alone, and without any merit in the imitated object, is capable of supporting the dignity of Painting: it cannot

support that of Statuary. There would seem, therefore, to be more merit in the one species of imitation than in the other.

8 In Statuary, scarcely any drapery is agreeable. The best of the ancient statues were either altogether naked or almost naked; and those of which any considerable part of the body is covered, are represented as clothed in wet linen—a species of clothing which most certainly never was agreeable to the fashion of any country. This drapery too is drawn so tight, as to express beneath its narrow foldings the exact form and outline of any limb, and almost of every muscle of the body. The clothing which thus approached the nearest to no clothing at all, had, it seems, in the judgment of the great artists of antiquity, been that which was most suitable to Statuary. A great painter of the Roman school, who had formed his manner almost entirely upon the study of the ancient statues, imitated at first their drapery in his pictures; but he soon found that in Painting it had the air of meanness and poverty, as if the persons who wore it could scarce afford clothes enough to cover them; and that larger folds, and a looser and more flowing drapery, were more suitable to the nature of his art. In Painting, the imitation of so very inferior an object as a suit of clothes is capable of pleasing; and, in order to give this object all the magnificence of which it is capable, it is necessary that the folds should be large, loose, and flowing. It is not necessary in Painting that the exact form and outline of every limb, and almost of every muscle of the body, should be expressed beneath the folds of the drapery; it is sufficient if these are so disposed as to indicate in general the situation and attitude of the principal limbs. Painting, by the mere force and merit of its imitation, can venture, without the hazard of displeasing, to substitute, upon many occasions, the inferior in the room of the superior object, by making the one, in this manner, cover and entirely conceal a great part of the other. Statuary can seldom venture to do this, but with the utmost reserve and caution; and the same drapery, which is noble and magnificent in the one art, appears clumsy and awkward in the other. Some modern artists, however, have attempted to introduce into Statuary the drapery which is peculiar to Painting. It may not, perhaps, upon every occasion, be quite so ridiculous as the marble periwigs in Westminster Abbey: but, if it does not always appear clumsy and awkward, it is at best always insipid and uninteresting.

9 It is not the want of colouring which hinders many things from pleasing in Statuary, which please in Painting; it is the want of that degree of disparity between the imitating and the imitated object, which is necessary, in order to render interesting the imitation of an object which is itself not interesting. Colouring, when added to

Statuary, so far from increasing, destroys almost entirely the pleasure which we receive from the imitation; because it takes away the great source of that pleasure, the disparity between the imitating and the imitated object. That one solid and coloured object should exactly resemble another solid and coloured object, seems to be a matter of no great wonder or admiration. A painted statue, though it certainly may resemble a human figure much more exactly than any statue which is not painted, is generally acknowledged to be a disagreeable, and even an offensive object; and so far are we from being pleased with this superior likeness, that we are never satisfied with it; and, after viewing it again and again, we always find that it is not equal to what we are disposed to imagine it might have been: though it should seem to want scarce any thing but the life, we could not pardon it for thus wanting what it is altogether impossible it should have. The works of Mrs. Wright,[1] a self-taught artist of great merit, are perhaps more perfect in this way than any thing I have ever seen. They do admirably well to be seen now and then as a show; but the best of them we should find, if brought home to our own house, and placed in a situation where it was to come often into view, would make, instead of an ornamental, a most offensive piece of household furniture. Painted statues, accordingly, are universally reprobated, and we scarce ever meet with them. To colour the eyes of statues is not altogether so uncommon: even this, however, is disapproved by all good judges. 'I cannot bear it,' (a gentleman used to say, of great knowledge and judgment in this art,) 'I cannot bear it; I always want them to speak to me.'

10   Artificial fruits and flowers sometimes imitate so exactly the natural objects which they represent, that they frequently deceive us. We soon grow weary of them, however; and, though they seem to want nothing but the freshness and the flavour of natural fruits and flowers, we cannot pardon them, in the same manner, for thus wanting what it is altogether impossible they should have. But we do not grow weary of a good flower and fruit painting. We do not grow weary of the foliage of the Corinthian capital, or of the flowers which sometimes ornament the frize of that order. Such imitations, however, never deceive us; their resemblance to the original objects is always much inferior to that of artificial fruits and flowers. Such as it is, however, we are contented with it; and, where there is such disparity between the imitating and the imitated objects, we find that it is as great as it can be, or as we expect that it should be. Paint that foliage

[1] Mrs. Patience Wright, born in New Jersey in 1725, moved to London in 1772 and remained there until her death in 1786. Her wax models, many life-sized, had a great vogue (*DNB*). [The *London Magazine* for 1775 (555) printed a notice of her work.]

and those flowers with the natural colours, and, instead of pleasing more, they will please much less. The resemblance, however, will be much greater; but the disparity between the imitating and the imitated objects will be so much less, that even this superior resemblance will not satisfy us. Where the disparity is very great, on the contrary, we are often contented with the most imperfect resemblance; with the very imperfect resemblance, for example, both as to figure and colour, of fruits and flowers in shell-work.

11   It may be observed, however, that, though in Sculpture the imitation of flowers and foliage pleases as an ornament of architecture, as a part of the dress which is to set off the beauty of a different and a more important object, it would not please alone, or as a separate and unconnected object, in the same manner as a fruit and flower painting pleases. Flowers and foliage, how elegant and beautiful soever, are not sufficiently interesting; they have not dignity enough, if I may say so, to be proper subjects for a piece of Sculpture, which is to please alone, and not as the ornamental appendage of some other object.

12   In Tapestry and Needle-work, in the same manner as in Painting, a plain surface is sometimes made to represent all the three dimensions of a solid substance. But both the shuttle of the weaver, and the needle of the embroiderer, are instruments of imitation so much inferior to the pencil of the painter, that we are not surprised to find a proportionable inferiority in their productions. We have all more or less experience that they usually are much inferior; and, in appreciating a piece of Tapestry or Needle-work, we never compare the imitation of either with that of a good picture, for it never could stand that comparison, but with that of other pieces of Tapestry or Needle-work. We take into consideration, not only the disparity between the imitating and the imitated object, but the awkwardness of the instruments of imitation; and if it is as well as any thing that can be expected from these, if it is better than the greater part of what actually comes from them, we are often not only contented but highly pleased.

13   A good painter will often execute in a few days a subject which would employ the best tapestry-weaver for many years; though, in proportion to his time, therefore, the latter is always much worse paid than the former, yet his work in the end comes commonly much dearer to market. The great expence of good Tapestry, the circumstance which confines it to the palaces of princes and great lords, gives it, in the eyes of the greater part of people, an air of riches and magnificence, which contributes still further to compensate the imperfection of its imitation. In arts which address themselves, not to

the prudent and the wise, but to the rich and the great, to the proud and the vain, we ought not to wonder if the appearance of great expence, of being what few people can purchase, of being one of the surest characteristics of great fortune, should often stand in the place of exquisite beauty, and contribute equally to recommend their productions.[2] As the idea of expence seems often to embellish, so that of cheapness seems as frequently to tarnish the lustre even of very agreeable objects. The difference between real and false jewels is what even the experienced eye of a jeweller can sometimes with difficulty distinguish. Let an unknown lady, however, come into a public assembly, with a head-dress which appears to be very richly adorned with diamonds, and let a jeweller only whisper in our ear that they are all false stones, not only the lady will immediately sink in our imagination from the rank of a princess to that of a very ordinary woman, but the head-dress, from an object of the most splendid magnificence, will at once become an impertinent piece of tawdry and tinsel finery.

14   It was some years ago the fashion to ornament a garden with yew and holly trees, clipped into the artificial shapes of pyramids, and columns, and vases, and obelisks. It is now the fashion to ridicule this taste as unnatural. The figure of a pyramid or obelisk, however, is not more unnatural to a yew-tree than to a block of porphyry or marble. When the yew-tree is presented to the eye in this artificial shape, the gardener does not mean that it should be understood to have grown in that shape: he means, first, to give it the same beauty of regular figure, which pleases so much in porphyry and marble; and, secondly, to imitate in a growing tree the ornaments of those precious materials: he means to make an object of one kind resemble another object of a very different kind; and to the original beauty of figure to join the relative beauty of imitation: but the disparity between the imitating and the imitated object is the foundation of the beauty of imitation. It is because the one object does not naturally resemble the other, that we are so much pleased with it, when by art it is made to do so. The shears of the gardener, it may be said, indeed, are very clumsy instruments of Sculpture. They are so, no doubt, when employed to imitate the figures of men, or even of animals. But in the simple and regular forms of pyramids, vases, and obelisks, even the shears of the gardener do well enough. Some allowance too is naturally made for

---

[2] [Cf. WN I.xi.c.31 ('Of the Produce of Land which sometimes does, and sometimes does not, afford Rent'), where this point is elaborated. Smith remarks of the rich: 'In their eyes the merit of an object which is in any degree either useful or beautiful, is greatly enhanced by its scarcity, or by the great labour which it requires to collect any considerable quantity of it, a labour which nobody can afford to pay but themselves. Such objects they are willing to purchase at a higher price than things much more beautiful and useful, but more common.']

the necessary imperfection of the instrument, in the same manner as in Tapestry and Needle-work. In short, the next time you have an opportunity of surveying those out-of-fashion ornaments, endeavour only to let yourself alone, and to restrain for a few minutes the foolish passion for playing the critic, and you will be sensible that they are not without some degree of beauty; that they give the air of neatness and correct culture at least to the whole garden; and that they are not unlike what the 'retired leisure, that' (as Milton says[3]) 'in trim gardens takes his pleasure,' might be amused with. What then, it may be said, has brought them into such universal disrepute among us? In a pyramid or obelisk of marble, we know that the materials are expensive, and that the labour which wrought them into that shape must have been still more so. In a pyramid or obelisk of yew, we know that the materials could cost very little, and the labour still less. The former are ennobled by their expence; the latter degraded by their cheapness. In the cabbage-garden of a tallow-chandler we may sometimes perhaps have seen as many columns and vases, and other ornaments in yew, as there are in marble and porphyry at Versailles: it is this vulgarity which has disgraced them. The rich and the great, the proud and the vain, will not admit into their gardens an ornament which the meanest of the people can have as well as they.[4] The taste for these ornaments came originally from France; where, notwithstanding that inconstancy of fashion with which we sometimes reproach the natives of that country, it still continues in good repute. In France, the conditions of the inferior ranks of people is seldom so happy as it frequently is in England;[5] and you will there seldom find even pyramids and obelisks of yew in the garden of a tallow-chandler. Such ornaments, not having in that country been degraded by their vulgarity, have not yet been excluded from the gardens of princes and great lords.

15   The works of the great masters in Statuary and Painting, it is to be observed, never produce their effect by deception. They never are, and it never is intended that they should be mistaken for the real objects which they represent. Painted Statuary may sometimes deceive an inattentive eye: proper Statuary never does. The little pieces of perspective in Painting, which it is intended should please

---

[3] *Il Penseroso*, 49–50.

[4] [Cf. WN I.xi.c.31: 'With the greater part of rich people, the chief enjoyment of riches consists in the parade of riches, which in their eyes is never so compleat as when they appear to possess those decisive marks of opulence which nobody can possess but themselves.']

[5] [Cf. WN I.ix.9: 'The wages of labour are lower in France than in England. When you go from Scotland to England, the difference which you may remark between the dress and countenance of the common people in the one country and in the other, sufficiently indicates the difference in their condition. The contrast is still greater when you return from France.']

by deception, represent always some very simple, as well as insignificant, object; a roll of paper, for example, or the steps of a staircase, in the dark corner of some passage or gallery. They are generally the works too of some very inferior artists. After being seen once, and producing the little surprise which it is meant they should excite, together with the mirth which commonly accompanies it, they never please more, but appear ever after insipid and tiresome.

16   The proper pleasure which we derive from those two imitative arts, so far from being the effect of deception, is altogether incompatible with it. That pleasure is founded altogether upon our wonder at seeing an object of one kind represent so well an object of a very different kind, and upon our admiration of the art which surmounts so happily that disparity which Nature had established between them. The nobler works of Statuary and Painting appear to us a sort of wonderful phaenomena, differing in this respect from the wonderful phaenomena of Nature, that they carry, as it were, their own explication along with them, and demonstrate, even to the eye, the way and manner in which they are produced. The eye, even of an unskilful spectator, immediately discerns, in some measure, how it is that a certain modification of figure in Statuary, and of brighter and darker colours in Painting, can represent, with so much truth and vivacity, the actions, passions, and behaviour of men, as well as a great variety of other objects. The pleasing wonder of ignorance is accompanied with the still more pleasing satisfaction of science. We wonder and are amazed at the effect; and we are pleased ourselves, and happy to find that we can comprehend, in some measure, how that wonderful effect is produced.

17   A good looking-glass represents the objects which are set before it with much more truth and vivacity than either Statuary or Painting. But, though the science of optics may explain to the understanding, the looking-glass itself does not at all demonstrate to the eye how this effect is brought about. It may excite the wonder of ignorance; and in a clown, who had never beheld a looking-glass before, I have seen that wonder rise almost to rapture and extasy; but it cannot give the satisfaction of science. In all looking-glasses the effects are produced by the same means, applied exactly in the same manner. In every different statue and picture the effects are produced; though by similar, yet not by the same means; and those means too are applied in a different manner in each. Every good statue and picture is a fresh wonder, which at the same time carries, in some measure, its own explication along with it. After a little use and experience, all looking-glasses cease to be wonders altogether; and even the ignorant become so familiar with them, as not to think that their effects require any

explication.[6] A looking-glass, besides, can represent only present objects; and, when the wonder is once fairly over, we choose, in all cases, rather to contemplate the substance than to gaze at the shadow. One's own face becomes then the most agreeable object which a looking-glass can represent to us, and the only object which we do not soon grow weary with looking at; it is the only present object of which we can see only the shadow: whether handsome or ugly, whether old or young, it is the face of a friend always, of which the features correspond exactly with whatever sentiment, emotion, or passion we may happen at that moment to feel.

18   In Statuary, the means by which the wonderful effect is brought about appear more simple and obvious than in Painting; where the disparity between the imitating and the imitated object being much greater, the art which can conquer that greater disparity appears evidently, and almost to the eye, to be founded upon a much deeper science, or upon principles much more abstruse and profound. Even in the meanest subjects we can often trace with pleasure the ingenious means by which Painting surmounts this disparity. But we cannot do this in Statuary, because the disparity not being so great, the means do not appear so ingenious. And it is upon this account, that in Painting we are often delighted with the representation of many things, which in Statuary would appear insipid, tiresome, and not worth the looking at.

19   It ought to be observed, however, that though in Statuary the art of imitation appears, in many respects, inferior to what it is in Painting, yet, in a room ornamented with both statues and pictures of nearly equal merit, we shall generally find that the statues draw off our eye from the pictures. There is generally but one, or little more than one, point of view from which a picture can be seen with advantage, and it always presents to the eye precisely the same object. There are many different points of view from which a statue may be seen with equal advantage, and from each it presents a different object. There is more variety in the pleasure which we receive from a good statue, than in that which we receive from a good picture; and one statue may frequently be the subject of many good pictures or drawings, all different from one another. The shadowy relief and projection of a picture, besides, is much flattened, and seems almost to vanish away altogether, when brought into comparison with the real and solid body which stands by it. How nearly soever these two arts may seem to be a-kin, they accord so very ill with one another, that their different productions ought, perhaps, scarce ever to be seen together.

[6] [Cf. Astronomy, II.11.]

Part II

1 After the pleasures which arise from the gratification of the bodily
appetites, there seem to be none more natural to man than Music and
Dancing. In the progress of art and improvement they are, perhaps,
the first and earliest pleasures of his own invention; for those which
arise from the gratification of the bodily appetites cannot be said to be
of his own invention. No nation has yet been discovered so uncivilized
as to be altogether without them. It seems even to be amongst the
most barbarous nations that the use and practice of them is both most
frequent and most universal, as among the negroes of Africa and the
savage tribes of America. In civilized nations, the inferior ranks of
people have very little leisure,[1] and the superior ranks have many
other amusements; neither the one nor the other, therefore, can spend
much of their time in Music and Dancing. Among savage nations,
the great body of the people have frequently great intervals of leisure,
and they have scarce any other amusement; they naturally, therefore,
spend a great part of their time in almost the only one they have.

2   What the ancients called Rhythmus, what we call Time or
Measure, is the connecting principle of those two arts; Music
consisting in a succession of a certain sort of sounds, and Dancing in
a succession of a certain sort of steps, gestures, and motions, regulated
according to time or measure, and thereby formed into a sort of whole
or system;[2] which in the one art is called a song or tune, and in the
other a dance; the time or measure of the dance corresponding always
exactly with that of the song or tune which accompanies and directs
it*.

3   The human voice, as it is always the best, so it would naturally be
the first and earliest of all musical instruments: in singing, or in its
first attempts towards singing, it would naturally employ sounds as
similar as possible to those which it had been accustomed to; that is,
it would employ words of some kind or other, pronouncing them
only in time and measure, and generally with a more melodious tone
than had been usual in common conversation. Those words, however,
might not, and probably would not, for a long time have any meaning,
but might resemble the syllables which we make use of in *sol-faing*, or

---

* The Author's Observations on the Affinity between Music, Dancing, and Poetry, are
annexed to the end of Part III of this Essay.

  [1] [Smith made much of this point in discussing the consequences of social stratification and
of the division of labour. See WN V.i.f.52–3 and generally this section: 'Of the Expence of the
Institutions for the Education of Youth'. See also V.i.g.15, where Smith defends the
encouragement of those who, 'without scandal or indecency', might amuse the people 'by
painting, poetry, musick, dancing; [and] by all sorts of dramatic representations'.]
  [2] [Smith's use of the word 'system' for a rhythmical series is clarified in II.29, below.]

the *derry-down-down* of our common ballads; and serve only to assist the voice in forming sounds proper to be modulated into melody, and to be lengthened or shortened according to the time and measure of the tune. This rude form of vocal Music, as it is by far the most simple and obvious, so it naturally would be the first and earliest.

4   In the succession of ages it could not fail to occur, that in the room of those unmeaning or musical words, if I may call them so, might be substituted words which expressed some sense or meaning, and of which the pronunciation might coincide as exactly with the time and measure of the tune, as that of the musical words had done before. Hence the origin of Verse or Poetry. The Verse would for.a long time be rude and imperfect. When the meaning words fell short of the measure required, they would frequently be eked out with the unmeaning ones, as is sometimes done in our common ballads. When the public ear came to be so refined as to reject, in all serious Poetry, the unmeaning words altogether, there would still be a liberty assumed of altering and corrupting, upon many occasions, the pronunciation of the meaning ones, for the sake of accommodating them to the measure. The syllables which composed them would, for this purpose, sometimes be improperly lengthened, and sometimes improperly shortened; and though no unmeaning words were made use of, yet an unmeaning syllable would sometimes be stuck to the beginning, to the end, or into the middle of a word. All these expedients we find frequently employed in the verses even of Chaucer, the father of the English Poetry.[3] Many ages might pass away before verse was commonly composed with such correctness, that the usual and proper pronunciation of the words alone, and without any other artifice, subjected the voice to the observation of a time and measure, of the same kind with the time and measure of Music.

5   The Verse would naturally express some sense which suited the grave or gay, the joyous or melancholy humour of the tune which it was sung to; being as it were blended and united with that tune, it would seem to give sense and meaning to what otherwise might not appear to have any, or at least any which could be clearly and distinctly understood, without the accompaniment of such an explication.

6   A pantomime dance may frequently answer the same purpose, and, by representing some adventure in love or war, may seem to give

---

[3] [Thomas Tyrwhitt's edition of *The Canterbury Tales* (1775–8), by printing final -e, -es, etc., where these are metrically required, refuted the common earlier notion that Chaucer's verse was quite irregular. See Dryden, Preface to the *Fables* (1700). The mistaken assumption, voiced here, that inclusion or omission of these 'unmeaning' syllables was an arbitrary metrical expedient, is still prevalent.]

sense and meaning to a Music which might not otherwise appear to have any. It is more natural to mimic, by gestures and motions, the adventures of common life, than to express them in Verse or Poetry. The thought itself is more obvious, and the execution is much more easy. If this mimicry was accompanied by music, it would of its own accord, and almost without any intention of doing so, accommodate, in some measure, its different steps and movements to the time and measure of the tune; especially if the same person both sung the tune and performed the mimicry, as is said to be frequently the case among the savage nations of Africa and America. Pantomime Dancing might in this manner serve to give a distinct sense and meaning to Music many ages before the invention, or at least before the common use of Poetry. We hear little, accordingly, of the Poetry of the savage nations of Africa and America, but a great deal of their pantomime dances.

7   Poetry, however, is capable of expressing many things fully and distinctly, which Dancing either cannot represent at all, or can represent but obscurely and imperfectly; such as the reasonings and judgments of the understanding; the ideas, fancies, and suspicions of the imagination; the sentiments, emotions, and passions of the heart. In the power of expressing a meaning with clearness and distinctness, Dancing is superior to Music, and Poetry to Dancing.

8   Of those three Sister Arts,[4] which originally, perhaps, went always together, and which at all times go frequently together, there are two which can subsist alone, and separate from their natural companions, and one which cannot. In the distinct observation of what the ancients called Rhythmus, of what we call Time and Measure, consists the essence both of Dancing and of Poetry or Verse; or the characteristical quality which distinguishes the former from all other motion and action, and the latter from all other discourse. But, concerning the proportion between those intervals and divisions of duration which constitute what is called time and measure, the ear, it would seem, can judge with much more precision than the eye; and Poetry, in the same manner as Music, addresses itself to the ear, whereas Dancing addresses itself to the eye. In Dancing, the rhythmus, the proper proportion, the time and measure of its motions, cannot distinctly be perceived, unless they are marked by the more distinct time and measure of Music. It is otherwise in Poetry; no

---

[4] [Eighteenth-century critics, who were fond of this expression, included painting rather than dancing in the three. They ascribed the metaphor to Cicero's remark on the kinship of the humane arts, *Pro Archia Poeta*, I.2; but obviously the Muses are the basis. The changing relations of music, dance, and poetry in different societies, savage and civilized, are treated at length by John Brown in *A Dissertation on the Rise, Union, and Power, the Progressions, Separations, and Corruptions, of Poetry and Music* (1763), III ff. See also Cartaud de la Villate, *Essais historiques et philosophiques sur le goût* (1734).]

accompaniment is necessary to mark the measure of good Verse. Music and Poetry, therefore, can each of them subsist alone; Dancing always requires the accompaniment of Music.

9   It is Instrumental Music which can best subsist apart, and separate from both Poetry and Dancing. Vocal Music, though it may, and frequently does, consist of notes which have no distinct sense or meaning, yet naturally calls for the support of Poetry. But 'Music, married to immortal Verse,' as Milton says,[5] or even to words of any kind which have a distinct sense or meaning, is necessarily and essentially imitative. Whatever be the meaning of those words, though, like many of the songs of ancient Greece, as well as some of those of more modern times, they may express merely some maxims of prudence and morality, or may contain merely the simple narrative of some important event, yet even in such didactic and historical songs there will still be imitation; there will still be a thing of one kind, which by art is made to resemble a thing of a very different kind; there will still be Music imitating discourse; there will still be rhythmus and melody, shaped and fashioned into the form either of a good moral counsel, or of an amusing and interesting story.

10   In this first species of imitation, which being essential to, is therefore inseparable from, all such Vocal Music, there may, and there commonly is, added a second. The words may, and commonly do, express the situation of some particular person, and all the sentiments and passions which he feels from that situation. It is a joyous companion who gives vent to the gaiety and mirth with which wine, festivity, and good company inspire him. It is a lover who complains, or hopes, or fears, or despairs. It is a generous man who expresses either his gratitude for the favours, or his indignation at the injuries, which may have been done to him. It is a warrior who prepares himself to confront danger, and who provokes or defies his enemy. It is a person in prosperity who humbly returns thanks for the goodness, or one in affliction who with contrition implores the mercy and forgiveness, of that invisible Power to whom he looks up as the Director of all the events of human life. The situation may comprehend, not only one, but two, three, or more persons; it may excite in them all either similar or opposite sentiments; what is a subject of sorrow to one, being an occasion of joy and triumph to another; and they may all express, sometimes separately and sometimes together, the particular way in which each of them is affected, as in a duo, trio, or a chorus.

11   All this it may, and it frequently has been said is unnatural; nothing being more so, than to sing when we are anxious to persuade,

[5] [*L'Allegro*, 137.]

or in earnest to express any very serious purpose. But it should be remembered, that to make a thing of one kind resemble another thing of a very different kind, is the very circumstance which, in all the Imitative Arts, constitutes the merits of imitation; and that to shape, and as it were to bend, the measure and the melody of Music, so as to imitate the tone and the language of counsel and conversation, the accent and the style of emotion and passion, is to make a thing of one kind resemble another thing of a very different kind.

12   The tone and the movements of Music, though naturally very different from those of conversation and passion, may, however, be so managed as to seem to resemble them. On account of the great disparity between the imitating and the imitated object, the mind in this, as in the other cases, cannot only be contented, but delighted, and even charmed and transported, with such an imperfect resemblance as can be had. Such imitative Music, therefore, when sung to words which explain and determine its meaning, may frequently appear to be a very perfect imitation. It is upon this account, that even the incomplete Music of a recitative seems to express sometimes all the sedateness and composure of serious but calm discourse, and sometimes all the exquisite sensibility of the most interesting passion. The more complete Music of an air is still superior, and, in the imitation of the more animated passions, has one great advantage over every sort of discourse, whether Prose or Poetry, which is not sung to Music. In a person who is either much depressed by grief or enlivened by joy, who is strongly affected either with love or hatred, with gratitude or resentment, with admiration or contempt, there is commonly one thought or idea which dwells upon his mind, which continually haunts him, which, when he has chaced it away, immediately returns upon him, and which in company makes him absent and inattentive. He can think but of one object, and he cannot repeat to them that object so frequently as it recurs upon him. He takes refuge in solitude, where he can with freedom either indulge the extasy or give way to the agony of the agreeable or disagreeable passion which agitates him;[6] and where he can repeat to himself, which he does sometimes mentally, and sometimes even aloud, and almost always in the same words, the particular thought which either delights or distresses him. Neither Prose nor Poetry can venture to imitate those almost endless repetitions of passion. They may describe them as I do now, but they dare not imitate them; they would become most insufferably tiresome if they did. The Music of a passionate air not only may, but frequently does, imitate them; and it never makes

6 [Cf. TMS I.i.4.7–10, where Smith emphasizes the contrary moderating effects of emotion on going into the company of others.]

its way so directly or so irresistibly to the heart as when it does so. It is upon this account that the words of an air, especially of a passionate one, though they are seldom very long, yet are scarce ever sung straight on to the end, like those of a recitative; but are almost always broken into parts, which are transposed and repeated again and again, according to the fancy or judgment of the composer. It is by means of such repetitions only, that Music can exert those peculiar powers of imitation which distinguish it, and in which it excels all the other Imitative Arts. Poetry and Eloquence, it has accordingly been often observed, produce their effect always by a connected variety and succession of different thoughts and ideas: but Music frequently produces its effects by a repetition of the same idea; and the same sense expressed in the same, or nearly the same, combination of sounds, though at first perhaps it may make scarce any impression upon us, yet, by being repeated again and again, it comes at last gradually, and by little and little, to move, to agitate, and to transport us.

13　　To these powers of imitating, Music naturally, or rather necessarily, joins the happiest choice in the objects of its imitation. The sentiments and passions which Music can best imitate are those which unite and bind men together in society; the social, the decent, the virtuous, the interesting and affecting, the amiable and agreeable, the awful and respectable,[7] the noble, elevating, and commanding passions. Grief and distress are interesting and affecting; humanity and compassion, joy and admiration, are amiable and agreeable; devotion is awful and respectable; the generous contempt of danger, the honourable indignation at injustice, are noble, elevating, and commanding. But it is these and such like passions which Music is fittest for imitating, and which it in fact most frequently imitates. They are, if I may say so, all Musical Passions; their natural tones are all clear, distinct, and almost melodious; and they naturally express themselves in a language which is distinguished by pauses at regular, and almost equal, intervals; and which, upon that account, can more easily be adapted to the regular returns of the correspondent periods of a tune. The passions, on the contrary, which drive men from one another, the unsocial, the hateful, the indecent, the vicious passions, cannot easily be imitated by Music. The voice of furious anger, for example, is harsh and discordant; its periods are all irregular, sometimes very long and sometimes very short, and distinguished by no regular pauses. The obscure and almost inarticulate grumblings of black malice and envy, the screaming outcries of dastardly fear, the hideous growlings of brutal and implacable revenge, are all equally discordant.

[7] [TMS I.i.5 distinguishes the 'amiable' virtues from the 'awful and respectable'.]

It is with difficulty that Music can imitate any of those passions, and the Music which does imitate them is not the most agreeable. A whole entertainment may consist, without any impropriety, of the imitation of the social and amiable passions. It would be a strange entertainment which consisted altogether in the imitation of the odious and the vicious. A single song expresses almost always some social, agreeable, or interesting passion. In an opera the unsocial and disagreeable are sometimes introduced, but it is rarely, and as discords are introduced into harmony, to set off by their contrast the superior beauty of the opposite passions. What Plato said of Virtue, that it was of all beauties the brightest,[8] may with some sort of truth be said of the proper and natural objects of musical imitation. They are either the sentiments and passions, in the exercise of which consist both the glory and the happiness of human life, or they are those from which it derives its most delicious pleasures, and most enlivening joys; or, at the worst and the lowest, they are those by which it calls upon our indulgence and compassionate assistance to its unavoidable weaknesses, its distresses, and its misfortunes.

14   To the merit of its imitation and to that of its happy choice in the objects which it imitates, the great merits of Statuary and Painting, Music joins another peculiar and exquisite merit of its own. Statuary and Painting cannot be said to add any new beauties of their own to the beauties of Nature which they imitate; they may assemble a greater number of those beauties, and group them in a more agreeable manner than they are commonly, or perhaps ever, to be found in Nature. It may perhaps be true, what the artists are so very fond of telling us, that no woman ever equalled, in all the parts of her body, the beauty of the Venus of Medicis, nor any man that of the Apollo of Belvidere. But they must allow, surely, that there is no particular beauty in any part or feature of those two famous statues, which is not at least equalled, if not much excelled, by what is to be found in many living subjects. But Music, by arranging, and as it were bending to its own time and measure, whatever sentiments and passions it expresses, not only assembles and groups, as well as Statuary and Painting, the different beauties of Nature which it imitates, but it clothes them, besides, with a new and an exquisite beauty of its own; it clothes them with melody and harmony, which, like a transparent mantle, far from concealing any beauty, serve only to give a brighter colour, a

---

[8] [Smith probably has in mind the myth of Plato's *Phaedrus*, 250 A–D, where Plato compares the invisible loveliness of the different virtues with the brightness of beauty, and says that if wisdom were visible to the eye it would be even more captivating than beauty. There is an allusion to the passage in Cicero, *De Finibus* (II.16.51–2), a work with which Smith was especially familiar.]

more enlivening lustre, and a more engaging grace to every beauty
which they infold.

15   To these two different sorts of imitation,—to that general one, by
which Music is made to resemble discourse, and to that particular
one, by which it is made to express the sentiments and feelings with
which a particular situation inspires a particular person,—there is
frequently joined a third. The person who sings may join to this
double imitation of the singer the additional imitation of the actor;
and express, not only by the modulation and cadence of his voice, but
by his countenance, by his attitudes, by his gestures, and by his
motions, the sentiments and feelings of the person whose situation is
painted in the song. Even in private company, though a song may
sometimes perhaps be said to be well sung, it can never be said to be
well performed, unless the singer does something of this kind; and
there is no comparison between the effect of what is sung coldly from
a music-book at the end of a harpsichord, and of what is not only
sung, but acted with proper freedom, animation, and boldness. An
opera actor does no more than this; and an imitation which is so
pleasing, and which appears even so natural, in private society, ought
not to appear forced, unnatural, or disagreeable upon the stage.

16   In a good opera actor, not only the modulations and pauses of his
voice, but every motion and gesture, every variation, either in the air
of his head, or in the attitude of his body, correspond to the time and
measure of Music: they correspond to the expression of the sentiment
or passion which the Music imitates, and that expression necessarily
corresponds to this time and measure. Music is as it were the soul
which animates him, which informs every feature of his countenance,
and even directs every movement of his eyes. Like the musical
expression of a song, his action adds to the natural grace of the
sentiment or action which it imitates, a new and peculiar grace of its
own; the exquisite and engaging grace of those gestures and motions,
of those airs and attitudes which are directed by the movement, by
the time and measure of Music; this grace heightens and enlivens
that expression. Nothing can be more deeply affecting than the
interesting scenes of the serious opera, when to good Poetry and good
Music, to the Poetry of Metastasio and the Music of Pergolese, is
added the execution of a good actor. In the serious opera, indeed, the
action is too often sacrificed to the Music; the castrati, who perform
the principal parts, being always the most insipid and miserable
actors. The sprightly airs of the comic opera are, in the same manner,
in the highest degree enlivening and diverting. Though they do not
make us laugh so loud as we sometimes do at the scenes of the
common comedy, they make us smile more frequently; and the

agreeable gaiety, the temperate joy, if I may call it so, with which they inspire us, is not only an elegant, but a most delicious pleasure. The deep distress and the great passions of tragedy are capable of producing some effect, though it should be but indifferently acted. It is not so with the lighter misfortunes and less affecting situations of comedy: unless it is at least tolerably acted, it is altogether insupportable. But the castrati are scarce ever tolerable actors; they are accordingly seldom admitted to play in the comic opera; which, being upon that account commonly better performed than the serious, appears to many people the better entertainment of the two.

17   The imitative powers of Instrumental are much inferior to those of Vocal Music; its melodious but unmeaning and inarticulated sounds cannot, like the articulations of the human voice, relate distinctly the circumstances of any particular story, or describe the different situations which those circumstances produced; or even express clearly, and so as to be understood by every hearer, the various sentiments and passions which the parties concerned felt from these situations: even its imitation of other sounds, the objects which it can certainly best imitate, is commonly so indistinct, that alone, and without any explication, it might not readily suggest to us what was the imitated object. The rocking of a cradle is supposed to be imitated in that concerto of Correlli, which is said to have been composed for the Nativity:[9] but, unless we were told beforehand, it might not readily occur to us what it meant to imitate, or whether it meant to imitate any thing at all; and this imitation (which, though perhaps as successful as any other, is by no means the distinguished beauty of that admired composition) might only appear to us a singular and odd passage in Music. The ringing of bells and the singing of the lark and nightingale are imitated in the symphony of Instrumental Music which Mr. Handel has composed for the Allegro and Penseroso of Milton:[10] these are not only sounds but musical sounds, and may therefore be supposed to be more within the compass of the powers of musical imitation. It is accordingly universally acknowledged, that in these imitations this great master has been remarkably successful; and yet, unless the verses of Milton explained the meaning of the Music, it might not even in this case readily occur to us what it meant to imitate, or whether it meant to imitate any thing at all. With the explication of the words, indeed, the imitation appears, what it certainly is, a very fine one; but without that explication it might

---

[9] The eighth *concerto grosso* contained in Corelli's Opus 6 is explicitly designated 'composed for the night of the nativity'. It was a *concerto di chiesa* and is known as the 'Christmas concerto'.

[10] Milton's two poems, together with one by Charles Jennens, were set to music by Handel under the title *L'Allegro, il Penseroso ed il Moderato*. The work, first performed on 27 February 1740, was several times revived.

perhaps appear only a singular passage, which had less connexion
either with what went before or with what came after it, than any
other in the Music.

18   Instrumental Music is said sometimes to imitate motion; but in
reality it only either imitates the particular sounds which accompany
certain motions, or it produces sounds of which the time and measure
bear some correspondence to the variations, to the pauses and
interruptions, to the successive accelerations and retardations of the
motion which it means to imitate: it is in this way that it sometimes
attempts to express the march and array of an army, the confusion and
hurry of a battle, etc. In all these cases, however, its imitation is so very
indistinct, that without the accompaniment of some other art, to
explain and interpret its meaning, it would be almost always
unintelligible; and we could scarce ever know with certainty, either
what it meant to imitate, or whether it meant to imitate any thing at all.

19   In the imitative arts, though it is by no means necessary that the
imitating should so exactly resemble the imitated object, that the one
should sometimes be mistaken for the other, it is, however, necessary
that they should resemble at least so far, that the one should always
readily suggest the other. It would be a strange picture which
required an inscription at the foot to tell us, not only what particular
person it meant to represent, but whether it meant to represent a man
or a horse, or whether it meant to be a picture at all, and to represent
any thing. The imitations of instrumental Music may, in some
respects, be said to resemble such pictures. There is, however, this
very essential difference between them, that the picture would not be
much mended by the inscription; whereas, by what may be
considered as very little more than such an inscription, instrumental
Music, though it cannot always even then, perhaps, be said properly
to imitate, may, however, produce all the effects of the finest and most
perfect imitation. In order to explain in what manner this is brought
about, it will not be necessary to descend into any great depth of
philosophical speculation.

20   That train of thoughts and ideas which is continually passing
through the mind does not always move on with the same pace, if I
may say so, or with the same order and connection. When we are gay
and cheerful, its motion is brisker and more lively, our thoughts
succeed one another more rapidly, and those which immediately
follow one another seem frequently either to have but little connection,
or to be connected rather by their opposition than by their mutual
resemblance. As in this wanton and playful disposition of mind we
hate to dwell long upon the same thought, so we do not much care to
pursue resembling thoughts; and the variety of contrast is more

agreeable to us than the sameness of resemblance. It is quite otherwise when we are melancholy and desponding; we then frequently find ourselves haunted, as it were, by some thought which we would gladly chase away, but which constantly pursues us, and which admits no followers, attendants, or companions, but such as are of its own kindred and complexion. A slow succession of resembling or closely connected thoughts is the characteristic of this disposition of mind; a quick succession of thoughts, frequently contrasted and in general very slightly connected, is the characteristic of the other. What may be called the natural state of the mind, the state in which we are neither elated nor dejected, the state of sedateness, tranquillity, and composure, holds a sort of middle place between those two opposite extremes; our thoughts succeed one another more slowly, and with a more distinct connection, than in the one; more quickly, and with a greater variety, than in the other.

21   Acute sounds are naturally gay, sprightly, and enlivening; grave sounds solemn, awful, and melancholy. There seems too to be some natural connection between acuteness in tune and quickness in time or succession, as well as between gravity and slowness: an acute sound seems to fly off more quickly than a grave one: the treble is more cheerful than the bass; its notes likewise commonly succeed one another more rapidly. But instrumental Music, by a proper arrangement, by a quicker or slower succession of acute and grave, of resembling and contrasted sounds, can not only accommodate itself to the gay, the sedate, or the melancholy mood; but if the mind is so far vacant as not to be disturbed by any disorderly passion, it can, at least for the moment, and to a certain degree, produce every possible modification of each of those moods or dispositions. We all readily distinguish the cheerful, the gay, and the sprightly Music, from the melancholy, the plaintive, and the affecting; and both these from what holds a sort of middle place between them, the sedate, the tranquil, and the composing. And we are all sensible that, in the natural and ordinary state of the mind, Music can, by a sort of incantation, sooth and charm us into some degree of that particular mood or disposition which accords with its own character and temper. In a concert of instrumental Music the attention is engaged, with pleasure and delight, to listen to a combination of the most agreeable and melodious sounds, which follow one another, sometimes with a quicker, and sometimes with a slower succession; and in which those that immediately follow one another sometimes exactly or nearly resemble, and sometimes contrast with one another in tune, in time, and in order of arrangement. The mind being thus successively occupied by a train of objects, of which the nature,

succession, and connection correspond, sometimes to the gay, sometimes to the tranquil, and sometimes to the melancholy mood or disposition, it is itself successively led into each of those moods or dispositions; and is thus brought into a sort of harmony or concord with the Music which so agreeably engages its attention.

22   It is not, however, by imitation properly, that instrumental Music produces this effect: instrumental Music does not imitate, as vocal Music, as Painting, or as Dancing would imitate, a gay, a sedate, or a melancholy person; it does not tell us, as any of those other arts could tell us, a pleasant, a serious, or a melancholy story. It is not, as in vocal Music, in Painting, or in Dancing, by sympathy with the gaiety, the sedateness, or the melancholy and distress of some other person, that instrumental Music soothes us into each of these dispositions: it becomes itself a gay, a sedate, or a melancholy object; and the mind naturally assumes the mood or disposition which at the time corresponds to the object which engages its attention. Whatever we feel from instrumental Music is an original, and not a sympathetic feeling: it is our own gaiety, sedateness, or melancholy; not the reflected disposition of another person.

23   When we follow the winding alleys of some happily situated and well laid out garden, we are presented with a succession of landscapes, which are sometimes gay, sometimes gloomy, and sometimes calm and serene; if the mind is in its natural state, it suits itself to the objects which successively present themselves, and varies in some degree its mood and present humour with every variation of the scene. It would be improper, however, to say that those scenes imitated the gay, the calm, or the melancholy mood of the mind; they may produce in their turn each of those moods, but they cannot imitate any of them. Instrumental Music, in the same manner, though it can excite all those different dispositions, cannot imitate any of them. There are no two things in nature more perfectly disparate than sound and sentiment; and it is impossible by any human power to fashion the one into any thing that bears any real resemblance to the other.

24   This power of exciting and varying the different moods and dispositions of the mind, which instrumental Music really possesses to a very considerable degree, has been the principal source of its reputation for those great imitative powers which have been ascribed to it. 'Painting,' says an Author, more capable of feeling strongly than of analising accurately, Mr. Rousseau of Geneva,[11] 'Painting, which

[11] J.-J. Rousseau, *Dictionnaire de musique* (1768), s.v. 'Imitation'; reprinted under 'Imitation' in the *Encyclopédie*, supp. vol. iii (1777) [and in Rousseau's *Essai sur l'origine des langues* (1781), chap. 16].

presents its imitations, not to the imagination, but to the senses, and
to only one of the senses, can represent nothing besides the objects of
sight. Music, one might imagine, should be equally confined to those
of hearing. It imitates, however, every thing, even those objects which
are perceivable by sight only. By a delusion that seems almost
inconceivable, it can, as it were, put the eye into the ear; and the
greatest wonder, of an art which acts only by motion and succession,
is, that it can imitate rest and repose. Night, Sleep, Solitude, and
Silence are all within the compass of musical imitation. Though all
Nature should be asleep, the person who contemplates it is awake;
and the art of the musician consists in substituting, in the room of an
image of what is not the object of hearing, that of the movements
which its presence would excite in the mind of the spectator.'—That
is, of the effects which it would produce upon his mood and
disposition. 'The musician' (continues the same Author) 'will
sometimes, not only agitate the waves of the sea, blow up the flames
of a conflagration, make the rain fall, the rivulets flow and swell the
torrents, but he will paint the horrors of a hideous desart, darken the
walls of a subterraneous dungeon, calm the tempest, restore serenity
and tranquillity to the air and the sky, and shed from the orchestre a
new freshness over the groves and the fields. He will not directly
represent any of these objects, but he will excite in the mind the same
movements which it would feel from seeing them.'

25   Upon this very eloquent description of Mr. Rousseau I must
observe, that without the accompaniment of the scenery and action
of the opera, without the assistance either of the scene-painter or of
the poet, or of both, the instrumental Music of the orchestre could
produce none of the effects which are here ascribed to it; and we
could never know, we could never even guess, which of the gay,
melancholy, or tranquil objects above mentioned it meant to represent
to us; or whether it meant to represent any of them, and not merely
to entertain us with a concert of gay, melancholy, or tranquil Music;
or, as the ancients called them, of the Diastaltic, of the Systaltic, or of
the Middle Music.[12] With that accompaniment, indeed, though it
cannot always even then, perhaps, be said properly to imitate, yet by
supporting the imitation of some other art, it may produce all the
same effects upon us as if itself had imitated in the finest and most
perfect manner. Whatever be the object or situation which the scene-

---

[12] [The threefold division (diastaltic, systaltic, hesychastic) by Aristides Quintilianus is
described in Charles Burney's 'Dissertation on the Music of the Ancients' (§5), prefixed to vol.
i (1776) of his *General History of Music*. Smith possessed a copy of Burney's work (J. Bonar,
Catalogue of the Library of Adam Smith, ed. 2, 39) and may well be drawing on it here. If so, the
passage provides confirmatory evidence of the late composition, or at least revision, of this essay
on the Imitative Arts (see the editor's Introduction, 171–2).]

painter represents upon the theatre, the Music of the orchestre, by disposing the mind[13] to the same sort of mood and temper which it would feel from the presence of that object, or from sympathy with the person who was placed in that situation, can greatly enhance the effect of that imitation: it can accommodate itself to every diversity of scene. The melancholy of the man who, upon some great occasion, only finds himself alone in the darkness, the silence and solitude of the night, is very different from that of one who, upon a like occasion, finds himself in the midst of some dreary and inhospitable desert; and even in this situation his feelings would not be the same as if he was shut up in a subterraneous dungeon. The different degrees of precision with which the Music of the orchestre can accommodate itself to each of those diversities, must depend upon the taste, the sensibility, the fancy and imagination of the composer: it may sometimes, perhaps, contribute to this precision, that it should imitate, as well as it can, the sounds which either naturally accompany, or which might be supposed to accompany, the particular objects represented. The Symphony in the French opera of Alcyone,[14] which imitated the violence of the winds and the dashing of the waves, in the tempest which was to drown Coix, is much commended by cotemporary writers. That in the opera of Isse,[15] which imitated that murmuring in the leaves of the oaks of Dodona, which might be supposed to precede the miraculous pronunciation of the oracle: and that in the opera of Amadis,[16] of which the dismal accents imitated the sounds which might be supposed to accompany the opening of the tomb of Ardan, before the apparition of the ghost of that warrior, are still more celebrated. Instrumental Music, however, without violating too much its own melody and harmony, can imitate but imperfectly the sounds of natural objects, of which the greater part have neither melody nor harmony. Great reserve, great discretion, and a very nice discernment are requisite, in order to introduce with

[13] Smith's emphasis on 'disposing the mind' provides a much more convincing account than Rousseau's.

[14] *Alcione* by Marin Marais (1656–1728), words by Houdar de La Motte, first produced at Paris in 1706, revived many times, and later much altered. Its *tempeste symphonique*, Act IV, sc.iv, has been described as 'one of the first essays in operatic realism' (A. Loewenberg, *Annals of Opera 1579–1940*, 2nd ed. revised (1955)).

[15] *Issé* by André (Cardinal) Destouches (1672–1749: not to be confused with the librettist Philippe Destouches-Néricault), words by Houdar de La Motte, first produced at Fontainebleau in 1697 and many times revived. [The scene referred to is Act II, sc.v.—or Act III, sc.v, in the five-act version of 1708.]

[16] *Amadis* (later *Amadis de Gaule*) by Jean-Baptiste Lully (1632–87), words by Philippe Quinault, first produced at Paris in 1684, several times revived, and finally rescored by J. C. Bach. [The scene referred to is Act III, sc.ii. The passages in the three operas to which Smith refers are in *Recueil général des opéra representez par l'Académie royale de musique*: vol. ix (1710), 103; vol. vi (1703), 211 (1708 version in vol. ix, 370); vol. ii (1703), 465.]

propriety such imperfect imitations, either into Poetry or Music; when repeated too often, when continued too long, they appear to be what they really are, mere tricks, in which a very inferior artist, if he will only give himself the trouble to attend to them, can easily equal the greatest. I have seen a Latin translation of Mr. Pope's Ode on St. Cecilia's Day,[17] which in this respect very much excelled the original. Such imitations are still easier in Music. Both in the one art and in the other, the difficulty is not in making them as well as they are capable of being made, but in knowing when and how far to make them at all: but to be able to accommodate the temper and character of the Music to every peculiarity of the scene and situation with such exact precision, that the one shall produce the very same effect upon the mind as the other, is not one of those tricks in which an inferior artist can easily equal the greatest; it is an art which requires all the judgment, knowledge, and invention of the most consummate master. It is upon this art, and not upon its imperfect imitation, either of real or imaginary sounds, that the great effects of instrumental Music depend; such imitations ought perhaps to be admitted only so far as they may sometimes contribute to ascertain the meaning, and thereby to enhance the effects of this art.

26   By endeavouring to extend the effects of scenery beyond what the nature of the thing will admit of, it has been much abused; and in the common, as well as in the musical drama, many imitations have been attempted, which, after the first and second time we have seen them, necessarily appear ridiculous: such are, the Thunder rumbling from the Mustard-bowl, and the Snow of Paper and thick Hail of Pease, so finely exposed by Mr. Pope.[18] Such imitations resemble those of painted Statuary; they may surprize at first, but they disgust ever after, and appear evidently such simple and easy tricks as are fit only for the amusement of children and their nurses at a puppet-show. The thunder of either theatre ought certainly never to be louder than that which the orchestre is capable of producing; and their most dreadful tempests ought never to exceed what the scene painter is capable of representing. In such imitations there may be an art which merits some degree of esteem and admiration. In the other there can be none which merits any.

27   This abuse of scenery has both subsisted much longer, and been carried to a much greater degree of extravagance, in the musical than in the common drama. In France it has been long banished from the latter; but it still continues, not only to be tolerated, but to be admired

[17] [*Carmen Alexandri Pope In S. Caeciliam Latine redditum* by Christopher Smart (1743; reprinted 1746).]
[18] [*Dunciad*, ii.226, 262.]

and applauded in the former. In the French operas, not only thunder and lightning, storms and tempests, are commonly represented in the ridiculous manner above mentioned, but all the marvellous, all the supernatural of Epic Poetry, all the metamorphoses of Mythology, all the wonders of Witchcraft and Magic, every thing that is most unfit to be represented upon the stage, are every day exhibited with the most complete approbation and applause of that ingenious nation. The Music of the orchestre producing upon the audience nearly the same effect which a better and more artful imitation would produce, hinders them from feeling, at least in its full force, the ridicule of those childish and aukward imitations which necessarily abound in that extravagant scenery. And in reality such imitations, though no doubt ridiculous every where, yet certainly appear somewhat less so in the musical than they would in the common drama. The Italian opera, before it was reformed by Apostolo Zeno[19] and Metastasio, was in this respect equally extravagant, and was upon that account the subject of the agreeable raillery of Mr. Addison in several different papers of the Spectator.[20] Even since that reformation it still continues to be a rule, that the scene should change at least with every act; and the unity of place never was a more sacred law in the common drama, than the violation of it has become in the musical: the latter seems in reality to require both a more picturesque and a more varied scenery, than is at all necessary for the former. In an opera, as the Music supports the effect of the scenery, so the scenery often serves to determine the character, and to explain the meaning of the Music; it ought to vary therefore as that character varies. The pleasure of an opera, besides, is in its nature more a sensual pleasure, than that of a common comedy or tragedy; the latter produce their effect principally by means of the imagination: in the closet, accordingly, their effect is not much inferior to what it is upon the stage. But the effect of an opera is seldom very great in the closet; it addresses itself more to the external senses, and as it soothes the ear by its melody and harmony, so we feel that it ought to dazzle the eye with the splendour and variety of its scenery.

28   In an opera the instrumental Music of the orchestre supports the imitation both of the poet and of the actor, as well as of the scene-painter. The overture disposes the mind to that mood which fits it for

---

[19] The original edition has 'Apostolo, Zeno,' but the redundant commas are probably an error of the printer (or conceivably of the copyist). Apostolo Zeno (1668–1750) was one librettist, not two. Metastasio (Pietro Trapassi, 1698–1782) succeeded him as imperial court poet in Vienna and was of course far more influential.

[20] *The Spectator*, i (1711), 5, 18, 29, 31. Though Addison was no musician, his articles inspired Johann Mattheson to translate and imitate them and to found the periodical *Critica Musica* in 1722. (See Grove's *Dictionary of Music*, article on 'Criticism'.)

the opening of the piece. The Music between the acts keeps up the
impression which the foregoing had made, and prepares us for that
which the following is to make. When the orchestre interrupts, as it
frequently does, either the recitative or the air, it is in order either to
enforce the effect of what had gone before, or to put the mind in the
mood which fits it for hearing what is to come after. Both in the
recitatives and in the airs it accompanies and directs the voice, and
often brings it back to the proper tone and modulation, when it is
upon the point of wandering away from them; and the correctness of
the best vocal Music is owing in a great measure to the guidance of
instrumental; though in all these cases it supports the imitation of
another art, yet in all of them it may be said rather to diminish than
to increase the resemblance between the imitating and the imitated
object. Nothing can be more unlike to what really passes in the world,
than that persons engaged in the most interesting situations, both of
public and private life, in sorrow, in disappointment, in distress, in
despair, should, in all that they say and do, be constantly accompanied
with a fine concert of instrumental Music. Were we to reflect upon it,
such accompaniment must in all cases diminish the probability of the
action, and render the representation still less like nature than it
otherwise would be. It is not by imitation, therefore, that instrumental
Music supports and enforces the imitations of the other arts; but it is
by producing upon the mind, in consequence of other powers, the
same sort of effect which the most exact imitation of nature, which
the most perfect observation of probability, could produce. To
produce this effect is, in such entertainments, the sole end and
purpose of that imitation and observation. If it can be equally well
produced by other means, this end and purpose may be equally well
answered.

29   But if instrumental Music can seldom be said to be properly
imitative, even when it is employed to support the imitation of some
other art, it is commonly still less so when it is employed alone. Why
should it embarrass its melody and harmony, or constrain its time
and measure, by attempting an imitation which, without the
accompaniment of some other art to explain and interpret its
meaning, nobody is likely to understand? In the most approved
instrumental Music, accordingly, in the overtures of Handel and the
concertos of Correlli,[21] there is little or no imitation, and where there
is any, it is the source of but a very small part of the merit of those
compositions. Without any imitation, instrumental Music can
produce very considerable effects; though its powers over the heart

[21] It is possible that the 'approval' of Vivaldi's lovely *Four Seasons* (1728) had declined by the
time Smith was writing.

and affections are, no doubt, much inferior to those of vocal Music, it has, however, considerable powers: by the sweetness of its sounds it awakens agreeably, and calls upon the attention; by their connection and affinity it naturally detains that attention, which follows easily a series of agreeable sounds, which have all a certain relation both to a common, fundamental, or leading note, called the key note; and to a certain succession or combination of notes, called the song or composition. By means of this relation each foregoing sound seems to introduce, and as it were prepare the mind for the following: by its rythmus, by its time and measure, it disposes that succession of sounds into a certain arrangement, which renders the whole more easy to be comprehended and remembered. Time and measure are to instrumental Music what order and method are to discourse; they break it into proper parts and divisions, by which we are enabled both to remember better what is gone before, and frequently to foresee somewhat of what is to come after: we frequently foresee the return of a period which we know must correspond to another which we remember to have gone before; and, according to the saying of an ancient philosopher and musician, the enjoyment of Music arises partly from memory and partly from foresight. When the measure, after having been continued so long as to satisfy us, changes to another, that variety, which thus disappoints, becomes more agreeable to us than the uniformity which would have gratified our expectation: but without this order and method we could remember very little of what had gone before, and we could foresee still less of what was to come after; and the whole enjoyment of Music would be equal to little more than the effect of the particular sounds which rung in our ears at every particular instant. By means of this order and method it is, during the progress of the entertainment, equal to the effect of all that we remember, and of all that we foresee; and at the conclusion, to the combined and accumulated effect of all the different parts of which the whole was composed.

30   A well-composed concerto[22] of instrumental Music, by the number and variety of the instruments, by the variety of the parts which are performed by them, and the perfect concord or correspondence of all these different parts; by the exact harmony or coincidence of all the different sounds which are heard at the same time, and by that happy variety of measure which regulates the succession of those which are heard at different times, presents an object so agreeable, so great, so various, and so interesting, that alone, and without suggesting any

[22] The term 'concerto' is used here in its 'correct' form of a group or 'concert' of instruments. Its virtual restriction to solo (or rarely double or triple) virtuoso works dates from the time of Haydn and Mozart.

other object, either by imitation or otherwise, it can occupy, and as it were fill up, completely the whole capacity of the mind, so as to leave no part of its attention vacant for thinking of any thing else. In the contemplation of that immense variety of agreeable and melodious sounds, arranged and digested, both in their coincidence and in their succession, into so complete and regular a system, the mind in reality enjoys not only a very great sensual, but a very high intellectual, pleasure, not unlike that which it derives from the contemplation of a great system in any other science.[23] A full concerto of such instrumental Music, not only does not require, but it does not admit of any accompaniment. A song or a dance, by demanding an attention which we have not to spare, would disturb, instead of heightening, the effect of the Music; they may often very properly succeed, but they cannot accompany it. That music seldom means to tell any particular story, or to imitate any particular event, or in general to suggest any particular object, distinct from that combination of sounds of which itself is composed. Its meaning, therefore, may be said to be complete in itself, and to require no interpreters to explain it. What is called the subject of such Music is merely, as has already been said, a certain leading combination of notes, to which it frequently returns, and to which all its digressions and variations bear a certain affinity. It is altogether different from what is called the subject of a poem or a picture, which is always something which is not either in the poem or in the picture, or something quite distinct from that combination, either of words on the one hand, or of colours on the other, of which they are respectively composed. The subject of a composition of instrumental Music is a part of that composition: the subject of a poem or picture is no part of either.

31   The effect of instrumental Music upon the mind has been called its expression. In the feeling it is frequently not unlike the effect of what is called the expression of Painting, and is sometimes equally interesting. But the effect of the expression of Painting arises always from the thought of something which, though distinctly and clearly suggested by the drawing and colouring of the picture, is altogether different from that drawing and colouring. It arises sometimes from sympathy with, sometimes from antipathy and aversion to, the sentiments, emotions, and passions which the countenance, the action, the air and attitude of the persons represented suggest. The melody and harmony of instrumental Music, on the contrary, do not distinctly and clearly suggest any thing that is different from that melody and harmony. Whatever effect it produces is the immediate

[23] [Cf.II.2, above, where Smith writes of a rhythmic succession in music or dance as 'a sort of whole or system'. Systems in science are discussed in Astronomy, IV.19.]

effect of that melody and harmony, and not of something else which is signified and suggested by them: they in fact signify and suggest nothing. It may be proper to say that the complete art of painting, the complete merit of a picture, is composed of three distinct arts or merits; that of drawing, that of colouring, and that of expression. But to say, as Mr. Avison does,[24] that the complete art of a musician, the complete merit of a piece of Music, is composed or made up of three distinct arts or merits, that of melody, that of harmony, and that of expression, is to say, that it is made up of melody and harmony, and of the immediate and necessary effect of melody and harmony: the division is by no means logical; expression in painting is not the necessary effect either of good drawing or of good colouring, or of both together; a picture may be both finely drawn and finely coloured, and yet have very little expression: but that effect upon the mind which is called expression in Music, is the immediate and necessary effect of good melody. In the power of producing this effect consists the essential characteristic which distinguishes such melody from what is bad or indifferent. Harmony may enforce the effect of good melody, but without good melody the most skilful harmony can produce no effect which deserves the name of expression; it can do little more than fatigue and confound the ear. A painter may possess, in a very eminent degree, the talents of drawing and colouring, and yet possess that of expression in a very inferior degree. Such a painter, too, may have great merit. In the judgment of Du Piles,[25] even the celebrated Titian was a painter of this kind. But to say that a musician possessed the talents of melody and harmony in a very eminent degree, and that of expression in a very inferior one, would be to say, that in his works the cause was not followed by its necessary and proportionable effect. A musician may be a very skilful harmonist, and yet be defective in the talents of melody, air, and expression; his songs may be dull and without effect. Such a musician too may have a certain degree of merit, not unlike that of a man of great learning, who wants fancy, taste, and invention.

32   Instrumental Music, therefore, though it may, no doubt, be considered in some respects as an imitative art, is certainly less so than any other which merits that appellation; it can imitate but a few objects, and even these so imperfectly, that without the accompani-

[24] Charles Avison (1709–70), composer and for much of his life organist in Newcastle-upon-Tyne. His original writings may be regarded as the beginning of English musical criticism. [The reference is to *An Essay on Musical Expression* (1752), 25 and *passim*.]

[25] [Roger de Piles (1635–1709)—usually called 'Du Piles' by English writers—analyses Titian's strengths and limitations in several of his works of art criticism. Smith here echoes a remark in *Abrégé de la vie des peintres* (1699), 265, which suggests that Titian was more concerned with fidelity to external nature than with 'une vive expression des Passions de l'Ame'. Cf. *Dissertations sur les ouvrages des plus fameux peintres* (1681), 19, 36, 73, etc.]

ment of some other art, its imitation is scarce ever intelligible: imitation is by no means essential to it, and the principal effects which it is capable of producing arises from powers altogether different from those of imitation.

Part III

1 The imitative powers of Dancing are much superior to those of instrumental Music, and are at least equal, perhaps superior, to those of any other art. Like instrumental Music, however, it is not necessarily or essentially imitative, and it can produce very agreeable effects, without imitating any thing. In the greater part of our common dances there is little or no imitation, and they consist almost entirely of a succession of such steps, gestures, and motions, regulated by the time and measure of Music, as either display extraordinary grace or require extraordinary agility. Even some of our dances, which are said to have been originally imitative, have, in the way in which we practise them, almost ceased to be so. The minuet, in which the woman, after passing and repassing the man several times, first gives him up one hand, then the other, and then both hands, is said to have been originally a Moorish dance, which emblematically represented the passion of love. Many of my readers may have frequently danced this dance, and, in the opinion of all who saw them, with great grace and propriety, though neither they nor their spectators once thought of the allegorical meaning which it originally intended to express.

2   A certain measured, cadenced step, commonly called a dancing step, which keeps time with, and as it were beats the measure of, the Music which accompanies and directs it, is the essential characteristic which distinguishes a dance from every other sort of motion. When the dancer, moving with a step of this kind, and observing this time and measure, imitates either the ordinary or the more important actions of human life, he shapes and fashions, as it were, a thing of one kind, into the resemblance of another thing of a very different kind: his art conquers the disparity which Nature has placed between the imitating and the imitated object, and has upon that account some degree of that sort of merit which belongs to all the imitative arts. This disparity, indeed, is not so great as in some other of those arts, nor consequently the merit of the imitation which conquers it. Nobody would compare the merit of a good imitative dancer to that of a good painter or statuary. The dancer, however, may have a very considerable degree of merit, and his imitation perhaps may

sometimes be capable of giving us as much pleasure as that of either of the other two artists. All the subjects, either of Statuary or of History Painting, are within the compass of his imitative powers; and in representing them, his art has even some advantage over both the other two. Statuary and History Painting can represent but a single instant[1] of the action which they mean to imitate: the causes which prepared, the consequences which followed, the situation of that single instant are altogether beyond the compass of their imitation. A pantomime dance can represent distinctly those causes and consequences; it is not confined to the situation of a single instant; but, like Epic Poetry, it can represent all the events of a long story, and exhibit a long train and succession of connected and interesting situations. It is capable therefore of affecting us much more than either Statuary or Painting. The ancient Romans used to shed tears at the representations of their pantomimes, as we do at that of the most interesting tragedies; an effect which is altogether beyond the powers of Statuary or Painting.

3   The ancient Greeks appear to have been a nation of dancers, and both their common and their stage dances seem to have been all imitative. The stage dances of the ancient Romans appear to have been equally so. Among that grave people it was reckoned indecent to dance in private societies; and they could therefore have no common dances. Among both nations imitation seems to have been considered as essential to dancing.

4   It is quite otherwise in modern times: though we have pantomime dances upon the stage, yet the greater part even of our stage dances are not pantomime, and cannot well be said to imitate any thing. The greater part of our common dances either never were pantomime, or, with a very few exceptions, have almost all ceased to be so.

5   This remarkable difference of character between the ancient and the modern dances seems to be the natural effect of a correspondent difference in that of the Music, which has accompanied and directed both the one and the other.

6   In modern times we almost always dance to instrumental Music, which being itself not imitative, the greater part of the dances which it directs, and as it were inspires, have ceased to be so. In ancient times, on the contrary, they seem to have danced almost always to vocal Music; which being necessary and essentially imitative, their dances became so too. The ancients seem to have had little or nothing of what is properly called instrumental Music, or of Music composed not to be sung by the voice, but to be played upon instruments, and

[1] [On History Painting, 'which represents an instant of time', cf. Hildebrand Jacob, *Of the Sister Arts, an Essay* (1734), 19.]

both their wind and their stringed instruments seem to have served only as an accompaniment and direction to the voice.

7   In the country it frequently happens that a company of young people take a fancy to dance, though they have neither fiddler nor piper to dance to. A lady undertakes to sing while the rest of the company dance: in most cases she sings the notes only, without the words, and then the voice being little more than a musical instrument, the dance is performed in the usual way, without any imitation. But if she sings the words, and if in those words there happens to be somewhat more than ordinary spirit and humour, immediately all the company, especially all the best dancers, and all those who dance most at their ease, become more or less pantomimes, and by their gestures and motions express, as well as they can, the meaning and story of the song. This would be still more the case, if the same person both danced and sung; a practice very common among the ancients: it requires good lungs and a vigorous constitution; but with these advantages and long practice, the very highest dances may be performed in this manner. I have seen a Negro dance to his own song, the war-dance of his own country, with such vehemence of action and expression, that the whole company, gentlemen as well as ladies, got up upon the chairs and tables, to be as much as possible out of the way of his fury. In the Greek language there are two verbs which both signify to dance;[2] each of which has its proper derivatives, signifying a dance and a dancer. In the greater part of Greek authors, these two sets of words, like all others which are nearly synonimous, are frequently confounded, and used promiscuously. According to the best critics, however, in strict propriety, one of these verbs signifies to dance and sing at the same time, or to dance to one's own music. The other to dance without singing, or to dance to the music of other people. There is said too to be a correspondent difference in the signification of their respective derivatives. In the choruses of the ancient Greek tragedies, consisting sometimes of more than fifty persons, some piped and some sung, but all danced, and danced to their own music.

[*The following Observations were found among Mr.* SMITH'S *Manuscripts, without any intimation whether they were intended as part of this, or of a different Essay. As they appeared too valuable to be suppressed, the Editors have availed themselves of their connection with the passage referred to in* ⟨II.2⟩ *and have annexed them to this Essay.*]

[2] Presumably χορεύειν and ὀρχεῖσθαι.

Of the Affinity between Music, Dancing, and Poetry

1   In the second part of this Essay I have mentioned the connection
between the two arts of *Music* and *Dancing* formed by the *Rythmus,*
as the ancients termed it, or, as we call it, the tune or measure that
equally regulates both.

2   It is not, however, every sort of step, gesture, or motion, of which
the correspondence with the tune or measure of Music will constitute
a Dance. It must be a step, gesture, or motion of a particular sort. In
a good opera-actor, not only the modulations and pauses of his voice,
but every motion and gesture, every variation, either in the air of his
head or in the attitude of his body, correspond to the time and
measure of Music. The best opera-actor, however, is not, according to
the language of any country in Europe, understood to dance, yet in
the performance of his part he generally makes use of what is called
the stage step; but even this step is not understood to be a dancing
step.

3   Though the eye of the most ordinary spectator readily distinguishes
between what is called a dancing step and any other step, gesture, or
motion, yet it may not perhaps be very easy to express what it is
which constitutes this distinction. To ascertain exactly the precise
limits at which the one species begins, and the other ends, or to give
an accurate definition of this very frivolous matter, might perhaps
require more thought and attention, than the very small importance
of the subject may seem to deserve. Were I, however, to attempt to do
this, I should observe, that though in performing any ordinary
action—in walking, for example—from the one end of the room to
the other, a person may show both grace and agility, yet if he betrays
the least intention of showing either, he is sure of offending more or
less, and we never fail to accuse him of some degree of vanity and
affectation. In the performance of any such ordinary action, every
person wishes to appear to be solely occupied about the proper
purpose of the action: if he means to show either grace or agility, he
is careful to conceal that meaning, and he is very seldom successful in
doing so: he offends, however, just in proportion as he betrays it, and
he almost always betrays it. In Dancing, on the contrary, every person
professes, and avows, as it were, the intention of displaying some
degree either of grace, or of agility, or of both. The display of one, or
other, or both of these qualities, is in reality the proper purpose of the
action; and there can never be any disagreeable vanity or affectation
in following out the proper purpose of any action. When we say of
any particular person, that he gives himself many affected airs and
graces in Dancing, we mean either that he gives himself airs and

graces which are unsuitable to the nature of the Dance, or that he executes aukwardly, perhaps exaggerates too much, (the most common fault in Dancing,) the airs and graces which are suitable to it. Every Dance is in reality a succession of airs and graces of some kind or other, and of airs and graces which, if I may say so, profess themselves to be such. The steps, gestures, and motions which, as it were, avow the intention of exhibiting a succession of such airs and graces, are the steps, gestures, and motions which are peculiar to Dancing, and when these are performed to the time and measure of Music, they constitute what is properly called a Dance.

4   But though every sort of step, gesture, or motion, even though performed to the time and measure of Music, will not alone make a Dance, yet almost any sort of sound, provided it is repeated with a distinct rythmus, or according to a distinct time and measure, though without any variation as to gravity or acuteness, will make a sort of Music, no doubt indeed, an imperfect one. Drums, cymbals, and, so far as I have observed, all other instruments of percussion, have only one note; this note, however, when repeated with a certain rythmus, or according to a certain time and measure, and sometimes, in order to mark more distinctly that time and measure, with some little variation as to loudness and lowness, though without any as to acuteness and gravity, does certainly make a sort of Music, which is frequently far from being disagreeable, and which even sometimes produces considerable effects. The simple note of such instruments, it is true, is generally a very clear, or what is called a melodious, sound. It does not however seem indispensably necessary that it should be so. The sound of the muffled drum, when it beats the dead march, is far from being either clear or melodious, and yet it certainly produces a species of Music, which is sometimes affecting. Even in the performance of the most humble of all artists, of the man who drums upon the table with his fingers, we may sometimes distinguish the measure, and perhaps a little of the humour, of some favourite song; and we must allow that even he makes some sort of Music. Without a proper step and motion, the observation of tune alone will not make a Dance; time alone, without tune, will make some sort of Music.

5   That exact observation of tune, or of the proper intervals of gravity and acuteness, which constitutes the great beauty of all perfect Music, constitutes likewise its great difficulty. The time or measure of a song are simple matters, which even a coarse and unpractised ear is capable of distinguishing and comprehending: but to distinguish and comprehend all the variations of the tune, and to conceive with precision, the exact proportion of every note, is what the finest and

most cultivated ear is frequently no more than capable of performing. In the singing of the common people we may generally remark a distinct enough observation of time, but a very imperfect one of tune. To discover and to distinguish with precision the proper intervals of tune, must have been a work of long experience and much observation. In the theoretical treatises upon Music, what the authors have to say upon time is commonly discussed in a single chapter of no great length or difficulty. The theory of tune fills commonly all the rest of the volume, and has long ago become both an extensive and an abstruse science, which is often but imperfectly comprehended, even by intelligent artists. In the first rude efforts of uncivilized nations towards singing, the niceties of tune could be but little attended to: I have, upon this account, been frequently disposed to doubt of the great antiquity of those national songs, which it is pretended have been delivered down from age to age by a sort of oral tradition, without having been ever noted, or distinctly recorded for many successive generations. The measure, the humour of the song, might perhaps have been delivered down in this manner, but it seems scarcely possible that the precise notes of the tune should have been so preserved. The method of singing some of what we reckon our old Scotch songs, has undergone great alterations within the compass of my memory, and it may have undergone still greater before.

6 The distinction between the sounds or tones of singing and those of speaking seems to be of the same kind with that between the steps, gestures, and motions of Dancing, and those of any other ordinary action; though in speaking a person may show a very agreeable tone of voice, yet if he seems to intend to show it, if he appears to listen to the sound of his own voice, and as it were to tune it into a pleasing modulation, he never fails to offend, as guilty of a most disagreeable affectation. In speaking, as in every other ordinary action, we expect and require that the speaker should attend only to the proper purpose of the action, the clear and distinct expression of what he has to say. In singing, on the contrary, every person professes the intention to please by the tone and cadence of his voice; and he not only appears to be guilty of no disagreeable affectation in doing so, but we expect and require that he should do so. To please by the choice and arrangement of agreeable sounds is the proper purpose of all Music, vocal as well as instrumental; and we always expect and require, that every person should attend to the proper purpose of whatever action he is performing. A person may appear to sing, as well as to dance, affectedly; he may endeavour to please by sounds and tones which are unsuitable to the nature of the song, or he may dwell too much on those which are suitable to it, or in some other way he may show an

overweening conceit of his own abilities, beyond what seems to be warranted by his performance. The disagreeable affectation appears to consist always, not in attempting to please by a proper, but by some improper modulation of the voice. It was early discovered that the vibrations of chords or strings, which either in their lengths, or in their densities, or in their degrees of tension, bear a certain proportion to one another, produce sounds which correspond exactly, or, as the musicians say, are the unisons of those sounds or tones of the human voice which the ear approves of in singing. This discovery has enabled musicians to speak with distinctness and precision concern-,ing the musical sounds or tones of the human voice; they can always precisely ascertain what are the particular sounds or tones which they mean, by ascertaining what are the proportions of the strings of which the vibrations produce the unisons of those sounds or tones. What are called the intervals; that is, the differences, in point of gravity and acuteness, between the sounds or tones of a singing voice, are much greater and more distinct than those of the speaking voice. Though the former, therefore, can be measured and appreciated by the proportions of chords or strings, the latter cannot. The nicest instruments cannot express the extreme minuteness of these intervals. The heptamerede of Mr. *Sauveur*[1] could express an interval so small as the seventh part of what is called a comma, the smallest interval that is admitted in modern Music. Yet even this instrument, we are informed by Mr. *Duclos*,[2] could not express the minuteness of the intervals in the pronunciation of the Chinese language; of all the languages in the world, that of which the pronunciation is said to approach the nearest to singing, or in which the intervals are said to be the greatest.

7   As the sounds or tones of the singing voice, therefore, can be ascertained or appropriated, while those of the speaking voice cannot; the former are capable of being noted or recorded, while the latter are not.

[1] Joseph Sauveur (1653–1716), though defective in speech and hearing, was virtually the founder of the science of musical acoustics, basing it on experimental and mathematical analysis of the frequency–pitch relation and the harmonies derivative therefrom. His division of the octave into *mérides* was never widely adopted. [He expounded it in a paper in *Mémoires de l'Académie des sciences* (1701). The octave was divided into forty-three *mérides*, each of these into seven *heptamérides*, and each of these into ten *decamérides*.]

[2] [Charles Pineau (or Pinot) -Duclos (1704–72) makes this comment in the 'Remarques' that he added to the *Grammaire générale et raisonnée* of C. Lancelot and A. Arnauld (1754 and later editions), chap. 4, 34: 'Ele [*sc.* la prosodie] doit se faire beaucoup sentir dans le Chinois, s'il est vrai que les diférentes inflexions d'une même mot servent à exprimer des idées diférentes.' He cites Dionysius of Halicarnassus on the musical interval between a grave and an acute accent in Greek.]

*Of the Affinity between certain English
and Italian Verses*

Introduction

The composition of this essay can be dated *c.* 1782. A fragmentary first draft in Adam Smith's hand survives among the Bannerman MSS.—Glasgow University Library MS. Gen. 1035(v)—written on a folded sheet whose watermark, T FRENCH, is not known to occur before 1780.[1] On 17 March 1783 Smith wrote from Edinburgh to Lady Frances Scott thanking her for returning him his 'paper upon Italian and English Verse' and renewing a promise to send her 'a more perfect copy as soon as he has compleated his plan'. The other business which, he says, will prevent this completion for some time— presumably the preparation of the new materials for the third edition of the *Wealth of Nations*—would not leave Smith free to rewrite this essay, if he ever did, until after 1784.

The critical background of the essay is established by the illustration used in §11. In 1738 Samuel Say (1676–1743),[2] a dissenting minister and minor poet, wrote 'An Essay on The Harmony, Variety, and Power of Numbers, Whether in Prose or Verse', in which he attacked the statement made by Edward Bysshe in his *Art of English Poetry* (1702) that English metre is based simply on the counting of syllables. To show that it is primarily a matter of stresses or accents and not syllables Say made up the couplet

> And mánỹ ăn ámŏroŭs, mánỹ ă húmŏroŭs Lāy,
> Whĭch mánỹ ă Bárd hăd chántĕd mánỹ ă Dāy

adapted from a line he claimed to have seen in a Chaucer manuscript—

> And mánỹ ă Rīme, ănd mánỹ ă Léchĕroŭs Lāy,

and one from *The Faerie Queene*, IV.vii.8—

> Whĭch mánỹ ă Knīght hăd soŭght, sŏ mánỹ ă Dāy.

His demonstration of the absurdity of scanning the lines as decasyllables by eliding certain vowels led to the frequent quotation

---

[1] W. A. Churchill, *Watermarks in paper . . . 17th and 18th centuries* (1935), 50 and watermark 144. The letter of 1783 (No. 225) has been pointed out by Prof. A. S. Skinner.

[2] Say's essay was published posthumously, with a second on Milton's prosody, in his *Poems on Several Occasions* (1745): reference to pp. 131–2. It was reprinted with introduction by Paul Fussell in 1955: Augustan Reprint Society Publications 55 (University of California, Los Angeles). Paul Fussell's *Theory of Prosody in Eighteenth Century England* (1954) surveys the subject.

and adaptation of his couplet, usually as in Smith's case without acknowledgement, by later prosodists. We find it in for instance John Mason's *Essay on the Power of Numbers and the Principles of Harmony in Poetical Compositions* (1749, 27); Thomas Sheridan's *Lectures on the Art of Reading* (1775, ii.4, 86–91); and John Rice's *Introduction to the Art of Reading with Energy and Propriety* (1765, 112). James Beattie was using it in the Aberdeen lectures on rhetoric which later appeared as *The Theory of Language* (1783, 279–80).

That Smith's essay was at once seen to belong to this tradition in prosodic debate is shown by Pierre Prevost's note to his translation of it in 1797 (*Essais philosophiques*, ii.142–5): the affinity between English and Italian verse is their accentual basis, as distinct from the quantitative basis of Latin and Greek verse and the syllabic basis of French. The point was made by Henry Pemberton in 1738 (*Observations on Poetry*, 125–6):

Trissino, a famous Italian poet, and an early writer on the measures of their verse, lays down this rule; that as the ancient feet were determined by the quantity of the syllables only, in his language they are determined by the accent. This is equally true in our tongue, and for this reason, that whereas the ancient accent is represented to be only a variation in the tone of the voice ... ours is constantly attended with an emphasis ...

The passage was quoted by John Mason (11 *n.*) and became influential. Jean-François Marmontel observed in his *Poëtique françoise* (1763; i.269) that English and Italian verse share a freedom in the placing of the pause—after the fourth, fifth, or sixth syllables— but he defends the rigidity of French practice in this; and his note was incorporated (with a denial of French superiority) in the *Lectures on Rhetoric and Belles Lettres* which Hugh Blair eventually published in 1783 (Lect. 38:ii.328) after many years of reading them in the University of Edinburgh. (Blair finds a pause after the seventh syllable most striking.) Monboddo included in his *Of the Origin and Progress of Language* (1787, iv.148 f.) a comparison of English and Italian methods in verse and a claim that they were both superior to French in variety. There is a brief application of Italian metrical terminology (*verso sdrucciolo*) to the opening lines of Rowe's *Fair Penitent* in Joseph Baretti's *Dictionary of the English and Italian Languages* (1760, xxxii); but this was justly criticized by William Mitford (*An Essay upon the Harmony of Language*, 1774, 187) for its insensitivity to the movement of English verse.

The immediate inspiration of Smith's essay was an unsigned article entitled 'Réflexions sur le Méchanisme de la Versification Italienne, Angloise et Allemande' contributed by the Marquis

François-Jean de Chastellux (1734–88) to the *Journal étranger* for June 1760 (Paris: 1–58). 'Le vers Italien et le vers Anglois ont une analogie frappante' (10): they are founded on the prosody of their languages and on the value (not merely the number) of the syllables (36). The affinity is worked out, as by Smith, in terms of the placing of accent and of pause, of elision, of the varieties of rhyme etc. in Heroic Verse of the two languages. Most significantly, the essayists share a misinterpretation of the term *verso cadente*—i.e. verse which 'falls away' at the close in unaccented syllables—as synonymous with *verso tronco*, i.e. verse ending in an accented syllable (op. cit., 14; Smith, § 9). Chastellux repeats the misuse of the terms in a long footnote to his *Essai sur l'union de la poésie et de la musique* (1765, 64–6)—a note which probably sent Smith to the 1760 article. Chastellux imagines *verso cadente* as making us hear 'une espèce de chûte, ... de résonnance dure' (*Essai*, 67). The work of Chastellux, which may have afforded hints for the treatment of poetry set to music in the essay on the Imitative Arts, suggests that this prosodic discussion had links with the lively controversy begun by Rousseau's *Lettre sur la musique françoise* (1753) as to the relative suitability of Italian and French for opera. Incidentally Chastellux, unlike Smith, acknowledges indebtedness to Johnson on the subject of the pause: 'M. *Rambler* est le seul auteur que je connoisse qui en ait parlé' ('Réflexions', 47).[3]

Adam Smith's interest in Italian literature dated from his Oxford days (Stewart, I. 10), and the fact that in 1781 his library[4] included the works of all the principal Italian poets—heroic, lyric, burlesque, dramatic—from Dante and Petrarch to his own day shows that he shared the catholic tastes of his Scottish contemporaries in this field of 'polite letters'. Perhaps the essay on verse (born of the same interest in the workings of rhythm as the essay on the Imitative Arts) would have found a place in the 'Philosophical History of all the different branches of Literature, of Philosophy, Poetry and Eloquence' which in 1785 he was still hoping to write.[5] As it stands it cannot be said to advance or to clarify its subject; and it is difficult to believe that its repetitions, its confusions (e.g. of phonetic and orthographic accents, §§ 19–20), and its obscurities (e.g. § 18) would have survived a revision. But it throws valuable light on Smith's familiarity with some of the critical discussions of his day.

[3] Only one verse example is common to Chastellux and Smith: the first line of the *Gerusalemme Liberata*, which Chastellux uses several times. Both read *l'arme* for *l'armi*. Smith had a copy of the 1765 *Essai*.
[4] See H. Mizuta, *Adam Smith's Library, a supplement to J. Bonar's Catalogue* (1967).
[5] Letter 248 addressed to Le Duc de La Rochefoucauld, dated 1 November 1785.

THE AFFINITY

BETWEEN CERTAIN

ENGLISH AND ITALIAN VERSES

1   The measure of the verses, of which the octave[1] of the Italians, their terzetti, and the greater part of their sonnets, are composed, seems to be as nearly the same with that of the English Heroic Rhyme, as the different genius and pronunciation of the two languages will permit.

2   The English Heroic Rhyme is supposed to consist sometimes of ten, and sometimes of eleven syllables: of ten, when the verse ends with a single; and of eleven, when it ends with a double rhyme.

3   The correspondent Italian verse is supposed to consist sometimes of ten, sometimes of eleven, and sometimes of twelve syllables, according as it happens to end with a single, a double, or a triple rhyme.

4   The rhyme ought naturally to fall upon the last syllable of the verse; it is proper likewise that it should fall upon an accented syllable, in order to render it more sensible. When, therefore, the accent happens to fall, not upon the last syllable, but upon that immediately before it, the rhyme must fall both upon the accented syllable and upon that which is not accented. It must be a double rhyme.

5   In the Italian language, when the accent falls neither upon the last syllable, nor upon that immediately before it, but upon the third syllable from the end, the rhyme must fall upon all the three. It must be a triple rhyme, and the verse is supposed to consist of twelve syllables:

Forsè era ver, non però credìbile, etc.[2]

Triple rhymes are not admitted into English Heroic Verse.

6   In the Italian language the accent falls much more rarely, either upon the third syllable from the end of a word, or upon the last syllable, than it does upon the one immediately before the last. In reality, this second syllable from the end seems, in that language, to

---

[1] Octave: *ottava rima*, abababcc. Terzetti: *terza rima*, the metre of the *Divina Commedia*, rhyming aba bcb cdc ... English Heroic Rhyme: pentameters rhyming in couplets.
[2] Ariosto, *Orlando Furioso*, i.56.1. Read '... ma non però credibile'.

be its most common and natural place. The Italian Heroic Poetry, therefore, is composed principally of double rhymes, or of verses supposed to consist of eleven syllables. Triple rhymes occur but seldom, and single rhymes still more seldom.

7   In the English language the accent falls frequently upon the last syllable of the word. Our language, besides, abounds in words of one syllable, the greater part of which do (for there are few which do not) admit of being accented. Words of one syllable are most frequently the concluding words of English rhymes. For both these reasons, English Heroic Rhyme is principally composed of single rhymes, or of verses supposed to consist of ten syllables. Double Rhymes occur almost as rarely in it, as either single or triple do in the Italian.

8   The rarity of double rhymes in English Heroic Verse makes them appear odd, and aukward, and even ludicrous, when they occur. By the best writers, therefore, they are reserved for light and ludicrous occasions; when, in order to humour their subject, they stoop to a more familiar style than usual. When Mr. Pope says;[3]

> Worth makes the man, and want of it the fellow;
> The rest is all but leather or prunello;

he means, in compliance with his subject, to condescend a good deal below the stateliness of his diction in the Essay on Man. Double rhymes abound more in Dryden than in Pope, and in Hudibras more than in Dryden.

9   The rarity both of single and of triple rhyme in Italian Heroic Verse, gives them the same odd and ludicrous air which double rhymes have in English Verse. In Italian, triple rhymes occur more frequently than single rhymes. The slippery, or if I may be allowed to use a very low, but a very expressive word, the glib pronunciation of the triple rhyme *(verso sdrucciolo[4])* seems tc depart less from the ordinary movement of the double rhyme, than the abrupt ending of the single rhyme *(verso tronco e cadente[5])* of the verse that appears to be cut off, and to fall short of the usual measure. Single rhymes accordingly appear in Italian verse much more burlesque than triple rhymes. Single rhymes occur very rarely in Ariosto; but frequently in the more burlesque poem of Ricciardetto.[6] Triple rhymes occur much oftener in all the best writers. It is thus, that what in English

[3] Pope, *Essay on Man*, iv.203–4. Read 'prunella'.
[4] All edd. (except Basel 1799) follow 1795 in misprinting as '*sotrucciolo*'; Pierre Prevost's French translation (1797) has '*strudciolo*'. 'Slippery' is a correct rendering.
[5] A misunderstanding: *tronco* describes single or monosyllabic rhyme, *cadente* disyllabic or 'falling' rhyme (not 'falling short of . . .').
[6] *Ricciardetto*, a burlesque chivalric epic by Niccolò Forteguerri (1674–1735) in thirty cantos, very popular in the mid-eighteenth century and translated into French in 1766 as *Richardet*. It was published in Venice (not 'Parigi') in 1738 as by 'Niccolò Carteromaco'.

appears to be the verse of the greatest gravity and dignity, appears in Italian to be the most burlesque and ludicrous; for no other reason, I apprehend, but because in the one language it is the ordinary verse, whereas in the other it departs the most from the movement of the ordinary verse.

10   The common Italian Heroic Poetry being composed of double rhymes, it can admit both of single and of triple rhymes; which seem to recede from the common movement on opposite sides to nearly equal distances. The common English Heroic Poetry, consisting of single rhymes, it can admit of double; but it cannot admit of triple rhymes, which would recede so far from the common movements as to appear perfectly burlesque and ridiculous. In English, when a word accented upon the third syllable from the end happens to make the last word of a verse, the rhyme falls upon the last syllable only. It is a single rhyme, and the verse consists of no more than ten syllables: but as the last syllable is not accented, it is an imperfect rhyme, which, however, when confined to the second verse of the couplet, and even there introduced but rarely, may have a very agreeable grace, and the line may even seem to run more easy and natural by means of it:

> Bùt of this fràme, the beàrings, and the tìes,
> The strìct connèctions, nìce depèndencies, etc.[7]

When by a well accented syllable in the end of the first line of a couplet, it has once been clearly ascertained what the rhyme is to be, a very slight allusion to it, such as can be made by a syllable of the same termination that is not accented, may often be sufficient to mark the coincidence in the second line; a word of this kind in the end of the first line seldom succeeds so well:

> Th' inhabitants of old Jerusalem
> Were Jebusites; the town so called from them.[8]

A couplet in which both verses were terminated in this manner, would be extremely disagreeable and offensive.

11   In counting the syllables, even of verses which to the ear appear sufficiently correct, a considerable indulgence must frequently be given, before they can, in either language, be reduced to the precise number of ten, eleven, or twelve, according to the nature of the rhyme. In the following couplet, for example, there are, strictly speaking, fourteen syllables in the first line, and twelve in the second.

---

[7] Pope, *Essay on Man*, i.29–30. Read 'strong connections'. Quoted (correctly) by Kames, *Elements of Criticism* (1762), chap. xviii, sect. 4, on versification.
[8] Dryden, *Absalom and Achitophel*, 85–6.

And many a hŭmoŭrous, many an amorous lay,
Was sung by many a bard, on many a day.[9]

By the rapidity, however, or, if I may use a very low word a second
time, by the glibness of the pronunciation, those fourteen syllables in
the first line, and those twelve in the second, appear to take up the
time but of ten ordinary syllables. The words *many a*, though they
plainly consist of three distinct syllables, or sounds, which are all
pronounced successively, or the one after the other, yet pass as but
two syllables; as do likewise these words *hŭmoŭroŭs* and *amorous*.
The words *heaven* and *given*, in the same manner, consist each of
them of two syllables, which, how rapidly soever they may be
pronounced, cannot be pronounced but successively, or the one after
the other. In verse, however, they are considered as consisting but of
one syllable each.

12   In counting the syllables of the Italian Heroic Verse, still greater
indulgences must be allowed: three vowels must there frequently be
counted as making but one syllable, though they are all pronounced,
rapidly indeed, but in succession, or the one after the other, and
though no two of them are supposed to make a dipththong. In these
licences too, the Italians seem not to be very regular, and the same
concourse of vowels which in one place makes but one syllable, will
in another sometimes make two. There are even some words which
in the end of a verse are constantly counted for two syllables, but
which in any other part of it are never counted for more than one;
such as *suo, tuo, suoi, tuoi*.

13   Ruscelli[10] observes, that in the Italian Heroic Verse the accent
ought to fall upon the fourth, the sixth, the eighth, and the tenth
syllables; and that if it falls upon the third, the fifth, the seventh, or
the ninth syllables, it spoils the verse.

14   In English, if the accent falls upon any of the above-mentioned odd
syllables, it equally[11] spoils the verse.

Bow'd their stiff necks, loaden with stormy blasts,[12]

though a line of Milton has not the ordinary movement of an English
Heroic Verse, the accent falls upon the third and fifth syllables.

---

[9] On Samuel Say's couplet see the editor's Introduction. The last two syllables of 'humorous' should have the breve, not the first.

[10] Girolamo Ruscelli (d. 1566), whose *Del modo di comporre in versi nella lingua italiana* (1559) enjoyed immense popularity because of its *rimario* or rhyming dictionary and was still in print at the end of the eighteenth century. The above metrical topics are treated in chapters iii–v, pp. xlviii–lxxxvi.

[11] 1795 has 'syllables it, qually'; corrected in Dublin 1795 ed.

[12] 1795 has 'blasts./ Though'. Pierre Prevost (1797) renders the sense correctly; and *Essays* (1869), 471, emends the punctuation as above. The line is *Paradise Regained*, iv.418. The whole storm passage is quoted and its metrics discussed by Samuel Say in his essay 'On the Numbers of *Paradise Lost*', in *Poems on Several Occasions* (1745), 166, with emphasis on this line.

15 In Italian frequently, and in English sometimes, an accent is with great grace thrown upon the first syllable: in which case it seldom happens that any other syllable is accented before the fourth:

Cánto l'armé pietóse e'l capitáno.[13]

Fírst in these fíelds I trý the sylvan stráins.[14]

16 Both in English and in Italian the second syllable may be accented with great grace, and it generally is so when the first syllable is not accented:

E in van l'inferno a' lui s' oppose; e in vano
S' armó d' Asia, e di Libia il popol misto, etc.[15]

10 Let us, since life can little more supply
11 Than just to look about us, and to die, etc.[16]

17 Both in English and in Italian Verse, an accent, though it must never be misplaced, may sometimes be omitted with great grace. In the last of the above-quoted English Verses there is no accent upon the eighth syllable; the conjunction *and* not admitting of any. In the following Italian Verse there is no accent upon the sixth syllable:

O Musa, tu, che di caduchi allori, etc.[17]

The preposition[18] *di* will as little admit of an accent as the conjunction *and.* In this case, however, when the even syllable is not accented, neither of the odd syllables immediately before or behind it must be accented.

18 Neither in English nor in Italian can two accents running be omitted.

19 It must be observed, that in Italian there are two accents, the grave and the acute: the grave accent is always marked by a slight stroke over the syllable to which it belongs; the acute accent has no mark.

20 The English language knows no distinction between the grave and the acute accents.

21 The same author observes, that in the Italian Verse the Pause, or what the grammarians call the Cesura, may with propriety be introduced after the third, the fourth, the fifth, the sixth, or the seventh syllables. The like observations have been made by several different writers upon the English Heroic Verse. Dobie admires particularly the verse in which there are two pauses; one after the

---

[13] Tasso, *Gerusalemme Liberata,* i.1. Read 'armi'.
[14] Pope, *Pastorals—Spring,* 1.
[15] Tasso, ibid.
[16] Pope, *Essay on Man,* i.3–4.
[17] Tasso, ibid. (st.2).
[18] 1795 has 'proposition'; corrected in Dublin 1795 ed.

fifth, and another after the ninth syllable. The example he gives is from Petrarch:

Nel dolce tempo de la prima etade, etc.[19]

In this verse, the second pause, which he says comes after the ninth syllable, in reality comes in between the two vowels, which, in the Italian way of counting syllables, compose the ninth syllable. It may be doubtful, therefore, whether this pause may not be considered as coming after the eighth syllable. I do not recollect any good English Verse in which the pause comes in after the ninth syllable. We have many in which it comes in after the eighth:

Yet oft, before his infant eyes, would run, *etc.*[20]

In which verse there are two pauses; one after the second, and the other after the eighth syllable. I have observed many Italian Verses in which the pause comes after the second syllable.

22   Both the English and the Italian Heroic Verse, perhaps, are not so properly composed of a certain number of syllables, which vary according to the nature of the rhyme; as of a certain number of intervals, (of five invariably,) each of which is equal in length, or time,[21] to two ordinary distinct syllables, though it may sometimes contain more, of which the extraordinary shortness compensates the extraordinary number. The close frequently of each of those intervals, but always of every second interval, is marked by a distinct accent. This accent may frequently, with great grace, fall upon the beginning of the first interval; after which, it cannot, without spoiling the verse, fall any where but upon the close of an interval. The syllable or syllables which come after the accent that closes the fifth interval are never accented. They make no distinct interval, but are considered as a sort of excrescence of the verse, and are in a manner counted for nothing.[22]

[19] Petrarch, *Rime*, xxiii.1. Ruscelli ('the same author') quotes the line to identify a canzone which exemplifies one of his types: op. cit., cxxxiii. Dobie has not been identified. On disposition of pauses see for example Johnson, *Rambler*, 90, 26 Jan. 1751; *The Beauties of Poetry Display'd* (1757), i.xxvii ff.; J. Rice, *Introd. to the Art of Reading* (1765), 155; S. Say (see the editor's Introduction), 136.

[20] Gray, *Progress of Poesy*, 118. Smith thought Gray's Odes 'the standard of lyric excellence' (report by 'Amicus', *The Bee or Literary Weekly Intelligencer*, iii (Edinburgh, 1791), 6). Cf. TMS III.ii.19; LRBL ii.96 (ed. Lothian, 123).

[21] This passage echoes the *Essai* by Chastellux (see the editor's Introduction), 79n., where short syllables 'ne valent qu'un tems'. They are *isochrone*.

[22] Chastellux several times says that these syllables 'ne sont comptées pour rien' (*Essai*, 64,66).

Contributions to the Edinburgh Review *of 1755–56*
Review of Johnson's Dictionary
A Letter to the Authors of the Edinburgh Review

Introduction

The short-lived *Edinburgh Review* of 1755–56 was launched and edited by Adam Smith's friend Alexander Wedderburn, later Lord Chancellor and Earl of Rosslyn, with the aim of reviewing every six months the Scottish publications of the previous half-year and, in an appendix, the most notable English and other books. Its motive was the prevailing Scottish thirst for 'self-improvement' and it expressed the curious mixture of national pride and a sense of inferiority (especially in the matter of language) so characteristic of eighteenth-century Scotland. Smith's choice of Johnson's *Dictionary* to review in the first number can thus be seen to be part of a programme, and his final sentences echo a passage which he himself probably contributed to the preface to that number (p. iii):

Two considerable obstacles have long obstructed the progress of science. One is, the difficulty of a proper expression in a country where there is either no standard of language, or at least one very remote: Some late instances, however, have discovered that this difficulty is not unsurmountable; and that a serious endeavour to conquer it, may acquire, to one born on the north side of the Tweed, a correct and even an elegant stile.

(The second obstacle had been the slow advance of printing in Scotland, now entirely remedied.) It is to this whole context that Smith's lectures on style and composition, i.e. 'rhetoric and belles lettres', in the University of Glasgow from 1751 to 1763 belong. The relevance to the 'Scottish Enlightenment' of Smith's effort, in the Letter he inserted in No. 2, to widen the *Review*'s horizon to take in the literature and learning of Europe, is obvious.[1] His notice of the *Dictionary* further illustrates a concern with 'those Principles in the Human Mind which Mr. Smith has pointed out to be the universal motives of Philosophical Researches', to quote the note at the end of the essay on the History of Astronomy; and it exhibits a semantic preoccupation similar to that of the opening of that essay.

The *Edinburgh Review* No. 1 (for 1 Jan. to 1 July 1755) appeared on 26 August 1755; No. 2 (for July 1755 to Jan. 1756) in March 1756. The early demise of the journal has been variously explained: most plausibly by A. F. Tytler (*Memoirs of the Life and Writings of Henry Home of Kames*, Edinburgh, 1807, i.233) as due to a violent outcry

---

[1] On Smith's 1755 lecture and his scientific, literary, and philosophical interests at this time see Stewart, IV.25.

from narrow churchmen over the theological views contained in notices of religious works. Certainly the reviews provoked a lively interest. Many extracts were printed and discussed in the monthly *Scots Magazine*, and in 1756 several polemical pamphlets appeared, such as *A View of the Edinburgh Review pointing out the Spirit and Tendency of that Paper* and a burlesque on this called *A New Groat's Worth of Wit for a Penny: or An Analysis or Compend of the Edinburgh Review.* The interest was abiding, and in 1818 Sir James Mackintosh brought out in London a second edition of both numbers, identifying the contributors (originally anonymous) and giving an account of the publication.

The authorship of Adam Smith's contributions was widely known long before Dugald Stewart mentioned them in his 'Life' (I.24). They had not escaped criticism: the *New Groat's Worth* (p. 5) says the specimen given of Johnson's *Dictionary* 'is dark and almost unintelligible'. Both articles were included in the 1811 edition of the *Works* (vol. v) with a note that they have often lately been referred to. The review of the *Dictionary* was reprinted in *The Scots Magazine* for November 1755 (xvii.539–44), and in *The European Magazine and London Review* for April 1802 (xli.249–54) with a remark that a great many readers who have sought without success the very scarce original edition will be gratified 'to see the opinion of so great a man on a subject he had so well considered, and was so perfect a master of'. This review was indeed influential. In the third edition of the *Encyclopaedia Britannica* (1797; viii.710) Smith's remarks on humour (§§ 5–13) constitute, with the addition of a sentence quoting the Duke of Buckingham's exaltation of humour over wit, the entire entry on HUMOUR—with no mention of the author. The entry remained in the fourth (1810), fifth (1817), and sixth (1823) editions of the *Encyclopaedia*, and was replaced only in the seventh (1842). Smith's association of wit with civility as opposed to buffoonish humour may have coloured the historical account of the matter given by his pupil John Millar (later Professor of Law at Glasgow) in *An historical view of the English Government from the settlement of the Saxons in Britain to the Revolution in 1688* (1803; iv.352–60). A refined and correct state of taste and literature are, according to this sociological theory, inimical to the cultivation of humour but 'peculiarly calculated to promote the circulation and improvement of wit' (358). Behind both Smith and Millar lie the distinctions made by Corbyn Morris in *An Essay towards fixing the true Standards of Wit, Humour, Raillery, Satire and Ridicule* (1744).

A curious piece of evidence of the impact made by the review of the *Dictionary* occurs in a savage attack on Johnson entitled *Deformities of Dr Samuel Johnson, selected from his Works* (Edinburgh, 1782: two editions), anonymous but the work of James Thomson Callender,[2] a journalist noted for later scurrilities in America. A footnote to a quotation (48) from the Letter to Chesterfield in which Johnson speaks of being 'bewildered, and in the mazes of such intricacy ... frequently entangled' reads: 'Perhaps he means, in defining *Thunder, Plum-porridge*, the particle *But*, etc. ' Without Smith the dictionary entry on *but* would scarcely have been singled out.

From Smith's second contribution, the 'Letter', the *Scots Magazine* for March 1756 (xviii.125-7) reprinted extracts representing 'what we shall call his *literary* character of the several nations': §§ 3-5, 9, 10, 17. Pierre Prevost included in his French translation of the *Essays on Philosophical Subjects—Essais philosophiques*, (1797), ii.273 ff.—a translation of the entire Letter, a copy of which Dugald Stewart had sent him for this purpose in November 1796. Clearly Prevost was impressed by the breadth and confidence of the Pisgah-view it provided over the continental intellectual scene at mid-century and (as well he might be) by the up-to-dateness of Smith's familiarity with that scene.

The texts are from the first edition: review of Johnson's *Dictionary* (Article III in the Appendix), No. 1 (1755), 61-73; Letter, No. 2 (1756), 63-79, Wedderburn's introductory note on p.62. The various reprints normalize such spellings as *synonomous, petulence, predominent, consistant, crystaline*. In view of Adam Smith's intense interest in the practice of translation, particularly from French (Stewart, I.9), the extracts from Rousseau translated in the Letter are here appended in the original for comparison. Smith will be seen frequently to sacrifice close fidelity to fluency and vigour. He is not impeccable: 'society' (*commerce*), 'thus' (*d'un autre côté*), 'situation' (*sort*), 'more surely' (*en sûreté*), 'concurrence' (*concurrence*), 'we have at last found out' (*on trouve enfin*), are at least misleading.

[2] On the authorship see Boswell, *Life of Johnson*, ed. Hill-Powell (1934-40), iv.499. Callender also wrote *A critical review of the works of Dr Samuel Johnson, containing a particular vindication of several eminent characters* (1783). In both books he praises Adam Smith and several other Scottish writers whose style avoids Johnsonian pedantry.

REVIEW OF JOHNSON'S *DICTIONARY*

A Dictionary of the English Language, by Samuel Johnson, *A. M. Knapton* 2 *Vols. Folio,* £4, 15*s.*

1   The present undertaking is very extensive. A dictionary of the English language, however useful, or rather necessary, has never been hitherto attempted with the least degree of success. To explain hard words and terms of art seems to have been the chief purpose of all the former compositions which have borne the title of English dictionaries. Mr. Johnson has extended his views much farther, and has made a very full collection of all the different meanings of each English word, justified by examples from authors of good reputation. When we compare this book with other dictionaries, the merit of its author appears very extraordinary. Those which in modern languages have gained the most esteem, are that of the French academy, and that of the academy Della Crusca.[1] Both these were composed by a numerous society of learned men, and took up a longer time in the composition, than the life of a single person could well have afforded. The dictionary of the English language is the work of a single person, and composed in a period of time very inconsiderable, when compared with the extent of the work. The collection of words appears to be very accurate, and must be allowed to be very ample. Most words, we believe, are to be found in the dictionary that ever were almost suspected to be English; but we cannot help wishing, that the author had trusted less to the judgment of those who may consult him, and had oftener passed his own censure upon those words which are not of approved use, tho' sometimes to be met with in authors of no mean name. Where a work is admitted to be highly useful, and the execution of it intitled to praise; the adding, that it might have been more useful, can scarcely, we hope, be deemed a censure of it. The merit of Mr. Johnson's dictionary is so great, that it cannot detract from it to take notice of some defects, the supplying which, would, in our judgment, add a considerable share of merit to that which it already possesses. Those defects consist chiefly in the plan, which appears to us not to be sufficiently grammatical. The different significations of a word are indeed collected; but they are seldom digested into general classes, or ranged under the meaning which the word principally expresses. And sufficient care has not

---

[1] *Le Dictionnaire de l'Académie Françoise* (1694; 3rd edn., rearranged, 1740). *Vocabolario degli Accademici della Crusca*, ed. L. Salviati (1612; 5th edn., 1746–8).

been taken to distinguish the words apparently synonomous.[2] The only method of explaining what we intend, is by inserting an article or two from Mr. Johnson, and by opposing to them the same articles, digested in the manner which we would have wished him to have followed.

2 BUT *conjunct.* [buze, buzan, Saxon.]

1. Except.

An emission of immateriate virtues we are a little doubtful to propound, it is so prodigious: *but* that it is so constantly avouched by many. *Bacon.*

Who can it be, ye gods! *but* perjur'd Lycon?
Who can inspire such storms of rage, *but* Lycon?
Where has my sword left one so black, *but* Lycon?
Smith's Phaedra and Hippolitus.

Your poem hath been printed, and we have no objection *but* the obscurity of several passages, by our ignorance in facts and persons. *Swift.*

2. Yet; nevertheless. It sometimes only enforces *yet.*

Then let him speak, and any that shall stand without, shall hear his voice plainly; *but* yet made extreme sharp and exile, like the voice of puppets: and yet the articulate sounds of the words will not be confounded. *Bacon's Nat. Hist.* N° 155.

Our wants are many, and grievous to be borne, *but* quite of another kind. *Swift.*

3. The particle which introduces the minor of a syllogism; now.

If there be a liberty and possibility for a man to kill himself to-day, then it is not absolutely necessary that he shall live till to-morrow; *but* there is such a liberty, therefore no such necessity.
Bramhall against Hobbes.

God will one time or another make a difference between the good and the evil. *But* there is little or no difference made in this world: therefore there must be another world, wherein this difference shall be made.
Watt's[3] *Logic, Introduct.*

4. Only; nothing more than.

If my offence be of mortal kind,
That not my service, past or present sorrows,
Can ransom me into his love again;
But to know so, must be my benefit. *Shakesp. Othello.*

And *but* infirmity,
Which waits upon worn times, hath something seiz'd

---

[2] The spelling based on ὄνομα is used throughout the review; but Dugald Stewart, quoting it in his 'Life' (I.24), has 'synonymous'.
[3] Johnson, correctly, has *Watts's.*

His wish'd ability, he had himself
The lands and waters measur'd.　　　　　　*Shak. Winter's Tale.*

What nymph soe'er his voice *but* hears,
Will be my rival, tho' she have *but* ears.　　　　　　*Ben. Johnson.*

No, Aurengzebe, you merit all my heart,
And I'm too noble *but* to give a part.　　　　　　*Dryden.*

Did *but* men consider the true notion of God, he would appear to be full of goodness.　　　　　　*Tillotson.*

If we do *but* put virtue and vice in equal circumstances, the advantages of ease and pleasure will be found to be on the side of religion. *Tillotson.*

The mischiefs or harms that come by play, inadvertency, or ignorance, are not at all, or *but* very gently, to be taken notice of.
　　　　　　Locke on Education.

If a reader examines Horace's art of poetry, he will find *but* very few precepts in it, which he may not meet with in Aristotle.
　　　　　　Addison. Spectator.

Prepar'd I stand: he was *but* born to try
The lot of man, to suffer and to die.　　　　　　*Pope's Odyssey.*

5. Than.

　　The full moon was no sooner up, and shining in all its brightness, *but* he privately opened the gate of paradise.　　　　　　*Guardian,* N° 167.

6. But that; without this consequence that.

　　Frosts that constrain the ground,
　　Do seldom their usurping power withdraw,
　　But raging floods pursue their hasty hand.　　　　　　*Dryden.*

7. Otherwise than that.

　　It cannot be *but* nature hath some director, of infinite power, to guide her in all her ways.　　　　　　*Hooker, b.* i. § 3.

　　　　Who shall believe,
　　But you misuse the reverence of your place?　　　　　　*Shakesp.*

8. Not otherwise than.

　　A genius so elevated and unconfined as Mr. Cowley's, was *but* necessary to make Pindar speak English.　　　　　　*Dryden.*

9. By any other means than.

　　Out of that will I cause those of Cyprus to mutiny: whose qualification shall come into no true taste again, *but* by transplanting of Cassio.
　　　　　　Shakesp. Othello.

10. If it were not for this; if this were not.

　　Believe me, I had rather have lost my purse
　　Full of cruzades. And *but* my noble Moor

Is true of mind, and made of no such baseness,
As jealous creatures are, it were enough
To put him to ill-thinking. *Shakesp. Othello.*

I here do give thee that with all my heart,
Which, *but* thou hast already, with all my heart
I would keep from thee. *Shakesp. Othello.*

11. However; howbeit.

I do not doubt but I have been to blame;
But, to pursue the end for which I came,
Unite your subjects first, then let us go,
And pour their common rage upon the foe. *Dryden.*

12. It is used after *no doubt, no question*, and such words, and signifies the same with *that*. It sometimes is joined with *that*.

They made no account, *but that* the navy should be absolutely master of the seas. *Bacon's War with Spain.*

I fancied to myself a kind of ease in the change of the paroxysm; never suspecting *but that* the humour would have wasted itself. *Dryden.*

There is no question *but* the King of Spain will reform most of the abuses. *Addison on Italy.*

13. That. This seems no proper sense in this place.

It is not therefore impossible, *but* I may alter the complexion of my play, to restore myself into the good graces of my fair criticks.
Dryden's Aurengzebe, Preface.

14. Otherwise than.

I should sin
To think *but* nobly of my grandmother. *Shakesp. Tempest.*

15. Even; not longer ago than.

Beroe *but* now I left; whom, pin'd with pain,
Her age and anguish from these rites detain. *Dryden.*

It is evident, in the instance I gave *but* now, the consciousness went along. *Locke.*

16. A particle by which the meaning of the foregoing sentence is bounded or restrained.

Thus fights Ulysses, thus his fame extends,
A formidable man, *but* to his friends. *Dryden.*

17. An objective particle; yet it may be objected.

But yet, Madam—
I do not like *but* yet; it does allay
The good precedence; fie upon *but* yet!
But yet is as a jaylour, to bring forth
Some monstrous malefactor. *Shakesp. Antony and Cleop.*

Must the heart then have been formed and constituted, before the blood was in being? *But* here again, the substance of the heart itself is most certainly made and nourished by the blood, which is conveyed to it by the coronary arteries.   *Bentl.*

18. But for; without; had not this been.

> Rash man! forbear, *but* for some unbelief,
> My joy had been as fatal as my grief.   *Waller.*

> Her head was bare,
> *But* for her native ornament of hair,
> Which in a simple knot was ty'd above.   *Dryden's Fables.*

> When the fair boy receiv'd the gift of right,
> And, *but* for mischief, you had dy'd for spight.   *Dryden.*

3   BUT, an English particle which denotes opposition, and which, according to the different modifications of the general sense of opposition, sometimes holds the place of an adverb, sometimes of a preposition, sometimes of a conjunction, and sometimes even of an interjection. It serves as a conjunction of four different species, as an adversitive, as an alternative, as a conductive, and as a transitive conjunction. In its original and most proper meaning, however, it seems to be an adversitive conjunction, in the sense in which it is synonomous with *however*; and in which it is expressed in Latin by *sed*, in French by *mais*. I should have done this, *but* was prevented: I should have done this; I was *however* prevented. The difference betwixt these two particles seems to consist chiefly in this, That *but* must always stand at the beginning of the sentence whose opposition it marks to what went before; whereas *however* is introduced more gracefully after the beginning of the opposed sentence: and that the construction may often be continued, when we make use of *but*; whereas, it must always be interrupted when we make use of *however*.

The use of *but*, upon this account, seems often to mark a more precipitate keenness in denoting the opposition, than the use of *however*. If, in talking of a quarrel, a person should say, I should have made some apology for my conduct, *but* was prevented by his insolence; he would seem to express more passion and keenness than if he had said, I should have made some apology for my conduct, I was *however* prevented by his insolence.

2. *But* is likewise an alternative conjunction in the sense in which it is nearly synonomous with the English *unless*, and *except*, with the Latin *nisi*, and with the French *sinon*.

The people are not to be satisfied, *but* by remitting them some of their taxes.

Unless by remitting them, *etc.*
Except by remitting them, *etc.*
The first expression seems to mark more peculiarly the insufficiency of every other means to pacify the people, but that which is proposed. The second seems to mark more peculiarly, that either this means must be employed, or the public disturbances will go on, and is therefore more alternative than the first. The third expression seems to mark the sense of one who out of all the means that can be proposed, chuses that which is most effectual. When we make use of *unless*, we do not mark that we have considered of any other means besides that which is proposed. Whereas, when we make use of *but* or *except*, we show that we have considered of some other means. *But* marks a negative rejection of every other means, but those proposed. *Except* a positive choice of the means proposed. *Unless* marks neither the one nor the other; and merely denotes an alternative, that either this must be done, or that will follow.

3. *But* is likewise a conductive conjunction in the sense in which it is nearly synonomous with the Latin *quin*, with the French *que*, and with the English *than* or *that*, when the first is preceded and the other followed by the particles of negation *no* or *not*.
The full moon was no sooner up, *than* he privately opened the gate of paradise.
But he privately opened, *etc.*
It cannot be doubted, that the King of Spain will not reform most of the abuses.
But the King of Spain will reform, *etc.*
Who shall believe, *but* you misuse the reverence of your place.
That you do not misuse, *etc.*
It cannot be *but* nature hath some director, *etc.*
It cannot be *that* nature has not some director.

4. *But* is likewise a transitive conjunction in the sense in which it is synonomous with the Latin *sed*, and with the French *or*.
All animals are mortal, *but* all men are animals, *etc.*

5. *But* is likeways[4] an adverb of quantity, and signifies *no more than*, and is nearly synonomous with the Latin *tantum*, and with the English *only*.
I saw *no more than* three plants.
I saw *but* three plants.
I saw three plants *only*.

---

[4] 'Likeways' survives in Scottish literary usage at least till the end of the eighteenth century.

A genius so elevated and unconfined as Mr. Cowley's was *no more than* necessary to make Pindar speak English.

Was *but* necessary, *etc.*

Was *only* necessary, *etc.*

This last expression might here, perhaps, be thought improper, because it might give occasion to an ambiguity; and might either signify, that nothing less than such a genius was capable of making Pindar speak English, or that nothing more was requisite for this purpose. Saving this ambiguity, the expression is, in every other respect, perfectly proper.

I should sin to think *but* nobly of my grandmother.

No more than nobly, *etc.*

Only nobly, *etc.*

Ulysses was formidable, *but* to his friends.

To his friends *only.*

Did *but* men consider the true notion of God.

Did men *only* consider, *etc.*

Beroe *but* now I left.

Beroe I left now *only.*

6. *But* is also a preposition, in which use it is synonomous with *except*, and would be expressed in Latin by *praeter*, in French by *hors*.

They are all dead *but* three.

They are all dead *except* three.

Who can it be ye gods *but* perjur'd Lycon?

Except perjur'd Lycon, *etc.*

7. *But* is also used as an interjection, tho' not frequently; as in this phrase, Good God, *but* she is handsom!

4 HUMOUR. n. s. [*humeur*, French; *humor*, Latin.]

1. Moisture.

The aqueous *humour* of the eye will not freeze; which is very admirable, seeing it hath the perspicuity and fluidity of common water.
Ray on the Creation.

2. The different kind of moisture in man's body, reckoned by the old physicians to be phlegm, blood, choler, and melancholy, which, as they predominated, were supposed to determine the temper of mind.

Believe not these suggestions, which proceed
From anguish of the mind and *humours* black,
That mingle with thy fancy.   *Milton's Agonistes.*

3. General turn or temper of mind.

As there is no *humour*, to which impudent poverty cannot make itself serviceable; so were there enow of those of desperate ambition, who would build their houses upon others ruin.   *Sidney, b.* ii.

There came with her a young lord, led hither with the *humour* of youth, which ever thinks that good whose goodness he sees not. *Sidney.*

King James, as he was a prince of great judgment, so he was a prince of a marvellous pleasant *humour*: as he was going through Lusen by Greenwich, he asked what town it was; they said Lusen. He asked, a good while after, what town is this we are now in? They said still it was Lusen: said the King, I will be King of Lusen.   *Bacon's Apophthegms.*

Examine how your *humour* is inclin'd,
And which the ruling passion of your mind.   *Roscom.*[5]

They, who were acquainted with him, know his *humour* to be such, that he would never constrain himself.   *Dryden.*

In cases where it is necessary to make examples, it is the *humour* of the multitude to forget the crime, and to remember the punishment.
                              Addison's Freeholder.

Good *humour* only teaches charms to last,
Still makes new conquests, and maintains the past.   *Pope.*

4. Present disposition.
    It is the curse of kings to be attended
    By slaves, that take their *humour*[6] for a warrant
    To break into the blood-house of life.   *Shak. K. John.*

    Another thought her nobler *humour* fed.   *Fairfax, b.* ii.

    Their *humours* are not to be won,
    But when they are impos'd upon.   *Hudibras, p.* iii.

          Tempt not his heavy hand;
    But one submissive word which you let fall,
    Will make him in good *humour* with us all.   *Dryden.*

5. Grotesque imagery; jocularity; merriment.

6. Diseased or morbid disposition.
    He was a man frank and generous; when well, denied himself nothing that he had a mind to eat or drink, which gave him a body full of *humours*, and made his fits of the gout frequent and violent.   *Temple.*

7. Petulence; peevishness.
    Is my friend all perfection, all virtue and discretion? Has he not *humours* to be endured, as well as kindness[7] to be enjoyed?
                              South's Sermons.

---

[5] Johnson has *Roscommon* in full.
[6] Johnson, correctly, has 'humours'; but the misreading of the next line (*KJ*, iv.ii.210: 'To break within the bloody house of life') is his.
[7] Johnson, correctly, has 'kindnesses'.

8. A trick; a practice.

> I like not the *humour* of lying: he hath wronged me in some *humours*:
> I should have borne the humour'd letter to her.
>> *Shak. Merry Wives of Windsor.*

9. Caprice; whim; predominant inclination.

> In private, men are more bold in their own *humours;* and in consort,
> men are more obnoxious to other[8] *humours;* therefore it is good to take
> both. *Bacon's Essays.*

5   HUMOUR, from the Latin *humor*, in its original signification, stands for moisture in general; from whence it has been restrained to signify the moisture of animal bodies, or those fluids which circulate thro' them.

6   It is distinguished from moisture in general in this, that *humours* properly express the fluids of the body, when, in a vitiated state, it would not be improper to say, that the fluids of such a person's body were full of *humours*.

7   The only fluids of the body, which, in their natural and healthful state, are called *humours*, are those in the eye; we talk of the aqueous *humour*, the crystaline *humour*, without meaning any thing that is morbid or diseased: yet, when we say in general, that such a person has got a *humour* in his eye, we understand it in the usual sense of a vitiated fluid.

8   As the temper of the mind is supposed to depend upon the state of the fluids in the body, *humour* has come to be synonomous with temper and disposition.

9   A person's humour however is different from his disposition in this, that humour seems to be the disease of a disposition; it would be proper to say that persons of a serious temper or disposition of mind, were subject to melancholy humours; that those of a delicate and tender disposition, were subject to peevish humours.

10   Humour may be agreeable, or disagreeable; but it is still humour, something that is whimsical, capricious, and not to be depended upon: an ill-natur'd man may have fits of good humour, which seem to come upon him accidentally, without any regard to the common moral cases of happiness or misery.

11   A fit of chearfulness constitutes the whole of good humour; and a man who has many such fits, is a good-humour'd man: yet he may not be good-natur'd; which is a character that supposes something more constant, equable, and uniform, than what was requisite to constitute good humour.

---

[8] Johnson, correctly, has 'others'.

12   Humour is often made use of to express the quality of the imagination which bears a considerable resemblance to wit.

13   Wit expresses something that is more designed, concerted, regular, and artificial; humour, something that is more wild, loose, extravagant, and fantastical; something which comes upon a man by fits, which he can neither command nor restrain, and which is not perfectly consistant with true politeness. Humour, it has been said, is often more diverting than wit; yet a man of wit is as much above a man of humour, as a gentleman is above a buffoon; a buffoon however will often divert more than a gentleman.

14   These instances may serve to explain the plan of a Dictionary which suggested itself to us. It can import no reflection upon Mr. Johnsons Dictionary that the subject has been viewed in a different light by others; and it is at least a matter of curiosity to consider the different views in which it appears. Any man who was about to compose a dictionary or rather a grammar of the English language, must acknowledge himself indebted to Mr. Johnson for abridging at least one half of his labour. All those who are under any difficulty with respect to a particular word or phrase, are in the same situation. The dictionary presents them a full collection of examples; from whence indeed they are left to determine, but by which the determination is rendered easy. In this country, the usefulness of it will be soon felt, as there is no standard of correct language in conversation; if our recommendation could in any degree incite to the perusal of it, we would earnestly recommend it to all those who are desirous to improve and correct their language, frequently to consult the dictionary. Its merit must be determined by the frequent resort that is had to it. This is the most unerring test of its value: criticisms may be false, private judgments ill-founded; but if a work of this nature be much in use, it has received the sanction of the public approbation.

LETTER TO THE *EDINBURGH REVIEW*

OF the letters which have been sent us by our learned Correspondents, we have room to publish no more in this number, except the following. It is long; but we are sure the public will reckon themselves indebted to us for it. We hope this ingenious and learned Gentleman, will continue to favour us with his assistance, for enlarging our plan in the manner which he proposes, and which we very much approve. We shall always acknowledge our obligations to any who favour us with literary memoirs, observations or criticisms, and take the first proper opportunity of transmitting them to the world.

[Alexander Wedderburn, editor][1]

A LETTER to the Authors of the *Edinburgh Review*.

GENTLEMEN,

1   It gives me pleasure to see a work so generally useful, as that which you have undertaken, likely to be so well executed in this country. I am afraid, however, you will find it impossible to support it with any degree of spirit, while you confine yourselves almost entirely to an account of the books published in Scotland. This country, which is but just beginning to attempt figuring in the learned world, produces as yet so few works of reputation, that it is scarce possible a paper which criticises upon them chiefly, should interest the public for any considerable time. The singular absurdity of some performances which you have so well represented in your first number, might divert your readers for once: But no eloquence could support a paper which consisted chiefly of accounts of such performances.

2   It is upon this account, that I take upon me, in the name of several of your readers, to propose to you, that you should enlarge your plan; that you should still continue to take notice, with the same humanity and candour, of every Scotch production that is tolerably decent. But that you should observe with regard to Europe in general the same plan which you followed with regard to England, examining such performances only, as, tho' they may not go down to the remotest posterity, have yet a chance of being remembered for thirty or forty years to come, and seem in the mean time to add something to that stock of literary amusement with which the world is at present provided. You will thus be able to give all proper encouragement to such efforts as this country is likely to make towards acquiring a

---

[1] [See Stewart, I.12. Wedderburn was Solicitor-General (1780), Lord Chancellor (1793–1801), Earl of Rosslyn (1801). In 1778 he invited Smith to write a memorandum on the likely outcome of the American War. The piece is reprinted in Corr., and was first published by G. H. Guttridge in the *American Historical Review*, xxxviii (1933).]

reputation in the learned world, which I imagine it was the well-natured design of your work to support; and you will oblige the public much more, by giving them an account of such books as are worthy of their regard, than by filling your paper with all the insignificant literary news of the times, of which not an article in a hundred is likely to be thought of a fortnight after the publication of the work that gave occasion to it.

3   Nor will this task be so very laborious as at first one might be apt to imagine. For tho' learning is cultivated in some degree in almost every part of Europe, it is in France and England only that it is cultivated with such success or reputation as to excite the attention of foreign nations. In Italy, the country in which it was first revived, it has been almost totally extinguished. In Spain, the country in which, after Italy, the first dawnings of modern genius appeared, it has been extinguished altogether. Even the art of printing seems to have been almost neglected in those two countries, from the little demand, I suppose, which there was for books: and tho' it has of late been revived in Italy, yet the expensive editions which have been published there of the Italian classics are plainly calculated for the libraries of Princes and monasteries, not to answer the demand of private persons. The Germans have never cultivated their own language; and while the learned accustom themselves to think and write in a language different from their own,[2] it is scarce possible that they should either think or write, upon any delicate or nice subject, with happiness and precision. In medicine, chemistry, astronomy, and mathematics, sciences which require only plain judgment joined to labour and assiduity, without demanding a great deal of what is called either taste or genius; the Germans have been, and still continue to be successful. The works of the Academies, indeed, both in Germany and Italy, and even in Russia, are the objects of some curiosity every where; but it is seldom that the works of any particular man are inquired for out of his own country. On the contrary, the works of many particular men both in France and England are more inquired for among foreign nations than those of any of their academies.

4   If we may pass any general judgment concerning the literary merit of those two great rivals in learning, trade, government and war: Imagination, genius and invention, seem to be the talents of the English; taste, judgment, propriety and order, of the French. In the old English poets, in Shakespear, Spencer and Milton, there often appears, amidst some irregularities and extravagancies, a strength of imagination so vast, so gigantic and supernatural, as astonishes and

[2] i.e. French.

confounds their reader into that admiration of their genius, which makes him despise, as mean and insignificant, all criticism upon the inequalities in their writings. In the eminent French writers, such sallies of genius are more rarely to be met with; but instead of them, a just arrangement, an exact propriety and decorum, joined to an equal and studied elegance of sentiment and diction, which, as it never strikes the heart like those violent and momentary flashes of imagination, so it never revolts the judgment by any thing that is absurd or unnatural, nor ever wearies the attention by any gross inequality in the stile, or want of connection in the method, but entertains the mind with a regular succession of agreeable, interesting and connected objects.

5   In natural philosophy, the science which in modern times has been most happily cultivated, almost all the great discoveries, which have not come from Italy or Germany, have been made in England. France has scarce produced any thing very considerable in that way. When that science was first revived in Europe, a fanciful, an ingenious and elegant, tho' fallacious, system was generally embraced in that country: nor can we with reason wonder that it was so. It may well be said of the Cartesian philosophy, now when it is almost universally exploded, that, in the simplicity, precision and perspicuity of its principles and conclusions, it had the same superiority over the Peripatetic system, which the Newtonian philosophy has over it.[3] A philosophy, which, upon its first appearance, had so many advantages over its rival system, was regarded by the French with peculiar fondness and admiration, when they considered it as the production of their own countryman, whose renown added new glory to their nation; and their attachment to it seems among them to have retarded and incumbered the real advancement of the science of nature. They seem now however to be pretty generally disengaged from the enchantment of that illusive philosophy; and it is with pleasure that

[3] [It is noted in LRBL ii.133–4 (ed. Lothian, 139–40), that there are two 'methods' which may be used in didactic (i.e. scientific) discourse, the Aristotelian and the Newtonian, and that the latter:

'is vastly more ingenious, and for that reason more engaging than the other. It gives us a pleasure to see the phenomena which we reckoned the most unaccountable, all deduced from some principle (commonly a well-known one) and all united in one chain far superior to what we feel from the unconnected method, where everything is accounted for by itself, without any reference to the others. We need not be surprised, then, that the Cartesian philosophy (for Descartes was in reality the first who attempted this method), though it does not perhaps contain a word of truth ... should nevertheless have been so universally received by all the learned in Europe at that time. The great superiority of the method over that of Aristotle, the only one then known, and the little enquiry that was then made into those matters, made them greedily receive a work which we justly esteem one of the most entertaining romances that have ever been wrote.'

Cf. TMS VII.ii.4.14 and Astronomy, IV.61 ff. and note. For comment see W. S. Howell, in *Essays on Adam Smith*, 32–3, and cf. LRBL ii.133 (ed. Lothian, 139).]

I observe in the new French Encyclopedia[4] the ideas of Bacon, Boyle, and Newton, explained with that order, perspicuity and good judgment, which distinguish all the eminent writers of that nation. As, since the union, we are apt to regard ourselves in some measure as the countrymen of those great men, it flattered my vanity, as a Briton, to observe the superiority of the English philosophy thus acknowledged by their rival nation. The two principal authors of that vast collection of every sort of literature, Mr. Diderot and Mr. Alembert, express every where the greatest passion for the science and learning of England, and insert into their work not only the discoveries and observations of those renowned philosophers I just now mentioned, but of many inferior English writers, whose names are now almost unknown, and whose works have been long disregarded in their own country. It mortified me, at the same time, to consider that posterity and foreign nations are more likely to be made acquainted with the English philosophy by the writings of others, than by those of the English themselves. It seems to be the peculiar talent of the French nation, to arrange every subject in that natural and simple order, which carries the attention, without any effort, along with it. The English seem to have employed themselves entirely in inventing, and to have disdained the more inglorious but not less useful labour of arranging and methodizing their discoveries, and of expressing them in the most simple and natural manner. There is not only no tolerable system of natural philosophy in the English language, but there is not even any tolerable system of any part of it. The Latin treatises of Keil and Gregory,[5] two Scotsmen, upon the principles of mechanics and astronomy, may be regarded as the best things that have been written in this way by any native of Great Britain, tho' in many respects confused, inaccurate and superficial. In Dr. Smith's Optics,[6] all the great discoveries which had before been made in that science are very compleatly recorded, along with many considerable corrections and improvements by that Gentleman himself. But if, in the knowledge of his science, he appears much superior to the two Scotsmen above mentioned, he is inferior

---

[4] *Encyclopédie, ou dictionnaire raisonné des sciences, des arts et des métiers,* ed. Denis Diderot and Jean le Rond d'Alembert (1751–72). Five volumes had appeared by 1755, and were purchased by Smith for Glasgow University Library. See Scott, *ASSP,* 179 and note.

[5] John Keill (1671–1721), the first to teach experimental physics at Oxford (Hart Hall), succeeded his Edinburgh professor David Gregory in the Savilian Chair of Astronomy at Oxford in 1712. His *Introductio ad Veram Physicam* (1701) is an introduction to Newton's *Principia. Introductio ad Veram Astronomiam* appeared in 1718.—David Gregory (1661–1708) taught Newtonian 'philosophy' and mathematics at Edinburgh till 1691, then at Oxford; wrote *Astronomiae Physicae et Geometriae Elementa* (1702).

[6] Robert Smith (1689–1768), Plumian Professor of Astronomy and Master of Trinity College, Cambridge, wrote the internationally famous *Compleat System of Opticks* (1738); and *Harmonics or the Philosophy of Musical Sounds* (1749), long the standard work on its subject.

even to them, who are far from being perfect, in the order and disposition of his work. It will not I hope be imputed to any mean motive, that I take notice of this fault, which in these subjects is not of the highest importance, and which that Gentleman himself would, I dare say, be willing to acknowledge; for whose knowledge and capacity I have the highest esteem, whose book has every other quality to recommend it, and who is himself, along with Dr. Bradley,[7] almost the only person now remaining in England to put us in mind of their illustrious predecessors. The learned world has been highly instructed by the labours and ingenuity of both these Gentlemen, and I will venture to say would have been much more so, if in their own country they had had more rivals and more judges. But the English of the present age, despairing perhaps to surpass the inventions, or to equal the renown of their forefathers, have disdained to hold the second place in a science in which they could not arrive at the first, and seem to have abandoned the study of it altogether.

6   The French work which I just now mentioned, promises to be the most compleat of the kind which has ever been published or attempted in any language. It will consist of many volumes in folio, illustrated with above six hundred plates, which make two volumes apart. There are above twenty Gentlemen engaged in it, all of them very eminent in their several professions, and many of them already known to foreign nations by the valuable works which they have published, particularly Mr. Alembert,[8] Mr. Diderot, Mr. Daubenton,[9] Mr. Rousseau of Geneva, Mr. Formey Secretary to the academy at Berlin, and many others. In the preliminary discourse, Mr. Alembert gives an account of the connection of the different arts and sciences, their genealogy and filiation as he calls it; which, a few alterations and corrections excepted, is nearly the same with that of my Lord Bacon.[10] In the body of the work, it is constantly marked, to what art or science, and to what branch of that art or science each particular article belongs. In the articles themselves, the reader will not find, as in other works of the same kind, a dry abstract of what is commonly known by the most superficial student of any science, but a compleat, reasoned and even critical examination of each subject. Scarce any thing seems to be omitted. Not only mathematics, natural philosophy and natural history, which commonly fill up the greater

[7] James Bradley (1693–1762), whom Newton called 'the best astronomer in Europe', was successively Savilian-Professor and Astronomer Royal; wrote on the aberration of light, the nutation of the Earth's axis, etc.

[8] d'Alembert was responsible for the mathematical and scientific entries in the *Encyclopédie*; Diderot was chief editor.

[9] Louis-Jean-Marie Daubenton (1716–1800): see below, 248. Jean-Henri-Samuel Formey (1711–97), secretary of Berlin Académie from 1748.

[10] In *Novum Organum* (1620).

part of works of this kind, are compleatly treated of; but all the mechanical arts are fully described, with the several machines which they make use of. Theology, morals, metaphysics, the art of criticism, the history of the *belles lettres*, philosophy, the literary history of sects, opinions and systems of all kinds, the chief doctrines of antient and modern jurisprudence, nay all the nicest subtleties of grammar, are explained in a detail that is altogether surprising. There are few men so learned in the science which they have peculiarly cultivated, as not to find in this work something even with regard to it which will both instruct and entertain them; and with regard to every other, they will seldom fail of finding all the satisfaction which they could desire. It promises indeed to be in every respect worthy of that magnificent eulogy which Mr. Voltaire bestows upon it, when, in the conclusion of his account of the artists who lived in the time of Louis the fourteenth, he tells us, 'That the last age has put the present in which we live in a condition to assemble into one body, and to transmit to posterity, to be by them delivered down to remoter ages, the sacred repository of all the arts and all the sciences, all of them pushed as far as human industry can go.' This, continues he, 'is what a society of learned men, fraught with genius and knowledge, are now labouring upon: an immense and immortal work, which seems to accuse the shortness of human life.'[11]

7   This work, which has several times been disagreeably interrupted by some jealousy either of the civil or of the ecclesiastical government of France,[12] to neither of which however the authors seem to have given any just occasion of suspicion, is not yet finished. The volumes of it which are yet to be published, will deserve, as they successively appear, to be particularly taken notice of in your future periodical reviews. You will observe, that tho' none of the authors of this collection appear to be mean or contemptible, yet they are not all equal. That the style of some of them is more declamatory, than is proper for a Dictionary; in which not only declamation, but any loose composition, is, more than any where, out of its place. That they seem too to have inserted some articles which might have been left out, and of which the insertion can serve only to throw a ridicule upon a work

[11] *Le Siècle de Louis XIV* (Berlin, 1751), ii.438: 'Enfin le siècle passé a mis celui où nous sommes en état de rassembler en un corps, et de transmettre à la postérité le dépôt de toutes les sciences et de tous les arts, tous poussés aussi loin que l'industrie humaine a pu aller; et c'est à quoi travaille aujourd'hui une société de savans, remplis d'esprit et de lumiéres. Cet ouvrage immense et immortel semble accuser la briéveté de la vie des hommes.'

[12] On 7 February 1752 the King's Council suppressed volumes i and ii after religious and other complaints, and suspended printing of more for eighteen months. The editors promised greater discretion, but five more volumes produced further complaints and on 8 March 1759 the Council revoked the *privilège*. Influential friends eventually enabled the remaining ten volumes of the main work to appear by 1772.

calculated for the propagation of every part of useful knowledge. The article of *Amour*,[13] for example, will tend little to the edification either of the learned or unlearned reader, and might, one should think, have been omitted even in an Encyclopedia of all arts, sciences and trades. These censures however fall but upon a few articles, and those of no great importance. The remaining parts of the work may give occasion to many other observations of more consequence, upon the candour or partiality with which they represent the different systems of philosophy or theology, antient or modern; the justness of their criticisms upon the celebrated authors of their own and of foreign nations; how far they have observed or neglected the just proportion betwixt the length of each article and the importance of the matter contained in it, and its fitness to be explained in a work of that kind; as well as many other observations of the same nature.

8   Nor is this the only great collection of science and literature at present carrying on in that country, to merit the attention of foreign nations. The description of the cabinet of the King,[14] which promises to comprehend a compleat system of natural history, is a work almost equally extensive. It was begun by the command of a minister whom France has long desired to see restored to the direction of the marine, and all Europe to that of the sciences, the Count de Maurepas. It is executed by two Gentlemen of most universally acknowledged merit, Mr. Buffon and Mr. Daubenton. A small part only of this work is yet published. The reasoning and philosophical part concerning the formation of plants, the generation of animals, the formation of the foetus, the development of the senses *etc.* is by Mr. Buffon. The system indeed of this Gentleman, it may be thought, is almost entirely hypothetical; and with regard to the causes of generation such, that it is scarce possible to form any very determinate idea of it. It must be acknowledged, however, that it is explained in an agreeable, copious, and natural eloquence, and that he has supported or connected it with many singular and curious observations and experiments of his own. The neatness, distinctness and propriety of all Mr. Daubenton's descriptions, seem to leave no room for criticism upon his part, which, tho' the least pompous, is by far the most important of the work.

9   None of the sciences indeed seem to be cultivated in France with more eagerness than natural history. Perspicuous description and

---

[13] i.367–74, by the Abbé Claude Yvon (1714–91). The future author of *The Theory of Moral Sentiments* might have been expected to look more kindly on an article beginning 'Il entre ordinairement beaucoup de sympathie dans l'*amour*'.

[14] *Histoire naturelle, générale et particulière, avec la description du Cabinet du Roi*, vols. i–xv (1749–67), ed. Georges Louis Leclerc, Comte de Buffon, and Louis-Jean-Marie Daubenton. Vols. i–v had appeared by 1755; xvi–xliv appeared by 1804.

just arrangement constitute a great part of the merit of a natural historian; and this study is perhaps upon that account peculiarly suited to the genius of that nation. In Mr. Reaumur's history of insects,[15] a work of which we are still to expect some volumes, your readers will find both these in the highest perfection, as well as the most attentive observation assisted by the most artful contrivances for inspecting into such things in the oeconomy and management of those little animals, as one would have imagined it impossible that he ever should have discovered. Those who complain of his tediousness, have never entered regularly upon his work, but have contented themselves with dipping into some parts of it. As mean as the subject may appear, he never fails to carry our attention along with him, and we follow him thro' all his observations and experiments with the same innocent curiosity and simple-hearted pleasure with which he appears to have made them. It will surprise your readers to find, that this Gentleman, amidst many other laborious studies and occupations, while he was composing, from his own experiments too, many other curious and valuable works, could find time to fill eight volumes in quarto with his own observations upon this subject, without ever once having recourse to the vain parade of erudition and quotation. These, and all other such works as these, which either seem to add something to the public stock of observations, if I may say so, or which collect more compleatly, or arrange in a better order, the observations that have already been made, the public will be pleased to see pointed out to them in your periodical *Review*, and will listen with attention to your criticisms upon the defects and perfections of what so well deserves to be criticised in general. As the works of all the academies in the different parts of Europe, are the objects of a pretty universal curiosity, tho' it would be impossible for you to give an account of every thing that is contained in them; it will not be very difficult to point out what are the most considerable improvements and observations which those societies have communicated to the public during the six months which preceed the publication of every *Review*.

10   The original and inventive genius of the English has not only discovered itself in natural philosophy, but in morals, metaphysics, and part of the abstract sciences. Whatever attempts have been made in modern times towards improvement in this contentious and unprosperous philosophy, beyond what the antients have left us, have been made in England. The Meditations of Des Cartes excepted, I know nothing in French that aims at being original upon these

---

[15] René Antoine Ferchault de Réaumur (1683–1757) published *Mémoires pour servir à l'histoire des insectes* in 1734–42, and left much material on ants, beetles, etc. in manuscript.

subjects; for the philosophy of Mr. Regis,[16] as well as that of Father Malbranche, are but refinements upon the Meditations of Des Cartes. But Mr. Hobbes, Mr. Lock, and Dr. Mandevil, Lord Shaftsbury, Dr. Butler, Dr. Clarke,[17] and Mr. Hutcheson,[18] have all of them, according to their different and inconsistent systems, endeavoured at least to be, in some measure, original; and to add something to that stock of observations with which the world had been furnished before them. This branch of the English philosophy, which seems now to be intirely neglected by the English themselves, has of late been transported into France. I observe some traces of it, not only in the Encyclopedia, but in the Theory of agreeable sentiments by Mr. De Pouilly,[19] a work that is in many respects original; and above all, in the late Discourse upon the origin and foundation of the inequality amongst mankind by Mr. Rousseau of Geneva.[20]

11   Whoever reads this last work with attention, will observe, that the second volume of the Fable of the Bees[21] has given occasion to the system of Mr. Rousseau, in whom however the principles of the English author are softened, improved, and embellished, and stript of all that tendency to corruption and licentiousness which has disgraced them in their original author. Dr. Mandeville represents the primitive state of mankind as the most wretched and miserable that can be imagined: Mr. Rousseau, on the contrary, paints it as the happiest and most suitable to his nature. Both of them however suppose, that there is in man no powerful instinct which necessarily determines him to seek society for its own sake: but according to the one, the misery of his original state compelled him to have recourse to this otherwise disagreeable remedy; according to the other, some unfortunate accidents having given birth to the unnatural passions of ambition and the vain desire of superiority, to which he had before been a stranger, produced the same fatal effect. Both of them suppose the same slow progress and gradual development of all the talents, habits, and arts which fit men to live together in society, and they

[16] Pierre-Sylvain Régis (1632–1707), author of *Système de philosophie* (1690); Nicolas Malebranche (1638–1715), author of *De la recherche de la vérité* (1674; English trans. 1694).

[17] No doubt the Newtonian Samuel Clarke (1675–1729), metaphysician and divine, whose collected works were published in 1738.

[18] Francis Hutcheson (1694–1746), Professor of Moral Philosophy at Glasgow and disciple of Shaftesbury; Smith was his pupil.

[19] *Théorie des sentimens agréables; où, après avoir indiqué les régles que la nature suit dans la distribution du plaisir, on établit les principes de la théologie naturelle et ceux de la philosophie morale* (1747), by Lévesque de Pouilly. This Shaftesburian treatise appeared in another version (*Réflexions sur les sentimens agréables*) in pirated editions in 1736 and 1743; and in an English translation 1749.

[20] *Discours sur l'origine et les fondemens de l'inégalité parmi les hommes.* Par Jean Jaques Rousseau citoyen de Genève (1755).

[21] Bernard Mandeville's *Fable of the Bees: or private vices publick benefits*, part ii, appeared in 1728. He adumbrated his views in 'An enquiry into the origin of moral virtue' in part i of the *Fable* (1714).

both describe this progress pretty much in the same manner. According to both, those laws of justice, which maintain the present inequality amongst mankind, were originally the inventions of the cunning and the powerful, in order to maintain or to acquire an unnatural and unjust superiority over the rest of their fellow-creatures. Mr. Rousseau however criticises upon Dr. Mandeville: he observes, that *pity*, the only amiable principle which the English author allows to be natural to man, is capable of producing all those virtues, whose reality Dr. Mandeville denies. Mr. Rousseau at the same time seems to think, that this principle is in itself no virtue, but that it is possessed by savages and by the most profligate of the vulgar, in a greater degree of perfection than by those of the most polished and cultivated manners; in which he perfectly agrees with the English author.

12   The life of a savage, when we take a distant view of it, seems to be a life either of profound indolence, or of great and astonishing adventures; and both these qualities serve to render the description of it agreeable to the imagination. The passion of all young people for pastoral poetry, which describes the amusements of the indolent life of a shepherd; and for books of chivalry and romance, which describe the most dangerous and extravagant adventures, is the effect of this natural taste for these two seemingly inconsistent objects. In the descriptions of the manners of savages, we expect to meet with both these: and no author ever proposed to treat of this subject who did not excite the public curiosity. Mr. Rousseau, intending to paint the savage life as the happiest of any, presents only the indolent side of it to view, which he exhibits indeed with the most beautiful and agreeable colours, in a style, which, tho' laboured and studiously elegant, is every where sufficiently nervous, and sometimes even sublime and pathetic. It is by the help of this style, together with a little philosophical chemistry, that the principles and ideas of the profligate Mandeville seem in him to have all the purity and sublimity of the morals of Plato, and to be only the true spirit of a republican carried a little too far. His work is divided into two parts: in the first, he describes the solitary state of mankind; in the second, the first beginnings and gradual progress of society. It would be to no purpose to give an analysis of either; for none could give any just idea of a work which consists almost entirely of rhetoric and description. I shall endeavour to present your readers therefore with a specimen of his eloquence, by translating one or two short passages.

13   'While men,' says he, *p.* 117. 'contented themselves with their first rustic habitations; while their industry had no object, except to pin together the skins of wild beasts for their original cloathing, to adorn

themselves with feathers and shells, to paint their bodies with different colours, to perfect or embellish their bows and arrows, to cut out with sharp stones some fishing canoes or some rude instruments of music; while they applied themselves to such works as a single person could execute, and to such arts as required not the concurrence of several hands; they lived free, healthful, humane and happy, as far as their nature would permit them, and continued to enjoy amongst themselves the sweets of an independent society. But from the instant in which one man had occasion for the assistance of another, from the moment that he perceived that it could be advantageous to a single person to have provisions for two, equality disappeared, property was introduced, labour became necessary, and the vast forrests of nature were changed into agreeable plains, which must be watered with the sweat of mankind, and in which the world beheld slavery and wretchedness begin to grow up and blosom with the harvest.'

14 'Thus, says he, *p.* 126. are all our faculties unfolded, memory and imagination brought into play, self-love interested, reason rendered active, and the understanding advanced almost to the term of its perfection. Thus are all our natural qualities exerted, the rank and condition of every man established, not only upon the greatness of his fortune and his power to serve or to hurt, but upon his genius, his beauty, his strength, or his address, upon his merit or his talents; and those qualities being alone capable of attracting consideration, he must either have them or affect them: he must for his advantage show himself to be one thing, while in reality he is another. To be and to appear to be, became two things entirely different; and from this distinction arose imposing ostentation, deceitful guile, and all the vices which attend them. Thus man, from being free and independent, became by a multitude of new necessities subjected in a manner, to all nature, and above all to his fellow creatures, whose slave he is in one sense even while he becomes their master; rich, he has occasion for their services; poor, he stands in need of their assistance; and even mediocrity does not enable him to live without them. He is obliged therefore to endeavour to interest them in his situation, and to make them find, either in reality or in appearance, their advantage in labouring for his. It is this which renders him false and artificial with some, imperious and unfeeling with others, and lays him under a necessity of deceiving all those for whom he has occasion, when he cannot terrify them, and does not find it for his interest to serve them in reality. To conclude, an insatiable ambition, an ardor to raise his relative fortune, not so much from any real necessity, as to set himself above others, inspires all men with a direful propensity to hurt one another; with a secret jealousy, so much the more dangerous, as to

strike its blow more surely, it often assumes the mask of good will; in short, with concurrence and rivalship on one side; on the other, with opposition of interest; and always with the concealed desire of making profit at the expence of some other person: All these evils are the first effects of property, and the inseparable attendants of beginning inequality.'

15   'Man,' says he afterwards, *p.* 179. 'in his savage, and man in his civilized state, differ so essentially in their passions and inclinations, that what makes the supreme happiness of the one, would reduce the other to despair. The savage breathes nothing but liberty and repose; he desires only to live and to be at leisure; and the *ataraxia* of the Stoic does not approach to his profound indifference for every other object. The citizen, on the contrary, toils, bestirs and torments himself without end, to obtain employments which are still more laborious; he labours on till his death, he even hastens it, in order to put himself in a condition to live, or renounces life to acquire immortality. He makes his court to the great whom he hates, and to the rich whom he despises; he spares nothing to obtain the honour of serving them; he vainly boasts of his own meanness and their protection, and, proud of his slavery, speaks with disdain of those who have not the honour to share it. What a spectacle to a *Caraib* would be the painful and envied labours of a European minister of state? how many cruel deaths would not that indolent savage prefer to the horror of such a life, which is often not even sweetened by the pleasure of doing well? but to see the end of so many cares, it is necessary that the words, *power* and *reputation,* should have an intelligible meaning in his understanding; that he should be made to comprehend that there is a species of men who count for something the looks of the rest of the universe; who can be happy and contented with themselves upon the testimony of another, rather than upon their own. For such in reality is the true cause of all those differences: the savage lives in himself; the man of society, always out of himself; cannot live but in the opinion of others, and it is, if I may say so, from their judgment alone that he derives the sentiment of his own existence. It belongs not to my subject to show, how from such a disposition arises so much real indifference for good and evil, with so many fine discourses of morality; how every thing being reduced to appearances, every thing becomes factitious and acted; honour, friendship, virtue, and often even vice itself, of which we have at last found out the secret of being vain; how in one word always demanding of others what we are, and never daring to ask ourselves the question, in the midst of so much philosophy, so much humanity, so much politeness, and so many sublime maxims we have nothing but a deceitful and frivolous

exterior; honour without virtue, reason without wisdom, and pleasure without happiness.'

16   I shall only add, that the dedication to the republic of Geneva, of which Mr. Rousseau has the honour of being a citizen, is an agreeable, animated, and I believe too, a just panegyric; and expresses that ardent and passionate esteem which it becomes a good citizen to entertain for the government of his country and the character of his countrymen.

17   It is not my intention, you may believe, to confine you to an account of the philosophical works that are published either at home or abroad. Tho' the poets of the present age seem in general to be inferior to those of the last, there are not however wanting, in England, France, and even in Italy, several who represent not unworthily their more renowned predecessors. The works of Metastasio are esteemed all over Europe; and Mr. Voltaire,[22] the most universal genius perhaps which France has ever produced, is acknowledged to be, in almost every species of writing, nearly upon a level with the greatest authors of the last age, who applied themselves chiefly to one. The original and inventive genius of that Gentleman never appeared more conspicuous than in his last tragedy, the orphan of China. It is both agreeable and surprising to observe how the atrocity, if I may say so, of Chinese virtue, and the rudeness of Tartar barbarity, have been introduced upon the French stage, without violating those nice decorums of which that nation are such delicate and scrupulous judges. In a letter to Mr. Rousseau of Geneva, he denies that the history of the last war, which has been published under his name in Holland, is to be regarded as his in the state in which it has been printed. There are indeed in it a great number of very gross misrepresentations with regard to the share which Great Britain had in the last war, for which, Mr. Voltaire, as it was published without his consent, is not answerable, and which will certainly be corrected in the first genuine edition that is published with the consent of the author.

I am,

Your most humble Servant, etc.

[22] The earliest of Smith's many expressions of admiration for Voltaire and for French drama: cf. Stewart, III.15. *L'Orphelin de la Chine* was presented in Paris on 20 August 1755 and published (with the letter to Rousseau, 30 August 1755, appended) in September. The story of the piracy by the publisher Prieur of Voltaire's *Histoire de la dernière guerre* is outlined by Georges Bengesco in *Voltaire, Bibliographie de ses œuvres* (1882), i.363–5. At least four editions (1755–6) of the piracy, with imprints Amsterdam, The Hague, or London, are known, as well as five of an English translation. Chapter V of *Histoire de la guerre de mil sept cent quarante-un* deals with Britain's role. Its quality may be judged by its treatment of names: 'Pwelney' (Pulteney), 'Posombi' (Ponsonby), 'Albermale', etc. For Voltaire's reactions to the event see his letters of late 1755: *Correspondence*, ed. T. Besterman, vol. cvii; Banbury, vol. xvi. Voltaire later incorporated parts of this work in *Essai sur l'histoire générale* (vol. viii, 1763), and with additions as *Précis du siècle de Louis XV* (1768).

APPENDIX: Passages quoted from Rousseau

Discours sur l'origine et les fondemens de l'inégalité parmi les hommes. Par Jean
Jaques Rousseau citoyen de Genève. Amsterdam: 1755.

pp. 117–18:
    Tant que les hommes se contentérent de leurs cabanes rustiques, tant
qu'ils se bornérent à coudre leurs habits de peaux avec des épines ou des
arrêtes, à se parer de plumes et de coquillages, à se peindre le corps de
diverses couleurs, à perfectionner ou embellir leurs arcs et leurs fleches, à
tailler avec des pierres tranchantes quelques Canots de pêcheurs ou quelques
grossiers instrumens de Musique; En un mot tant qu'ils ne s'appliquérent
qu'à des ouvrages qu'un seul pouvoit faire, et qu'à des arts qui n'avoient pas
besoin du concours de plusieurs mains, ils vécurent libres, sains, bons, et
heureux autant qu'ils pouvoient l'être par leur Nature, et continuérent à
joüir entre eux des douceurs d'un commerce independant: mais dès l'instant
qu'un homme eut besoin du secours d'un autre; dès qu'on s'apperçut qu'il
étoit utile à un seul d'avoir des provisions pour deux, l'égalité disparut, la
propriété s'introduisit, Le travail dévint nécessaire et les vastes forêts se
changérent en des Campagnes riantes qu'il falut arroser de la sueur des
hommes, et dans lesquelles on vit bientôt l'esclavage et la misére germer et
croître avec les moissons.

pp. 126–9:
    Voilà donc toutes nos facultés développées, la mémoire et l'imagination en
jeu, l'amour propre intéressé, la raison rendüe active, et l'esprit arrivé
presqu'au terme de la perfection, dont il est susceptible. Voilà toutes les
qualités naturelles mises en action, le rang et le sort de chaque homme établi,
non seulement sur la quantité des biens et le pouvoir de servir ou de nuire,
mais sur l'esprit, la beauté, la force ou l'adresse, sur le mérite ou les talens, et
ces qualités étant les seules qui pouvoient attirer de la consideration, il falut
bientôt les avoir ou les affecter; Il falut pour son avantage se montrer autre
que ce qu'on étoit en effet. Etre et paraître devinrent deux choses tout à fait
différentes, et de cette distinction sortirent le faste imposant, la ruse
trompeuse, et tous les vices qui en sont le cortége. D'un autre côté, de libre
et independant qu'étoit auparavant l'homme, le voilà par une multitude de
nouveaux besoins assujéti, pour ainsi dire, à toute la Nature, et surtout à ses
semblables dont il devient l'esclave en un sens, même en devenant leur
maître; riche, il a besoin de leurs services; pauvre, il a besoin de leur secours,
et la médiocrité ne le met point en état de se passer d'eux. Il faut donc qu'il
cherche sans cesse à les intéresser à son sort, et à leur faire trouver en effet ou
en apparence leur profit à travailler pour le sien: ce qui le rend fourbe et
artificieux avec les uns, imperieux et dur avec les autres, et le met dans la

nécessité d'abuser tous ceux dont il a besoin, quand il ne peut s'en faire craindre, et qu'il ne trouve pas son intérêt à les servir utilement. Enfin l'ambition dévorante, l'ardeur d'élever sa fortune relative, moins par un veritable besoin que pour se mettre au-dessus des autres, inspire à tous les hommes un noir penchant à se nuire mutuellement, une jalousie secrete d'autant plus dangereuse que, pour faire son coup plus en sûreté, elle prend souvent le masque de la bienveillance; en un mot, concurrence et rivalité d'une part, de l'autre opposition d'intérêt, et toujours le désir caché de faire son profit au depends d'autrui; Tous ces maux sont le premier effet de la propriété et le cortége inséparable de l'inégalité naissante.

pp. 179–82:

L'homme Sauvage et l'homme policé différent tellement par le fond du coeur et des inclinations, que ce qui fait le bonheur suprême de l'un, réduiroit l'autre au désespoir. Le premier ne respire que le repos et la liberté, il ne veut que vivre et rester oisif, et l'ataraxie même du Stoïcien n'approche pas de sa profonde indifférence pour tout autre objet. Au contraire, le Citoyen toujours actif suë, s'agite, se tourmente sans cesse pour chercher des occupations encore plus laborieuses: il travaille jusqu'à la mort, il y court même pour se mettre en état de vivre, ou renonce à la vie pour acquerir l'immortalité. Il fait sa cour aux grands qu'il hait et aux riches qu'il méprise; il n'épargne rien pour obtenir l'honneur de les servir; il se vante orgueilleusement de sa bassesse et de leur protection, et fier de son esclavage, il parle avec dédain de ceux qui n'ont pas l'honneur de le partager. Quel Spectacle pour un Caraïbe que les travaux pénibles et enviés d'un Ministre Européen! Combien de morts cruelles ne préféreroit pas cet indolent Sauvage à l'horreur d'une pareille vie qui souvent n'est pas même adoucie par le plaisir de bien faire? Mais pour voir le but de tant de soins, il faudroit que ces mots, *puissance* et *réputation*, eussent un sens dans son esprit, qu'il apprît qu'il y a une sorte d'hommes qui comptent pour quelque chose les regards du reste de l'univers, qui savent être heureux et contens d'eux mêmes sur le témoignage d'autrui plûtôt que sur le leur propre. Telle est, en effet, la véritable cause de toutes ces différences: le Sauvage vit en lui-même; l'homme sociable toûjours hors de lui ne sait vivre que dans l'opinion des autres, et c'est, pour ainsi dire, de leur seul jugement qu'il tire le sentiment de sa propre existence. Il n'est pas de mon sujet de montrer comment d'une telle disposition naît tant d'indifférence pour le bien et le mal, avec de si beaux discours de morale; comment tout se réduisant aux apparences, tout devient factice et joüé; honneur, amitié, vertu, et souvent jusqu'aux vices mêmes, dont on trouve enfin le secret de se glorifier; comment, en un mot, demandant toujours aux autres ce que nous sommes et n'osant jamais nous interroger là-dessus nous mêmes, au milieu de tant de Philosophie, d'humanité, de politesse et de maximes Sublimes, nous n'avons qu'un extérieur trompeur et frivole, de l'honneur sans vertu, de la raison sans sagesse, et du plaisir sans bonheur.

Preface and Dedication to William Hamilton's
Poems on Several Occasions

Introduction

Adam Smith's first published writing was an unsigned preface to *Poems on Several Occasions* (Glasgow: Printed and sold by Robert and Andrew Foulis, M.D.CC.XLVIII), a small octavo volume of work by the Jacobite poet William Hamilton, later laird of Bangour, who had gone into exile in France after the defeat of his cause at Culloden in April 1746. The authorship of the preface is attested by a statement from the poet's intimate friend Andrew Lumisden to George Chalmers, preserved in the Chalmers–Laing manuscript notes on Scots poets in Edinburgh University Library.[1] There is no evidence that Smith helped to edit the poems, but it seems unlikely that he was called in merely to write a short foreword. His enlistment was probably due to Henry Home (later Lord Kames), at whose instance he had just begun delivering his first course of lectures on rhetoric and belles-lettres at Edinburgh and who had been the poet's literary mentor since the early 1720s.

The advertisement of the book in the *Glasgow Courant* for 23 January 1749 suggests that the date on the title-page was premature. A second issue, with preliminary pages reset, appeared in 1749, and a reprint with some corrections and bearing the poet's name in 1758—the 'Second Edition'. Hamilton had died in 1754; and in 1755 William Crawford, the 'friend' mentioned in the preface, to whom Hamilton had long been in the habit of entrusting his poems and whose granddaughter Elizabeth Dalrymple became Hamilton's second wife in July 1752, also died. When the second edition of the poems was being prepared the poet's brother-in-law (Sir) John Dalrymple wrote from Edinburgh, on 1 December 1757, to Robert Foulis:

I have changed my mind about the Dedication to Mr Hamilton's Poems. I would have had it stand 'the friend of William Hamilton', but I assent to your opinion to have something more to express Mr. Crawfurd's Character. I know none so able to do this as my friend Mr. Smith; I beg it therefore earnestly that he will write the Inscription and with all the elegance and all the feelingness which he, above the rest of mankind, is able to express. This is a thing that touches me very nearly, and therefore I beg a particular answer as to what he says to it. The many happy and the many flattering hours which he has spent with Mr. Hamilton and Mr. Crawfurd makes me think that he will account his usual indolence a crime upon this occasion. I

[1] Laing MSS., 359: quoted by Nelson S. Bushnell, *William Hamilton of Bangour, Jacobite and Poet* (1957), 132, n.17.

beg you will make my excuse for not wryting him this night about this. I consider wryting to you upon this head to be wryting to him.[2]

The close network of friendships involved makes it unthinkable that Adam Smith could have refused this request, and the 1758 Dedication is here included as his. Neither it nor the Preface was reprinted in the much fuller collection of Hamilton's poems—containing more than twice the number in the 1748 volume—published in Edinburgh in 1760; but the foreword to this, by David Rae (later Lord Eskgrove) echoes some of Smith's phrases.

Hamilton's poems appeared in various miscellanies from 1724 onwards and twenty-two of the 1748 thirty-nine had already been published. The long poem *Contemplation; or, The triumph of love*, finished in 1739, was issued in Edinburgh in February 1747 as a fourpenny pamphlet, abridged and (it seems) pirated; only the 1760 version is complete. Of it the most perceptive appreciation came from another Glasgow professor, William Richardson of the Chair of Humanity, in *The Lounger* No. 42, 19 November 1785. As Smith hints, Hamilton excelled particularly in the 'imitation' and free translation or adaptation of originals as diverse as Pindar, Anacreon, Sophocles, Virgil, Horace (Odes and Epistles), Shakespeare, Racine. He was the first to render Homer into English blank verse: the Glaucus and Diomed episode from *Iliad*, vi. His best-known poem is the imitation-ballad *The Braes of Yarrow*, which in turn inspired imitations by Wordsworth.

Text reproduced: Preface, from *Poems* 1748 and 1758, p.v (1749 has six spelling variants); Dedication, from *Poems* 1758, pp.iii–iv.

---

[2] W. J. Duncan, *Notices and Documents illustrative of the Literary History of Glasgow* (Maitland Club: Glasgow, 1831), 23–4, taken from the Foulis Press papers.

PREFACE TO WILLIAM HAMILTON'S
POEMS ON SEVERAL OCCASIONS (1748)

No writings of this kind ever had a better claim to the indulgence of the public, than the following poems; as this collection is published not only without the author's consent, but without his knowledge, and therefore in justice to him, the editors must take upon themselves any faults or imperfections that may be found in it.

It is hoped, that the many beauties of language and sentiment which appear in this little volume, and the fine genius the author every where discovers, will make it acceptable to every reader of taste, and will in some measure attone for our presumption in presenting the publick with poems, of which none have had the author's finishing hand, and many of them only first essays in his early youth.

One inducement to print them, was to draw from the author a more perfect edition, when he returns to this country, and if our faulty attempt shall be the occasion of producing a work that may be an honour to this part of the kingdom, we shall glory in what we have done.

What brought us at first to think of this little undertaking was the concern some of the author's friends express'd to us, at the imperfect edition of his noble poem of CONTEMPLATION lately published from an incorrect manuscript; this determin'd us to give an edition of it, less unworthy of the author, and to join to it every little piece of his that had been printed at different times; and we prevailed likewise on a friend of his, tho' with some difficulty, to give us a small number of pieces that had never before been printed, some of which had been handed about in manuscript, and might have been printed with the transcribers errors by others. It is owing to the delicacy of this friend of the author's, that this edition is not enriched with many original poems, and some beautiful translations from Pindar and other ancient poets, both Greek and Roman, that are in his possession, but which he would not permit to be published.

Glasgow, December 21. 1748.

DEDICATION TO WILLIAM HAMILTON'S
POEMS ON SEVERAL OCCASIONS (1758)

TO
THE MEMORY OF
MR. WILLIAM CRAUFURD,
MERCHANT IN GLASGOW,
.THE FRIEND OF MR. HAMILTON,

WHO to that exact frugality, that downright probity and plainness of manners so suitable to his profession, joined a love of learning and of all the ingenious arts, an openness of hand and a generosity of heart that was free both from vanity and from weakness, and a magnanimity that could support, under the prospect of approaching and unavoidable death, the most torturing pains of body with an unalterable chearfulness of temper, and without once interrupting, even to his last hour, the most manly and the most vigorous activity in a vast variety of business;

This Edition of the Works of a Gentleman for whom he, who was candid and penetrating, circumspect and sincere, always expressed the highest and the most affectionate esteem, is inscribed by the Editors, as the only monument which it is in their power to raise of their veneration and of their regret.

Dugald Stewart: *Account of the Life and Writings of Adam Smith, LL.D.*

Introduction

'I hate biography' was the confession of Dugald Stewart (1753–1828) in a letter of 1797, but it appears that of the three pieces of this kind which he wrote for presentation to the Royal Society of Edinburgh, the one on Adam Smith was most to his taste (*Works*, ed. Hamilton, x. lxxv, *n.*1). Indeed, as a member of Smith's circle, and like him a Scots professor of moral philosophy, inheriting and transmitting the same intellectual tradition, Stewart was a logical choice as a memorialist of Smith, and he must have felt some affinity for this project.

The first news of it comes in a letter of 10 August 1790 to Smith's heir, David Douglas, in which John Millar, distinguished Professor of Civil Law at Glasgow University, and a former pupil of Smith, welcomes the idea of publishing the posthumous essays (EPS), and states: 'It will give me the greatest pleasure to contribute any hints to Mr Stuart with regard to Mr Smiths professorial talents, or any other particular you mention, while he remained at Glasgow' (Glasgow University Library, MS. Gen. 1035/178). True to his word, Millar sent 'some particulars about Dr. Smith' to Stewart in December of the same year, and on 17 August 1792 the latter reported to the publisher Thomas Cadell as follows: 'Mr Smith's papers with the Account of his life will be ready for the press the beginning of next winter' (National Library of Scotland, MS. 5319, f. 34). Cadell offered terms for the book to Henry Mackenzie, one of the 'privy council' advising Douglas about the publication, on 21 December 1792 (GUL, MS. Gen. 1035/177), and Stewart wrote to Cadell on 13 March of the following year to say that he had finished the 'Account' and was ready to send it to the press 'immediately'. (In fact, he read it at meetings of the Royal Society of Edinburgh on 21 January and 18 March 1793.) In the same letter to Cadell, Stewart mentions that neither the RSE *Transactions* nor EPS is likely to appear 'this Season', and he asks if a separate publication could be considered: 'more especially, as [my papers] have Swelled to Such a Size, that I suspect they must be printed in an abridged form in the Transactions' (NLS, MS. 5319, ff. 35–6).

As matters turned out, the first edition of the 'Account' was published in the third volume of the RSE *Transactions* (1794), and when EPS was published in 1795, under the editorship of Joseph Black and James Hutton, Smith's literary executors, the 'Account' was printed as the first piece, with some minor changes from the RSE text. In 1810, Stewart withdrew from active teaching at Edinburgh University because of failing health, and among other projects undertook the revision of his RSE papers for publication as *Biographical Memoirs of Adam Smith, William Robertson, and Thomas Reid* (1811).

In the preface to this book, the author stated his belief that for Smith and Reid he had nearly exhausted all the information available, and that he had been induced to connect 'with the slender thread of [his] narration a variety of speculative discussions and illustration' (vi). These provide a useful commentary on some of Smith's ideas, and include such valuable material as Millar's description of Smith's course of lectures at Glasgow (I.16–22). Also, discussing Smith's thought in relation to that of the French economists, Stewart presented a fragment of a paper written by Smith in 1755, in which some of his leading ideas are outlined (IV.25). Stewart's version of both documents is all that has survived, the originals perhaps being destroyed with Stewart's own papers by his son when suffering from paranoia (*Works*, viii. x–xi; x. iii). In the preface to the *Memoirs*, Stewart further states that he left the text of the 'Account of Smith' as it was (i.e. in 1794–5), 'with the exception of some trifling verbal corrections', and added to it notes that were 'entirely new' (vii).

In the same year as the *Memoirs* appeared, Stewart published an edition of Smith's *Works* (1811–12), incorporating in the fifth volume the *Memoirs* text of the 'Account', but omitting at the conclusion two paragraphs describing EPS, and one dealing with the preference of Smith and his circle for the plain style of 'Mr' rather than the honorific 'Doctor'. In a letter to ?William Davies, Cadell's partner, dated 26 July 1810, Stewart suggests that since Smith's *Works* are to be printed in London, they should be put 'into the hands of some corrector' whose accuracy can be relied on, 'desiring him to follow the text of the last Editions published before Mr Smith's death'. Stewart will correct EPS himself, and he asks that the 'Account of Smith' be printed last, 'as I have some Slight alterations to make on it, and intend to add a few paragraphs to some of the Sections'. Stewart continues that 'in a Week or two I propose to begin to print the 4to Edition of Lives [i.e. *Memoirs*]', presumably in Edinburgh under his own eye (NLS, MS. 5319, ff.39–40).

Subsequently, Stewart's *Works* (1854–60) were themselves edited by Sir William Hamilton (1788–1856) at the end of his life, and the 'Account of Smith' found its place in the tenth volume (1858). The advertisement to this volume, written by John Veitch (1829–94), states that the memoirs of Smith, Robertson, and Reid were 'printed under ... Hamilton's revision and superintendence, from private copies belonging to [Stewart] which contained a few manuscript additions by him' (x. vii). One such 'private copy' survives in Edinburgh University Library (MS. Df. 4. 52*), consisting of an EPS text of the 'Account of Smith' with marginal corrections in Stewart's hand (pp. 46, 57, 63) and indicators for notes, followed by Notes A to I of the present edition, all in Stewart's hand save that of Note D, which is in that of an amanuensis. Stewart must have worked on this 'private copy' after 1821, because Note E refers to Morellet's *Mémoires* published in that year.

All the 'last additions' of the EUL 'private copy' are incorporated in Hamilton's text of the 'Account of Smith', with the trifling exception of the 'la' in 'la Rochefoucauld' (303, below), and it is tempting to use the 1858 edition as the copy-text for our present purpose. However, in his *Memoir of Hamilton* (1869), John Veitch prints letters indicating that Hamilton was fatally ill during the editing of Stewart's *Works*, and was assisted by a Miss Petre, formerly governess to his daughter (362–3). Indeed, Hamilton died before the tenth volume appeared and its publication was supervised by Veitch. In view of these facts, it has been thought best to make the 1811 *Memoirs* version of the 'Account of Smith' the copy-text for this edition, as the one containing the fullest amount of biographical material directly authorized by Stewart himself, also as the text he personally revised for publication. A letter of 1798 by Stewart makes the claim, at least, that he read proof carefully: 'The very great alterations and corrections which I have been in the habit of making during the time that the printing of my books was going on, put it out of my power to let anything out of my hands till it has undergone the very last revisal' (*Works*, x. xxxi, *n.*4.).

Within each section of the text paragraphs have been numbered to facilitate references and citations. Asterisks and daggers point Stewart's notes, and the signal 5 after a note indicates that it comes from Hamilton's 1858 edition. Superscript letters refer the reader to textual notes preserving substantive readings from the editions of 1794 and 1795, identified as *1* and *2*. The *author's last additions* of the EUL 'private copy' mentioned above are identified by that very phrase. The modern convention for indicating quotations has been adopted, and translations of Latin quotations have been supplied, in some cases from Stewart's *Works* edited by Hamilton. The present editor's notes are numbered consecutively, with material added by him placed within round brackets, and the General Editors' notes are placed within square brackets.

Whereas Smith 'considered every species of note as a blemish or imperfection; indicating, either an idle accumulation of superfluous particulars, or a want of skill and comprehension in the general design' (Stewart, *Works*, x.169–70), Stewart followed the practice of Robertson in placing discursive notes at the end of the text. For the sake of convenience, these endnotes have been retained below, with the 'last additions', principally D and E, duly identified.

List of the Editions of 'Account of the Life and Writings of Adam Smith, LL.D.'

1	1794	*Transactions of the Royal Society of Edinburgh* (T. Cadell: London; J. Dickson and E. Balfour: Edinburgh), iii.55–137.
2	1795	EPS, ix–cxxiii.
3	1811	*Biographical memoirs of Adam Smith, LL.D. of William Robertson, D.D. and of Thomas Reid, D.D.* (W. Creech, Bell and Bradfute, and A. Constable: Edinburgh; F. and C. Rivington *et al.* [including Cadell and Davies]: London), 3–152.
4	1811	*The Works of Adam Smith, LL.D.*, ed. Dugald Stewart, 5 vols. (T. Cadell and W. Davies *et al.*: London; W. Creech, and Bell and Bradfute: Edinburgh), v.403–552.
5	1858	*The Collected Works of Dugald Stewart, Esq., F.R.S.*, ed. Sir William Hamilton, Bart., 11 vols. (Thomas Constable and Co.: Edinburgh; Little, Brown, and Co.: Boston), x.1–98.

ACCOUNT

OF THE

LIFE AND WRITINGS

OF

ADAM SMITH, LL.D.

From the Transactions of the Royal Society of Edinburgh

[Read by Mr STEWART, January 21, and March 18, 1793]

SECTION I

*From Mr Smith's Birth till the publication of the
Theory of Moral Sentiments*

1 ADAM SMITH, author of the Inquiry into the Nature and Causes of
the Wealth of Nations, was the son of Adam Smith, comptroller of
the customs at Kirkaldy*, and of Margaret Douglas, daughter of Mr
Douglas of Strathenry. He was the only child of the marriage, and
was born at Kirkaldy on the 5th of June 1723, a few months after the
death of his father.

2   His constitution during infancy was infirm and sickly, and
required all the tender solicitude of his surviving parent. She was
blamed for treating him with an unlimited indulgence; but it
produced no unfavourable effects on his temper or his dispositions:—
and he enjoyed the rare satisfaction of being able to repay her
affection, by every attention that filial gratitude could dictate, during
the long period of sixty years.

3   An accident which happened to him when he was about three
years old, is of too interesting a nature to be omitted in the account of
so valuable a life. He had been carried by his mother to Strathenry,
on a visit to his uncle Mr Douglas, and was one day amusing himself
alone at the door of the house, when he was stolen by a party of that

---

* Mr Smith, the father, was a native of Aberdeenshire, and, in the earlier part of his life,
practised at Edinburgh as a writer to the signet. He was afterwards private secretary to the Earl
of Loudoun (during the time he held the offices of principal secretary of state for Scotland, and
of keeper of the great seal), and continued in this situation till 1713 or 1714, when he was
appointed comptroller of the customs at Kirkaldy. He was also clerk to the courts-martial and
councils of war for Scotland; an office which he held from 1707 till his death. As it is now
seventy years since he died, the accounts I have received of him are very imperfect; but, from
the particulars already mentioned, it may be presumed, that he was a man of more than
common abilities.

set of vagrants who are known in Scotland by the name of tinkers. Luckily he was soon missed by his uncle, who, hearing that some vagrants had passed, pursued them, with what assistance he could find, till he overtook them in Leslie wood; and was the happy instrument of preserving to the world a genius, which was destined, not only to extend the boundaries of science, but to enlighten and reform the commercial policy of Europe.

4   The school of Kirkaldy, where Mr Smith received the first rudiments of his education, was then taught by Mr David Miller, a teacher, in his day, of considerable reputation, and whose name deserves to be recorded, on account of the eminent men whom that very obscure seminary produced while under his direction. Of this number were Mr Oswald of Dunikeir*; his brother, Dr John Oswald, afterwards Bishop of Raphoe; and our late excellent colleague, the Reverend Dr John Drysdale: all of them nearly contemporary with Mr Smith, and united with him through life by the closest ties of friendship.—One of his school-fellows is still alive†; and to his kindness I am principally indebted for the scanty materials which form the first part of this narrative.

5   Among these companions of his earliest years, Mr Smith soon attracted notice, by his passion for books, and by the extraordinary powers of his memory. The weakness of his bodily constitution prevented him from partaking in their more active amusements; but he was much beloved by them on account of his temper, which, though warm, was to an uncommon degree friendly and generous. Even then he was remarkable for those habits which remained with him through life, of speaking to himself when alone, and of *absence* in company.

6   From the grammar-school of Kirkaldy, he was sent, in 1737, to the university of Glasgow, where he remained till 1740, when he went to Baliol college, Oxford, as an exhibitioner‡ on Snell's foundation.

7   Dr Maclaine of the Hague, who was a fellow-student of Mr Smith's at Glasgow, told me some years ago, that his favourite pursuits while at that university were mathematics and natural philosophy; and I

---

* See Note (A.)

† George Drysdale, Esq. of Kirkaldy, brother of the late Dr Drysdale.

‡ As the word *exhibitioner* has misled a French author, to whose critical acquaintance with the English language I am indebted for a very elegant translation of this memoir, I think it proper to mention, that it is used here to denote a student who enjoys a salary to assist him in carrying on his academical education. 'The word *Exhibition*' (says Johnson) 'is much used for pensions allowed to scholars at the university.'—In the translation above referred to, as well as in the *Notice* prefixed to M. Garnier's translation of the Wealth of Nations, the clause in the text is thus rendered: *il entra au college de Baliol à Oxford, en qualité de démonstrateur de la fondation de Snell.*

    With respect to Snell's foundation ('the largest, perhaps, and most liberal in Britain'), see the Statistical Account of the University of Glasgow ᵃby Dr. Thomas Reidᵃ.

---

a–a added in 5

remember to have heard my father remind him of a geometrical problem of considerable difficulty, about which he was occupied at the time when their acquaintance commenced, and which had been proposed to him as an exercise by the celebrated Dr Simpson.

8   These, however, were certainly not the sciences in which he was formed to excel; nor did they long divert him from pursuits more congenial to his mind. What Lord Bacon says of Plato may be justly applied to him: 'Illum, licet ad rempublicam non accessisset, tamen naturâ et inclinatione omnino ad res civiles propensum, vires eo praecipue intendisse; neque de Philosophia Naturali admodum sollicitum esse; nisi quatenus ad Philosophi nomen et celebritatem tuendam, et ad majestatem quandam moralibus et civilibus doctrinis addendam et aspergendam sufficeret*.' The study of human nature in all its branches, more particularly of the political history of mankind, opened a boundless field to his curiosity and ambition; and while it afforded scope to all the various powers of his versatile and comprehensive genius, gratified his ruling passion, of contributing to the happiness and the improvement of society. To this study, diversified at his leisure hours by the less severe occupations of polite literature, he seems to have devoted himself almost entirely from the time of his removal to Oxford; but he still retained, and retained even in advanced years, a recollection of his early acquisitions, which not only added to the splendour of his conversation, but enabled him to exemplify some of his favourite theories concerning the natural progress of the mind in the investigation of truth, by the history of those sciences in which the connection and succession of discoveries may be traced with the greatest advantage. If I am not mistaken too, the influence of his early taste for the Greek geometry may be remarked in the elementary clearness and fulness, bordering sometimes upon prolixity, with which he frequently states his political reasonings.—The lectures of the profound and eloquent Dr Hutcheson, which he had attended previous to his departure from Glasgow, and of which he always spoke in terms of the warmest admiration, had, it may be reasonably presumed, a considerable effect in directing his talents to their proper objects†.

9   I have not been able to collect any information with respect to that part of his youth which was spent in England. I have heard him say, that he employed himself frequently in the practice of translation,

---

* Redargutio Philosophiarum. ('Although he had not taken up politics, he was by nature and entire disposition inclined towards civil affairs, and his talents tended chiefly in that direction; nor was he particularly concerned about Natural Philosophy, except to the degree it should suffice for maintaining the good name and fame of Philosopher, and adding to moral and civil disciplines and shedding on them a kind of majesty.')
† See Note (B.)

(particularly from the French), with a view to the improvement of his own style: and he used often to express a favourable opinion of the utility of such exercises, to all who cultivate the art of composition. It is much to be regretted, that none of his juvenile attempts in this way have been preserved; as the few specimens which his writings contain of his skill as a translator, are sufficient to shew the eminence he had attained in a walk of literature, which, in our country, has been so little frequented by men of genius.

10   It was probably also at this period of his life, that he cultivated with the greatest care the study of languages. The knowledge he possessed of these, both ancient and modern, was uncommonly extensive and accurate; and, in him, was subservient, not to a vain parade of tasteless erudition, but to a familiar acquaintance with every thing that could illustrate the institutions, the manners, and the ideas of different ages and nations. How intimately he had once been conversant with the more ornamental branches of learning; in particular, with the works of the Roman, Greek, French, and Italian poets, appeared sufficiently from the hold which they kept of his memory, after all the different occupations and inquiries in which his maturer faculties had been employed*. In the English language, the variety of poetical passages which he was not only accustomed to refer to occasionally, but which he was able to repeat with correctness, appeared surprising even to those, whose attention had never been directed to more important acquisitions.

11   After a residence at Oxford of seven years, he returned to Kirkaldy, and lived two years with his mother; engaged in study, but without any fixed plan for his future life. He had been originally destined for the Church of England, and with that view had been sent to Oxford; but not finding the ecclesiastical profession suitable to his taste, he chose to consult, in this instance, his own inclination, in preference to the wishes of his friends; and abandoning at once all the schemes which their prudence had formed for him, he resolved to return to his own country, and to limit his ambition to the uncertain prospect of obtaining, in time, some one of those moderate preferments, to which literary attainments lead in Scotland.

12   In the year 1748, he fixed his residence at Edinburgh, and during that and the following years, read lectures on rhetoric and belles lettres, under the patronage of Lord Kames. About this time, too, he

---

* The uncommon degree in which Mr Smith retained possession, even to the close of his life, of different branches of knowledge which he had long ceased to cultivate, has been often remarked to me by my learned colleague and friend, Mr Dalzel, Professor of Greek in this University.—Mr Dalzel mentioned particularly the readiness and correctness of Mr Smith's memory on philological subjects, and the acuteness and skill he displayed in various conversations with him on some of the *minutiae* of Greek grammar.

contracted a very intimate friendship, which continued without interruption till his death, with Mr Alexander Wedderburn,[1] now Lord Loughborough, and with Mr William Johnstone, now Mr Pulteney.

13   At what particular period his acquaintance with Mr David Hume commenced, does not appear from any information that I have received; but from some papers, now in the possession of Mr Hume's nephew, and which he has been so obliging as to allow me to peruse, their acquaintance seems to have grown into friendship before the year 1752. It was a friendship on both sides founded on the admiration of genius, and the love of simplicity; and, which forms an interesting circumstance in the history of each of these eminent men, from the ambition which both have shewn to record it to posterity.

14   In 1751, he was elected Professor of Logic in the University of Glasgow; and, the year following, he was removed to the Professorship of Moral Philosophy in the same University, upon the death of Mr Thomas Craigie, the immediate successor of Dr Hutcheson. In this situation he remained thirteen years; a period he used frequently to look back to, as the most useful and happy of his life.[2] It was indeed a situation in which he was eminently fitted to excel, and in which the daily labours of his profession were constantly recalling his attention to his favourite pursuits, and familiarizing his mind to those important speculations he was afterwards to communicate to the world. In this view, though it afforded, in the meantime, but a very narrow scene for his ambition, it was probably instrumental, in no inconsiderable degree, to the future eminence of his literary character.

15   Of Mr Smith's lectures while a Professor at Glasgow, no part has been preserved, excepting what he himself published in the Theory of Moral Sentiments, and in the Wealth of Nations. The Society therefore, I am persuaded, will listen with pleasure to the following short account of them, for which I am indebted to a gentleman who was formerly one of Mr Smith's pupils, and who continued till his death to be one of his most intimate and valued friends*.

16   'In the Professorship of Logic, to which Mr Smith was appointed on his first introduction into this University, he soon saw the necessity of departing widely from the plan that had been followed by his predecessors, and of directing the attention of his pupils to studies of a more interesting and useful nature than the logic and

* Mr. Millar, the late celebrated Professor of Law in the University of Glasgow. [See the editor's Introduction, 265, above.]

[1] [See above, 172, 229, 242n.]
[2] [See below, V.10, where Stewart cites Smith's letter to the Principal of the University accepting the office of Rector.]

metaphysics of the schools. Accordingly, after exhibiting a general view of the powers of the mind, and explaining so much of the ancient logic as was requisite to gratify curiosity with respect to an artificial method of reasoning, which had once occupied the universal attention of the learned, he dedicated all the rest of his time to the delivery of a system of rhetoric and belles lettres. The best method of explaining and illustrating the various powers of the human mind,[3] the most useful part of metaphysics, arises from an examination of the several ways of communicating our thoughts by speech, and from an attention to the principles of those literary compositions which contribute to persuasion or entertainment. By these arts, every thing that we perceive or feel, every operation of our minds, is expressed and delineated in such a manner, that it may be clearly distinguished and remembered. There is, at the same time, no branch of literature more suited to youth at their first entrance upon philosophy than this, which lays hold of their taste and their feelings.

17   'It is much to be regretted, that the manuscript containing Mr Smith's lectures on this subject was destroyed before his death. The first part, in point of composition, was highly finished; and the whole discovered strong marks of taste and original genius. From the permission given to students of taking notes, many observations and opinions contained in these lectures have either been detailed in separate dissertations, or engrossed in general collections, which have since been given to the public. But these, as might be expected, have lost the air of originality and the distinctive character which they received from their first author, and are often obscured by that multiplicity of common-place matter in which they are sunk and involved.

18   'About a year after his appointment to the Professorship of Logic, Mr Smith was elected to the chair of Moral Philosophy. His course of lectures on this subject was divided into four parts. The first contained Natural Theology; in which he considered the proofs of the being and attributes of God, and those principles of the human mind upon which religion is founded. The second comprehended Ethics, strictly so called, and consisted chiefly of the doctrines which he afterwards published in his Theory of Moral Sentiments. In the third part, he treated at more length of that branch of morality which relates to *justice*, and which, being susceptible of precise and accurate rules, is for that reason capable of a full and particular explanation.

19   'Upon this subject he followed the plan that seems to be suggested by Montesquieu; endeavouring to trace the gradual progress of jurisprudence, both public and private, from the rudest to the most

3 [And see below, Note D.]

refined ages, and to point out the effects of those arts which contribute
to subsistence, and to the accumulation of property, in producing
correspondent improvements or alterations in law and government.[4]
This important branch of his labours he also intended to give to the
public; but this intention, which is mentioned in the conclusion of
the Theory of Moral Sentiments, he did not live to fulfil.[5]

20   'In the last part of his lectures, he examined those political
regulations which are founded, not upon the principle of *justice*, but
that of *expediency*, and which are calculated to increase the riches, the
power, and the prosperity of a State. Under this view, he considered
the political institutions relating to commerce, to finances, to
ecclesiastical and military establishments. What he delivered on these
subjects contained the substance of the work he afterwards published
under the title of An Inquiry into the Nature and Causes of the
Wealth of Nations.

21   'There was no situation in which the abilities of Mr Smith appeared
to greater advantage than as a Professor. In delivering his lectures, he
trusted almost entirely to extemporary elocution. His manner, though
not graceful, was plain and unaffected; and, as he seemed to be
always interested in the subject, he never failed to interest his hearers.
Each discourse consisted commonly of several distinct propositions,
which he successively endeavoured to prove and illustrate.[6] These
propositions, when announced in general terms, had, from their
extent, not unfrequently something of the air of a paradox.[7] In his
attempts to explain them, he often appeared, at first, not to be
sufficiently possessed of the subject, and spoke with some hesitation.
As he advanced, however, the matter seemed to crowd upon him, his
manner became warm and animated, and his expression easy and
fluent. In points susceptible of controversy, you could easily discern,
that he secretly conceived an opposition to his opinions, and that he

[4] [Dugald Stewart comments further on this subject below, II.50. Millar himself observed in
his *Historical View of the English Government* (1787; ed. in 4 vols., 1803):

'I am happy to acknowledge the obligations I feel myself under to this illustrious philosopher,
by having, at an early period of life, had the benefit of hearing his lectures on the History of
Civil Society, and of enjoying his unreserved conversation on the same subject. The great
Montesquieu pointed out the road. He was the Lord Bacon in this branch of philosophy. Dr.
Smith is the Newton'. *H.V.*ii.429–30*n*.]

[5] [The promise was recalled in the advertisement to the 6th edition of TMS (1790) where
Smith also observed that he was now unlikely to fulfil it. The subject is treated in LJ and also
to a considerable extent in WN III and V.]

[6] [Smith throws some light on this statement in LRBL ii.125–6 (ed. Lothian, 136–7), when
discussing didactic eloquence, where 'the design of the writer is to lay down a proposition and
prove this by the different arguments that lead to that conclusion ... But it will often happen
that, in order to prove the capitall proposition, it will be necessary to prove severall subordinate
ones ... We are to observe however, that these subordinate propositions should not be above 5
at most. When they exceed this number, the mind cannot easily comprehend them at one view,
and the whole runs into confusion. Three, or thereabout, is a very proper number ...']

[7] [In Astronomy, IV.34, Smith refers to 'that love of paradox, so natural to the learned'.]

was led upon this account to support them with greater energy and vehemence. By the fulness and variety of his illustrations, the subject gradually swelled in his hands, and acquired a dimension which, without a tedious repetition of the same views, was calculated to seize the attention of his audience, and to afford them pleasure, as well as instruction, in following the same object, through all the diversity of shades and aspects in which it was presented, and afterwards in tracing it backwards to that original proposition or general truth from which this beautiful train of speculation had proceeded.

22   'His reputation as a Professor was accordingly raised very high, and a multitude of students from a great distance resorted to the University, merely upon his account. Those branches of science which he taught became fashionable at this place, and his opinions were the chief topics of discussion in clubs and literary societies. Even the small peculiarities in his pronunciation or manner of speaking, became frequently the objects of imitation.'

23   While Mr Smith was thus distinguishing himself by his zeal and ability as a public teacher, he was gradually laying the foundation of a more extensive reputation, by preparing for the press his system of morals. The first edition of this work appeared in 1759, under the title of 'The Theory of Moral Sentiments.'

24   Hitherto Mr Smith had remained unknown to the world as an author; nor have I heard that he had made a trial of his powers in any anonymous publications, excepting in a periodical work called *The Edinburgh Review*, which was begun in the year 1755, by some gentlemen of distinguished abilities, but which they were prevented by other engagements from carrying farther than the two first numbers. To this work Mr Smith contributed a review of Dr Johnson's Dictionary of the English Language, and also a letter, addressed to the editors, containing some general observations on the state of literature in the different countries of Europe. In the former of these papers, he points out some defects in Dr Johnson's plan, which he censures as not sufficiently grammatical. 'The different significations of a word (he observes) are indeed collected; but they are seldom digested into general classes, or ranged under the meaning which the word principally expresses: And sufficient care is not taken to distinguish the words apparently synonymous.' To illustrate this criticism, he copies from Dr Johnson the articles BUT and HUMOUR, and opposes to them the same articles digested agreeably to his own idea. The various significations of the word BUT are very nicely and happily discriminated. The other article does not seem to have been executed with equal care.[8]

[8] [See above, 232 ff. The quotation is not quite exact.]

25   The observations on the state of learning in Europe are written
with ingenuity and elegance; but are chiefly interesting, as they shew
the attention which the Author had given to the philosophy and
literature of the Continent, at a period when they were not much
studied in this island.

26   In the same volume with the Theory of Moral Sentiments, Mr
Smith published a Dissertation 'on the Origin of Languages, and on
the different Genius of those which are original and compounded.'⁹
The remarks I have to offer on these two discourses, I shall, for the
sake of distinctness, make the subject of a separate section.

⁹ [First published in *Philological Miscellany* (1761) and included in ed. 3 of TMS (1767).
Stewart himself states that he believed the work was first appended to ed. 2 (1761); below, II.44.]

SECTION II

Of the Theory of Moral Sentiments, and the Dissertation on the Origin of Languages

1 THE science of Ethics has been divided by modern writers into two parts; the one comprehending the theory of Morals, and the other its practical doctrines. The questions about which the former is employed, are chiefly the two following. *First*, By what *principle* of our constitution are we led to form the notion of moral distinctions;— whether by that faculty which, in the other branches of human knowledge, perceives the distinction between truth and falsehood; or by a peculiar power of perception (called by some the Moral Sense) which is *pleased* with one set of qualities, and *displeased* with another? *Secondly*, What is the proper *object* of moral approbation? or, in other words, What is the common quality or qualities belonging to all the different modes of virtue?[1] Is it benevolence; or a rational self-love; or a disposition (resulting from the ascendant of Reason over Passion) to act suitably to the different relations in which we are placed? These two questions seem to exhaust the whole theory of Morals. The scope of the one is to ascertain the origin of our moral ideas; that of the other, to refer the phenomena of moral perception to their most simple and general laws.

2 The practical doctrines of morality comprehend all those rules of conduct which profess to point out the proper ends of human pursuit, and the most effectual means of attaining them; to which we may add all those literary compositions, whatever be their particular form, which have for their aim to fortify and animate our good dispositions, by delineations of the beauty, of the dignity, or of the utility of Virtue.

3 I shall not inquire at present into the justness of this division. I shall only observe, that the words Theory and Practice are not, in this instance, employed in their usual acceptations. The theory of Morals does not bear, for example, the same relation to the practice of Morals, that the theory of Geometry bears to practical Geometry. In this last science, all the practical rules are founded on theoretical principles previously established: But in the former science, the practical rules are obvious to the capacities of all mankind; the theoretical principles form one of the most difficult subjects of discussion that *have* ever exercised the ingenuity of metaphysicians.

---

a–a has 5

[1] [TMS VII.1.1.]

4   In illustrating the doctrines of practical morality, (if we make allowance for some unfortunate prejudices produced or encouraged by violent and oppressive systems of policy), the ancients seem to have availed themselves of every light furnished by nature to human reason; and indeed those writers who, in later times, have treated the subject with the greatest success, are they who have followed most closely the footsteps of the Greek and the Roman philosophers. The theoretical question, too, concerning the essence of virtue, or the proper *object* of moral approbation, was a favourite topic of discussion in the ancient schools. The question concerning the *principle* of moral approbation, though not entirely of modern origin, has been chiefly agitated since the writings of Dr Cudworth, in opposition to those of Mr Hobbes; and it is this question accordingly (recommended at once by its novelty and difficulty to the curiosity of speculative men), that has produced most of the theories which characterize and distinguish from each other the later systems of moral philosophy.

5   It was the opinion of Dr Cudworth, and also of Dr Clarke, that moral distinctions are perceived by that power of the mind, which distinguishes truth from falsehood.[2] This system it was one great object of Dr Hutcheson's philosophy to refute, and in opposition to it, to show that the words Right and Wrong express certain agreeable and disagreeable qualities in actions, which it is not the province of reason but of feeling to perceive; and to that power of perception which renders us susceptible of pleasure or of pain from the view of virtue or of vice, he gave the name of the Moral Sense.[3] His reasonings upon this subject are in the main acquiesced in, both by Mr Hume and Mr Smith; but they differ from him in one important particular,—Dr Hutcheson plainly supposing, that the moral sense is a simple principle of our constitution, of which no account can be given; whereas the other two philosophers have both attempted to analyze it into other principles more general. Their systems, however, with respect to it are very different from each other. According to Mr Hume, all the qualities which are denominated virtuous, are useful either to ourselves or to others, and the pleasure which we derive from the view of them is the pleasure of utility.[4] Mr Smith, without rejecting entirely Mr Hume's doctrine, proposes another of his own, far more comprehensive; a doctrine with which he thinks all the most celebrated theories of morality invented by his predecessors coincide in part, and from some partial view of which he apprehends that they have all proceeded.

6   Of this very ingenious and original theory, I shall endeavour to

---

[2] [TMS VII.iii.2.]   [3] [TMS VII.iii.3.]   [4] [TMS IV.1-2.]

give a short abstract. To those who are familiarly acquainted with it as it is stated by its author, I am aware that the attempt may appear superfluous; but I flatter myself that it will not be wholly useless to such as have not been much conversant in these abstract disquisitions, by presenting to them the leading principles of the system in one connected view, without those interruptions of the attention which necessarily arise from the author's various and happy illustrations, and from the many eloquent digressions which animate and adorn his composition.

7   The fundamental principle of Mr Smith's theory is, that the primary objects of our moral perceptions are the actions of other men; and that our moral judgments with respect to our own conduct are only applications to ourselves of decisions which we have already passed on the conduct of our neighbour. His work accordingly *b*includes two distinct inquiries, which, although sometimes blended together in the execution of his general design, it is necessary for the reader to discriminate carefully from each other, in order to comprehend all the different bearings of the author's argument. The aim of the former inquiry is, to explain in what manner we learn to judge of the conduct of our neighbour; that of the latter, to shew how, by applying these judgments to ourselves, we acquire *a sense of duty*, and a feeling of its paramount authority over all our other principles of action.*b*

8   Our moral judgments, both with respect to our own conduct and that of others, include two distinct perceptions: *first,* A perception of conduct as right or wrong; and, *secondly,* A perception of the merit or demerit of the agent. To that quality of conduct which moralists, in general, express by the word Rectitude, Mr Smith gives the name of Propriety; and he begins his theory with inquiring in what it consists, and how we are led to form the idea of it. The leading principles of his doctrine on this subject are comprehended in the following propositions.

9   1. It is from our own experience alone, that we can form any idea of what passes in the mind of another person on any particular occasion; and the only way in which we can form this idea, is by supposing ourselves in the same circumstances with him, and conceiving how we should be affected if we were so situated. It is impossible for us, however, to conceive ourselves placed in any situation, whether agreeable or otherwise, without feeling an effect of the same kind with what would be produced by the situation itself;

---

b–b consists of two parts. In the former, he explains in what manner we learn to judge of the conduct of our neighbour; in the latter, in what manner, by applying these judgments to ourselves, we acquire *a sense of duty. 1–2* and of consequence the attention we give at any time to the circumstances of our neighbour, must affect us somewhat in the same manner, although by no means in the same degree, as if these circumstances were our own.

10   That this imaginary change of place with other men, is the real source of the interest we take in their fortunes, Mr Smith attempts to prove by various instances. 'When we see a stroke aimed, and just ready to fall upon the leg or arm of another person, we naturally shrink and draw back our own leg or our own arm; and when it does fall, we feel it in some measure, and are hurt by it as well as the sufferer. The mob, when they are gazing at a dancer on the slack-rope, naturally writhe and twist and balance their own bodies, as they see him do, and as they feel that they themselves must do if in his situation.'[5] The same thing takes place, according to Mr Smith, in every case in which our attention is turned to the condition of our neighbour. 'Whatever is the passion which arises from any object in the person principally concerned, an analogous emotion springs up, at the thought of his situation, in the breast of every attentive spectator. In every passion of which the mind of man is susceptible, the emotions of the bystander always correspond to what, by bringing the case home to himself, he imagines should be the sentiments of the sufferer.'[6]

11   To this principle of our nature which leads us to enter into the situations of other men, and to partake with them in the passions which these situations have a tendency to excite, Mr Smith gives the name of *sympathy* or *fellow-feeling*, which two words he employs as synonymous. Upon some occasions, he acknowledges, that sympathy arises merely from the view of a certain emotion in another person; but in general it arises, not so much from the view of the emotion, as from that of the situation which excites it.

12   2. A sympathy or fellow-feeling between different persons is always agreeable to both. When I am in a situation which excites any passion, it is pleasant to me to know, that the spectators of my situation enter with me into all its various circumstances, and are affected with them in the same manner as I am myself. On the other hand, it is pleasant to the spectator to observe this correspondence of his emotions with mine.

13   3. When the spectator of another man's situation, upon bringing home to himself all its various circumstances, feels himself affected in the same manner with the person principally concerned, he approves of the affection or passion of this person as just and proper, and suitable to its object. The exceptions which occur to this observation

[5] (TMS I.i.1.3.)   [6] (TMS I.i.1.4.)

are, according to Mr Smith, only apparent. 'A stranger, for example,[7] passes by us in the street with all the marks of the deepest affliction: and we are immediately told, that he has just received the news of the death of his father. It is impossible that, in this case, we should not approve of his grief; yet it may often happen, without any defect of humanity on our part, that, so far from entering into the violence of his sorrow, we should scarce conceive the first movements of concern upon his account.[8] We have learned, however, from experience, that such a misfortune naturally excites such a degree of sorrow; and we know, that if we took time to examine his situation fully, and in all its parts, we should, without doubt, most sincerely sympathize with him. It is upon the consciousness of this conditional sympathy that our approbation of his sorrow is founded, even in those cases in which that sympathy does not actually take place; and the general rules derived from our preceding experience of what our sentiments would commonly correspond with, correct upon this, as upon many other occasions, the impropriety of our present emotions.'[9]

14   By the *propriety* therefore of any affection or passion exhibited by another person, is to be understood its suitableness to the object which excites it. Of this suitableness I can judge only from the coincidence of the affection with that which I feel, when I conceive myself in the same circumstances; and the perception of this coincidence is the foundation of the sentiment of *moral approbation*.

15   4. Although, when we attend to the situation of another person, and conceive ourselves to be placed in his circumstances, an emotion of the same kind with that which he feels naturally arises in our own mind, yet this sympathetic emotion bears but a very small proportion, in point of degree, to what is felt by the person principally concerned. In order, therefore, to obtain the pleasure of mutual sympathy, nature teaches the spectator to strive, as much as he can, to raise his emotion to a level with that which the object would really produce: and, on the other hand, she teaches the person whose passion this object has excited, to bring it down, as much as he can, to a level with that of the spectator.

16   5. Upon these two different efforts are founded two different sets of virtues. Upon the effort of the spectator to enter into the situation of the person principally concerned, and to raise his sympathetic emotions to a level with the emotions of the actor, are founded the gentle, the amiable virtues; the virtues of candid condescension and indulgent humanity. Upon the effort of the person principally

---

[7] [The words 'for example' do not occur in the actual text of TMS, nor is the punctuation of this quotation exact.]

[8] [A complete sentence is omitted at this point.]   [9] (TMS I.i.3.4.)

concerned to lower his own emotions, so as to correspond as nearly as possible with those of the spectator, are founded the great, the awful, and respectable virtues; the virtues of self-denial, of self-government, of that command of the passions, which subjects all the movements of our nature to what our own dignity and honour, and the propriety of our own conduct, require.

17 As a farther illustration of the foregoing doctrine, Mr Smith considers particularly the degrees of the different passions which are consistent with propriety, and endeavours to shew, that, in every case, it is decent or indecent to express a passion strongly, according as mankind are disposed, or not disposed to sympathize with it. It is unbecoming, for example, to express strongly any of those passions which arise from a certain condition of the body; because other men, who are not in the same condition, cannot be expected to sympathize with them. It is unbecoming to cry out with bodily pain; because the sympathy felt by the spectator bears no proportion to the acuteness of what is felt by the sufferer. The case is somewhat similar with those passions which take their origin from a particular turn or habit of the imagination.

18 In the case of the unsocial passions of hatred and resentment, the sympathy of the spectator is divided between the person who feels the passion, and the person who is the object of it. 'We are concerned for both, and our fear for what the one may suffer damps our resentment for what the other has suffered.'[10] Hence the imperfect degree in which we sympathize with such passions; and the propriety, when we are under their influence, of moderating their expression to a much greater degree than is required in the case of any other emotions.

19 The reverse of this takes place with respect to all the social and benevolent affections. The sympathy of the spectator with the person who feels them, coincides with his concern for the person who is the object of them. It is this redoubled sympathy which renders these affections so peculiarly becoming and agreeable.

20 The selfish emotions of grief and joy, when they are conceived on account of our own private good or bad fortune, hold a sort of middle place between our social and our unsocial passions. They are never so graceful as the one set, nor so odious as the other. Even when excessive, they are never so disagreeable as excessive resentment; because no opposite sympathy can ever interest us against them: and when most suitable to their objects, they are never so agreeable as impartial humanity and just benevolence; because no double sympathy can ever interest us for them.

[10] (TMS I.ii.3.1. The punctuation does not exactly follow the printed text.)

21   After these general speculations concerning the propriety of
actions, Mr Smith examines how far the judgments of mankind
concerning it are liable to be influenced, in particular cases, by the
prosperous or the adverse circumstances of the agent. The scope of
his reasoning on this subject is directed to shew (in opposition to the
common opinion), that when there is no envy in the case, our
propensity to sympathize with joy is much stronger than our
propensity to sympathize with sorrow; and, of consequence, that it is
more easy to obtain the approbation of mankind in prosperity than
in adversity. From the same principle he traces the origin of ambition,
or of the desire of rank and pre-eminence; the great object of which
passion is, to attain that situation which sets a man most in the view
of general sympathy and attention, and gives him an easy empire
over the affections of others.

22   Having finished the analysis of our sense of propriety and of
impropriety, Mr Smith proceeds to consider our sense of merit and
demerit; which he thinks has also a reference, in the first instance, not
to our own characters, but to the characters of our neighbours. In
explaining the origin of this part of our moral constitution, he avails
himself of the same principle of sympathy, into which he resolves the
sentiment of moral approbation.

23   The words *propriety* and *impropriety*, when applied to an affection
of the mind, are used in this theory (as has been already observed) to
express the suitableness or unsuitableness of the affection to its
exciting *cause*. The words *merit* and *demerit* have always a reference
(according to Mr Smith) to the *effect* which the affection tends to
produce. When the tendency of an affection is beneficial, the agent
appears to us a proper object of reward; when it is hurtful, he appears
the proper object of punishment.

24   The principles in our nature which most directly prompt us to
reward and to punish, are gratitude and resentment. To say of a
person, therefore, that he is deserving of reward or of punishment, is
to say, in other words, that he is a proper object of gratitude or of
resentment; or, which amounts to the same thing, that he is to some
person or persons the object of a gratitude or of a resentment, which
every reasonable man is ready to adopt and sympathize with.

25   It is however very necessary to observe, that we do not thoroughly
sympathize with the gratitude of one man towards another, merely
because this other has been the cause of his good fortune, unless he
has been the cause of it from motives which we entirely go along
with. Our sense, therefore, of the good desert of an action, is a
compounded sentiment, made up of an indirect sympathy with the

person to whom the action is beneficial, and of a direct sympathy with the affections and motives of the agent.——The same remark applies, *mutatis mutandis*, to our sense of demerit, or of ill-desert.

26 From these principles, it is inferred, that the only actions which appear to us deserving of reward, are actions of a beneficial tendency, proceeding from proper motives; the only actions which seem to deserve punishment, are actions of a hurtful tendency, proceeding from improper motives. A mere want of beneficence exposes to no punishment; because the mere want of beneficence tends to do no real positive evil. A man, on the other hand, who is barely innocent, and contents himself with observing strictly the laws of justice with respect to others, can merit only, that his neighbours, in their turn, should observe religiously the same laws with respect to him.

27 These observations lead Mr Smith to anticipate a little the subject of the second great division of his work, by a short inquiry into the origin of our sense of justice, *as applicable to our own conduct*; and also of our sentiments of remorse, and of good desert.

28 The origin of our sense of justice, as well as of all our other moral sentiments, he accounts for by means of the principle of sympathy. When I attend only to the feelings of my own breast, my own happiness appears to me of far greater consequence than that of all the world besides. But I am conscious, that, in this excessive preference, other men cannot possibly sympathize with me, and that to them I appear only one of the crowd, in whom they are no more interested than in any other individual. If I wish, therefore, to secure their sympathy and approbation (which, according to Mr Smith, are the objects of the strongest desire of my nature), it is necesssary for me to regard my happiness, not in that light in which it appears to myself, but in that light in which it appears to mankind in general. If an unprovoked injury is offered to me, I know that society will sympathize with my resentment; but if I injure the interests of another, who never injured me, merely because they stand in the way of my own, I perceive evidently, that society will sympathize with *his* resentment, and that I shall become the object of general indignation.

29 When, upon any occasion, I am led by the violence of passion to overlook these considerations, and, in the case of a competition of interests, to act according to my own feelings, and not according to those of impartial spectators, I never fail to incur the punishment of remorse. When my passion is gratified, and I begin to reflect coolly on my conduct, I can no longer enter into the motives from which it proceeded; it appears as improper to me as to the rest of the world; I lament the effects it has produced; I pity the unhappy sufferer whom I have injured; and I feel myself a just object of indignation to

mankind. 'Such,' says Mr Smith, 'is the nature of that sentiment which is properly called remorse.[11] It is made up of shame from the sense of the impropriety of past conduct; of grief for the effects of it; of pity for those who suffer by it; and of the dread and terror of punishment from the consciousness of the justly provoked resentment of all rational creatures.'[12]

30   The opposite behaviour of him who, from proper motives, has performed a generous action, inspires, in a similar manner, the opposite sentiment of conscious merit, or of deserved reward.

31   The foregoing observations contain a general summary of Mr Smith's principles with respect to the origin of our moral sentiments, in so far at least as they relate to the conduct of others. He acknowledges, at the same time, that the sentiments of which we are conscious, on particular occasions, do not always coincide with these principles; and that they are frequently modified by other consider-ations, very different from the propriety or impropriety of the affections of the agent, and also from the beneficial or hurtful tendency of these affections. The good or the bad consequences which accidently follow from an action, and which, as they do not depend on the agent, ought undoubtedly, in point of justice, to have no influence on our opinion, either of the propriety or the merit of his conduct, scarcely ever fail to influence considerably our judgment with respect to both; by leading us to form a good or a bad opinion of the prudence with which the action was performed, and by animating our sense of the merit or demerit of his design. These facts, however, do not furnish any objections which are peculiarly applicable to Mr Smith's theory; for whatever hypothesis we may adopt with respect to the origin of our moral perceptions, all men must acknowledge, that, in so far as the prosperous or the unprosperous event of an action depends on fortune or on accident, it ought neither to increase nor to diminish our moral approbation or disapprobation of the agent. And accordingly it has, in all ages of the world, been the complaint of moralists, that the actual sentiments of mankind should so often be in opposition to this equitable and indisputable maxim. In examining, therefore, this irregularity of our moral sentiments, Mr Smith is to be considered, not as obviating an objection peculiar to his own system, but as removing a difficulty which is equally connected with every theory on the subject which has ever been proposed. So far as I know, he is the first philosopher who has been fully aware of the importance of the difficulty, and he has indeed treated it with great ability and success. The explanation which he gives of it is not

[11] [The quotation omits the words '; of all the sentiments which can enter the human breast the most dreadful'.]   [12] (TMS II.ii.2.3.)

warped in the least by any peculiarity in his own scheme; and, I must own, it appears to me to be the most solid and valuable improvement he has made in this branch of science. It is impossible to give any abstract of it in a sketch of this kind; and therefore I must content myself with remarking, that it consists of three parts. The first explains the causes of this irregularity of sentiment; the second, the extent of its influence; and the third, the important purposes to which it is subservient. His remarks on the last of these heads are more particularly ingenious and pleasing; as their object is to shew, in opposition to what we should be disposed at first to apprehend, that when nature implanted the seeds of this irregularity in the human breast, her leading intention was, to promote the happiness and perfection of the species.

32   The remaining part of Mr Smith's theory is employed in shewing, in what manner *our sense of duty* comes to be formed, in consequence of an application to ourselves of the judgments we have previously passed on the conduct of others.

33   In entering upon this inquiry, which is undoubtedly the most important in the work, and for which the foregoing speculations are, according to Mr Smith's theory, a necessary preparation, he begins with stating *the fact* concerning our consciousness of merited praise or blame; and it must be owned, that the first aspect of the fact, as he himself states it, appears not very favourable to his principles. That the great object of a wise and virtuous man is not to act in such a manner as to obtain the actual approbation of those around him, but to act so as to render himself the *just* and *proper* object of their approbation, and that his satisfaction with his own conduct depends much more on the consciousness of *deserving* this approbation than from that of really enjoying it, he candidly acknowledges; but still he insists, that although this may seem, at first view, to intimate the existence of some moral faculty which is not borrowed from without, our moral sentiments have always some secret reference, either to what are, or to what upon a certain condition would be, or to what we imagine ought to be, the sentiments of others; and that if it were possible, that a human creature could grow up to manhood without any communication with his own species, he could no more think of his own character, or of the propriety or demerit of his own sentiments and conduct, than of the beauty or deformity of his own face. There is indeed a tribunal within the breast, which is the supreme arbiter of all our actions, and which often mortifies us amidst the applause, and supports us under the censure of the world; yet still, he contends, that if we inquire into the origin of its institution, we shall find, that its jurisdiction is, in a great measure, derived from the authority of that very tribunal whose decisions it so often and so justly reverses.

34 When we first come into the world, we, for some time, fondly pursue the impossible project of gaining the good-will and approbation of everybody. We soon however find, that this universal approbation is unattainable; that the most equitable conduct must frequently thwart the interests or the inclinations of particular persons, who will seldom have candour enough to enter into the propriety of our motives, or to see that this conduct, how disagreeable soever to them, is perfectly suitable to our situation. In order to defend ourselves from such partial judgments, we soon learn to set up in our own minds, a judge between ourselves and those we live with. We conceive ourselves as acting in the presence of a person, who has no particular relation, either to ourselves, or to those whose interests are affected by our conduct; and we study to act in such a manner as to obtain the approbation of this supposed impartial spectator. It is only by consulting him that we can see whatever relates to ourselves in its proper shape and dimensions.

35 There are two different occasions, on which we examine our own conduct, and endeavour to view it in the light in which the impartial spectator would view it. First, when we are about to act; and, secondly, after we have acted. In both cases, our views are very apt to be partial.

36 When we are about to act, the eagerness of passion seldom allows us to consider what we are doing with the candour of an indifferent person. When the action is over, and the passions which prompted it have subsided, although we can undoubtedly enter into the sentiments of the indifferent spectator much more coolly than before, yet it is so disagreeable to us to think ill of ourselves, that we often purposely turn away our view from those circumstances which might render our judgment unfavourable.—Hence that self-deceit which is the source of half the disorders of human life.

37 In order to guard ourselves against its delusions, nature leads us to form insensibly, by our continual observations upon the conduct of others, certain general rules concerning what is fit and proper either to be done or avoided. Some of their actions shock all our natural sentiments; and when we observe other people affected in the same manner with ourselves, we are confirmed in the belief, that our disapprobation was just. We naturally therefore lay it down as a general rule, that all such actions are to be avoided, as tending to render us odious, contemptible, or punishable; and we endeavour, by habitual reflection, to fix this general rule in our minds, in order to correct the misrepresentations of self-love, if we should ever be called on to act in similar circumstances. The man of furious resentment, if he were to listen to the dictates of that passion, would perhaps regard

the death of his enemy as but a small compensation for a trifling wrong. But his observations on the conduct of others have taught him how horrible such sanguinary revenges are; and he has impressed it on his mind as an invariable rule, to abstain from them upon all occasions. This rule preserves its authority with him, checks the impetuosity of his passion, and corrects the partial views which self-love suggests; although, if this had been the first time in which he considered such an action, he would undoubtedly have determined it to be just and proper, and what every impartial spectator would approve of.—A regard to such general rules of morality constitutes, according to Mr Smith, what is properly called *the sense of duty.*

38   I before hinted, that Mr Smith does not reject entirely from his system that principle of *utility*, of which the perception in any action or character constitutes, according to Mr Hume, the sentiment of moral approbation. That no qualities of the mind are approved of as virtues, but such as are useful or agreeable, either to the person himself or to others, he admits to be a proposition that holds universally; and he also admits, that the sentiment of approbation with which we regard virtue, is enlivened by the perception of this utility, or, as he explains the fact, it is enlivened by our sympathy with the happiness of those to whom the utility extends: But still he insists, that it is not the view of this utility which is either the first or principal source of moral approbation.

39   To sum up the whole of his doctrine in a few words. 'When we approve of any character or action, the sentiments which we feel are[13] derived from four different sources.[14] First, we sympathize with the motives of the agent; secondly, we enter into the gratitude of those who receive the benefit of his actions; thirdly, we observe that his conduct has been agreeable to the general rules by which those two sympathies generally act; and, lastly,[15] when we consider such actions as making a part of a system of behaviour which tends to promote the happiness either of the individual or of society,[16] they appear to derive a beauty from this utility, not unlike that which we ascribe to any well-contrived machine.'[17] These different sentiments, he thinks, exhaust completely, in every instance that can be supposed, the compounded sentiment of moral approbation. 'After deducting, says he, in any one particular case, all that must be acknowledged to proceed from some one or other of these four principles, I should be glad to know what remains; and I shall freely allow this overplus to

---

[13] [TMS reads: 'according to the foregoing system'.]
[14] [TMS reads: 'four sources, which are in some respects different from one another'.]
[15] [TMS reads 'last of all'.]
[16] [TMS reads 'or of the society'.]
[17] [TMS VII.iii.3.16. The punctuation does not exactly follow the printed texts.]

be ascribed to a moral sense, or to any other peculiar faculty, provided any body will ascertain precisely what this overplus is.'[18]

40   Mr Smith's opinion concerning the nature of virtue, is involved in his theory concerning the principle of moral approbation. The idea of virtue, he thinks, always implies the idea of propriety, or of the suitableness of the affection to the object which excites it; which suitableness, according to him, can be determined in no other way than by the sympathy of impartial spectators with the motives of the agent. But still he apprehends, that this description of virtue is incomplete; for although in every virtuous action propriety is an essential ingredient, it is not always the sole ingredient. Beneficent actions have in them another quality, by which they appear, not only to deserve approbation, but recompense, and excite a superior degree of esteem, arising from a double sympathy with the motives of the agent, and the gratitude of those who are the objects of his affection. In this respect, beneficence appears to him to be distinguished from the inferior virtues of prudence, vigilance, circumspection, temperance, constancy, firmness, which are always regarded with approbation, but which confer no merit. This distinction, he apprehends, has not been sufficiently attended to by moralists; the principles of some affording no explanation of the approbation we bestow on the inferior virtues; and those of others accounting as imperfectly for the peculiar excellency which the supreme virtue of beneficence is acknowledged to possess.*

41   Such are the outlines of Mr Smith's Theory of Moral Sentiments; a work which, whatever opinion we may entertain of the justness of its conclusions, must be allowed by all to be a singular effort of invention, ingenuity, and subtilty. For my own part I must confess, that it does not coincide with my notions concerning the foundation of Morals: but I am convinced, at the same time, that it contains a large mixture of important truth, and that, although the author has sometimes been misled by too great a desire of generalizing his principles, he has had the merit of directing the attention of philosophers to a view of human nature which had formerly in a great measure escaped their notice. Of the great proportion of just and sound reasoning which the theory involves its striking plausibility is a sufficient proof; for, as the author himself has remarked, no system in morals can well gain our assent, if it does not border, in some respects, upon the truth. 'A system of natural philosophy (he observes) may appear very plausible, and be for a long time very

---

ᶜ*See Note (C.)ᶜ

ᶜ⁻ᶜ *added in* 5

[18] (Ibid.)

generally received in the world, and yet have no foundation in nature;
but the author who should assign as the cause of any natural
sentiment, some principle which neither had any connection with it,
nor resembled any other principle which had some connection,
would appear absurd and ridiculous to the most injudicious and
inexperienced reader.'[19] The merit, however, of Mr Smith's performance does not rest here. No work, undoubtedly, can be mentioned,
ancient or modern, which exhibits so complete a view of those facts
with respect to our moral perceptions, which it is one great object of
this branch of science to refer to their general laws; and upon this
account, it well deserves the careful study of all whose taste leads
them to prosecute similar inquiries. These facts are indeed frequently
expressed in a language which involves the author's peculiar theories:
But they are always presented in the most happy and beautiful lights;
and it is easy for an attentive reader, by stripping them of hypothetical
terms, to state them to himself with that logical precision, which, in
such very difficult disquisitions, can alone conduct us with certainty
to the truth.

42   It is proper to observe farther, that with the theoretical doctrines of
the book, there are everywhere interwoven, with singular taste and
address, the purest and most elevated maxims concerning the
practical conduct of life; and that it abounds throughout with
interesting and instructive delineations of characters and manners. A
considerable part of it too is employed in collateral inquiries, which,
upon every hypothesis that can be formed concerning the foundation
of morals, are of equal importance. Of this kind is the speculation
formerly mentioned, with respect to the influence of fortune on our
moral sentiments, and another speculation, no less valuable, with
respect to the influence of custom and fashion on the same part of our
constitution.

43   The style in which Mr Smith has conveyed the fundamental
principles on which his theory rests, does not seem to me to be so
perfectly suited to the subject as that which he employs on most other
occasions. In communicating ideas which are extremely abstract and
subtle, and about which it is hardly possible to reason correctly,
without the scrupulous use of appropriated terms, he sometimes
presents to us a choice of words, by no means strictly synonymous, so
as to divert the attention from a precise and steady conception of his
proposition: and a similar effect is, in other instances, produced by
that diversity of forms which, in the course of his copious and
seducing composition, the same truth insensibly assumes. When the

[19] [The quotation runs together passages from the second and concluding sentences of TMS
VII.ii.4.14, and does not follow the punctuation or spelling of the printed text exactly.]

subject of his work leads him to address the imagination and the heart, the variety and felicity of his illustrations; the richness and fluency of his eloquence; and the skill with which he wins the attention and commands the passions of his readers, leave him, among our English moralists, without a rival.

---

44   The Dissertation on the Origin of Languages, which now forms a part of the same volume with the Theory of Moral Sentiments, was, I believe, first annexed to the second edition of that work.[20] It is an essay of great ingenuity, and on which the author himself set a high value; but, in a general review of his publications, it deserves our attention less, on account of the opinions it contains, than as a specimen of a particular sort of inquiry, which, so far as I know, is entirely of modern origin, and which seems, in a peculiar degree, to have interested Mr Smith's curiosity.* Something very similar to it may be traced in all his different works, whether moral, political, or literary; and on all these subjects he has exemplified it with the happiest success.

45   When, in such a period of society as that in which we live, we compare our intellectual acquirements, our opinions, manners, and institutions, with those which prevail among rude tribes, it cannot fail to occur to us as an interesting question, by what gradual steps the transition has been made from the first simple efforts of uncultivated nature, to a state of things so wonderfully artificial and complicated. Whence has arisen that systematical beauty which we admire in the structure of a cultivated language; that analogy which runs through the *mixture* of languages spoken by the most remote and unconnected nations; and those peculiarities by which they are all distinguished from each other? Whence the origin of the different sciences and of the different arts; and by what chain has the mind been led from their first rudiments to their last and most refined improvements? Whence the astonishing fabric of the political union; the fundamental principles which are common to all governments; and the different forms which civilized society has assumed in different ages of the world? On most of these subjects very little information is to be expected from history; for long before that stage of society when men begin to think of recording their transactions, many of the most important steps of their progress have been made. A few insulated facts may perhaps be collected from the casual observations of travellers, who have viewed the arrangements of rude

---

d *See the letter quoted in Note (D.)*d*

d–d added in 5   *e–e* texture *1*

[20] (In fact ed. 3. See above, I.26 and note.)

nations; but nothing, it is evident, can be obtained in this way, which approaches to a regular and connected detail of human improvement.

46   In this want of direct evidence, we are under a necessity of supplying the place of fact by conjecture; and when we are unable to ascertain how men have actually conducted themselves upon particular occasions, of considering in what manner they are likely to have proceeded, from the principles of their nature, and the circumstances of their external situation. In such inquiries, the detached facts which travels and voyages afford us, may frequently serve as land-marks to our speculations; and sometimes our conclusions *a priori*, may tend to confirm the credibility of facts, which, on a superficial view, appeared to be doubtful or incredible.

47   Nor are such theoretical views of human affairs subservient merely to the gratification of curiosity. In examining the history of mankind, as well as in examining the phenomena of the material world, when we cannot trace the process by which an event *has been* produced, it is often of importance to be able to show how it *may have been* produced by natural causes. Thus, in the instance which has suggested these remarks, although it is impossible to determine with certainty what the steps were by which any particular language was formed, yet if we can shew, from the known principles of human nature, how all its various parts might gradually have arisen, the mind is not only to a certain degree satisfied, but a check is given to that indolent philosophy, which refers to a miracle, whatever appearances, both in the natural and moral worlds, it is unable to explain.

48   To this species of philosophical investigation, which has no appropriated name in our language, I shall take the liberty of giving the title of *Theoretical* or *Conjectural History*; an expression which coincides pretty nearly in its meaning with that of *Natural History*, as employed by Mr Hume*, and with what some French writers have called *Histoire Raisonnée*.

49   The mathematical sciences, both pure and mixed, afford, in many of their branches, very favourable subjects for theoretical history; and a very competent judge, the late M. d'Alembert, has recommended this arrangement of their elementary principles, which is founded on the natural succession of inventions and discoveries, as the best adapted for interesting the curiosity and exercising the genius of students. The same author points out as a model a passage

---

* See his Natural History of Religion. [Stewart also commented on the distinctive nature of 'natural history' in his 'Account of the Life and Writings of William Robertson, D.D.' where he remarked on: 'the ability and address with which he has treated some topics that did not fall within the ordinary sphere of his studies, more especially those which border on the province of the natural historian'. *Works*, x (1858), 156.]

in Montucla's History of Mathematics,[21] where an attempt is made to exhibit the gradual progress of philosophical speculation, from the first conclusions suggested by a general survey of the heavens, to the doctrines of Copernicus. It is somewhat remarkable, that a theoretical history of this very science (in which we have, perhaps, a better opportunity than in any other instance whatever, of comparing the natural advances of the mind with the actual succession of hypothetical systems) was one of Mr Smith's earliest compositions, and is one of the very small number of his manuscripts which he did not destroy before his death.

50   I already hinted, that inquiries perfectly analogous to these may be applied to the modes of government, and to the municipal institutions which have obtained among different nations. It is but lately, however, that these important subjects have been considered in this point of view; the greater part of politicians before the time of Montesquieu, having contented themselves with an historical statement of facts, and with a vague reference of laws to the wisdom of particular legislators, or to accidental circumstances, which it is now impossible to ascertain.[22] Montesquieu, on the contrary, considered laws as originating chiefly from the circumstances of society; and attempted to account, from the changes in the condition of mankind, which take place in the different stages of their progress, for the corresponding alterations which their institutions undergo.[23] It is thus that, in his occasional elucidations of the Roman jurisprudence, instead of bewildering himself among the erudition of scholiasts and of antiquaries, we frequently find him borrowing his lights from the most remote and unconnected quarters of the globe, and combining the casual observations of illiterate travellers and navigators, into a philosophical commentary on the history of law and of manners.

51   The advances made in this line of inquiry since Montesquieu's time have been great.[24] Lord Kames, in his Historical Law Tracts,[25]

---

[21] [First published in 1758, i.e. after the composition of the Astronomy; see above, 7.]

[22] [See above, I.19 and note 4.]

[23] [While Montesquieu does not neglect time in *L' Esprit*, it is more a feature of his *Considérations sur les causes de la grandeur des Romains et de leur décadence* (1734).]

[24] [Stewart returned to this theme in his 'Account of the Life and Writings of William Robertson, D.D.' read before the Royal Society of Edinburgh, 21 March 1796:

'It will not, I hope, be imputed to me as a blameable instance of national vanity, if I conclude this Section with remarking the rapid progress that has been made in our own country during the last fifty years, in tracing the origin and progress of the present establishments in Europe. Montesquieu undoubtedly led the way, but much has been done since the publication of his works, by authors whose names are enrolled among the members of this Society'.

Stewart no doubt had in view Hume, Robertson, Smith, and Adam Ferguson. *Works*, x (1858), 147.]

[25] [First published in 1758.]

has given some excellent specimens of it, particularly in his Essays on the History of Property and of Criminal Law, and many ingenious speculations of the same kind occur in the works of Mr Millar.[26]

52   In Mr Smith's writings, whatever be the nature of his subject, he seldom misses an opportunity of indulging his curiosity, in tracing from the principles of human nature, or from the circumstances of society, the origin of the opinions and the institutions which he describes. I formerly mentioned a fragment concerning the History of Astronomy which he has left for publication; and I have heard him say more than once, that he had projected, in the earlier part of his life, a history of the other sciences on the same plan. In his Wealth of Nations, various disquisitions are introduced which have a like object in view, particularly the theoretical delineation he has given of the natural progress of opulence in a country; and his investigation of the causes which have inverted this order in the different countries of modern Europe.[27] His lectures on jurisprudence seem, from the account of them formerly given, to have abounded in such inquiries.

53   I am informed by the same gentleman who favoured me with the account of Mr Smith's lectures at Glasgow, that he had heard him sometimes hint an intention of writing a treatise upon the Greek and Roman republics. 'And after all that has been published on that subject, I am convinced (says he), that the observations of Mr Smith would have suggested many new and important views concerning the internal and domestic circumstances of those nations, which would have displayed their several systems of policy, in a light much less artificial than that in which they have hitherto appeared.'

54   The same turn of thinking was frequently, in his social hours, applied to more familiar subjects; and the fanciful theories which, without the least affectation of ingenuity, he was continually starting upon all the common topics of discourse, gave to his conversation a novelty and variety that were quite inexhaustible. Hence too the minuteness and accuracy of his knowledge on many trifling articles, which, in the course of his speculations, he had been led to consider from some new and interesting point of view; and of which his lively and circumstantial descriptions amused his friends the more, that he seemed to be habitually inattentive, in so remarkable a degree, to what was passing around him.

55   I have been led into these remarks by the Dissertation on the Formation of Languages, which exhibits a very beautiful specimen of theoretical history, applied to a subject equally curious and

---

[26] (John Millar, *The Origin of the Distinction of Ranks* (1771; ed. 3, 1779): *An Historical View of the English Government* (1787; ed. in 4 vols., 1803)).
[27] [WN III.]

difficult. The analogy between the train of thinking from which it has taken its rise, and that which has suggested a variety of his other disquisitions, will, I hope, be a sufficient apology for the length of this digression; more particularly, as it will enable me to simplify the account which I am to give afterwards, of his inquiries concerning political economy.

56   I shall only observe farther on this head, that when different theoretical histories are proposed by different writers, of the progress of the human mind in any one line of exertion, these theories are not always to be understood as standing in opposition to each other. If the progress delineated in all of them be plausible, it is possible at least, that they may all have been realized; for human affairs never exhibit, in any two instances, a perfect uniformity. But whether they have been realized or no, is often a question of little consequence. In most cases, it is of more importance to ascertain the progress that is most simple, than the progress that is most agreeable to fact; for, paradoxical as the proposition may appear, it is certainly true, that the real progress is not always the most natural. It may have been determined by particular accidents, which are not likely again to occur, and which cannot be considered as forming any part of that general provision which nature has made for the improvement of the race.

_____

57   IN order to make some amends for the length (I am afraid I may add for the tediousness) of this section, I shall subjoin to it an original letter of Mr Hume's addressed to Mr Smith, soon after the publication of his Theory. It is strongly marked with that easy and affectionate pleasantry which distinguished Mr Hume's epistolary correspondence, and is entitled to a place in this Memoir, on account of its connection with an important event of Mr Smith's life, which soon after removed him into a new scene, and influenced, to a considerable degree, the subsequent course of his studies. The letter is dated from London, 12th April 1759.[28]

58   'I give you thanks for the agreeable present of your Theory. Wedderburn and I made presents of our copies to such of our acquaintances as we thought good judges, and proper to spread the reputation of the book. I sent one to the Duke of Argyll, to Lord Lyttleton, Horace Walpole, Soame Jennyns, and Burke, an Irish gentleman, who wrote lately a very pretty treatise on the Sublime. Millar desired my permission to send one in your name to Dr Warburton. I have delayed writing to you till I could tell you something of the success of the book, and could prognosticate with

[28] (The corrected text is published in Corr., Letter 31.)

some probability, whether it should be finally damned to oblivion, or should be registered in the temple of immortality. Though it has been published only a few weeks, I think there appear already such strong symptoms, that I can almost venture to foretel its fate. It is in short this———— But I have been interrupted in my letter by a foolish impertinent visit of one who has lately come from Scotland. He tells me that the University of Glasgow intend to declare Rouet's office vacant, upon his going abroad with Lord Hope. I question not but you will have our friend Ferguson in your eye, in case another project for procuring him a place in the University of Edinburgh should fail. Ferguson has very much polished and improved his treatise on Refinement*, and with some amendments it will make an admirable book, and discovers an elegant and a singular genius. The Epigoniad, I hope, will do; but it is somewhat up-hill work. As I doubt not but you consult the reviews sometimes at present, you will see in the Critical Review a letter upon that poem; and I desire you to employ your conjectures in finding out the author. Let me see a sample of your skill in knowing hands by your guessing at the person. I am afraid of Lord Kames's Law Tracts. A man might as well think of making a fine sauce by a mixture of wormwood and aloes, as an agreeable composition by joining metaphysics and Scotch law. However, the book, I believe, has merit; though few people will take the pains of diving into it. But, to return to your book, and its success in this town, I must tell you————. A plague of interruptions! I ordered myself to be denied; and yet here is one that has broke in upon me again. He is a man of letters, and we have had a good deal of literary conversation. You told me that you was curious of literary anecdotes, and therefore I shall inform you of a few that have come to my knowledge. I believe I have mentioned to you already Helvetius's book *de l'Esprit*. It is worth your reading, not for its philosophy, which I do not highly value, but for its agreeable composition. I had a letter from him a few days ago, wherein he tells me that my name was much oftener in the manuscript, but that the Censor of books at Paris obliged him to strike it out. Voltaire has lately published a small work called *Candide, ou l'Optimisme*. I shall give you a detail of it———— But what is all this to my book? say you.—My dear Mr Smith, have patience: Compose yourself to tranquillity: Shew yourself a philosopher in practice as well as profession: Think on the emptiness, and rashness, and futility of the common judgments of men: How little they are regulated by reason in any subject, much more in philosophical subjects, which so far exceed the comprehension of the vulgar.

* Published afterwards under the title of 'An Essay on the History of Civil Society'. (1767)

————————Non si quid turbida Roma,
Elevet, accedas: examenve improbum in illa
Castiges trutina: nec te quaesiveris extra.[29]

A wise man's kingdom is his own breast; or, if he ever looks farther, it will only be to the judgment of a select few, who are free from prejudices, and capable of examining his work. Nothing indeed can be a stronger presumption of falsehood than the approbation of the multitude; and Phocion, you know, always suspected himself of some blunder, when he was attended with the applauses of the populace.

59   'Supposing, therefore, that you have duly prepared yourself for the worst by all these reflections, I proceed to tell you the melancholy news, that your book has been very unfortunate; for the public seem disposed to applaud it extremely. It was looked for by the foolish people with some impatience; and the mob of literati are beginning already to be very loud in its praises. Three Bishops called yesterday at Millar's shop in order to buy copies, and to ask questions about the author. The Bishop of Peterborough said he had passed the evening in a company where he heard it extolled above all books in the world. The Duke of Argyll is more decisive than he uses to be in its favour. I suppose he either considers it as an exotic, or thinks the author will be serviceable to him in the Glasgow elections. Lord Lyttleton says, that Robertson and Smith and Bower are the glories of English literature. Oswald protests he does not know whether he has reaped more instruction or entertainment from it. But you may easily judge what reliance can be put on his judgment who has been engaged all his life in public business, and who never sees any faults in his friends. Millar exults and brags that two-thirds of the edition are already sold, and that he is now sure of success. You see what a son of the earth that is, to value books only by the profit they bring him. In that view, I believe it may prove a very good book.

60   'Charles Townsend, who passes for the cleverest fellow in England, is so taken with the performance, that he said to Oswald he would put the Duke of Buccleuch under the author's care, and would make it worth his while to accept of that charge. As soon as I heard this I called on him twice, with a view of talking with him about the matter, and of convincing him of the propriety of sending that young Nobleman to Glasgow: For I could not hope, that he could offer you any terms which would tempt you to renounce your Professorship. But I missed him. Mr Townsend passes for being a little uncertain in his resolutions: so perhaps you need not build much on this sally.

[29] (Persius, *Satires*, i.5–7: If confused Rome makes light of anything, do not go up and correct the deceitful tongue in that balance of theirs, or look to anyone except yourself.)

61   'In recompence for so many mortifying things, which nothing but truth could have extorted from me, and which I could easily have multiplied to a greater number, I doubt not but you are so good a Christian as to return good for evil; and to flatter my vanity by telling me, that all the godly in Scotland abuse me for my account of John Knox and the Reformation. I suppose you are glad to see my paper end, and that I am obliged to conclude with

Your humble servant,
DAVID HUME.'

SECTION III

From the Publication of The Theory of Moral Sentiments, till that of The Wealth of Nations

1 AFTER the publication of the Theory of Moral Sentiments, Mr Smith remained four years at Glasgow, discharging his official duties with unabated vigour, and with increasing reputation. During that time, the plan of his lectures underwent a considerable change. His ethical doctrines, of which he had now published so valuable a part, occupied a much smaller portion of the course than formerly: and accordingly, his attention was naturally directed to a more complete illustration of the principles of jurisprudence and of political economy.

2 To this last subject, his thoughts appear to have been occasionally turned from a very early period of life. It is probable, that the uninterrupted friendship he had always maintained with his old companion Mr Oswald,[1] had some tendency to encourage him in prosecuting this branch of his studies; and the publication of Mr Hume's political discourses, in the year 1752, could not fail to confirm him in those liberal views of commercial policy which had already opened to him in the course of his own inquiries. His long residence in one of the most enlightened mercantile towns in this island, and the habits of intimacy in which he lived with the most respectable of its inhabitants, afforded him an opportunity of deriving what commercial information he stood in need of, from the best sources; and it is a circumstance no less honourable to their liberality than to his talents, that notwithstanding the reluctance so common among men of business to listen to the conclusions of mere speculation, and the direct opposition of his leading principles to all the old maxims of trade, he was able, before he quitted his situation in the university, to rank some very eminent merchants in the number of his proselytes*.

3 Among the students who attended his lectures, and whose minds were not previously warped by prejudice, the progress of his opinions, it may be reasonably supposed, was much more rapid. It was this class of his friends accordingly that first adopted his system with eagerness, and diffused a knowledge of its fundamental principles over this part of the kingdom.

---

* I mention this fact on the respectable authority of James Ritchie, Esq. of Glasgow.

   [1] [See above, I.4 and Note A. Dugald Stewart also pointed out with regard to the division of factor rewards into wages, rent, and profit that: 'It appears from a manuscript of Mr. Smith's now in my own possession, that the foregoing analysis or division was first suggested to him by Mr. Oswald of Dunnikier.' *Works*, ix (1856), 6.]

4   Towards the end of 1763, Mr Smith received an invitation from
Mr Charles Townsend to accompany the Duke of Buccleuch on his
travels; and the liberal terms in which the proposal was made to him,
added to the strong desire he had felt of visiting the Continent of
Europe, induced him to resign his office at Glasgow. With the
connection which he was led to form in consequence of this change
in his situation, he had reason to be satisfied in an uncommon degree,
and he always spoke of it with pleasure and gratitude. To the public,
it was not perhaps a change equally fortunate; as it interrupted that
studious leisure for which nature seems to have destined him, and in
which alone he could have hoped to accomplish those literary projects
which had flattered the ambition of his youthful genius.

5   The alteration, however, which, from this period, took place in his
habits, was not without its advantages. He had hitherto lived chiefly
within the walls of an university; and although to a mind like his, the
observation of human nature on the smallest scale is sufficient to
convey a tolerably just conception of what passes on the great theatre
of the world, yet it is not to be doubted, that the variety of scenes
through which he afterwards passed, must have enriched his mind
with many new ideas, and corrected many of those misapprehensions
of life and manners which the best descriptions of them can scarcely
fail to convey.—But whatever were the lights that his travels afforded
to him as a student of human nature, they were probably useful in a
still greater degree, in enabling him to perfect that system of political
economy, of which he had already delivered the principles in his
lectures at Glasgow, and which it was now the leading object of his
studies to prepare for the public. The coincidence between some of
these principles and the distinguishing tenets of the French
economists, who were at that very time in the height of their
reputation, and the intimacy in which he lived with some of the
leaders of that sect, could not fail to assist him in methodizing and
digesting his speculations; while the valuable collection of facts,
accumulated by the zealous industry of their numerous adherents,
furnished him with ample materials for illustrating and confirming
his theoretical conclusions.

6   After leaving Glasgow, Mr Smith joined the Duke of Buccleuch at
London early in the year 1764, and set out with him for the continent
in the month of March following. At Dover they were met by Sir
James Macdonald, who accompanied them to Paris, and with whom
Mr Smith laid the foundation of a friendship, which he always
mentioned with great sensibility, and of which he often lamented the
short duration. The panegyrics with which the memory of this
accomplished and amiable person has been honoured by so many

distinguished characters in the different countries of Europe, are a proof how well fitted his talents were to command general admiration. The esteem in which his abilities and learning were held by Mr Smith, is a testimony to his extraordinary merit of still superior value. Mr Hume, too, seems, in this instance, to have partaken of his friend's enthusiasm. 'Were you and I together (says he in a letter to Mr Smith), we should shed tears at present for the death of poor Sir James Macdonald. We could not possibly have suffered a greater loss than in that valuable young man.'[2]

7   In this first visit to Paris, the Duke of Buccleuch and Mr Smith employed only ten or twelve days*, after which they proceeded to Thoulouse, where they fixed their residence for eighteen months; and where, in addition to the pleasure of an agreeable society, Mr Smith had an opportunity of correcting and extending his information concerning the internal policy of France, by the intimacy in which he lived with some of the principal persons of the Parliament.

8   From Thoulouse they went, by a pretty extensive tour, through the south of France to Geneva. Here they passed two months. The late Earl Stanhope, for whose learning and worth Mr Smith entertained a sincere respect, was then an inhabitant of that republic.

9   About Christmas 1765, they returned to Paris, and remained there till October following. The society in which Mr Smith spent these ten months, may be conceived from the advantages he enjoyed, in consequence of the recommendations of Mr Hume. Turgot, Quesnai, *Morellet,†* Necker, d'Alembert, Helvetius, Marmontel, Madame

* The day after his arrival at Paris, Mr Smith sent a formal resignation of his Professorship to the Rector of the University of Glasgow. 'I never was more anxious (says he in the conclusion of this letter) for the good of the College, than at this moment; and I sincerely wish, that whoever is my successor may not only do credit to the office by his abilities, but be a comfort to the very excellent men with whom he is likely to spend his life, by the probity of his heart, and the goodness of his temper.' (Corr., Letter 81.)

The following extract from the records of the University, which follows immediately after Mr Smith's letter of resignation, is at once a testimony to his assiduity as a Professor, and a proof of the just sense which that learned body entertained of the talents and worth of the colleague they had lost:

'The meeting accept of Dr Smith's resignation, in terms of the above letter, and the office of Professor of Moral Philosophy in this University is therefore hereby declared to be vacant. The University, at the same time, cannot help expressing their sincere regret at the removal of Dr Smith, whose distinguished probity and amiable qualities procured him the esteem and affection of his colleagues; and whose uncommon genius, great abilities, and extensive learning, did so much honour to this society; his elegant and ingenious Theory of Moral Sentiments having recommended him to the esteem of men of taste and literature throughout Europe. His happy talent in illustrating abstracted subjects, and faithful assiduity in communicating useful knowledge, distinguished him as a Professor, and at once afforded the greatest pleasure and the most important instruction to the youth under his care.' [Scott, *ASSP*, 221.]

† See note (E.)

---

a–a Author's last additions

---

[2] (Corr., Letter 96.)

Riccoboni, were among the number of his acquaintances; and some
of them he continued ever afterwards to reckon among his friends.
From Madam *ᵇd'Anville,ᵇ* the respectable mother of the late excellent
and much lamented Duke of *ᶜlaᶜ* Rochefoucauld*, he received many
attentions, which he always recollected with particular gratitude.

10   It is much to be regretted, that he preserved no journal of this very
interesting period of his history; and such was his aversion to write
letters, that I scarcely suppose any memorial of it exists in his
correspondence with his friends. The extent and accuracy of his
memory, in which he was equalled by few, made it of little
consequence to himself to record in writing what he heard or saw;
and from his anxiety before his death to destroy all the papers in his
possession, he seems to have wished, that no materials should remain
for his biographers, but what were furnished by the lasting
monuments of his genius, and the exemplary worth of his private life.

* The following letter, which has been very accidentally preserved, while it serves as a
memorial of Mr Smith's connection with the family of Rochefoucauld, is so expressive of the
virtuous and liberal mind of the writer, that I am persuaded it will give pleasure to the Society
to record it in their Transactions. (Corr., Letter 194.)

Paris, 3. Mars 1778.

'Le desir de se rappeller à votre souvenir, Monsieur, quand on a eu l'honneur de vous
connoître, doit vous paroitre fort naturel; permettez que nous saisissions pour cela, ma Mère et
moi, l'occasion d'une edition nouvelle des *Maximes de la Rochefoucauld,* dont nous prenons la
liberté de vous offrir un exemplaire. Vous voyez que nous n'avons point de rancune, puisque le
mal que vous avez dit de lui dans la *Théorie des Sentimens Moraux,* ne nous empêche point de
vous envoyer ce même ouvrage. Il s'en est même fallu de peu que je ne fisse encore plus, car
j'avois eu peut-être la témérité d'entreprendre une traduction de votre *Théorie;* mais comme je
venois de terminer la première partie, j'ai vu paroître la traduction de M. l'Abbé Blavet, et j'ai
été forcé de renoncer au plaisir que j'aurois eu de faire passer dans ma langue un des meilleurs
ouvrages de la vôtre†.

'Il auroit bien fallu pour lors entreprendre une justification de mon grandpère. Peut-être
n'auroit-il pas été difficile, premièrement de l'excuser, en disant, qu'il avoit toujours vu les
hommes à la Cour, et dans la guerre civile, *deux théatres sur lesquels ils sont certainement plus
mauvais qu'ailleurs;* et ensuite de justifier par la conduite personelle de l'auteur, les principes qui
sont certainement trop généralisés dans son ouvrage. Il a pris la partie pour le tout; et parceque
les gens qu'il avoit eu le plus sous les yeux étoient animés par *l'amour propre,* il en a fait le mobile
général de tous les hommes. Au reste, quoique son ouvrage merite à certains égards d'être
combattu, il est cependant estimable même pour le fond, et beaucoup pour la forme.

'Permettez-moi de vous demander, si nous aurons bientôt une édition complette des œuvres
de votre illustre ami M. Hume? Nous l'avons sincèrement regretté.

'Recevez, je vous supplie, l'expression sincère de tous les sentimens d'estime et d'attachement
avec lesquels j'ai l'honneur d'être, Monsieur, votre très humble et très obeissant serviteur,

Le Duc de la ROCHEFOUCAULD.'

Mr Smith's last intercourse with this excellent man was in the year 1789, when he
informed him, by means of a friend who happened to be then at Paris, that in the future
editions of his *Theory* the name of Rochefoucauld should be no longer classed with that of
Mandeville. In the enlarged edition, accordingly, of that work, published a short time before
his death, he has suppressed his censure of the author of the *Maximes;* who seems indeed
(however exceptionable many of his principles may be) to have been actuated, both in his life
and writings, by motives very different from those of Mandeville. The real scope of these
maxims is placed, I think, in a just light by the ingenious author of the *notice* prefixed to the
edition of them published at Paris in 1778. (The friend above mentioned was Dugald Stewart
himself.)

† See Note (F.)

ᵇ⁻ᵇ D'Enville, 5
ᶜ⁻ᶜ *Author's last additions*

11   The satisfaction he enjoyed in the conversation of Turgot may be easily imagined. Their opinions on the most essential points of political economy were the same; and they were both animated by the same zeal for the best interests of mankind. The favourite studies, too, of both, had directed their inquiries to subjects on which the understandings of the ablest and the best informed are liable to be warped, to a great degree, by prejudice and passion; and on which, of consequence, a coincidence of judgment is peculiarly gratifying. We are told by one of the biographers of Turgot, that after his retreat from the ministry, he occupied his leisure in a philosophical correspondence with some of his old friends; and, in particular, that various letters on important subjects passed between him and Mr Smith. I take notice of this anecdote chiefly as a proof of the intimacy which was understood to have subsisted between them; for in other respects, the anecdote seems to me to be somewhat doubtful. It is scarcely to be supposed, that Mr Smith would destroy the letters of such a correspondent as Turgot; and still less probable, that such an intercourse was carried on between them without the knowledge of any of Mr Smith's friends. From some inquiries that have been made at Paris by a gentleman of this Society since Mr Smith's death, I have reason to believe, that no evidence of the correspondence exists among the papers of M. Turgot, and that the whole story has taken its rise from a report suggested by the knowledge of their former intimacy. This circumstance I think it of importance to mention, because a good deal of curiosity has been excited by the passage in question, with respect to the fate of the supposed letters.[3]

12   Mr Smith was also well known to M. Quesnai, the profound and original author of the Economical Table; a man (according to Mr Smith's account of him) 'of the greatest modesty and simplicity;'[4] and whose system of political economy he has pronounced, 'with all its imperfections,' to be 'the nearest approximation to the truth that has yet been published on the principles of that very important science.'[5] If he had not been prevented by Quesnai's death, Mr Smith had once an intention (as he told me himself) to have inscribed to him his 'Wealth of Nations.'

13   It was not, however, merely the distinguished men who about this

---

[3] [The relations between Turgot and Smith are explored in P. D. Groenewegen, 'Turgot and Adam Smith', *Scottish Journal of Political Economy*, xvi (1969). See also Corr., Letters 93 and 248.]

[4] (WN IV.ix.38.) [See also Corr., Letters 94 and 97. In the latter place Smith described Quesnay as 'one of the worthiest men in France and one of the best Physicians that is to be met with in any country. He was not only the Physician but the friend and confident of Madame Pompadour a woman who was no contemptible Judge of merit.' Smith comments at length on physiocratic teaching in WN IV.ix.]

[5] (WN IV.ix.38. The quotation occurs at the beginning of the paragraph.)

period fixed so splendid an aera in the literary history of France, that excited Mr Smith's curiosity while he remained in Paris. His acquaintance with the polite literature both of ancient and modern times was extensive; and amidst his various other occupations, he had never neglected to cultivate a taste for the fine arts;—less, it is probable, with a view to the peculiar enjoyments they convey, (though he was by no means without sensibility to their beauties,) than on account of their connection with the general principles of the human mind; to an examination of which they afford the most pleasing of all avenues. To those who speculate on this very delicate subject, a comparison of the modes of taste that prevail among different nations, affords a valuable collection of facts; and Mr Smith, who was always disposed to ascribe to custom and fashion their full share in regulating the opinions of mankind with respect to beauty, may naturally be supposed to have availed himself of every opportunity which a foreign country afforded him of illustrating his former theories.

14   Some of his peculiar notions, too, with respect to the imitative arts, seem to have been much confirmed by his observations while abroad. In accounting for the pleasure we receive from these arts, it had early occurred to him as a fundamental principle, that a very great part of it arises from the difficulty of the imitation;[6] a principle which was probably suggested to him by that of the *difficulté surmontée*, by which some French critics had attempted to explain the effect of versification and of rhyme*. This principle Mr Smith pushed to the greatest possible length, and referred to it, with singular ingenuity, a great variety of phenomena in all the different fine arts. It led him, however, to some conclusions, which appear, at first view at least, not a little paradoxical; and I cannot help thinking, that it warped his judgment in many of the opinions which he was accustomed to give on the subject of poetry.

15   The principles of dramatic composition had more particularly attracted his attention; and the history of the theatre, both in ancient and modern times, had furnished him with some of the most remarkable facts on which his theory of the imitative arts was founded. From this theory it seemed to follow as a consequence, that the same circumstances which, in tragedy, give to blank verse an advantage over prose, should give to rhyme an advantage over blank verse; and Mr Smith had always inclined to that opinion.[7] Nay, he

---

* See the Preface to Voltaire's *Oedipe*, edit. of 1729.

[6] [See, for example, Imitative Arts, I.16.]
[7] [Rae, *Life*, 35, records that Boswell had acquainted Johnson with Smith's preference for
(*continued*)

had gone so far as to extend the same doctrine to comedy; and to regret that those excellent pictures of life and manners which the English stage affords, had not been executed after the model of the French school. The admiration with which he regarded the great dramatic authors of France tended to confirm him in these opinions; and this admiration (resulting originally from the general character of his taste, which delighted more to remark that pliancy of genius which accommodates itself to established rules, than to wonder at the bolder flights of an undisciplined imagination) was increased to a great degree, when he saw the beauties that had struck him in the closet, heightened by the utmost perfection of theatrical exhibition. In the last years of his life, he sometimes amused himself, at a leisure hour, in supporting his theoretical conclusions on these subjects, by the facts which his subsequent studies and observations had suggested; and he intended, if he had lived, to have prepared the result of these labours for the press. Of this work he has left for publication a short fragment;[d] but he had not proceeded far enough to apply his doctrine to versification and to the theatre. As his notions, however, with respect to these were a favourite topic of his conversation, and were intimately connected with his general principles of criticism, it would have been improper to pass them over in this sketch of his life; and I even thought it proper to detail them at greater length than the comparative importance of the subject would have justified, if he had carried his plans into execution. Whether his love of system, added to his partiality for the French drama, may not have led him, in this instance, to generalize a little too much his conclusions, and to overlook some peculiarities in the language and versification of that country, I shall not take upon me to determine.

16   In October 1766, the Duke of Buccleuch returned to London. His Grace, to whom I am indebted for several particulars in the foregoing narrative, will, I hope, forgive the liberty I take in transcribing one paragraph in his own words: 'In October 1766, we returned to London, after having spent near three years together, without the slightest disagreement or coolness;—on my part, with every advantage that could be expected from the society of such a man. We continued to live in friendship till the hour of his death; and I shall always remain with the impression of having lost a friend whom I

---

[d] the first part of which is, in my judgment, more finished in point of style than any of his compositions; *added in 1*

rhyme over blank verse 'always, no doubt, on the same principle that the greater the difficulty the greater the beauty. This delighted the heart of Johnson, and he said: "Sir, I was once in company with Smith, and we did not take to each other, but had I known that he loved rhyme as much as you tell me he does, I should have hugged him."']

loved and respected, not only for his great talents, but for every private virtue.'

17   The retirement in which Mr Smith passed his next ten years, formed a striking contrast to the unsettled mode of life he had been for some time accustomed to, but was so congenial to his natural disposition, and to his first habits, that it was with the utmost difficulty he was ever persuaded to leave it. During the whole of this period, (with the exception of a few visits to Edinburgh and London,) he remained with his mother at Kirkaldy; occupied habitually in intense study, but unbending his mind at times in the company of some of his old school-fellows, whose 'sober wishes' had attached them to the place of their birth. In the society of such men, Mr Smith delighted; and to them he was endeared, not only by his simple and unassuming manners, but by the perfect knowledge they all possessed of those domestic virtues which had distinguished him from his infancy.

18   Mr Hume, who (as he tells us himself) considered 'a town as the true scene for a man of letters,'[8] made many attempts to seduce him from his retirement. In a letter, dated in 1772, he urges him to pass some time with him in Edinburgh. 'I shall not take any excuse from your state of health, which I suppose only a subterfuge invented by indolence and love of solitude. Indeed, my dear Smith, if you continue to hearken to complaints of this nature, you will cut yourself out entirely from human society, to the great loss of both parties.'[9] In another letter, dated in 1769, from his house in James's Court, (which commanded a prospect of the Frith of Forth, and of the opposite coast of Fife,) 'I am glad (says he) to have come within sight of you; but as I would also be within speaking terms of you, I wish we could concert measures for that purpose. I am mortally sick at sea, and regard with horror and a kind of hydrophobia the great gulf that lies between us. I am also tired of travelling, as much as you ought naturally to be of staying at home. I therefore propose to you to come hither, and pass some days with me in this solitude. I want to know what you have been doing, and propose to exact a rigorous account of the method in which you have employed yourself during your retreat. I am positive you are in the wrong in many of your speculations, especially where you have the misfortune to differ from me. All these are reasons for our meeting, and I wish you would make me some reasonable proposal for that purpose. There is no habitation in the island of Inchkeith, otherwise I should challenge you to meet me on that spot, and neither of us ever to leave the place, till we were fully agreed on all points of controversy. I expect General Conway here

8 (*My Own Life.*)   9 (Corr., Letter 129.)

tomorrow, whom I shall attend to Roseneath, and I shall remain there a few days. On my return, I hope to find a letter from you, containing a bold acceptance of this defiance.'[10]

19   At length (in the beginning of the year 1776) Mr Smith accounted to the world for his long retreat, by the publication of his 'Inquiry into the Nature and Causes of the Wealth of Nations.' A letter of congratulation on this event, from Mr Hume, is now before me. It is dated 1st April 1776 (about six months before Mr Hume's death), and discovers an amiable solicitude about his friend's literary fame.[11] *'Euge! Belle!* Dear Mr Smith: I am much pleased with your performance, and the perusal of it has taken me from a state of great anxiety. It was a work of so much expectation, by yourself, by your friends, and by the public, that I trembled for its appearance; but am now much relieved. Not but that the reading of it necessarily requires so much attention, and the public is disposed to give so little, that I shall still doubt for some time of its being at first very popular. But it has depth and solidity and acuteness, and is so much illustrated by curious facts, that it must at last take the public attention. It is probably much improved by your last abode in London. If you were here at my fire-side, I should dispute some of your principles.......
.... But these, and a hundred other points, are fit only to be discussed in conversation.[12] I hope it will be soon; for I am in a very bad state of health, and cannot afford a long delay.'

20   Of a book which is now so universally known as 'The Wealth of Nations,' it might be considered perhaps as superfluous to give a particular analysis; and, at any rate, the limits of this essay make it impossible for me to attempt it at present. A few remarks, however, on the object and tendency of the work, may, I hope, be introduced without impropriety. The history of a philosopher's life can contain little more than the history of his speculations; and in the case of such an author as Mr Smith, whose studies were systematically directed from his youth to subjects of the last importance to human happiness, a review of his writings, while it serves to illustrate the peculiarities of his genius, affords the most faithful picture of his character as a man.

[10] (Corr., Letter 121.)
[11] (Corr., Letter 150.)
[12] [The quotation omits: '; which, till you tell me the contrary, I shall still flatter myself with soon'.]

SECTION IV

*Of the Inquiry into the Nature and Causes of the Wealth of Nations**

1   AN historical view of the different forms under which human affairs
have appeared in different ages and nations,[1] naturally suggests the
question, Whether the experience of former times may not now
furnish some general principles to enlighten and direct the policy of
future legislators? The discussion, however, to which this question
leads, is of singular difficulty: as it requires an accurate analysis of by
far the most complicated class of phenomena that can possibly engage
our attention, those which result from the intricate and often the
imperceptible mechanism of political society;—a subject of observation which seems, at first view, so little commensurate to our faculties,
that it has been generally regarded with the same passive emotions of
wonder and submission,[2] with which, in the material world, we
survey the effects produced by the mysterious and uncontroulable
operation of physical causes. It is fortunate that upon this, as upon
many other occasions, the difficulties which had long baffled the
efforts of solitary genius begin to appear less formidable to the united
exertions of the race; and that in proportion as the experience and the
reasonings of different individuals are brought to bear upon the same
objects, and are combined in such a manner as to illustrate and to
limit each other, the science of politics assumes more and more that
systematical form which encourages and aids the labours of future
inquirers.

2   In prosecuting the science of politics on this plan, little assistance
is to be derived from the speculations of ancient philosophers, the
greater part of whom, in their political inquiries, confined their
attention to a comparison of the different forms of government, and
to an examination of the provisions they made for perpetuating their
own existence, and for extending the glory of the state. It was reserved
for modern times to investigate those universal principles of justice
and of expediency,[3] which ought, under every form of government,
to regulate the social order; and of which the object is, to make as

---

*The length to which this Memoir has already extended, together with some other reasons
which it is unnecessary to mention here, have induced me, in printing the following section, to
confine myself to a much more general view of the subject than I once intended. See Note (G.)

[1] [See above, II. 45–52.]
[2] [Stewart's view seems to be quite different from that of Smith himself. See Astronomy, I-
II.]
[3] [See I.20 above, where the term is used by Millar in describing Smith's lectures on
economics.]

equitable a distribution as possible, among all the different members of a community, of the advantages arising from the political union.

3   The invention of printing was perhaps necessary to prepare the way for these researches. In those departments of literature and of science, where genius finds within itself the materials of its labours; in poetry, in pure geometry, and in some branches of moral philosophy; the ancients have not only laid the foundations on which we are to build, but have left great and finished models for our imitation. But in physics, where our progress depends on an immense collection of facts, and on a combination of the accidental lights daily struck out in the innumerable walks of observation and experiment; and in politics, where the materials of our theories are equally scattered, and are collected and arranged with still greater difficulty, the means of communication afforded by the press have, in the course of two centuries, accelerated the progress of the human mind, far beyond what the most sanguine hopes of our predecessors could have imagined.

4   The progress already made in this science, inconsiderable as it is in comparison of what may be yet expected, has been sufficient to shew, that the happiness of mankind depends, not on the share which the people possesses, directly or indirectly, in the enactment of laws, but on the equity and expediency of the laws that are enacted. The share which the people possesses in the government is interesting chiefly to the small number of men whose object is the attainment of political importance; but the equity and expediency of the laws are interesting to every member of the community: and more especially to those whose personal insignificance leaves them no encouragement, but what they derive from the general spirit of the government under which they live.

5   It is evident, therefore, that the most important branch of political science is that which has for its object to ascertain the philosophical principles of jurisprudence; or (as Mr Smith expresses it) to ascertain 'the general principles which ought to run through and be the foundation of the laws of all nations*.' In countries where the prejudices of the people are widely at variance with these principles, the political liberty which the constitution bestows, only furnishes them with the means of accomplishing their own ruin: And if it were possible to suppose these principles completely realized in any system of laws, the people would have little reason to complain, that they were not immediately instrumental in their enactment. The only infallible criterion of the excellence of any constitution is to be found in the detail of its municipal code; and the value which wise men set

* See the conclusion of his Theory of Moral Sentiments. (VII. iv. 37.)

on political freedom, arises chiefly from the facility it is supposed to afford, for the introduction of those legislative improvements which the general interests of the community recommend*a*; combined with the security it provides in the light and spirit of the people, for the pure and equal administration of justice*a*.—I cannot help adding, that the capacity of a people to exercise political rights with utility to themselves and to their country, presupposes a diffusion of knowledge and of good morals, which can only result from the previous operation of laws favourable to industry, to order, and to freedom.

6   Of the truth of these remarks, enlightened politicians seem now to be in general convinced; for the most celebrated works which have been produced in the different countries of Europe, during the last thirty years, by Smith, Quesnai, Turgot, Campomanes, Beccaria, and others, have aimed at the improvement of society,—not by delineating plans of new constitutions, but by enlightening the policy of actual legislators. Such speculations, while they are more essentially and more extensively useful than any others, have no tendency to unhinge established institutions, or to inflame the passions of the multitude. The improvements they recommend are to be effected by means too gradual and slow in their operation, to warm the imaginations of any but of the speculative few; and in proportion as they are adopted, they consolidate the political fabric, and enlarge the basis upon which it rests.

7   To direct the policy of nations with respect to one most important class of its laws, those which form its system of political economy, is the great aim of Mr Smith's *Inquiry*:[4] And he has unquestionably had the merit of presenting to the world, the most comprehensive and perfect work that has yet appeared, on the general principles of any branch of legislation. The example which he has set will be followed, it is to be hoped, in due time, by other writers, for whom the internal policy of states furnishes many other subjects of discussion no less curious and interesting; and may accelerate the progress of that science which Lord Bacon has so well described in the following passage: 'Finis et scopus quem leges intueri, atque ad quem jussiones et sanctiones suas dirigere debent, non alius est, quam ut cives feliciter degant; id fiet, si pietate et religione recte instituti; moribus honesti; armis adversus hostes externos tuti; legum auxilio adversus seditiones et privatas injurias muniti; imperio et magistratibus obsequentes; copiis et opibus locupletes et florentes fuerint.—Certe cognitio ista ad

---

a–a Author's last additions

4 [While not neglecting Smith's analytical achievement, e.g. §27 below, Stewart's preoccupation with policy may explain his defence of Smith's originality in terms of the doctrine of natural liberty at §23 and §25.]

viros civiles proprie spectat; qui optime nôrunt, quid ferat societas humana, quid salus populi, quid aequitas naturalis, quid gentium mores, quid rerumpublicarum formae diversae: ideoque possint de legibus, ex principiis et praeceptis tam aequitatis naturalis, quam politices decernere. Quamobrem id nunc agatur, ut fontes justitiae et utilitatis publicae petantur, et in singulis juris partibus character quidam et idea justi exhibeatur, ad quam particularium regnorum et rerumpublicarum leges probare, atque inde emendationem moliri, quisque, cui hoc cordi erit et curae, possit.'5 The enumeration contained in the foregoing passage, of the different objects of law, coincides very nearly with that given by Mr Smith in the conclusion of his Theory of Moral Sentiments; and the precise aim of the political speculations which he then announced, and of which he afterwards published so valuable a part in his Wealth of Nations, was to ascertain the general principles of justice and of expediency, which ought to guide the institutions of legislators on these important articles;—in the words of Lord Bacon, to ascertain those *leges legum*, 'ex quibus informatio peti possit, quid in singulis legibus bene aut perperam positum aut constitutum sit.'6

8   The branch of legislation which Mr Smith has made choice of as the subject of his work, naturally leads me to remark a very striking contrast between the spirit of ancient and of modern policy in respect to the Wealth of Nations*. The great object of the former was to counteract the love of money and a taste for luxury, by positive institutions; and to maintain in the great body of the people, habits of frugality, and a severity of manners. The decline of states is uniformly ascribed by the philosophers and historians, both of Greece and Rome, to the influence of riches on national character; and the laws

---

* Science de la Legislation, par le Chev. Filangieri, Liv. i. chap. 13.

5 (*Exemplum Tractatus de Fontibus Juris*, Aphor. 5: 'The ultimate object which legislators ought to have in view, and to which all their enactments and sanctions ought to be subservient, is, *that the citizens may live happily.* For this purpose, it is necessary that they should receive a religious and pious education; that they should be trained to good morals; that they should be secured from foreign enemies by proper military arrangements; that they should be guarded by an effectual policy against seditions and private injuries; that they should be loyal to government, and obedient to magistrates; and finally, that they should abound in wealth, and in other national resources.' *De Augmentis Scientiarum*, lib. viii. cap. iii: 'The science of such matters certainly belongs more particularly to the province of men who, by habits of public business, have been led to take a comprehensive survey of the social order; of the interests of the community at large; of the rules of natural equity; of the manners of nations; of the different forms of government; and who are thus prepared to reason concerning the wisdom of laws, both from considerations of justice and of policy. The great desideratum, accordingly, is, by investigating the principles of *natural justice*, and those of *political expediency*, to exhibit a theoretical model of legislation, which, while it serves as a standard for estimating the comparative excellence of municipal codes, may suggest hints for their correction and improvement, to such as have at heart the welfare of mankind.' Stewart's translation, from *Works*, i. 71–2.)

6 (*De Fontibus Juris*, Aphor. 6: 'Laws of Laws from which we can determine what is right or wrong in the appointments of each individual law.' Stewart, *Works*, xi.2.)

of Lycurgus, which, during a course of ages, banished the precious metals from Sparta, are proposed by many of them as the most perfect model of legislation devised by human wisdom.—How opposite to this is the doctrine of modern politicians! Far from considering poverty as an advantage to a state, their great aim is to open new sources of national opulence, and to animate the activity of all classes of the people, by a taste for the comforts and accommodations of life.

9   One principal cause of this difference between the spirit of ancient and of modern policy, may be found in the difference between the sources of national wealth in ancient and in modern times. In ages when commerce and manufactures were yet in their infancy, and among states constituted like most of the ancient republics, a sudden influx of riches from abroad was justly dreaded as an evil, alarming to the morals, to the industry, and to the freedom of a people. So different, however, is the case at present, that the most wealthy nations are those where the people are the most laborious, and where they enjoy the greatest degree of liberty. Nay, it was the general diffusion of wealth among the lower orders of men, which first gave birth to the spirit of independence in modern Europe, and which has produced under some of its governments, and especially under our own, a more equal diffusion of freedom and of happiness than took place under the most celebrated constitutions of antiquity.[7]

10   Without this diffusion of wealth among the lower orders, the important effects resulting from the invention of printing would have been extremely limited; for a certain degree of ease and independence is necessary to inspire men with the desire of knowledge, and to afford them the leisure which is requisite for acquiring it; and it is only by the rewards which such a state of society holds up to industry and ambition, that the selfish passions of the multitude can be interested in the intellectual improvement of their children. The extensive propagation of light and refinement arising from the influence of the press, aided by the spirit of commerce, seems to be the remedy provided by nature, against the fatal effects which would otherwise by produced, by the subdivision of labour accompanying the progress of the mechanical arts: Nor is any thing wanting to make the remedy effectual, but wise institutions to facilitate general instruction, and to adapt the education of individuals to the stations they are to occupy. The mind of the *b*artist*b*,

b–b artisan 5

[7] [See, for example, WN III and especially III. iv together with the notes to the Glasgow edition. For comment, see A. Skinner. 'Adam Smith: An Economic Interpretation of History', and D. Forbes, 'Sceptical Whiggism, Commerce, and Liberty', in *Essays on Adam Smith*. The point made in the text was repeated by John Millar, *Historical View*, iv.124.]

which, from the limited sphere of his activity,[8] would sink below the level of the peasant or the savage, might receive in infancy the means of intellectual enjoyment, and the seeds of moral improvement; and even the insipid uniformity of his professional engagements, by presenting no object to awaken his ingenuity or to distract his attention, might leave him at liberty to employ his faculties, on subjects more interesting to himself, and more extensively useful to others.

11   These effects, notwithstanding a variety of opposing causes which still exist, have already resulted, in a very sensible degree, from the liberal policy of modern times. Mr Hume, in his Essay on Commerce, after taking notice of the numerous armies raised and maintained by the small republics in the ancient world, ascribes the military power of these states to their want of commerce and luxury. 'Few artisans were maintained by the labour of the farmers, and therefore more soldiers might live upon it.' He adds, however, that 'the policy of ancient times was VIOLENT, and contrary to the NATURAL course of things;'[9]—by which, I presume, he means, that it aimed too much at modifying, by the force of positive institutions, the order of society, according to some preconceived idea of expediency; without trusting sufficiently to those principles of the human constitution, which, wherever they are allowed free scope, not only conduct mankind to happiness, but lay the foundation of a progressive improvement in their condition and in their character. The advantages which modern policy possesses over the ancient, arise principally from its conformity, in some of the most important articles of political economy, to an order of things recommended by nature; and it would not be difficult to shew, that, where it remains imperfect, its errors may be traced to the restraints it imposes on the natural course of human affairs. Indeed, in these restraints may be discovered the latent seeds of many of the prejudices and follies which infect modern manners, and which have so long bid defiance to the reasonings of the philosopher and the ridicule of the satirist.

12   The foregoing very imperfect hints appeared to me to form, not only a proper, but in some measure a necessary introduction to the few remarks I have to offer on Mr Smith's Inquiry; as they tend to illustrate a connection between his system of commercial politics, and those speculations of his earlier years, in which he aimed more professedly at the advancement of human improvement and happiness. It is this view of political economy that can alone render

[8] [See WN V.i.f.51 and this section generally, i.e. 'Of the Expence of the Institutions for the Education of Youth'.]

[9] [*Essays Moral, Political and Literary*, ed. Green and Grose (1882), i.291. The quotation reads: 'contrary to the more natural and usual course of things'.]

it interesting to the moralist, and can dignify calculations of profit and loss in the eye of the philosopher.[10] Mr Smith has alluded to it in various passages of his work, but he has nowhere explained himself fully on the subject; and the great stress he has laid on the effects of the division of labour in increasing its productive powers, seems, at first sight, to point to a different and very melancholy conclusion;— that the same causes which promote the progress of the arts, tend to degrade the mind of the artist; and, of consequence, that the growth of national wealth implies a sacrifice of the character of the people.[11]

13   The fundamental doctrines of Mr Smith's system are now so generally known, that it would have been tedious to offer any recapitulation of them in this place; even if I could have hoped to do justice to the subject, within the limits which I have prescribed to myself at present. ᶜ I shall content myself, therefore, with remarking, in general terms, that the great and leading object of his speculations is, to illustrate the provision made by nature in the principles of the human mind, and in the circumstances of man's external situation, for a gradual and progressive augmentation in the means of national wealth; and to demonstrate, that the most effectual plan for advancing a people to greatness, is to maintain that order of things which nature has pointed out; by allowing every man, as long as he observes the rules of justice, to pursue his own interest in his own way, and to bring both his industry and his capital into the freest competition with those of his fellow-citizens.[12] Every system of policy which endeavours, either by extraordinary encouragements to draw towards a particular species of industry a greater share of the capital of the society than what would naturally go to it, or, by extraordinary restraints, to force from a particular species of industry some share of the capital which would otherwise be employed in it, is, in reality, subversive of the great purpose which it means to promote.[13]

14   What the circumstances are, which, in modern Eurc.)e, have contributed to disturb this order of nature, and, in particular, to encourage the industry of towns, at the expence of that of the country, Mr Smith has investigated with great ingenuity;[14] and in such a

ᶜ A distinct analysis of his work might indeed be useful to many readers; but it would itself form a volume of considerable magnitude. I may perhaps, at some future period, present to the Society, an attempt towards such an analysis, which I began long ago, for my own satisfaction, and which I lately made considerable progress in preparing for the press, before I was aware of the impossibility of connecting it, with the general plan of this paper. In the mean time *1–2* (See the article *Smith, Adam*, in the Index to Stewart, *Works*, xi, for references to analysis of parts of WN.)

[10] [This statement, together with the broadly liberal sentiments of the preceding paragraphs, may bear upon Stewart's own experience. See for example, *Works* x. xlvi–liv.]
[11] [See, for example, WN V.i.f.50.]
[12] [WN IV.ix.51.]
[13] [WN IV.ix.50.]
[14] [Smith makes this point in WN II.v.37, drawing attention to the two following books.]

manner, as to throw much new light on the history of that state of society which prevails in this quarter of the globe. His observations on this subject tend to shew, that these circumstances were, in their first origin, the natural and the unavoidable result of the peculiar situation of mankind during a certain period; and that they took their rise, not from any general scheme of policy, but from the private interests and prejudices of particular orders of men.

15   The state of society, however, which at first arose from a singular combination of accidents, has been prolonged much beyond its natural period, by a false system of political economy, propagated by merchants and manufacturers; a class of individuals, whose interest is not always the same with that of the public, and whose professional knowledge gave them many advantages, more particularly in the infancy of this branch of science, in defending those opinions which they wished to encourage. By means of this system, a new set of obstacles to the progress of national prosperity has been created. Those which arose from the disorders of the feudal ages, tended directly to disturb the internal arrangements of society, by obstructing the free circulation of labour and of stock, from employment to employment, and from place to place. The false system of political economy which has been hitherto prevalent, as its professed object has been to regulate the commercial intercourse between different nations, has produced its effect in a way less direct and less manifest, but equally prejudicial to the states that have adopted it.

16   On this system, as it took its rise from the prejudices, or rather from the interested views of mercantile speculators, Mr Smith bestows the title of the Commercial or Mercantile System;[15] and he has considered at great length its two principal expedients for enriching a nation; restraints upon importation, and encouragements to exportation.[16] Part of these expedients, he observes, have been dictated by the spirit of monopoly, and part by a spirit of jealousy against those countries with which the balance of trade is supposed to be disadvantageous.[17] All of them appear clearly, from his reasonings, to have a tendency unfavourable to the wealth of the nation which imposes them.—His remarks with respect to the jealousy of commerce are expressed in a tone of indignation, which he seldom assumes in his political writings.

17   'In this manner (says he) the sneaking arts of underling tradesmen are erected into political maxims for the conduct of a great empire.[18]

[15] [The title of WN IV.i. In the introduction to this book, the commercial system is described as 'the modern system, and is best understood in our own country and in our own times'.]
[16] [WN IV.i.35.]
[17] [See, for example, the conclusion of WN IV.iii.a.1.]
[18] [WN IV.iii.c.8. The quotation occurs at the end of the paragraph and reads 'are thus erected'.]

By such maxims as these,[19] nations have been taught that their interest consisted in beggaring all their neighbours. Each nation has been made to look with an invidious eye upon the prosperity of all the nations with which it trades, and to consider their gain as its own loss. Commerce, which ought naturally to be among nations as among individuals, a bond of union and friendship, has become the most fertile source of discord and animosity. The capricious ambition of Kings and Ministers has not, during the present and the preceding century, been more fatal to the repose of Europe, than the impertinent jealousy of merchants and manufacturers. The violence and injustice of the rulers of mankind is an ancient evil, for which[20] perhaps the nature of human affairs can scarce admit of a remedy. But the mean rapacity, the monopolizing spirit of merchants and manufacturers, who neither are nor ought to be the rulers of mankind, though it cannot perhaps be corrected, may very easily be prevented from disturbing the tranquillity of any body but themselves.'[21]

18   Such are the liberal principles which, according to Mr Smith, ought to direct the commercial policy of nations; and of which it ought to be the great object of legislators to facilitate the establishment. In what manner the execution of the theory should be conducted in particular instances, is a question of a very different nature, and to which the answer must vary, in different countries, according to the different circumstances of the case. In a speculative work, such as Mr Smith's, the consideration of this question did not fall properly under his general plan; but that he was abundantly aware of the danger to be apprehended from a rash application of political theories, appears not only from the general strain of his writings, but from some incidental observations which he has expressly made upon the subject. 'So unfortunate (says he, in one passage) are the effects of all the regulations of the mercantile system, that they not only[22] introduce very dangerous disorders into the state of the body politic, but disorders which it is often difficult to remedy, without occasioning, for a time at least, still greater disorders.—In what manner, therefore,[23] the natural system of perfect liberty and justice ought gradually to be restored, we must leave to the wisdom of future statesmen and legislators to determine.'[24] In the last edition of his

---

[19] [The original reads 'By such maxims as these, however, . . .'.]

[20] [The original text reads 'for which, I am afraid, the nature . . .'.]

[21] (WN IV.iii.c.9.)

[22] [The original reads 'Such are the unfortunate effects of all the regulations of the mercantile system! They not only . . .'.]

[23] [The original continues 'the colony trade ought gradually to be opened; what are the restraints which ought first, and what are those which ought last to be taken away; or in what manner'.]

[24] (WN IV.vii.c.44.)

Theory of Moral Sentiments, he has introduced some remarks, which have an obvious reference to the same important doctrine. The following passage seems to refer more particularly to those derangements of the social order which derived their origin from the feudal institutions:

19   'The man whose public spirit is prompted altogether by humanity and benevolence, will respect the established powers and privileges even of individuals, and still more[25] of the great orders and societies into which the state is divided. Though he should consider some of them as in some measure abusive, he will content himself with moderating, what he often cannot annihilate without great violence. When he cannot conquer the rooted prejudices of the people by reason and persuasion, he will not attempt to subdue them by force; but will religiously observe what, by Cicero, is justly called the divine maxim of Plato, never to use violence to his country no more than to his parents. He will accommodate, as well as he can, his public arrangements to the confirmed habits and prejudices of the people; and will remedy, as well as he can, the inconveniencies which may flow from the want of those regulations which the people are averse to submit to. When he cannot establish the right, he will not disdain to ameliorate the wrong; but, like Solon, when he cannot establish the best system of laws, he will endeavour to establish the best that the people can bear.'[26]

20   These cautions with respect to the practical application of general principles were peculiarly necessary from the Author of 'The Wealth of Nations;' as the unlimited freedom of trade, which it is the chief aim of his work to recommend, is extremely apt, by flattering the indolence of the statesman, to suggest to those who are invested with absolute power, the idea of carrying it into immediate execution. 'Nothing is more adverse to the tranquillity of a statesman (says the author of an Eloge on the Administration of Colbert) than a spirit of moderation; because it condemns him to perpetual observation, shews him every moment the insufficiency of his wisdom, and leaves him the melancholy sense of his own imperfection; while, under the shelter of a few general principles, a systematical politician enjoys a perpetual calm. By the help of one alone, that of a perfect liberty of trade, he would govern the world, and would leave human affairs to arrange themselves at pleasure, under the operation of the prejudices and the self-interests of individuals. If these run counter to each other, he gives himself no anxiety about the consequence; he insists that the result cannot be judged of till after a century or two shall

[25] [The original reads 'still more those . . .'.]
[26] (TMS VI.ii.2.16.)

have elapsed. If his contemporaries, in consequence of the disorder into which he has thrown public affairs, are scrupulous about submitting quietly to the experiment, he accuses them of impatience. They alone, and not he, are to blame for what they have suffered; and the principle continues to be inculcated with the same zeal and the same confidence as before.' These are the words of the ingenious and eloquent author of the Eloge on Colbert, which obtained the prize from the French Academy in the year 1763; a performance which, although confined and erroneous in its speculative views, abounds with just and important reflections of a practical nature. How far his remarks apply to that particular class of politicians whom he had evidently in his eye in the foregoing passage, I shall not presume to decide.

21   It is hardly necessary for me to add to these observations, that they do not detract in the least from the value of those political theories which attempt to delineate the principles of a perfect legislation. Such theories (as I have elsewhere observed*) ought to be considered merely as descriptions of the *ultimate* objects at which the statesman ought to aim. The tranquillity of his administration, and the immediate success of his measures, depend on his good sense and his practical skill; and his theoretical principles only enable him to direct his measures steadily and wisely, to promote the improvement and happiness of mankind, and prevent him from being ever led astray from these important ends, by more limited views of temporary expedience. 'In all cases (says Mr Hume) it must be advantageous to know what is most perfect in the kind, that we may be able to bring any real constitution or form of government as near it as possible, by such gentle alterations and innovations as may not give too great disturbance to society.'[27]

22   The limits of this Memoir make it impossible for me to examine particularly the merit of Mr Smith's work in point of originality. That his doctrine concerning the freedom of trade and of industry coincides remarkably with that which we find in the writings of the French Economists, appears from the slight view of their system which he himself has given.[28] But it surely cannot be pretended by the warmest admirers of that system, that any one of its numerous expositors has approached to Mr Smith in the precision and perspicuity with which he has stated it, or in the scientific and luminous manner in which he has deduced it from elementary

---

* Elements of the Philosophy of the Human Mind, p.261. (Stewart, *Works*, ii.240.)

[27] ('Idea of a Perfect Commonwealth', *Essays Moral, Political and Literary*, ed. Green and Grose, i.481.)

[28] [Not perhaps a wholly fair assessment of WN. ix: cf. A. Skinner, 'Adam Smith: The Development of a System', *Scottish Journal of Political Economy*, xxiii (1976).]

principles. The awkwardness of their technical language, and the paradoxical form in which they have chosen to present some of their opinions, are acknowledged even by those who are most willing to do justice to their merits; whereas it may be doubted, with respect to Mr Smith's Inquiry, if there exists any book beyond the circle of the mathematical and physical sciences, which is at once so agreeable in its arrangement to the rules of a sound logic, and so accessible to the examination of ordinary readers. Abstracting entirely from the author's peculiar and original speculations, I do not know that, upon any subject whatever, a work has been produced in our times, containing so methodical, so comprehensive, and so judicious a digest of all the most profound and enlightened philosophy of the age*.

23   In justice also to Mr Smith, it must be observed, that although some of the economical writers had the start of him in publishing their doctrines to the world, these doctrines appear, with respect to him, to have been altogether original, and the result of his own reflections.[29] Of this, I think, every person must be convinced, who reads the Inquiry with due attention, and is at pains to examine the gradual and beautiful progress of the author's ideas: But in case any doubt should remain on this head, it may be proper to mention, that Mr. Smith's political lectures, comprehending the fundamental principles of his Inquiry, were delivered at Glasgow as early as the year 1752 or 1753; at a period, surely, when there existed no French performance on the subject, that could be of much use to him in guiding his researches†. In the year 1756, indeed, M. Turgot (who is said to have imbibed his first notions concerning the unlimited freedom of commerce from an old merchant, M. Gournay), published in the *Encyclopédie*, an article which sufficiently shews how completely his mind was emancipated from the old prejudices in favour of commercial regulations: But that even then, these opinions were confined to a few speculative men in France, appears from a passage in the *Mémoires sur la Vie et les Ouvrages de M. Turgot*; in which, after a short quotation from the article just mentioned, the author adds: 'These ideas were *then* considered as paradoxical; they are since become common, and they will one day be adopted universally.'

24   The Political Discourses of Mr Hume were evidently of greater

---

* See Note (H.)

† In proof of this, it is sufficient for me to appeal to a short history of the progress of political economy in France, published in one of the volumes of *Ephémérides du Citoyen*. See the first part of the volume for the year 1769. The paper is entitled, *Notice abrégée des différens Ecrits modernes, qui ont concouru en France à former la science de l'économie politique.*

[29] [It is pointed out above (III.5), however, that contact with the physiocrats 'could not fail to assist him in methodizing and digesting his speculations'.]

use to Mr Smith, than any other book that had appeared prior to his
lectures. Even Mr Hume's theories, however, though always plausible
and ingenious, and in most instances profound and just, involve
some fundamental mistakes; and, when compared with Mr. Smith's,
afford a striking proof, that, in considering a subject so extensive and
so complicated, the most penetrating sagacity, if directed only to
particular questions, is apt to be led astray by first appearances;[30] and
that nothing can guard us effectually against error, but a comprehensive survey of the whole field of discussion, assisted by an accurate
and patient analysis of the ideas about which our reasonings are
employed.—It may be worth while to add, that Mr. Hume's Essay 'on
the Jealousy of Trade,' with some other of his Political Discourses,
received a very flattering proof of M. Turgot's approbation, by his
undertaking the task of translating them into the French language*.

25   I am aware that the evidence I have hitherto produced of Mr
Smith's originality may be objected to as not perfectly decisive, as it
rests entirely on the recollection of those students who attended his
first courses of moral philosophy at Glasgow; a recollection which, at
the distance of forty years, cannot be supposed to be very accurate.
There exists, however, fortunately, a short manuscript drawn up by
Mr. Smith in the year 1755, and presented by him to a society of
which he was then a member;[31] in which paper, a pretty long
enumeration is given of certain leading principles, both political and
literary, to which he was anxious to establish his exclusive right; in
order to prevent the possibility of some rival claims which he thought
he had reason to apprehend, and to which his situation as a Professor,
added to his unreserved communications in private companies,
rendered him peculiarly liable. This paper is at present in my
possession. It is expressed with a good deal of that honest and
indignant warmth, which is perhaps unavoidable by a man who is
conscious of the purity of his own intentions, when he suspects that
advantages have been taken of the frankness of his temper. On such
occasions, due allowances are not always made for those plagiarisms,[32]
which, however cruel in their effects, do not necessarily imply bad

---

* See Note (I.)

[30] [Possibly a reference to sentiments which Smith was known to have expressed. In LJ(B)
253 (ed. Cannan, 197), for example, Smith refers to the ingenuity of Hume's reasoning on the
subject of money, while noting that: 'He seems however to have gone a little into the notion that
public opulence consists in money.']

[31] [Scott comments on this paper in *ASSP*, 117 ff.]

[32] [Smith writes briefly of plagiarism, but with no especial warmth of feeling, in TMS
III.2.15: 'A weak man ... pretends to have done what he never did, to have written what
another wrote, to have invented what another discovered; and is led into all the miserable vices
of plagiarism and common lying.' See also TMS VII.ii.4.8: 'the foolish plagiary who gives
himself out for the author of what he has no pretensions to' is 'properly accused' of vanity.]

faith in those who are guilty of them; for the bulk of mankind, incapable themselves of original thought, are perfectly unable to form a conception of the nature of the injury done to a man of inventive genius, by encroaching on a favourite speculation. For reasons known to some members of this Society, it would be improper, by the publication of this manuscript, to revive the memory of private differences; and I should not have even alluded to it, if I did not think it a valuable document of the progress of Mr Smith's political ideas at a very early period.[33] Many of the most important opinions in *The Wealth of Nations* are there detailed; but I shall quote only the following sentences: 'Man is generally considered by statesmen and projectors as the materials of a sort of political mechanics. Projectors disturb nature in the course of her operations in human affairs; and it requires no more than to let her alone, and give her fair play in the pursuit of her ends, that she may establish her own designs.'—And in another passage: 'Little else is requisite to carry a state to the highest degree of opulence from the lowest barbarism, but peace, easy taxes, and a tolerable administration of justice; all the rest being brought about by the natural course of things. All governments which thwart this natural course, which force things into another channel, or which endeavour to arrest the progress of society at a particular point, are unnatural, and to support themselves are obliged to be oppressive and tyrannical.—A great part of the opinions (he observes) enumerated in this paper is treated of at length in some lectures which I have still by me, and which were written in the hand of a clerk who left my service six years ago. They have all of them been the constant subjects of my lectures since I first taught Mr Craigie's class, the first winter I spent in Glasgow, down to this day, without any considerable variation. They had all of them been the subjects of lectures which I read at Edinburgh the winter before I left it, and I can adduce innumerable witnesses, both from that place and from this, who will ascertain them sufficiently to be mine.'

26   After all, perhaps the merit of such a work as Mr Smith's is to be estimated less from the novelty of the principles it contains, than from the reasonings employed to support these principles, and from the scientific manner in which they are unfolded in their proper order and connection.[34] General assertions with respect to the advantages of a free commerce, may be collected from various writers of an early date. But in questions of so complicated a nature as occur in political economy, the credit of such opinions belongs of right to the author who first established their solidity, and followed them out

[33] [Cf. Scott, *ASSP*, 118–20.]
[34] [A rather similar judgement of TMS is given in Note C, §4.]

to their remote consequences; not to him who, by a fortunate accident, first stumbled on the truth.

27   Besides the principles which Mr Smith considered as more peculiarly his own, his Inquiry exhibits a systematical view of the most important articles of political economy, so as to serve the purpose of an elementary treatise on that very extensive and difficult science. The skill and the comprehensiveness of mind displayed in his arrangement, can be judged of by those alone who have compared it with that adopted by his immediate predecessors. And perhaps, in point of utility, the labour he has employed in connecting and methodizing their scattered ideas, is not less valuable than the results of his own original speculations: For it is only when digested in a clear and natural order, that truths make their proper impression on the mind, and that erroneous opinions can be combated with success.

28   It does not belong to my present undertaking (even if I were qualified for such a task) to attempt a separation of the solid and important doctrines of Mr Smith's book from those opinions which appear exceptionable or doubtful. I acknowledge, that there are some of his conclusions to which I would not be understood to subscribe implicitly; more particularly in that chapter, where he treats of the principles of taxation^d;—a subject, which he has certainly examined in a manner more loose and unsatisfactory than most of the others which have fallen under his review*.^{d}

29   It would be improper for me to conclude this section without taking notice of the manly and dignified freedom with which the author uniformly delivers his opinions, and of the superiority which he discovers throughout, to all the little passions connected with the factions of the times in which he wrote. Whoever takes the trouble to compare the general tone of his composition with the period of its first publication, cannot fail to feel and acknowledge the force of this remark.—It is not often that a disinterested zeal for truth has so soon met with its just reward. Philosophers (to use an expression of Lord Bacon's) are 'the servants of posterity;' and most of those who have devoted their talents to the best interests of mankind, have been obliged, like Bacon, to 'bequeath their fame' to a race yet unborn, and to console themselves with the idea of sowing what another generation was to reap:

Insere Daphni pyros, carpent tua poma nepotes.^{35}

* See Note (J.)

$^{d-d}$ and which is certainly executed in a manner more loose and unsatisfactory than the other parts of his system. *1–2*

^{35} (Virgil, *Eclogues*, ix.50: 'Graft your pears, Daphnis, your descendants will gather your fruits'.)

Mr Smith was more fortunate; or rather, in this respect, his fortune was singular. He survived the publication of his work only fifteen years; and yet, during that short period, he had not only the satisfaction of seeing the opposition it at first excited, gradually subside, but to witness the practical influence of his writings on the commercial policy of his country.

SECTION V

Conclusion of the Narrative

1   About two years after the publication of 'The Wealth of Nations,' Mr Smith was appointed one of the Commissioners of his Majesty's Customs in Scotland; a preferment which, in his estimation, derived an additional value from its being bestowed on him at the request of the Duke of Buccleuch. The greater part of these two years he passed in London, enjoying a society too extensive and varied to afford him any opportunity of indulging his taste for study. His time, however, was not lost to himself; for much of it was spent with some of the first names in English literature. Of these no unfavourable specimen is preserved by Dr Barnard, in his well-known 'Verses addressed to Sir Joshua Reynolds and his friends.'

> If I have thoughts, and can't express 'em,
> Gibbon shall teach me how to dress 'em
>   In words select and terse:
> Jones teach me modesty and Greek,
> Smith how to think, Burke how to speak,
>   And Beauclerc to converse.*

2   In consequence of Mr Smith's appointment to the Board of Customs, he removed, in 1778, to Edinburgh, where he spent the last twelve years of his life; enjoying an affluence which was more than equal to all his wants; and, what was to him of still greater value, the prospect of passing the remainder of his days among the companions of his youth.

3   His mother, who, though now in extreme old age, still possessed a considerable degree of health, and retained all her faculties unimpaired, accompanied him to town; and his cousin Miss Jane Douglas, (who had formerly been a member of his family at Glasgow, and for whom he had always felt the affection of a brother) while she divided with him those tender attentions which her aunt's infirmities required, relieved him of a charge for which he was peculiarly ill qualified, by her friendly superintendence of his domestic economy.

4   The accession to his income which his new office brought him, enabled him to gratify, to a much greater extent than his former circumstances admitted of, the natural generosity of his disposition; and the state of his funds at the time of his death, compared with his very moderate establishment, confirmed, beyond a doubt, what his

* See Annual Register for the year 1776.

intimate acquaintances had often suspected, that a large proportion of his annual savings was allotted to offices of secret charity. A small, but excellent library, which he had gradually formed with great judgment in the selection; and a simple, though hospitable table, where, without the formality of an invitation, he was always happy to receive his friends, were the only expences that could be considered as his own.*

5　　The change in his habits which his removal to Edinburgh produced, was not equally favourable to his literary pursuits. The duties of his office, though they required but little exertion of thought, were yet sufficient to waste his spirits and to dissipate his attention; and now that his career is closed, it is impossible to reflect on the time they consumed, without lamenting, that it had not been employed in labours more profitable to the world, and more equal to his mind.

6　　During the first years of his residence in this city, his studies seemed to be entirely suspended; and his passion for letters served only to amuse his leisure, and to animate his conversation. The infirmities of age, of which he very early began to feel the approaches, reminded him at last, when it was too late, of what he yet owed to the public, and to his own fame. The principal materials of the works which he had announced, had been long ago collected; and little probably was wanting, but a few years of health and retirement, to bestow on them that systematical arrangement in which he delighted; and the ornaments of that flowing, and apparently artless style, which he had studiously cultivated, but which, after all his experience in composition, he adjusted, with extreme difficulty, to his own taste.†

7　　The death of his mother in 1784, which was followed by that of Miss Douglas in 1788, contributed, it is probable, to frustrate these projects. They had been the objects of his affection for more than sixty years; and in their society he had enjoyed, from his infancy, all that he ever knew of the endearments of a family.‡ He was now alone,

---

* Some very affecting instances of Mr Smith's beneficence, in cases where he found it impossible to conceal entirely his good offices, have been mentioned to me by a near relation of his, and one of his most confidential friends, Miss Ross, daughter of the late Patrick Ross, Esq. of Innernethy. They were all on a scale much beyond what might have been expected from his fortune; and were accompanied with circumstances equally honourable to the delicacy of his feelings and the liberality of his heart.

† Mr Smith observed to me, not long before his death, that after all his practice in writing, he composed as slowly, and with as great difficulty, as at first. He added, at the same time, that Mr Hume had acquired so great a facility in this respect, that the last volumes of his History were printed from his original copy, with a few marginal corrections.

It may gratify the curiosity of some readers to know, that when Mr Smith was employed in composition, he generally walked up and down his apartment, dictating to a secretary. All Mr Hume's works (I have been assured) were written with his own hand. A critical reader may, I think, perceive in the different styles of these two classical writers, the effects of their different modes of study.

‡ See Note (K.)

and helpless; and, though he bore his loss with equanimity, and regained apparently his former cheerfulness, yet his health and strength gradually declined till the period of his death, which happened in July 1790, about two years after that of his cousin, and six after that of his mother. His last illness, which arose from a chronic obstruction in his bowels, was lingering and painful; but had every consolation to sooth it which he could derive from the tenderest sympathy of his friends, and from the complete resignation of his own mind.

8   A few days before his death, finding his end approach rapidly, he gave orders to destroy all his manuscripts, excepting some detached essays, which he entrusted to the care of his executors; and they were accordingly committed to the flames. What were the particular contents of these papers, is not known even to his most intimate friends; but there can be no doubt that they consisted, in part, of the lectures on rhetoric, which he read at Edinburgh in the year 1748, and of the lectures on natural religion and on jurisprudence, which formed part of his course at Glasgow. That this irreparable injury to letters proceeded, in some degree, from an excessive solicitude in the author about his posthumous reputation, may perhaps be true; but with respect to some of his manuscripts, may we not suppose, that he was influenced by higher motives? It is but seldom that a philosopher, who has been occupied from his youth with moral or with political inquiries, succeeds completely to his wish in stating to others, the grounds upon which his own opinions are founded; and hence it is, that the known principles of an individual, who has approved to the public his candour, his liberality, and his judgment, are entitled to a weight and an authority, independent of the evidence which he is able, upon any particular occasion, to produce in their support. A secret consciousness of this circumstance, and an apprehension that, by not doing justice to an important argument, the progress of truth may be rather retarded than advanced, have probably induced many authors to withhold from the world the unfinished results of their most valuable labours; and to content themselves with giving the general sanction of their suffrages to truths which they regarded as peculiarly interesting to the human race.*

---

* Since writing the above, I have been favoured by Dr Hutton with the following particulars. 'Some time before his last illness, when Mr Smith had occasion to go to London, he enjoined his friends, to whom he had entrusted the disposal of his manuscripts, that, in the event of his death, they should destroy all the volumes of his lectures, doing with the rest of his manuscripts what they pleased. When now he had become weak, and saw the approaching period of his life, he spoke to his friends again upon the same subject. They entreated him to make his mind easy, as he might depend upon their fulfilling his desire. He was then satisfied. But some days afterwards, finding his anxiety not entirely removed, he begged one of them to destroy the volumes immediately. This accordingly was done; and his mind was so much relieved, that he was able to receive his friends in the evening with his usual complacency.

(*continued*)

9 The additions to the Theory of Moral Sentiments, most of which were composed under severe disease, had fortunately been sent to the press in the beginning of the preceding winter; and the author lived to see the publication of the work.[1] The moral and serious strain that prevails through these additions, when connected with the circumstance of his declining health, adds a peculiar charm to his pathetic eloquence, and communicates a new interest, if possible, to those sublime truths, which, in the academical retirement of his youth, awakened the first ardours of his genius, and on which the last efforts of his mind reposed.

10 In a letter addressed, in the year 1787, to the Principal of the University of Glasgow, in consequence of being elected Rector of that learned body, a pleasing memorial remains of the satisfaction with which he always recollected that period of his literary career, which had been more peculiarly consecrated to these important studies. 'No preferment (says he) could have given me so much real satisfaction. No man can owe greater obligations to a society than I do to the University of Glasgow. They educated me; they sent me to Oxford. Soon after my return to Scotland, they elected me one of their own members; and afterwards preferred me to another office, to which the abilities and virtues of the never to be forgotten Dr

'They had been in use to sup with him every Sunday; and that evening there was a pretty numerous meeting of them. Mr Smith not finding himself able to sit up with them as usual, retired to bed before supper; and, as he went away, took leave of his friends by saying, "I believe we must adjourn this meeting to some other place." He died a very few days afterwards.'

Mr Riddell, an intimate friend of Mr Smith's, who was present at one of the conversations on the subject of the manuscripts, mentioned to me, in addition to Dr Hutton's note, that Mr Smith regretted 'he had done so little.' But I meant (said he) to have done more; and there are materials in my papers, of which I could have made a great deal. But that is now out of the question.'

That the idea of destroying such unfinished works as might be in his possession at the time of his death, was not the effect of any sudden or hasty resolution, appears from the following letter to Mr Hume, written by Mr Smith in 1773, at a time when he was preparing himself for a journey to London, with the prospect of a pretty long absence from Scotland.

My dear Friend, *Edinburgh, 16th April 1773.*
As I have left the care of all my literary papers to you, I must tell you, that except those which I carry along with me, there are none worth the publication, but a fragment of a great work, which contains a history of the astronomical systems that were successively in fashion down to the time of Des Cartes. Whether that might not be published as a fragment of an intended juvenile work, I leave entirely to your judgment, though I begin to suspect myself that there is more refinement than solidity in some parts of it. This little work you will find in a thin folio paper book in my back room. All the other loose papers which you will find in that desk, or within the glass folding doors of a bureau which stands in my bed-room, together with about eighteen thin paper folio books, which you will likewise find within the same glass folding doors, I desire to be destroyed without any examination. Unless I die very suddenly, I shall take care that the papers I carry with me shall be carefully sent to you.
I ever am, my dear Friend, most faithfully your's,

ADAM SMITH.
To David Hume, Esq.
St Andrew's Square.
(The corrected text appears in Corr., Letter 137.)

[1] (Ed. 6, 2 vols. 8vo, 1790.)

Hutcheson had given a superior degree of illustration. The period of thirteen years which I spent as a member of that society, I remember as by far the most useful, and therefore as by far the happiest and most honourable period of my life; and now, after three and twenty years absence, to be remembered in so very agreeable a manner by my old friends and protectors, gives me a heart-felt joy which I cannot easily express to you.'[2]

11   The short narrative which I have now finished, however barren of incident, may convey a general idea of the genius and character of this illustrious Man. Of the intellectual gifts and attainments by which he was so eminently distinguished;—of the originality and comprehensiveness of his views; the extent, the variety, and the correctness of his information; the inexhaustible fertility of his invention; and the ornaments which his rich and beautiful imagination had borrowed from classical culture;— he has left behind him lasting monuments. To his private worth the most certain of all testimonies may be found in that confidence, respect, and attachment, which followed him through all the various relations of life. The serenity and gaiety he enjoyed, under the pressure of his growing infirmities, and the warm interest he felt to the last, in every thing connected with the welfare of his friends, will be long remembered by a small circle, with whom, as long as his strength permitted, he regularly spent an evening in the week; and to whom the recollection of his worth still forms a pleasing, though melancholy bond of union.

12   The more delicate and characteristical features of his mind, it is perhaps impossible to trace. That there were many peculiarities, both in his manners, and in his intellectual habits, was manifest to the most superficial observer; but although, to those who knew him, these peculiarities detracted nothing from the respect which his abilities commanded; and although, to his intimate friends, they added an inexpressible charm to his conversation, while they displayed, in the most interesting light, the artless simplicity of his heart; yet it would require a very skilful pencil to present them to the public eye. He was certainly not fitted for the general commerce of the world, or for the business of active life. The comprehensive speculations with which he had been occupied from his youth, and the variety of materials which his own invention continually supplied to his thoughts, rendered him habitually inattentive to familiar objects, and to common occurrences; and he frequently exhibited instances of absence, which have scarcely been surpassed by the fancy of La Bruyère. Even in company, he was apt to be engrossed with his studies; and appeared, at times, by the motion of his lips, as

[2] (Corr., Letter 274.)

well as by his looks and gestures, to be in the fervour of composition. I have often, however, been struck, at the distance of years, with his accurate memory of the most trifling particulars; and am inclined to believe, from this and some other circumstances, that he possessed a power, not perhaps uncommon among absent men, of recollecting, in consequence of subsequent efforts of reflection, many occurrences, which, at the time when they happened, did not seem to have sensibly attracted his notice.

13   To the defect now mentioned, it was probably owing, in part, that he did not fall in easily with the common dialogue of conversation, and that he was somewhat apt to convey his own ideas in the form of a lecture. When he did so, however, it never proceeded from a wish to engross the discourse, or to gratify his vanity. His own inclination disposed him so strongly to enjoy in silence the gaiety of those around him, that his friends were often led to concert little schemes, in order to engage him in the discussions most likely to interest him. Nor do I think I shall be accused of going too far, when I say, that he was scarcely ever known to start a new topic himself, or to appear unprepared upon those topics that were introduced by others. Indeed, his conversation was never more amusing than when he gave a loose to his genius, upon the very few branches of knowledge of which he only possessed the outlines.

14   The opinions he formed of men, upon a slight acquaintance, were frequently erroneous; but the tendency of his nature inclined him much more to blind partiality, than to ill-founded prejudice. The enlarged views of human affairs, on which his mind habitually dwelt, left him neither time nor inclination to study, in detail, the uninteresting peculiarities of ordinary characters; and accordingly, though intimately acquainted with the capacities of the intellect, and the workings of the heart, and accustomed, in his theories, to mark, with the most delicate hand, the nicest shades, both of genius and of the passions; yet, in judging of individuals, it sometimes happened, that his estimates were, in a surprising degree, wide of the truth.

15   The opinions, too, which, in the thoughtlessness and confidence of his social hours, he was accustomed to hazard on books, and on questions of speculation, were not uniformly such as might have been expected from the superiority of his understanding, and the singular consistency of his philosophical principles. They were liable to be influenced by accidental circumstances, and by the humour of the moment; and when retailed by those who only saw him occasionally, suggested false and contradictory ideas of his real sentiments. On these, however, as on most other occasions, there was always much truth, as well as ingenuity, in his remarks; and if the different

opinions which, at different times, he pronounced upon the same subject, had been all combined together, so as to modify and limit each other, they would probably have afforded materials for a decision, equally comprehensive and just. But, in the society of his friends, he had no disposition to form those qualified conclusions that we admire in his writings; and he generally contented himself with a bold and masterly sketch of the object, from the first point of view in which his temper, or his fancy, presented it. Something of the same kind might be remarked, when he attempted, in the flow of his spirits, to delineate those characters which, from long intimacy, he might have been supposed to understand thoroughly. The picture was always lively, and expressive; and commonly bore a strong and amusing resemblance to the original, when viewed under one particular aspect; but seldom, perhaps, conveyed a just and complete conception of it in all its dimensions and proportions.—In a word, it was the fault of his unpremeditated judgments, to be too systematical, and too much in extremes.

16   But, in whatever way these trifling peculiarities in his manners may be explained, there can be no doubt, that they were intimately connected with the genuine artlessness of his mind. In this amiable quality, he often recalled to his friends, the accounts that are given of good La Fontaine; a quality which in him derived a peculiar grace from the singularity of its combination with those powers of reason and of eloquence, which, in his political and moral writings, have long engaged the admiration of Europe.

17   In his external form and appearance, there was nothing uncommon. When perfectly at ease, and when warmed with conversation, his gestures were animated, and not ungraceful: and, in the society of those he loved, his features were often brightened with a smile of inexpressible benignity. In the company of strangers, his tendency to absence, and perhaps still more his consciousness of this tendency, rendered his manner somewhat embarrassed;—an effect which was probably not a little heightened by those speculative ideas of propriety, which his recluse habits tended at once to perfect in his conception, and to diminish his power of realizing. He never sat for his picture; but the medallion of Tassie conveys an exact idea of his profile, and of the general expression of his countenance.

18   His valuable library, together with the rest of his property, was bequeathed to his cousin Mr David Douglas, Advocate.* In the education of this young gentleman, he had employed much of his leisure; and it was only two years before his death (at a time when he

---

*a** Ultimately a Senator of the College of Justice, under the title of Lord Reston.*a*

a–a added in 5

could ill spare the pleasure of his society), that he had sent him to study law at Glasgow, under the care of Mr Millar;—the strongest proof he could give of his disinterested zeal for the improvement of his friend, as well as of the esteem in which he held the abilities of that eminent Professor.

19   The executors of his will were Dr Black and Dr Hutton; with whom he had long lived in habits of the most intimate and cordial friendship; and who, to the many other testimonies which they had given him of their affection, added the mournful office of witnessing his last moments.

NOTES

to the

LIFE OF ADAM SMITH, LL.D.

Note (A.), p. 270

'Of this number were Mr Oswald of Dunikeir,' etc.]—The late James Oswald, Esq.—for many years one of the most active, able and public-spirited of our Scottish representatives in Parliament. He was more particularly distinguished by his knowledge in matters of finance, and by his attention to whatever concerned the commercial or the agricultural interests of the country. From the manner in which he is mentioned in a paper of Mr Smith's which I have perused, he appears to have combined, with that detailed information which he is well known to have possessed as a statesman and man of business, a taste for the more general and philosophical discussions of political economy. He lived in habits of great intimacy with Lord Kames and Mr Hume; and was one of Mr Smith's earliest and most confidential friends.[1]

Note (B.), p. 271

'The lectures of the profound and eloquent Dr Hutcheson,' etc.] Those who have derived their knowledge of Dr Hutcheson solely from his publications, may, perhaps, be inclined to dispute the propriety of the epithet *eloquent*, when applied to any of his compositions; more particularly, when applied to *the System of Moral Philosophy*, which was published after his death, as the substance of his lectures in the University of Glasgow. His talents, however, as a public speaker, must have been of a far higher order than what he has displayed as a writer; all his pupils whom I have happened to meet with (some of them, certainly, very competent judges) having agreed exactly with each other in their accounts of the extraordinary impression which they made on the minds of his hearers. I have mentioned, in the text, Mr Smith as one of his warmest admirers; and to *his* name I shall take this opportunity of adding those of the late Earl of Selkirk; the late Lord President Miller; and the late Dr Archibald Maclaine, the very learned and judicious translator of Mosheim's Ecclesiastical History. My father, too, who had attended Dr Hutcheson's lectures for several years, never spoke of them without much sensibility. On this occasion we can only say, as Quinctilian has done of the eloquence of Hortensius; 'Apparet placuisse aliquid eo dicente, quod legentes non invenimus.'[2]

[1] (In a note to ed. 1 (94), Stewart acknowledged inaccuracy in mentioning Oswald and Smith as school-fellows: 'the former was born in 1715; the latter in 1723. It appears, however, that their intimacy had commenced before Mr Smith went to the University.')

[2] (*Institutio Oratoria*, XI.iii.8: 'his speaking appears to have pleased in some manner, which we do not find in reading.')

Dr Hutcheson's Inquiry into our Ideas of Beauty and Virtue; his Discourse on the Passions; and his Illustrations of the Moral Sense, are much more strongly marked with the characteristical features of his genius, than his posthumous work. His great and deserved fame, however, in this country, rests *now* chiefly on the traditionary history of his academical lectures, which appear to have contributed very powerfully to diffuse, in Scotland, that taste for analytical discussion, and that spirit of liberal inquiry, to which the world is indebted for some of the most valuable productions of the eighteenth century.

Note (C.), p. 290

According to < John Gillies > the learned English translator of 'Aristotle's Ethics and Politics,' the general idea which runs through Mr Smith's Theory, was obviously borrowed from the following passage of Polybius: 'From the union of the two sexes, to which all are naturally inclined, children are born. When any of these, therefore, being arrived at perfect age, instead of yielding suitable returns of gratitude and assistance to those by whom they have been bred, on the contrary, attempt to injure them by words or actions, it is manifest that those who behold the wrong, after having also seen the sufferings and the anxious cares that were sustained by the parents in the nourishment and education of their children, must be greatly offended and displeased at such proceeding. For man, who among all the various kinds of animals is alone endowed with the faculty of reason, cannot, like the rest, pass over such actions: but will make reflection on what he sees; and comparing likewise the future with the present, will not fail to express his indignation at this injurious treatment; to which, as he foresees, he may also, at some time, be exposed. Thus again, when any one who has been succoured by another in the time of danger, instead of shewing the like kindness to this benefactor, endeavours at any time to destroy or hurt him; it is certain, that all men must be shocked by such ingratitude, through sympathy with the resentment of their neighbour; and from an apprehension also, that the case may be their own. And from hence arises, in the mind of every man, a certain *notion* of the nature and force of duty, in which consists both the beginning and the end of justice. In like manner, the man, who, in defence of others, is seen to throw himself the foremost into every danger, and even to sustain the fury of the fiercest animals, never fails to obtain the loudest acclamations of applause and veneration from all the multitude; while he who shews a different conduct is pursued with censure and reproach. And thus it is, that the people begin to discern the nature of things honourable and base, and in what consists the difference between them; and to perceive that the former, on account of the advantage that attends them, are fit to be admired and imitated, and the latter to be detested and avoided.'

'The doctrine' (says Dr Gillies) 'contained in this passage is expanded by Dr Smith into a theory of moral sentiments. But he departs from *his author*, in placing the perception of right and wrong, in sentiment or feeling, ultimately and simply.———Polybius, on the contrary, maintains with Aristotle, that these notions arise from reason, or intellect, operating on affection or appetite; or, in other words, that the moral faculty is a compound, and may be resolved into two simpler principles of the mind.'—(Gillies's Aristotle, Vol. I. pp. 302, 303, 2d Edit.)

The only expression I object to in the two preceding sentences, is the phrase, *his author*, which has the appearance of insinuating a charge of plagiarism against Mr Smith;—a charge which, I am confident, he did not deserve; and to which the above extract does not, in my opinion, afford any plausible colour. It exhibits, indeed, an instance of a curious coincidence between two philosophers in their views of the same subject; and as such, I have no doubt that Mr Smith himself would have remarked it, had it occurred to his memory, when he was writing his book. Of such accidental coincidences between different minds, examples present themselves every day to those, who, after having drawn from their internal resources all the lights they could supply on a particular question, have the curiosity to compare their own conclusions with those of their predecessors: And it is extremely worthy of observation, that, in proportion as any conclusion approaches to the truth, the number of previous approximations to it may be reasonably expected to be multiplied.

In the case before us, however, the question about originality is of little or no moment; for the peculiar merit of Mr Smith's work does not lie in his general principle, but in the skilful use he has made of it to give a systematical arrangement to the most important discussions and doctrines of Ethics. In this point of view, the Theory of Moral Sentiments may be justly regarded as one of the most original efforts of the human mind in that branch of science to which it relates; and even if we were to suppose that it was first suggested to the author by a remark of which the world was in possession for two thousand years before, this very circumstance would only reflect a stronger lustre on the novelty of his design, and on the invention and taste displayed in its execution.

I have said, in the text, that my own opinion about the foundation of morals does not agree with that of Mr Smith; and I propose to state, in another publication, the grounds of my dissent from his conclusions on that question.* At present, I shall only observe, that I consider the defects of his Theory as originating rather in a *partial*, than in a *mistaken* view of the subject; while, on some of the most essential points of ethics, it appears to me to approximate very nearly to a correct statement of the truth. I must not omit to add, in justice to the author, that his zeal to support his favourite system never has led him to vitiate or misrepresent the phenomena which he has employed it to explain; and that the connected order which he has given to a multiplicity of isolated facts, must facilitate greatly the studies of any of his successors, who may hereafter prosecute the same inquiry, agreeably to the severe rules of the inductive logic.

After the passage which I have quoted in the beginning of this note, I hope I shall be pardoned if I express my doubts, whether the learned and ingenious *ᵇwriterᵇ* has not, upon this, as well as on some other occasions,

ᵃ* Vide <*Stewart*>, *Works*, vol. vii, pp. 35, 36, 329, *seq.*, 407, *seq.*ᵃ

ᵃ⁻ᵃ added in 5
ᵇ⁻ᵇ author 5

allowed his partiality to the ancients to blind him a little too much to the merits of his contemporaries. Would not his laborious and interesting researches into the remains of the Greek philosophy, have been employed still more usefully in revealing to us the systems and discoveries to which our successors may yet lay claim, than in conjectures concerning the origin of those with which we are already acquainted? How does it happen that those men of profound erudition, who can so easily trace every *past* improvement to the fountain-head of antiquity, should not sometimes amuse themselves, and instruct the world, by anticipating the *future* progress of the human mind.

In studying the connection and *filiation* of successive Theories, when we are at a loss, in any instance, for a link to complete the continuity of philosophical speculation, it seems much more reasonable to search for it in the systems of the immediately preceding period, and in the inquiries which *then* occupied the public attention, than in detached sentences, or accidental expressions gleaned from the relics of distant ages. It is thus only, that we can hope to seize the precise point of view, in which an author's subject first presented itself to his attention; and to account, to our own satisfaction, from the particular aspect under which he saw it, for the subsequent direction which was given to his curiosity. In following such a plan, our object is not to detect plagiarisms, which we suppose men of genius to have intentionally concealed; but to fill up an apparent chasm in the history of Science, by laying hold of the thread which insensibly guided the mind from one station to another. By what easy and natural steps Mr Smith's Theory arose from the state of ethical discussion in Great Britain, when he began his literary career, I shall endeavour elsewhere to explain.[3]

A late author, of taste and learning, has written a pleasing and instructive essay on the *Marks of Poetical Imitation.* The marks of *Philosophical Plagiarism,* are not less discernible by an unprejudiced and discriminating eye; and are easily separable from that occasional similarity of thought and of illustration, which we may expect to meet with in writers of the most remote ages and countries, when employed in examining the same questions, or in establishing the same truths.

As the foregoing observations apply with fully as great force to the Wealth of Nations, as to the Theory of Moral Sentiments, I trust some allowance will be made for the length of this note.*

* I shall have occasion afterwards to vindicate Mr Smith's claims to originality in the former of these works, against the pretensions of some foreign writers. As I do not mean, however, to recur again to his alleged plagiarisms from the ancients, I shall introduce here, though somewhat out of place, two short quotations; from which it will appear, that the germ of his speculations concerning national wealth, as well as concerning the principles of ethics, is (according to Dr Gillies) to be found in the Greek philosophers.

'By adopting Aristotle's principles on the subjects of exchangeable value, and of national wealth, Dr Smith has rescued the science of political economy from many false subtilties and many gross errors.' Vol. I. p. 377, 2d edit.

'The subject of money is treated above, Vol. I. p. 374, *et seq.* In that passage, compared with another in the Magna Moralia, we find the fundamental principles of the modern economists.' Vol. II. p. 43.

In reply to these observations, I have only to request my readers to compare them with the well-

[3](See Stewart, *Works,* vi.412–14.)

^dNote (D.), p. 292

Extracted by Mr. Stewart from (John) Nichols's *Illustrations of the Literary History of the Eighteenth Century*, etc., Vol III (1818), pp. 515, 516; and appended in manuscript to one of his own copies of this *Memoir*. (Edinburgh University Library, MS. Df.4.52*.)

Dr. Adam Smith to Mr. George Baird[4]

Glasgow, February 7, 1763.

'DEAR SIR,—I have read over the contents of your friend's* work with very great pleasure; and heartily wish it was in my power to give, or to procure him all the encouragement which his ingenuity and industry deserve. I think myself greatly obliged to him for the very obliging notice he has been pleased to take of me, and should be glad to contribute anything in my power towards completing his design. I approve greatly of his plan for a Rational Grammar, and am convinced that a work of this kind, executed with his abilities and industry, may prove not only the best system of grammar, but the best system of logic in any language, as well as the best history of the natural progress of the human mind in forming the most important abstractions upon which all reasoning depends. From the short abstract which Mr. Ward has been so good as to send me, it is impossible for me to form any very decisive judgement concerning the propriety of every part of his method, particularly of some of his divisions. If I was to treat the same subject, I should endeavour to begin with the consideration of *verbs*; these being, in my apprehension, the original parts of speech, first invented to express in one word a complete event: I should then have endeavoured to show how the subject was divided from the attribute; and afterwards, how the object was distinguished from both; and in this manner I should have tried to investigate the origin and use of all the different parts of speech, and of all their different modifications, considered as necessary to express all the different qualifications and relations of any single event. Mr. Ward, however, may have excellent reasons for following his own method; and, perhaps, if I was engaged in the same task, I should find it necessary to follow the same,—things frequently appearing in a very different light when taken in a general view, which is the only view that I can pretend to have taken of them, and when considered in detail.

known passage in the first book of Aristotle's Politics, with respect to the lawfulness of usury. When we consider how much the interest of money enters as an element into all our modern disquisitions concerning commercial policy, is it possible to imagine, that there should be any thing more than the most general and fortuitous coincidence between the reasonings of such writers as Smith, or Hume, or Turgot; and those of an author whose experience of the nature and effects of commerce was so limited, as to impress his mind with a conviction, that to receive a *premium* for the use of money was inconsistent with the rules of morality? ^cCompare the subsequent edition of Gillies's *Ethics and Politics of Aristotle.*^c

* Probably William Ward, A.M. master of the Grammar School of Beverley, Yorkshire, who, among other grammatical works, published *An Essay on Grammar as it may be applied to the English Language, in two Treatises*, etc., 4to, 1765, which is perhaps the most philosophical Essay on the English language extant.

^{c—c} *added in 5*
^d *This Note was added in 5*

[4] (Corr., Letter 69.)

Mr. Ward, when he mentions the definitions which different authors have given of nouns substantive, takes no notice of that of the Abbé Girard, the author of a book called *Les vrais Principes de la Langue Française*, which made me think it might be possible he had not seen it. It is a book which first set me a thinking upon these subjects, and I have received more instruction from it than from any other I have yet seen upon them. If Mr. Ward has not seen it, I have it at his service. The grammatical articles, too, in the French *Encyclopédie* have given me a good deal of entertainment. Very probably Mr. Ward has seen both these works, and, as he may have considered the subject more than I have done, may think less of them. Remember me to Mrs. Baird, and Mr. Oswald; and believe me to be, with great truth, dear Sir, sincerely yours,

(Signed) ADAM SMITH.'

*e*Note (E.), p. 302

I ought to have mentioned, among the number of Mr. Smith's friends at Paris, the Abbé Morellet, of whom I have frequently heard him speak with much respect. But his name, with which I was not then very well acquainted, happened to escape my recollection while writing this *Memoir*; nor was I at all aware that they had been so well known to each other, as I have since learned that they were. On this subject I might quote the Abbé Morellet himself, of whom I had the pleasure to see much in the year 1806; but I prefer a reference to his own words, which coincide exactly with what he stated to myself. 'J'avais connu Smith dans un voyage qu'il avait fait en France, vers 1762; il parlait fort mal notre langue; mais *La Théorie des Sentimens Moraux*, publiée en 1758, m'avait donné une grande idée de sa sagacité et de sa profondeur. Et véritablement je le regarde encore aujourd'hui comme un des hommes qui a fait les observations et les analyses les plus complètes dans toutes les questions qu'il a traitées. M. Turgot, qui aimait ainsi que moi la métaphysique, estimait beaucoup son talent. Nous le vîmes plusieurs fois; il fut présenté chez Helvétius; nous parlâmes de la théorie commerciale, banque, crédit public, et de plusieurs points du grand ouvrage qu'il méditait.'—*Mémoires de l'Abbé Morellet*, Tome I. p. 257, (Paris, 1821).

Note (F.), p. 303

The Theory of Moral Sentiments does not seem to have attracted so much notice in France as might have been expected, till after the publication of the Wealth of Nations. Mr Smith used to ascribe this in part to the Abbé Blavet's translation, which he thought was but indifferently executed. A better reason, however, may perhaps be found in the low and stationary condition of Ethical and Metaphysical science in that country, previous to the publication of the *Encyclopédie*. On this head I beg leave to transcribe a few sentences from an anonymous paper of his own, printed in the

---

e *This Note was added in 5* (It was appended in manuscript to one of Stewart's own copies of this *Memoir*: Edinburgh University Library, MS. Df.4.52*. See the editor's Introduction, 267–8, above.)

Edinburgh Review for the year 1755. The remarks contained in them, so far as they are admitted to be just, tend strongly to confirm an observation which I have elsewhere quoted from D'Alembert, with respect to the literary taste of his countrymen. (See Philosophical Essays, pp. 110–111.) ⌠Part I, Essay iii; <Stewart>, *Works* Vol.V. p. 126.⌡

'The original and inventive genius of the English, has not only discovered itself in Natural Philosophy, but in morals, metaphysics, and part of the abstract sciences. Whatever attempts have been made in modern times towards improvement in this contentious and unprosperous philosophy, beyond what the ancients have left us, have been made in England. The meditations of Des Cartes excepted, I know nothing in French that aims at being original on that subject; for the philosophy of M. Regis, as well as that of Father Malebranche, are but refinements on the meditations of Des Cartes. But Mr Hobbes, Mr Locke, and Dr Mandeville, Lord Shaftesbury, Dr Butler, Dr Clarke, and Mr Hutcheson, have all of them, according to their different and inconsistent systems, endeavoured at least, to be, in some measure, original; and to add something to that stock of observations with which the world had been furnished before them. This branch of the English Philosophy, which seems now to be entirely neglected by the English themselves, has, *of late*, been transported into France. I observe some traces of it, not only in the *Encyclopédie*, but in the Theory of agreeable sentiments by M. de Pouilly, a work that is in many respects original; and above all, in the late Discourse upon the origin and foundation of the inequality amongst mankind, by M. Rousseau of Geneva.'

A new translation of Mr Smith's Theory, (including his last additions), was published at Paris in 1798 by Madame de Condorcet, with some ingenious letters on Sympathy annexed to it, written by the translator.

Note (G.), p. 309

By way of explanation of what is hinted at in the foot-note, p. 309, I think it proper for me *now* to add, that at the period when this memoir was read before the Royal Society of Edinburgh, it was not unusual, even among men of some talents and information, to confound, studiously, the speculative doctrines of Political Economy, with those discussions concerning the first principles of Government which happened unfortunately at that time to agitate the public mind.[5] The doctrine of a Free Trade was itself represented as of a revolutionary tendency; and some who had formerly prided themselves on their intimacy with Mr. Smith, and on their zeal for the propagation of his liberal system, began to call in question the expediency of subjecting to the disputations of philosophers, the arcana of State Policy, and the unfathomable wisdom of the feudal ages. In reprinting this Section at present, I have, from obvious motives, followed scrupulously the text of the first edition, without any alterations or additions whatsoever; reserving any comments and criticisms which I have to offer on Mr. Smith's work, for a different publication. (1810.)

⌠–⌡ *added in* 5

[5] (See John Veitch, 'Memoir of Stewart', in Stewart, *Works*, x. lxx–lxxv.)

Note (H.), p. 320

Notwithstanding the unqualified praise I have bestowed, in the text, on Mr Smith's arrangement, I readily admit, that some of his incidental discussions and digressions might have been more skilfully and happily incorporated with his general design. Little stress, however, will be laid on blemishes of this sort, by those who are aware of the extreme difficulty of giving any thing like a systematic shape to researches so various, and, at first view, so unconnected, as his plan embraces:—Some of them having for their aim to establish abstract principles of universal application; and others bearing a particular reference to the circumstances and policy of our own country.——It ought to be remembered, besides, how much our taste, in matters of arrangement, is liable to be influenced by our individual habits of thought; by the accidental conduct of our early studies; and by other circumstances which may be expected to present the same objects under different aspects to different inquirers. Something of this kind is experienced even in those more exact Sciences, where the whole business of an elementary writer is to state known and demonstrated truths, in a logical and pleasing series. It has been experienced most remarkably in pure geometry, the elements of which have been modelled into a hundred different forms by the first mathematicians of modern Europe; while none of them has yet been able to unite the suffrages of the public in favour of any one arrangement as indisputably the best. What allowances, then, are those entitled to, who, venturing upon a vast and untrodden field, aspire to combine with the task of original speculation, a systematical regard to luminous method, if they should sometimes happen to mistake the historical order of their own conclusions for the natural procedure of the human understanding!

Note (I.), p. 321*

When this memoir was first written, I was not fully aware to what an extent the French Economists had been anticipated in some of their most important conclusions, by writers (chiefly British) of a much earlier date. I had often, indeed, been struck with the coincidence between their reasonings concerning the advantages of their territorial tax, and Mr Locke's speculations on the same subject, in one of his political discourses published sixty years before; as well as with the coincidence of their argument against corporations and exclusive companies, with what had been urged at a still earlier period, by the celebrated John de Witt; by Sir Josiah Child; by John Cary of Bristol; and by various other speculative men, who appeared in the latter part of the seventeenth century. To these last writers, my attention had been directed by some quotations and references of the Abbé Morellet, in his very able Memoir on the East India Company of France, printed in 1769. Many passages, however, much more full and explicit than those

---

*g** In regard to Adam Smith's originality on various points of Political Economy, I may refer, in general, to Vols. VIII and IX (of Stewart's *Works*), in which Mr. Stewart's *Lectures* on this science are contained. See also in Vol. IX, art. *Smith, Adam*, etc., of the *Index.g*

g—g added in 5

which had fallen in his way, have been pointed out to me by the Earl of Lauderdale, in his curious and valuable collection of rare English Tracts relating to political economy. In some of these, the argument is stated in a manner so clear and so conclusive, as to render it surprising, that truths of which the public has been so long in possession, should have been so completely overborne by prejudice and misrepresentation, as to have had, to a large proportion of readers, the appearance of novelty and paradox, when revived in the philosophical theories of the present age*.

The system of political economy which professes to regulate the commercial intercourse of different nations, and which Mr Smith has distinguished by the title of the Commercial, or Mercantile System, had its root in prejudices still more inveterate than those which restrained the freedom of commerce and industry among the members of the same community. It was supported not only by the prejudices with which all innovations have to contend, and by the talents of very powerful bodies of men interested to defend it, but by the mistaken and clamorous patriotism of many good citizens, and their blind hostility to supposed enemies or rivals abroad. The absurd and delusive principles, too, formerly so prevalent, with respect to the nature of national wealth, and the essential importance of a favourable balance of trade (principles which, though now so clearly and demonstrably exploded by the arguments of Mr Smith, must be acknowledged to fall in naturally, and almost inevitably, with the first apprehensions of the mind when it begins to speculate concerning the Theory of Commerce), communicated to the Mercantile System a degree of plausibility, against which the most acute reasoners of our own times are not always sufficiently on their guard. It was accordingly, at a considerably later period, that the wisdom of its maxims came to be the subject of general discussion; and, even at this day, the controversy to which the discussion gave rise cannot be said to be completely settled, to the satisfaction of all parties. A few enlightened individuals, however, in different parts of Europe, very early got a glimpse of the truth†; and it is but justice, that the scattered hints which they threw out should be treasured up as materials for literary history. I have sometimes thought of attempting a slight sketch on that subject myself; but am not without hopes that this suggestion may have the effect of recommending the task to some abler hand. At present, I shall only quote

---

* That the writers of this Island should have had the start of those in the greater part of Europe, in adopting enlightened ideas concerning commerce, will not appear surprising, when we consider that 'according to the Common Law of England, the freedom of trade is the birthright of the subject.' For the opinions of Lord Coke and of Lord Chief-Justice Fortescue, on this point, see a pamphlet by Lord Lauderdale, entitled, 'Hints to the Manufacturers of Great Britain,' etc. (printed in 1805); where also may be found a list of statutes containing recognitions and declarations of the above principle.

† According to the statement of Lord Herbert of Cherbury, the following doctrine was delivered in the English House of Commons by Sir Thomas More (then speaker), almost three centuries ago. 'I say confidently, you need not fear this penury or scarceness of money; the intercourse of things being so establish'd throughout the whole world, that there is a perpetual derivation of all that can be necessary to mankind. Thus, your commodities will ever find out money; while, not to go far, I shall produce our own merchants only, who, (let me assure you) will be always as glad of your corn and cattel as you can be of any thing they bring you.'—The Life and Reign of King Henry the Eighth, London, 1672, p. 135.

It is not a little discouraging to reflect, that the mercantile prejudice here combated by this great man, has not yet yielded entirely to all the philosophical lights of the 18th century.

one or two paragraphs from a pamphlet published in 1734, by Jacob Vanderlint*; an author whose name has been frequently referred to of late years, but whose book never seems to have attracted much notice till long after the publication of the Wealth of Nations. He describes himself, in his Preface, as an *ordinary tradesman, from whom the conciseness and accuracy of a scholar* is not to be expected; and yet the following passages will bear a comparison, both in point of good sense and of liberality, with what was so ably urged by Mr Hume twenty years afterwards, in his Essay on the Jealousy of Trade.

'All nations have some commodities peculiar to them, which, therefore, are undoubtedly designed to be the foundation of commerce between the several nations, and produce a great deal of maritime employment for mankind, which probably, without such peculiarities, could not be; and in this respect, I suppose, we are distinguished, as well as other nations; and I have before taken notice, that if one nation be by nature more distinguished in this respect than another, as they will, by that means, gain more money than such other nations, so the prices of all their commodities and labour will be higher in such proportion, and consequently, they will not be richer or more powerful for having more money than their neighbours.

'But, if we import any kind of goods cheaper than we can now raise them, which otherwise might be as well raised at home; in this case, undoubtedly, we ought to attempt to raise such commodities, and thereby furnish so many new branches of employment and trade for our own people; and remove the inconvenience of receiving any goods from abroad, which we can anywise raise on as good terms ourselves: and, as this should be done to prevent every nation from finding their account with us by any such commodities whatsoever, so this would more effectually shut out all such foreign goods than any law can do.

'And as this is all the prohibitions and restraints whereby any foreign trade should be obstructed, so, if this method were observed, our gentry would find themselves the richer, notwithstanding their consumption of such other foreign goods, as being the peculiarities of other nations, we may be obliged to import. For if, when we have thus raised all we can at home, the goods we import after this is done be cheaper than we can raise such goods ourselves, (which they must be, otherwise we shall not import them), it is plain, the consumption of any such goods cannot occasion so great an expence as they would, if we could shut them out by an act of parliament, in order to raise them ourselves.

'From hence, therefore, it must appear, that it is impossible any body should be poorer, for using any foreign goods at cheaper rates than we can raise them ourselves, after we have done all we possibly can to raise such goods as cheap as we import them, and find we cannot do it; nay, this very circumstance makes all such goods come under the character of the *peculiarities* of those countries, which are able to raise any such goods cheaper than we can do; for they will necessarily operate as such.'—(pp. 97, 98, 99.)

The same author, in another part of his work, quotes from Erasmus Philips, a maxim which he calls a *glorious one*: 'That a trading nation should

* 'Money Answers all Things,' etc. etc. London, 1734.

be an open warehouse, where the merchant may buy what he pleases, and sell what he can. Whatever is brought to you, if you don't want it, you won't purchase it; if you do want it, the largeness of the impost don't keep it from you.'

'All nations of the world, therefore,' (says Vanderlint) 'should be regarded as one body of tradesmen, exercising their various occupations for the mutual benefit and advantage of each other.'—(p. 42.) 'I will not contend,' (he adds, evidently in compliance with national prejudices,) 'I will not contend for a free and unrestrained trade with respect to France, though I can't see it could do us any harm even in that case.'—(p. 45.)

In these last sentences, an argument is suggested for a free commerce all over the globe, founded on the same principle on which Mr Smith has demonstrated the beneficial effects of a division and distribution of labour among the members of the same community. The happiness of the whole race would, in fact, be promoted by the former arrangement, in a manner exactly analogous to that in which the comforts of a particular nation are multiplied by the latter.

In the same Essay, Mr. Vanderlint, following the footsteps of Locke, maintains, with considerable ingenuity, the noted doctrine of the Economists, that all taxes fall ultimately on land; and recommends the substitution of a land-tax, in place of those complicated fiscal regulations, which have been everywhere adopted by the statesmen of modern Europe; and which, while they impoverish and oppress the people, do not, in the same degree, enrich the sovereign*.

The doctrine which more exclusively distinguishes this celebrated sect, is neither that of the freedom of trade, nor of the territorial tax, (on both of which topics they had been, in part, anticipated by English writers), but what they have so ingeniously and forcibly urged, with respect to the tendency of the existing regulations and restraints, to encourage the industry of towns in preference to that of the country. To revive the languishing agriculture of France was the first and the leading aim of their speculations; and it is impossible not to admire the metaphysical acuteness and subtlety, with which all their various discussions are so combined as to bear systematically upon this favourite object. The influence of their labours in turning the attention of French statesmen, under the old monarchy, to the encouragement of this essential branch of national industry, was remarked by Mr Smith more than thirty years ago; nor has it altogether ceased to

---

* Lord Lauderdale has traced some hints of what are commonly considered as the peculiarities of the economical system, in various British publications now almost forgotten. The following extract, from a Treatise published by Mr Asgill, in 1696, breathes the very spirit of Quesnay's philosophy.

'What we call commodities is nothing but land severed from the soil. Man deals in nothing but earth. The merchants are the factors of the world, to exchange one part of the earth for another. The king himself is fed by the labour of the ox: and the clothing of the army, and victualling of the navy, must all be paid for to the owner of the soil as the ultimate receiver. All things in the world are originally the produce of the ground, and there must all things be raised.'—(Inquiry into the Nature and Origin of Public Wealth, p. 113.)

The title of Asgill's Treatise is, 'Several assertions proved, in order to create another species of Money than Gold.' Its object was to support Dr Chamberlayne's proposition for a Land Bank, which he laid before the English House of Commons in 1693, and before the Scottish Parliament in 1703.

operate in the same direction, under all the violent and fantastic metamorphoses which the government of that country has since exhibited*.

In combating the policy of commercial privileges, and in asserting the reciprocal advantages of a free trade among different nations, the founders of the economical sect candidly acknowledged, from the beginning, that their first lights were borrowed from England. The testimony of M. Turgot upon this point is so perfectly decisive, that I hope to gratify some of my readers (in the present interrupted state of our communication with the continent), by the following quotations from a memoir, which, till lately, was very little known, even in France. They are transcribed from his Eloge on M. Vincent de Gournay; a name which has always been united with that of Quesnay, by the French writers who have attempted to trace the origin and progress of the *now* prevailing opinions on this branch of legislation.— (Oeuvres de M. Turgot, Tome III. Paris, 1808.)

'JEAN-CLAUDE-MARIE VINCENT, Seigneur DE GOURNAY, etc. est mort à Paris le 27. Juin dernier (1759) âgé de quarante sept ans.

'Il etoit né à Saint-Malo, au moi de Mai 1712, de Claude VINCENT, l'un des plus considérables négocians de cette ville, et secrétaire du roi.

'Ses parens le destinèrent au commerce, et l'envoyèrent à Cadix en 1729, à peine âgé de dix sept ans.'—(p. 321.)

'Aux lumières que M. de Gournay tiroit de sa propre expérience et de ses réflexions, il joignit la lecture des meilleurs ouvrages que possèdent sur cette matière les différentes nations de l'Europe, *et en particulier la nation Angloise, la plus riche de toutes en ce genre, et dont il s'étoit rendu, pour cette raison, la langue familière.* Les ouvrages qu'il lut avec plus de plaisir, et dont il goûta le plus la doctrine, furent les traités du fameux Josias Child, qu'il a traduits depuis en François, et les mémoires du Grand Pensionnaire Jean de Witt. On sait que ces deux grands hommes sont considérés, l'un en Angleterre, l'autre en Hollande, comme les législateurs du commerce; que leurs principes sont devenus les principes nationaux, et que l'observation de ces principes est regardée comme une des sources de la prodigieuse supériorité que ces deux nations ont acquise dans le commerce sur toutes les autres puissances. M. de Gournay trouvoit sans cesse dans la pratique d'un commerce étendu la vérification de ces principes simples et lumineux, il se les rendoit propres sans prévoir qu'il étoit destiné à en repandre un jour la lumière en France, et à mériter de sa patrie le même tribut de reconnoissance, que l'Angleterre et la Hollande rendent à la mémoire de ces deux bienfaiteurs de leur nation et de l'humanité.'—(pp. 324, 325.)

'M. de Gournay, après avoir quitté l'Espagne, prit la resolution d'employer quelques années à voyager dans les différentes parties de l'Europe, soit pour augmenter ses connoissances, soit pour étendre ses correspondances et former des liaisons avantageuses pour le commerce, qu'il se proposoit de continuer. Il voyagea à Hambourg; il parcourut la Hollande et l'Angleterre; partout il faisoit des observations et rassembloit des mémoires sur l'état du commerce et de la marine, et sur les principes d'administration adoptés par ces différentes nations relativement à ces grands objets. Il entretenoit

---

* It is but justice to the Economists to add, that they have laid more stress than any other class of writers whatsoever, on the principles of political economy, considered in their connection with the intellectual and moral character of a people.

pendant ses voyages une correspondance suivie avec M. de Maurepas, auquel il faisoit part des lumières qui'il recueilloit.'—(pp. 325, 326.)

'M. de Gournay acheta, en 1749, une charge de conseiller au grand conseil; et une place d'intendant du commerce etant venue à vâquer au commencement de 1751, M. de Machault, à qui le mérite de M. de Gournay etoit très-connu, la lui fit donner. C'est de ce moment que la vie de M. de Gournay devint celle d'un homme public: son entrée au Bureau du commerce parut être l'epoque d'une révolution. M. de Gournay, dans une pratique de vingt ans du commerce le plus étendu et le plus varié, *dans la fréquentation des plus habiles négocians de Hollande et d'Angleterre, dans la lecture des auteurs les plus estimés de ces deux nations, dans l'observation attentive des causes de leur étonnante prospérité,* s'êtoit fait des principes qui parurent nouveaux à quelques-uns des magistrats qui composoient le Bureau du Commerce.'—(pp. 327, 328.)

'M. de Gournay n'ignoroit pas que plusieurs des abus auxquels il s'opposoit, avoient été autrefois établis dans une grande partie de l'Europe, et qu'il en restoit même encore des vestiges en Angleterre; mais il savoit aussi que le gouvernement Anglois en avoit détruit une partie; que s'il en restoit encore quelques-unes, bien loin de les adopter comme des établissemens utiles, il cherchoit à les restreindre, à les empêcher de s'étendre, et ne les tóleroit encore, que parceque la constitution républicaine met quelquefois des obstacles à la réformation de certains abus, lorsque ces abus ne peuvent être corrigés que par une autorité dont l'exercice le plus avantageux au peuple excite toujours sa défiance. *Il savoit enfin que depuis un siècle toutes les personnes éclairées, soit en Hollande, soit en Angleterre, regardoient ces abus comme des restes de la barbarie Gothique et de la foiblesse de tous les gouvernemens qui n'avoient ni connu l'importance de la liberté publique, ni su la protéger des invasions de l'esprit monopoleur et de l'intérêt particulier*.*

'M. de Gournay avoit fait et vu faire, pendant vingt ans, le plus grand commerce de l'univers sans avoir eu occasion d'apprendre autrement que par les livres l'existence de toutes ces loix auxquelles il voyoit attacher tant

---

* Some of these liberal principles found their way into France before the end of the 17th century.—See a very curious book entitled, *Le Détail de la France sous le Règne Présent.* The first edition (which I have never met with), appeared in 1698 or 1699; the second was printed in 1707. Both editions are anonymous; but the author is well known to have been M. de Bois-Guilbert; to whom Voltaire has also (erroneously) ascribed the *Projet d'une dixme Royale,* published in the name of the Maréchal de Vauban. (See the Ephémérides du Citoyen for the year 1769, Tome IX. pp. 12, 13.)

The fortunate expression, *laissez nous faire,* which an old merchant (Le Gendre) is said to have used in a conversation with Colbert; and the still more significant maxim of the Marquis d'Argenson, *pas trop gouverner,* are indebted chiefly for that proverbial celebrity which they have now acquired, to the accidental lustre reflected upon them by the discussions of more modern times. They must, at the same time, be allowed to evince in their authors, a clear perception of the importance of a problem, which Mr Burke has somewhere pronounced to be '*one of the finest in legislation;—to ascertain, what the state ought to take upon itself to direct by the public wisdom; and what it ought to leave, with as little interference as possible, to individual discretion.*' [6] The solution of this problem, in some of its most interesting cases, may be regarded as one of the principal objects of Mr Smith's Inquiry; and, among the many happy changes which that work has gradually produced in prevailing opinions, none is, perhaps, of greater consequence, than its powerful effect in discrediting that empirical spirit of tampering Regulation, which the multitude is so apt to mistake for the provident sagacity of political experience.

[6] (The reference to Burke is to his 'Thoughts and Details on Scarcity', originally presented to the Right Hon. William Pitt (1795). *Works* (1802), iv.287.)

d'importance, et il ne croyoit point alors qu'on le prendroit pour un *novateur* et un *homme à systêmes*, lorsqu' il ne feroit que développer les principes que l'experience lui avoit enseignés, et qu'il voyoit universellement reconnus par les négocians les plus éclairés avec lesquels il vivoit.

'Ces principes, qu'on qualifioit de *systême nouveau*, ne lui paroissoient que les maximes du plus simple bon sens. Tout ce prétendu *systême* étoit appuyé sur cette maxime, qu'en general tout homme connoit mieux son propre intérêt qu'un autre homme à qui cet intérêt est entièrement indifférent*.

'De là M. de Gournay concluoit, que lorsque l'intérêt des particuliers est précisément le même que l'intérêt general, ce qu'on peut faire de mieux est de laisser chaque homme libre de faire ce qu'il veut.—Or il trouvoit impossible que dans le commerce abandonné à lui-meme, l'intérêt particulier ne concourût pas avec l'intérêt général.'—(pp. 334, 335, 336.)

In mentioning M. de Gournay's opinion on the subject of taxation, M. Turgot does not take any notice of the source from which he derived it. But on *this* head (whatever may be thought of the justness of that opinion) there can be no doubt among those who are acquainted with the writings of Locke and of Vanderlint. 'Il pensoit' (says Turgot) 'que tous les impôts, sont en derniere analyse, toujours payés par le propriétaire, qui vend d'autant moins les produits de sa terre, et que si tous les impôts étoient répartis sur les fonds, les propriétaires et le royaume y gagneroient tout ce qu' absorbent les fraix de régie, toute la consommation ou l'emploi stérile des hommes perdus, soit à percevoir les impôts, soit à faire la contrebande, soit à l'empecher, sans compter la prodigieuse augmentation des richesses et des valeurs résultantes de l'augmentation du commerce.'—(pp. 350, 351.)

In a note upon this passage by the Editor, this project of a territorial tax, together with that of a free trade, are mentioned among the most important points in which Gournay and Quesnay agreed perfectly together†: and it is not a little curious, that the same two doctrines should have been combined together as parts of the same system, in the Treatise of Vanderlint, published almost twenty years before.‡

* I have endeavoured, in a former work, to vindicate, upon the very same principle, some of Mr Smith's political speculations against the charge of being founded rather on theory than on actual experience. I was not aware, till very lately, that this view of the subject had been sanctioned by such high authorities as M. de Gournay and M. Turgot.—See Philosophy of the Human Mind, pp. 254, 255, 256, 3d edit. ʰchap. iv §8: < Stewart >, *Works*, Vol. II. p. 235 *seq.*ʰ

† Ceci est, avec la liberté du commerce et du travail, un des principaux points sur lesquels M. de Gournay et M. Quesnay ont été complettement d'accord.

‡ I have already quoted, from Vanderlint, his opinion about the freedom of trade. His ideas with respect to taxation I shall also state in his own words: 'I can't dismiss this head without shewing, that if all the taxes were taken off goods, and levied on lands and houses only, the gentlemen would have more *nett rent* left out of their estates, than they have now when the taxes are almost wholly levied on goods.' For his argument in proof of this proposition, see his Essay on Money, p. 109, *et seq.* See also Locke's Considerations on the lowering of interest and raising the Value of Money; published in 1691.

As to the *discovery* (as it has been called) of the *luminous distinction between the 'produit total' and the 'produit net de la culture*§,' it is not worth while to dispute about its author. Whatever merit this theory of taxation may possess, the whole credit of it evidently belongs to those who first proposed the doctrine stated in the foregoing paragraph. The calculations of M. Quesnay, however interesting and useful they may have appeared in a country where so great a proportion of the territory was cultivated by *Métayers* or *Coloni Partiarii*, cannot surely be considered as throwing any new light on the general principles of Political Economy.

§ See the Ephémérides du Citoyen for the year 1769, T.I. pp. 13, 25 and 26, and T.IX. p. 9.

ʰ⁻ʰ *added in 5*

It does not appear from Turgot's account of M. de Gournay, that any of his original works were ever published; nor have I heard that he was known even in the capacity of a translator, prior to 1752. 'Il eut le bonheur' (says M. Turgot) 'de rencontrer dans M. Trudaine, le même amour de la vérité et du bien public qui l'animoit; comme il n'avoit encore développé ses principes que par occasion, dans la discussion des affaires ou dans la conversation, M. Trudaine l'engagea à donner comme une espèce de corps de sa doctrine; et c'est dans cette vue qu'il a traduit, en 1752, les traités sur le commerce et sur l'intérêt de l'argent, de Josias Child et de Thomas Culpepper.'—(p. 354.) I quote this passage, because it enables me to correct an inaccuracy in point of dates, which has excaped the learned and ingenious writer to whom we are indebted for the first complete edition which has yet appeared of Turgot's works. After dividing the Economists into two schools, that of Gournay, and that of Quesnay, he classes under the former denomination (among some other very illustrious names), Mr David Hume; whose Political Discourses, I must take the liberty of remarking, were published as early as 1752, the very year when M. Gournay published his translations of Child and of Culpepper.

The same writer afterwards adds: 'Entre ces deux écoles, profitant de l'une et de l'autre, mais évitant avec soin de paroître tenir à aucune, se sont élevés quelques philosophes éclectiques, à la tête desquels il faut placer M. Turgot, l'Abbé de Condillac, et le célèbre Adam Smith; et parmi lesquels on doit compter très-honorablement le traducteur de celui-ci, M. le Sénateur Germain Garnier, en Angleterre my Lord Landsdown, à Paris M. Say. à Genève M. Simonde.'

How far Mr Smith has availed himself of the writings of the Economists in his Wealth of Nations, it is not my present business to examine. All that I wish to establish is, his indisputable claim to the same opinions which he professed in common with them, several years before the names of either Gournay or of Quesnay were at all heard of in the republic of letters.

With respect to a very distinguished and enlightened English statesman,[7] who is here included along with Mr Smith among the *eclectic* disciples of Gournay and of Quesnay, I am enabled to state, from his own authority, the accidental circumstance which first led him into this train of thought. In a letter which I had the honour to receive from his Lordship in 1795, he expresses himself thus:

'I owe to a journey I made with Mr Smith from Edinburgh to London, the difference between light and darkness through the best part of my life. The novelty of his principles, added to my youth and prejudices, made me unable to comprehend them at the time, but he urged them with so much benevolence, as well as eloquence, that they took a certain hold, which, though it did not develope itself so as to arrive at full conviction for some few years after, I can fairly say, has constituted, ever since, the happiness of my life, as well as any little consideration I may have enjoyed in it.'

As the current of public opinion, at a particular period (or at least the prevailing habits of study), may be pretty accurately judged of by the books which were *then* chiefly in demand, it may be worth mentioning, before I conclude this note, that in the year 1751 (the same year in which Mr Smith

[7] (First Marquess of Lansdowne and second Earl of Shelburne.)

was promoted to his professorship), several of our choicest tracts on subjects connected with political economy were re-published by Robert and Andrew Foulis, printers to the University of Glasgow. A book of Mr Law's entitled, Proposals and Reasons for constituting a Council of Trade in Scotland, etc. reprinted in that year, is now lying before me; from which it appears, that the following works had recently issued from the university press:—Child's Discourse of Trade; Law's Essay on Money and Trade; Gee's Trade and Navigation of Great Britain considered; and Berkeley's Querist. In the same list, Sir William Petty's Political Arithmetic is advertised as being then *in the press.*

Mr Smith's Lectures, it must be remembered (to the fame of which he owed his appointment at Glasgow), were read at Edinburgh as early as 1748.

Note (J.), p. 323

Among the questionable doctrines to which Mr Smith has lent the sanction of his name, there is perhaps none that involves so many important consequences as the opinion he has maintained concerning the expediency of legal restrictions on the rate of interest. The inconclusiveness of his reasoning on this point, has been evinced, with a singular degree of logical acuteness, by Mr Bentham, in a short treatise entitled *A Defence of Usury*;[8] a performance to which (notwithstanding the long interval that has elapsed since the date of its publication), I do not know that any answer has yet been attempted; and which a late writer, eminently acquainted with the operations of commerce, has pronounced (and, in my opinion, with great truth), to be 'perfectly unanswerable*.' It is a remarkable circumstance, that Mr Smith should, in this solitary instance, have adopted, on such slight grounds, a conclusion so strikingly contrasted with the general spirit of his political discussions, and so manifestly at variance with the fundamental principles which, on other occasions, he has so boldly followed out, through all their practical applications. This is the more surprising, as the French Economists had, a few years before, obviated the most plausible objections which are apt to present themselves against this extension of the doctrine of commercial freedom. See, in particular, some observations in M. Turgot's Reflections on the Formation and Distribution of Riches; and a separate Essay, by the same author, entitled, 'Mémoire sur le prêt à interêt, et sur le Commerce des Fers†.'

* Sir Francis Baring. Pamphlet on the Bank of England. (The full title of this work is: *Observations on the Establishment of the Bank of England*, 1797.)

† In an Essay read before a literary society in Glasgow, some years before the publication of the Wealth of Nations, Dr Reid disputed the expediency of legal restrictions on the rate of interest; founding his opinion on some of the same considerations which were afterwards so forcibly stated by Mr Bentham. His attention had probably been attracted to this question by a very weak defence of these restrictions in Sir James Stewart's Political Economy; a book which had then been recently published, and which (though he differed widely from many of its doctrines), he was accustomed, in his academical lectures, to recommend warmly to his students. It was indeed the only systematical work on the subject that had appeared in our language, previous to Mr Smith's Inquiry.

[Sir James Steuart's *Principles* was first published in 1767. The defence of regulation of the rate of interest will be found in Book IV, Part I, especially chapters 5 and 6. Dugald Stewart

8 (Corr., Appendix C, 'Bentham's Letters to Adam Smith', 386–404.)

Upon this particular question, however, as well as upon those mentioned in the preceding Note, I must be allowed to assert the prior claims of our own countrymen to those of the Economists. From a memoir presented by the celebrated Mr Law (before his elevation to the ministry), to the Regent Duke of Orleans, that very ingenious writer appears to have held the same opinion with M. Turgot; and the arguments he employs in support of it are expressed with that clearness and conciseness which, in general, distinguish his compositions. The memoir to which I refer is to be found in a French work entitled, *Recherches et Considérations sur les Finances de France, depuis* 1595 *jusqu'en* 1721. (See Vol. VI. p. 181. Edit. printed at Liège, 1758.) In the same volume, this doctrine is ascribed by the editor, to Mr Law as its author, or, at least, as its first broacher in France. '*Une opinion apportée en France pour la première fois par M. Law,* c'est que l'etat ne doit jamais donner de réglemens sur le taux de l'interêt.'—p. 64.

To this opinion Law appears evidently to have been led by Locke, whose reasonings (although he himself declares in favour of a legal rate of interest), seem, all of them, to point at the opposite conclusion. Indeed the apology he suggests for the existing regulations is so trifling and so slightly urged, that one would almost suppose he was prevented merely by a respect for established prejudices, from pushing his argument to its full extent. The passage I allude to, considering the period when it was written, does no small credit to Locke's sagacity.—(See the folio edit. of his Works < 1714 >, Vol. II. p. 31, et seq.)

_____

I would not have entered here into the historical details contained in the two last Notes, if I had not been anxious to obviate the effect of that weak, but inveterate prejudice which shuts the eyes of so many against the most manifest and important truths, when they are supposed to proceed from an obnoxious quarter. The leading opinions which the French Economists embodied and systematized were, in fact, all of British origin; and most of them follow as necessary consequences, from a maxim of natural law, which (according to Lord Coke), is identified with the first principles of English jurisprudence. '*La loi de la liberté entière de tout commerce est un corollaire du droit de propriété.*'

The truly exceptionable part of the economical system (as I have elsewhere remarked), is that which relates to the power of the Sovereign. Its original authors and patrons were the decided opposers of political liberty, and, in their zeal for the right of property and the freedom of commerce, lost sight of the only means by which either the one or the other can be effectually protected.

Note (K.), p. 326

In the early part of Mr Smith's life it is well known to his friends, that he was for several years attached to a young lady of great beauty and

recommended his students to *begin* their studies with the WN and then to consult Steuart's work as one which contains 'a great mass of accurate details... ascertained by his own personal observation during his long residence on the Continent': *Works*, ix.458; *Principles*, ed. A. Skinner (1966), 4*n*.]

accomplishment. How far his addresses were favourably received, or what the circumstances were which prevented their union, I have not been able to learn; but I believe it is pretty certain that, after this disappointment, he laid aside all thoughts of marriage. The lady to whom I allude died also unmarried. She survived Mr Smith for a considerable number of years, and was alive long after the publication of the first edition of this Memoir. I had the pleasure of seeing her when she was turned of eighty, and when she still retained evident traces of her former beauty. The powers of her understanding and the gaiety of her temper seemed to have suffered nothing from the hand of time.

END OF THE NOTES

P.S. Soon after the foregoing account of Mr Smith was read before the Royal Society, a Volume of his Posthumous Essays was published by his executors and friends, Dr Black and Dr Hutton. In this volume are contained three Essays on the Principles which lead and direct Philosophical Inquiries;—illustrated, in the first place, by the History of Astronomy; in the second, by the History of the Ancient Physics; in the third, by the History of the Ancient Logics and Metaphysics. To these are subjoined three other Essays;—on the Imitative Arts; on the Affinity between certain English and Italian Verses; and on the External Senses. 'The greater part of them appear' (as is observed in an advertisement subscribed by the Editors) 'to be parts of a plan the Author had once formed, for giving a connected history of the liberal sciences and elegant arts.'—'This plan' (we are informed by the same authority) 'he had long abandoned as far too extensive; and these parts of it lay beside him neglected till his death.'

As this posthumous volume did not appear till after the publication of the foregoing Memoir, it would be foreign to the design of these Notes, to offer any observations on the different Essays which it contains. Their merits were certainly not overrated by the two illustrious editors, when they expressed their hopes, 'that the reader would find in them that happy connection, that full and accurate expression, and that clear illustration which are conspicuous in the rest of the author's works; and that, though it is difficult to add much to the great fame he so justly acquired by his other writings, these would be read with satisfaction and pleasure.' The three first Essays, more particularly the fragment on the History of Astronomy, are perhaps as strongly marked as any of his most finished compositions, with the peculiar characteristics of his rich, original, and comprehensive mind.

In order to obviate a cavil which may possibly occur to some of those readers who were not personally acquainted with Mr Smith, I shall take this opportunity of mentioning, that in suppressing, through the course of the foregoing narrative, his honorary title of LL. D. (which was conferred on him by the University of Glasgow a very short time before he resigned his Professorship), I have complied not only with his own taste, but with the uniform practice of that circle in which I had the happiness of enjoying his society. To have given him, so soon after his death, a designation, which he never assumed but on the title-pages of his books; and by which he is never mentioned in the letters of Mr Hume and of his other most intimate friends, would have subjected me justly to the charge of affectation from the audience before whom my paper was read; but the truth is (so little was my ear *then* accustomed to the name of Doctor Smith), that I was altogether unconscious of the omission, till it was pointed out to me, several years afterwards, as a circumstance which, however trifling, had been magnified by more than one critic, into a subject of grave animadversion.

Index of Persons